The Age of
Reconnaissance

J. H. PARRY

UNIVERSITY OF CALIFORNIA PRESS

Berkeley · Los Angeles · London

University of California Press
Berkeley and Los Angeles
University of California Press Ltd.
London, England

Printed in the United States of America

2 3 4 5 6 7 8 9

CONTENTS

PREFACE

The purpose of this book is to tell in outline the story of European geographical exploration, trade and settlement outside the bounds of Europe in the fifteenth, sixteenth and seventeenth centuries; to define the factors that stimulated expansion and made it possible; and to describe briefly the consequences that followed from it. The western European maritime empires, whose early beginnings I have tried to compare, have disappeared into the limbo of History; but that does not make the study of their origins less interesting or less worthwhile.

The original edition of this work, published by Weidenfeld and Nicolson in 1963, is now out of print. In the course of eighteen years, research and re-interpretation have rendered parts of it also out of date. The text of this edition has been extensively revised, to take account of new work, and to reflect my own changes of mind during that period. Much of the work of checking and revising was done, with customary skill and precision, by my assistant Phoebe Wilson. She did not live to see the published result. I would wish to record here my overdue gratitude. I should like also to thank Jim Clark and Susan Defosset, of the University of California Press, not only for undertaking the publication of the work, but also for their unfailing patience with the idiosyncracies of a dilatory author.

Harvard University   J. H. Parry
                                                         29 July 1981

vii

INTRODUCTION

BETWEEN the middle of the fifteenth century and the late seventeenth, Europeans learned to think of the world as a whole and of all seas as one. Their lessons were those of experience and eye-witness report. During those two and a half centuries European explorers actually visited most of the habitable regions of the globe; nearly all those, in fact, which were accessible by sea. They found vast territories formerly unknown to them, and drew the rough outlines of the world which we know. The period, especially the earlier half of it, is commonly called the Age of Discovery, and with reason. Geographical exploration, however, is only one of many kinds of discovery. The age saw not only the most rapid extension of geographical knowledge in the whole of European history; it saw also the first major victories of empirical inquiry over authority, the beginnings of that close association of pure science, technology, and everyday work which is an essential characteristic of the modern western world. During this period, especially the latter half of it, European scientists sketched the outline of the physical universe which, broadly speaking, is that accepted by the ordinary educated man today, and formulated the laws they deduced from the movement and interaction of its parts. All forms of discovery, all forms of original thought, are connected in some way, however distant: and it is natural to see a connection between these particular forms. The seaman, exploring uncharted seas, needed the help of learned men, especially men learned in mathematics, astronomy, and physical science; also, though this came later, in medical science. The student of science, seeing the achievements of geographical exploration (most empirical of all forms of inquiry, and most destructive of purely *a priori* reasoning) was naturally stimulated to further exploration in his chosen field. Both kinds of discovery further stimulated, and were stimulated by, the work of philosophers, poets and pamphleteers.

Connection there undoubtedly was; but its precise nature was both complex and elusive. The modern historian, accustomed to finding as the result of seeking, to discovery as the product of research, is tempted both to exaggerate and to anticipate. It is confidently expected today

I

that every decade will produce new and important additions to the mounting sum of human knowledge. In the fifteenth and sixteenth centuries people—even educated people—had no such confident expectation. The intellectual temper of the sixteenth century, particularly, was conservative, respectful of authority. Even with evidence before their eyes that seamen were in fact finding lands formerly unknown and unsuspected, learned men were slow to draw analogies in other fields of inquiry. The idea that there was an America of learning and understanding beyond the horizon of the classics, ancient philosophy and the teachings of religion, was still in those years new and strange—the vision of comparatively few men. Students of science were concerned less with research than with attempts to provide neat and consistent explanations of known phenomena. It is significant that Copernicus—perhaps the most original figure in sixteenth-century science—reached his momentous conclusions by a mixture of reasoning and intuition, and made little or no attempt to check his hypotheses by actual observation. The first major European astronomical research to be based upon careful detailed observation over a long span of years was undertaken in the late sixteenth century and the early seventeenth by that perverse and unmanageable enthusiast, Tycho Brahe, and by Kepler, the mathematical genius into whose hands Tycho's mass of raw data providentially fell. Until towards the end of our period, certainly until the time of Tycho and Kepler, scientific inquiry in general tended to remain hypothetical and tentative, more given to broad speculation than to precise observation and experiment. Scientists had still, moreover, to be a little wary of charges of heresy; a danger which they commonly avoided by framing as hypotheses conclusions which in some instances they really regarded as proven fact. Galileo's difficulties with the ecclesiastical authorities arose chiefly from his neglect of this elementary precaution. In these circumstances, it was only by very slow degrees that science and technology, intuition and experience, experiment and everyday skill, could be brought together freely to illuminate one another.

It is commonly assumed today, at least among educated people, not only that knowledge can be indefinitely extended, but that all extensions are potentially useful—that all new knowledge will somehow or other, sooner or later, be turned to practical account. Conversely, it is fairly generally accepted that a technological approach need not inhibit pure inquiry; on the contrary, it can prove fruitful in giving rise to problems of a purely theoretical kind. It can help the inquirer, whether in the natural or the social sciences, in the fundamental task of selecting problems; and it imposes a discipline upon his speculative inclinations, by forcing him to submit his theories to definite standards of clarity and testability. These ideas and assumptions were also foreign to the intellectual temper of the period we are discussing. Science was then very far from being harnessed to technology, as it is sometimes said to be today; or as some say it should be. Possibly it gained in originality and intuitive strength by this very fact; but its immediate usefulness was limited, and less was expected of it by practical men. Scientific discoveries of obvious practical value were incidental, often fortuitous. The system of mutual check and stimulation between pure science and technology—the regular submission of theories to standards of clarity and testability—operated only in very limited fields. Geographical exploration, with its associated skills of navigation and cartography, was not merely the principal field of human endeavour in which scientific discovery and everyday technique became closely associated before the middle of the seventeenth century; except for the arts of war and of military engineering and (to a very limited extent) medical practice, it was almost the only field; hence its immense significance in the history of science and of thought. Even in this field, association was slow and hard to establish. The sailors and explorers received only meagre crumbs from the table of the philosophers and scientists. The elementary processes of arithmetic were naturally among the first to be seized and accepted. Arithmetic, which freed men from dependence upon the abacus, was made practicable by Hindu numerals, first introduced into Europe by Leonardo of Pisa's book of arithmetic at the beginning of the thirteenth century. Leonardo was exceptional, a well-travelled man, of merchant stock, who kept the needs of practical men in mind. His book took the reader as far as the Rule of Three. He wrote helpfully also on geometry and its application to measurement. Later came the trigonometry of the plane right-angled triangle, a simple and essential tool of dead-reckoning navigation, but slow to find application in regular use. The influence of astronomy came much later still. At first and for long, only the simplest celestial phenomena—the apparent immobility of the pole star and the movement of the sun relative to the earth—were seen to have any practical significance for the ocean traveller; and not until the fifteenth century was a technique evolved for making use even of these. Long after that, great discoveries continued to be confined to the learned world. The influence of Copernicus upon the development of astronomy was tremendous. His influence on the development of navigation was negligible. Galileo made great indirect contributions to navigation, but not—at least in our period—by his astronomical reasoning and observation. It was his work in the field of optics which, by facilitating the making of instruments, eventually made the task of the navigator easier and more precise. That the invention of the telescope, by making possible an estimation of the relative distances of heavenly bodies, also revolutionized the study of astronomy, was, from the point of view of contemporary seamen, irrelevant. Similarly, navigators were scarcely, and only indirectly, affected by Kepler's resounding declaration, in the introduction to the *New Astronomy*, that the earth 'is round, circumhabited by antipodes, of a most insignificant smallness, and a swift wanderer among the stars.'

If the discoveries and the hypotheses of the scientists were only occasionally and fortuitously helpful to seamen, most seamen—even sometimes sea-going explorers and compilers of navigation manuals—tended for their part to be sceptical and unreceptive of scientific ideas. Seamen were then, much more than now, a race apart, practical, conservative, employing traditional skills, relying on accumulated experience. To say this is not to belittle the skill or the experience. Hydrography and pilotage developed steadily in the later Middle Ages. Practical use had given the sailor, well before the fifteenth century, charts and sailing directions of good working accuracy for the known trade routes of the Mediterranean, the Black Sea, and the coasts of western Europe, and instruments—straight-edge and dividers, compass and lead-line—accurate enough to lay off and follow courses on those charts. The charts, the rutters and the instruments, however, were adequate only for the limited area and the relatively short passages of the regular trade routes. Information about the world outside that area, guidance on how to navigate on long ocean passages, could come only from books; and sailors, traditionally suspicious of book-learning, absorbed it very slowly. Even arithmetic, the elementary arithmetic of Leonardo of Pisa, to take a simple instance, made very slow headway. For short, familiar passages it was unnecessary. Well into the sixteenth century, accounts of ships' stores, records of mileages run, were still often kept in Roman figures. Most sailors, moreover, had naturally little wish to leave the familiar trade routes where their living lay, unless they could see a clear advantage in doing so. Even the great discoverers of the fifteenth and sixteenth centuries were not primarily interested in discovery for its own sake. Their main interest, the main task entrusted to them by the rulers and investors who sent them out, was to link Europe, or particular European countries, with other areas known or believed to be of economic importance. The discovery of distant, unknown islands and continents, like much scientific discovery, was incidental, often fortuitous. Sometimes it was positively unwelcome. In the fifteenth and sixteenth centuries an immense body of geographical knowledge was accumulated by this somewhat haphazard process; but this knowledge, despite (or because of) its vast extent, was still rough and sketchy. For the most part it revealed only coastlines, roughly explored, and harbours. It lacked precision and unity; it left many gaps and perpetuated some long-lived myths. In the story of discovery in the broadest sense, then, our period was a time of tentative, though splendid, beginnings. 'The Age of Reconnaissance' seems the most appropriate name by which to describe it.

Even in so far as they were willing to turn to books for help, the early pioneers of the Reconnaissance had little to guide them. Books about the world outside Europe, available to Europeans in the early fifteenth century, may be divided roughly into two classes: academic treatises and travellers' tales. The travellers' tales included both the accounts of genuine travellers and the romances of imaginary ones. Both dealt chiefly with Asia and—very sketchily—with Africa. The American continent was, of course, unknown. Greenland, and other lands vaguely reported to the west of it, were thought, by the few who had heard of them, to be either islands, or westerly capes of the Eurasian continent stretching across the Arctic. This knowledge such as it was, derived from Norse voyages; but the Norse settlements in Greenland, by the fifteenth century, had lost regular contact with Europe and were dying out. They had long been neglected and latterly were almost forgotten.[1] Similarly with the voyages which Norse adventurers had made in the eleventh century to Baffin Land, Labrador, Newfoundland, perhaps New England. These exploits were splendidly described in Scandinavian epic tales; but such oral recitals are by their nature imprecise. No reliable cartographical evidence, so far as we know, has survived. The celebrated Vinland map,[2] the only early, or apparently early, map to show that equivocal country by name, is now thought to be a forgery. Neither sagas, nor contemporary Scandinavian maps, if any were made, can have been much known elsewhere in Europe. Recollections of voyages to Arctic America can have had little direct influence in the development of the Reconnaissance.

African travel was a little better recorded. The accounts of the great Arab travellers—Masudi, Ibn Haukal, El-Bekri, Ibn Battuta —were unknown to Europeans in their original form, but traces of their influence appeared in Europe from time to time. Edrisi, writing in Norman Sicily in the twelfth century, transmitted scraps of Arab knowledge to western Europe. Much of this information was not only inaccurate, but from the point of view of the maritime explorer, positively discouraging. Masudi, for example, described accurately enough the places he had visited, but beyond them relied upon hearsay and guess. He believed the 'green sea of darkness' (the Atlantic) to be unnavigable, and the frigid and torrid zones of the earth to be uninhabitable; and in these opinions he was followed by many later writers, both Muslim and Christian. A more practical channel of information was the school of Jewish cartographers and instrument-makers working in Majorca in the later fourteenth century. Iberian Jews were well placed as intermediaries between Christendom and Islam, and the Majorcan Jews had particular advantages because of their connection, through Aragon, with Sicily, and because of their commercial contacts in the Maghreb. They were familiar with both the Arab and (such as they were) the European travellers' tales from Africa. The famous Catalan Atlas,[3] drawn in Majorca by Abraham Cresques about 1375, was perhaps the best and most accurate, certainly the most beautifully executed medieval chart collection in the practical maritime tradition. It represents the first, and for long the only, attempt to apply medieval hydrographical techniques to the world outside Europe. It contains in addition, however, a considerable amount of inland information. It includes an elaborate drawing of Mansa Musa, the greatest of the fourteenth-century Mandingo kings;[4] it places Timbuktu in approximately its true position, and shows near it a lake from which one river, clearly the Senegal, flows westward to the sea, and another, presumably intended to represent the Niger, eastward to join the Nile. The implications of this supposedly continuous waterway were to be noted by Portuguese promoters of exploration in the following centuries.

For Asia, Europeans were less dependent upon Arab sources; the travellers' tales available to them were more numerous and more detailed. They were, however, even more out of date. Most of them were written in the late thirteenth and early fourteenth centuries, during the longest respite which Christendom enjoyed, between the seventh century and the seventeenth, from Muslim pressure on its eastern and southern borders. This respite was due not to the efforts of crusading armies, nor to the intervention of any Prester John beloved of medieval legend, but to the conquests of Chingis Khan. Swift and devastating campaigns, by Mongol cavalry operating over immense areas, had led to the establishment of an empire embracing China and most of central Asia. The Tatar Khans, Chingis' successors, were tolerant in religion, desirous of trade, curious about the world outside their great dominions. Their authority was effective enough to make travel safe for those whom they protected. For a little over a hundred years it was possible for Europeans to travel to the Far East, and a few did so. In 1245 John of Plano Carpini, a Franciscan friar, was sent by the Pope on a mission to the great Khan at his camp-capital at Karakorum. This remarkable journey was well recorded. John himself wrote a *Description of the Mongols* with an account of his experiences;[5] one of his companions wrote an independent narrative; a third contemporary account, the *Tartar Relation*, has recently come to light, and is of particular interest because

6

of its association with the Vinland map.[6] Another friar, William of Rubruck, undertook a similar mission in 1253 on behalf of Louis IX, and similarly recorded his discoveries.[7] The Venetian merchants Nicolo and Maffeo Polo set out in 1256 on a journey which took them eventually to Peking, where the Tatar Khans had recently established their permanent capital; and in 1271–3 they returned there with Nicolo's son Marco, on a visit which lasted until 1292. In the early fourteenth century more ecclesiastics—John of Monte Corvino, Odoric of Pordenone, Andrew of Perugia, Jordan of Severac, John of Marignolli, to mention only the best known[8]—visited China, some by way of the Indian coast, and wrote accounts of their travels. The existence of a mid-fourteenth-century merchants' handbook,[9] containing a detailed section on mid- and far-eastern trade routes, suggests that a considerable number of itinerant merchants, who left no surviving records, made similar journeys. All this coming and going of European travellers was sharply interrupted in the middle of the fourteenth century. The Black Death, which swept both Asia and Europe, brought most long-distance travel temporarily to a standstill. The incursion from the Steppe of yet another pillaging mounted horde—the Ottoman Turks, quickly converted to Islam and engaged in holy war against Christendom—interposed a further barrier between east and west. Finally the Tatar Empire broke up; in 1368, the descendants of Kublai Khan were driven from their Peking throne by a native Chinese dynasty, the Mings, who brought back the traditional official dislike and contempt for western barbarians. The Tatar Khans, for their part, embraced Islam, and made no attempt to re-establish the broken contact. Fifteenth-century Europe, therefore, was almost entirely dependent upon thirteenth-century writers for eye-witness knowledge of the Far East.

Of all the accounts of Asia written by medieval European travellers, the *Travels* of Marco Polo[10] is the best, the most complete and the most informative. His long residence at Peking; the privileged position which he achieved as a trusted official in the service of Kublai Khan; the missions with which he was charged in many widely separated parts of the Khan's dominions; all combined to give him unique opportunities for collecting information. He was an assiduous, though not very penetrating observer; he had a good memory, and a talent for describing what he had seen in plain, sober detail. In writing of what he had heard about but not seen, he preserved, on the whole, a judicious scepticism. His accounts are factual, unsophisticated and—so far as can be judged—accurate. They are relatively free from the tales of the grotesque and the marvellous, in which medieval readers delighted and which formed the staple of much of the travel literature of the time. The *Travels* was widely read and copied. It was undoubtedly the source of

7

the information on Asia set out in the Catalan Atlas, which was one of the very few maps of the practical *portolano* type to include such information. Its superiority over other contemporary writings on similar subjects was not, however, universally or immediately recognized. The *Travels* of Odoric of Pordenone[11] enjoyed an equal popularity in the fourteenth century. Odoric gives a better description of Chinese customs than Marco, and his work is more freely enlivened with marvels and curiosities. Significantly, the popularity of both was exceeded by that of a famous collection of spurious travellers' tales—the *Travels* of 'Sir John Mandeville'.[12] Nothing illustrates European geographical ignorance better than the long inability of the reading public to discriminate between Polo's eye-witness accounts and Mandeville's lying wonders, whether as entertainment or as serious information. Polo's description of the 'black stones' which the Chinese burned as fuel was received with no more, and no less, credulity than Mandeville's dog-headed men. Mandeville had his importance in the Reconnaissance; for probably no book did more to arouse interest in travel and discovery, and to popularize the idea of a possible circumnavigation of the globe. Gradually, however, as the search for India by sea got seriously under way, the unique value of Marco Polo's *Travels* as a reliable source of information came to be generally recognized among the more penetrating amateurs of geography. It influenced most of the pioneers of the Reconnaissance. Prince Henry of Portugal knew it in manuscript. It was printed at Gouda in 1483, and frequently thereafter. Columbus had a printed copy. Polo's description of the immense east-west extent of Asia, and his reference to Japan, lying far to the east of the China coast, may have helped to form Columbus' geographical convictions; at least it lent them strong support. It was still, in Columbus' time, the best account of the Far East available to Europeans; but since it described a political situation which had long passed away, it was bound to mislead as well as to encourage.

Marco Polo, and the travellers generally, had very little influence upon the academic geographers and cosmographers of the later Middle Ages; so wide was the gap between theory and knowledge. The academic treatises available to Europeans fall, like the travellers' tales, into two broad groups: those in the strait scholastic tradition, drawing their information chiefly from scriptural and patristic sources and from the handful of ancient writers long accepted as respectable, and those which made use of the more recently recovered works of ancient science, coming to Europe chiefly through Arabic translations. Of the first group little need be said. Just as the *Travels* of Marco Polo and similar travel books had their cartographical counterparts in the Catalan Atlas and other maps in the *portolano* tradition, so the scholastic geographies

8

had their counterpart in the great *mappae-mundi*, such as the Hereford and Ebstorf maps,[13] with their central Jerusalem and their symmetrically disposed continents—all-embracing in scope, splendid in execution, and for practical purposes useless. Symmetry and orthodoxy rather than scientific verisimilitude were in general the guiding principles of these works. The most important, indeed almost the only, departure from this tradition before the fifteenth century, was the geographical section of Roger Bacon's *Opus Majus* of 1264. Bacon had, for his day, an unusually wide acquaintance with Arab writers. He believed, on literary evidence, that Asia and Africa extended southwards across the equator, and (contrary to Masudi and his followers) that the torrid zone was habitable. Both in his specific geographical opinions, and in his objective approach to scientific problems in general, Bacon was almost unique among the schoolmen. Not quite unique, however; for he exerted a powerful influence on the last great scholastic geographer, whose work not only summarized the best medieval thought, but also provided a significant link with later developments. The *Imago Mundi* of Cardinal Pierre d'Ailly, the leading geographical theorist of his time, was written about 1410.[14] It is a vast mine of scriptural and Aristotelian erudition, bearing little relation to travellers' experience—its author knew nothing, for instance, of Marco Polo. D'Ailly was a prolific writer on many topics, whose works enjoyed an immense prestige among scholars. The *Imago Mundi* had a widespread influence throughout the fifteenth century. It was printed at Louvain about 1483. Columbus' copy, with his marginal annotations, survives in the Colombina at Seville. Like all theorists of whom Columbus approved, d'Ailly exaggerated the east-west extent of Asia and the proportion of land to sea in the area of the globe. His section on this subject was copied almost word for word from Bacon's *Opus Majus*. Apart from his influence on Columbus, d'Ailly's main interest lies in his acquaintance, much wider than that of his predecessors, even than Bacon, with Arab authors and with little-known classical writers. He made relatively little use of them; he knew Ptolemy's *Almagest* well, for example, but where they conflicted he considered Aristotle and Pliny to be of greater authority. Nevertheless, for all his scholastic conservatism, d'Ailly was the herald of a new and exciting series of classical recoveries, and of geographical works based on their inspiration.

Throughout the period of the Reconnaissance, the normal educated man believed not only that the Ancients had been more civilized, more elegant in behaviour and expression, more sagacious in the conduct of affairs than his contemporaries; save in the field of revealed religion (a large exception, admittedly) he believed them to have been better informed. At the beginning of our period, in the middle of the fifteenth century, this belief was general, and, in general, reasonable; and nowhere more so than in geographical study. The Ancients had indeed a better knowledge of geography and cosmography than fifteenth-century Europeans. It is true that some ancient writers—Pliny and Macrobius, for examples—widely read in the Middle Ages, had retailed information little more reliable than that of Sir John Mandeville; but in the early fifteenth century readers had the same difficulty in discriminating between Pliny and—say—Strabo, as between Mandeville and Marco Polo. To scholars, the way to clearer understanding seemed, naturally enough, to lie in more extensive study, in more careful interpretation, of all the relevant ancient writings which scholarship could discover; and in fact, in the field of geography, fifteenth-century study of neglected or hitherto unknown classical writers yielded rich rewards. It revealed to Europe Strabo's compendious gazetteer of the world of his time, and—more important and influential still—the *Geography* of Claudius Ptolemaeus.

Ptolemy was a Hellenized Egyptian who wrote about the middle of the second century AD. It was natural, at the time of the greatest extension of the Roman Empire, that there should be a demand for a complete description of the empire itself and of the *oikoumene* of which it appeared to form the major part. Ptolemy set out to summarize, in his writings, the entire geographical and cosmographical knowledge of his day. He was not himself a discoverer or a particularly original thinker, but rather an assiduous compiler. He inherited and made use of the works of a long series of Greek geographers, mathematicians and astronomers, many of whom had lived and worked in his own city of Alexandria. His fame rests on two works: the *Geography*, and an *Astronomy*, usually known by its Arabic name, *Almagest*, 'the Greatest'. Both books were well known and highly respected in the Middle Ages among Arab scholars, who were the most direct inheritors of classical Greek learning; but among them the *Almagest* attracted far the greater attention. It was a book for the learned practitioner, serving the esoteric purposes of astrology rather than the satisfaction of general scientific curiosity—still less the task of finding one's way at sea. It enlarged upon the austerely beautiful Aristotelian picture of transparent concentric spheres, revolving round the earth and carrying the sun and the stars with them; and added an immensely elaborate and ingenious system of circles and 'epicycles' to account for the eccentric movements of the planets and other heavenly bodies relative to the earth. The *Almagest* was translated into Latin in the twelfth century by Gerard of Cremona, an avid student of Arabic learning, working at Toledo. In the course of the thirteenth century it came to be known and accepted in the learned world of the schoolmen; though less understood, and much less revered, than Aristotle's own works, most of which had reached western Europe about the same time and by similar routes. The Aristotelian-Ptolemaic system with its celestial spheres and its epicycles remained—albeit with many variants—the standard academic picture of the universe until Copernicus, distrusting its over-strained complexity, began its demolition in the sixteenth century.

The indirect influence of the *Almagest* was not, however, confined to the erudite. An abstract of Gerard of Cremona's translation was made about the middle of the thirteenth century by John Holywood or Sacrobosco, an English scholar then lecturing in Paris (who, incidentally, also composed one of the earliest European arithmetic primers, only a little later than the famous *Arithmetic* of Leonardo of Pisa). Sacrobosco's little book, *De Sphaera Mundi*, became and for nearly three centuries remained the best-known elementary textbook. It was not, of course, a textbook of navigation; though later it was often bound up with navigation manuals. Its importance lay in its wide diffusion. It survives in more than thirty *incunabula* editions, besides many manuscripts. Most university students in the later Middle Ages must have read it. Sacrobosco did more than any other writer to discredit flat-earth fundamentalists such as Cosmas Indicopleustes, who had exerted a formidable, though never quite unchallenged, influence upon cosmographical thought for seven centuries. Thanks to Sacrobosco, it was at least common knowledge among educated people in the fifteenth century that the world was round.

Ptolemy's *Geography* made its impact upon Europe much later and in a very different manner. It is curious that so famous a book remained so long unknown. Edrisi, the gifted Ceuta Moor who worked for many years at the Court of Roger II of Sicily, drew largely upon Ptolemy in compiling his own Geography, the celebrated *Book of Roger*; but Edrisi's influence was less than the merits of his work deserved, and no European scholar tried to investigate the sources he had used.[15] Ptolemy's *Geography* was first translated into Latin not from an Arabic manuscript, but from a Greek one brought from Constantinople. The translation was made by Jacobus Angelus, a pupil of the celebrated Crysoloras, and was completed about 1406 or a little after. Its appearance was one of the most important events in the growth of European geographical knowledge.

The main part of Ptolemy's text is an exhaustive gazetteer of places, arranged by regions, with a latitude and longitude assigned to each place. Ptolemy divided his sphere into the familiar 360 degrees of latitude and of longitude, and from his estimate of the circumference of the earth he deduced the length of a degree of the equator or of a meridian. He gives a method of adjusting the length of a degree of longitude for any given latitude, and explains how to construct a 'grid' of parallels and meridians for maps drawn on a conical projection. The idea of using co-ordinates of latitude and longitude for defining the position of points on the earth's surface was not entirely new to medieval Europe. Astrologers' *Ephemerides* were constructed with reference to positions in the Zodiac, and estimated differences of longitude were necessarily used for the 'rectification' of these tables for places other than those for which they were compiled. Roger Bacon had even attempted an actual map based on co-ordinates. The map, which he sent to Pope Clement IV, is lost; and Bacon, before his time in this as in other ways, exerted no influence upon cartography and inspired no imitators. Ptolemy's use of co-ordinates as a base and a frame of reference in the construction of maps reappeared in the fifteenth century as a new and revolutionary invention. The second part of the *Geography* is a collection of maps, a world map and regional maps. Whether Ptolemy himself drew maps to accompany his text is doubtful. He implied that any intelligent reader, using the information contained in the text, could prepare his own maps; and the maps which reached fifteenth-century Europe—whoever drew them, and whenever they were made—were based on his co-ordinates and drawn on his projection. They show, in addition to a detailed and reasonably accurate (though elongated) Mediterranean, the continents of Europe, Asia and Africa. Africa is broad and truncated, India even more truncated, Ceylon greatly exaggerated in size. To the east of India is drawn another and larger peninsula, the Golden Chersonese; to the east of that again, a great arm of the sea, the Great Gulf; and finally, near the easternmost extremity of the map, the country of the Sinae. The interior of Asia contains towns and river systems which cannot easily be related to any actual places. The interior of Africa is drawn with some attempt at detail, showing not only the 'Mountains of the Moon', but also the lacustrine source of the Nile and other rivers; but South Africa is joined to the country of the Sinae, making the Indian Ocean a land-locked sea; and all around, to the east and south, is solid land, *Terra Incognita*.

Ptolemy was a compiler, not an originator. His ideas on the measure-ment of the earth, for example, came from Marinus of Tyre, who had them from Posidonius; the concepts of a sphere divided into degrees of angular distance, and of co-ordinates of latitude and longitude, were derived from Hipparchus; the immense catalogue of names and places was compiled from various *Periploi*—sailing directions—for the Medi-terranean, from Marinus, perhaps from Strabo; though Ptolemy gives little of Strabo's descriptive detail. Compilation involves selection, and the authorities used by Ptolemy did not always represent the best classical thought on the subject. In adopting Marinus' measurement of the earth, for example, he perpetuated and popularized an under-estimate of the size of the earth, and consequently of the length of a degree: 500 *Stadia* or 62½ Roman miles. This figure was too small by about one quarter. Eratosthenes, centuries earlier, had by a very clever and very lucky calculation reached a much more accurate figure. Ptolemy assumed, moreover—and in this he differed from Marinus—that the 'known' world of his day covered exactly 180 degrees of longitude; he numbered these off from the furthest reported land to the West—the Canaries or Fortunate Isles—and stretched the continent of Asia eastward accordingly. These errors, together with those of the enclosed Indian Ocean, the twin peninsulas and gulf of south-eastern Asia, and the interior waterways of Africa, were to have momentous consequences.

Ptolemy had, of course, no compass and no practicable means of observing longitude. The number of reliably observed latitudes actually known to him was, as he admitted, small. He could ascertain the positions of little-known places only by plotting their reported distance, along vaguely indicated lines of direction, from places better known; and calculating differences of latitude and longitude by means of plane right-angled—not spherical—triangles. Consequently, the positions which he gives for many places outside the well-known area of the Mediterranean are wildly inaccurate. Further, a text such as Ptolemy's, with its long lists of names and figures, is peculiarly vulnerable to corruption in copying. It may be supposed that, over the centuries, many copyists' errors came to be added to Ptolemy's own.

The scholars of early fifteenth-century Europe, however, had no reliable criteria for criticizing Ptolemy, just as they had none for criticizing Marco Polo. His compendiousness suited their requirements and their own literary habits, and much of what he wrote was to them new, exciting and incontrovertible. The maps based on his information, despite their many errors, were vastly superior to the medieval *mappae-mundi* and covered areas not usually touched by the makers of *portolani*. His use of co-ordinates was a major advance which—though still unintelligible to seamen—could not be ignored by scholars. We have seen that Cardinal Pierre d'Ailly wrote his first major work, the *Imago Mundi*, about 1410, before he had seen the Latin Ptolemy. In 1413, after the recovery of the *Geography*, d'Ailly wrote a second work, the *Compendium Cosmographiae*, in which he summarized—albeit in a distorted form—the opinions of Ptolemy. In one respect this was, curiously, a retrograde step, for in the *Imago Mundi* d'Ailly had described an insular Africa and an open Indian Ocean; in the *Compendium* he deferred to Ptolemy. More august recognition followed. The *Historia rerum ubique gestarum* of Pope Pius II—that erudite and cultivated humanist—is largely a digest of Ptolemy, though not an uncritical one, for the Pope maintained the circumnavigability of Africa. Columbus had a printed copy of this book, and drew from it such knowledge of Ptolemy's *Geography* as he possessed. From its first appearance, then, the Latin *Geography* was received among scholars with great, though not entirely uncritical deference. Hundreds of manuscript copies were made. The first of the many printed editions which were to give Ptolemy's ideas wider and wider currency, appeared in Vicenza in 1475; the earliest to include maps in Bologna in 1477 and—a much better edition—in Rome in 1478.[16]

Growing dissatisfaction with Ptolemy's archaic maps did little, at first, to diminish the popularity of his text, for improved maps, incorporating the results of sailing experience, were bound up with it from 1482 onwards. The splendid Strasburg edition of 1513 contains forty-seven maps, eleven of them new—the first modern atlas, and the best for many years; until 1570, in fact, when Ortelius set new standards with his great *Theatrum Orbis Terrarum*. Editions of Ptolemy, some of great beauty and distinction, continued to appear in Rome, in Venice and in Basel. They were only displaced from serious use (and not then, of course, from historical interest) by the rise of the Dutch school of geography and cartography at the end of the sixteenth century. For nearly two hundred years, therefore, Ptolemy was the leading academic source of geographical knowledge. His ideas, in geography as in astronomy, were both stimulating and enslaving, and the advancement of knowledge in both fields required that his theories should first be mastered and then superseded. It was a principal task of the Reconnaissance to challenge belief in the necessary superiority of ancient wisdom. Not only in the specific field of geography, but in almost every branch of science, at some time during our period there came a moment when western Europe, so to speak, at last caught up with the ancient world, and a few bold men, understanding and revering what the ancients had taught, were, nevertheless, ready to dispute their conclusions. So in the process of Reconnaissance, explorers by sea, pushing rashly out into a world unknown, but for Ptolemy, and finding it bigger and more varied than they expected, began first to doubt Ptolemy, then to prove him wrong in many particulars, and finally to draw on maps and globes a new and more convincing picture. Similarly, but independently, Copernicus and his successors, studying their Ptolemy and watching the heavens, noticed certain celestial phenomena which Ptolemy's theories failed adequately to explain. They began, timidly and tentatively, first, to question, then to dismantle the Aristotelian-Ptolemaic geocentric scheme of the universe, and to postulate a heliocentric system in its place. In both studies, the whole progress from deferential acceptance to doubt, from doubt to discard and replacement, took many years. Eventually, in all branches of science, Reconnaissance became Revolution.

But how did Reconnaissance begin? Information about the world outside Europe, available to Europeans in the first half of the fifteenth century, was all, as we have seen, misleading to a greater or less degree. It was either purely theoretical and academic, ignoring practical experience; or out-of-date; or merely fanciful, compounded of myth and guess-work. Technical knowledge of means of communication with African or Asian coasts outside the Mediterranean by sea—the only practicable way, in view of Turkish power, save on the Turks' own terms—was even more inadequate. The political situation, on the face of it, could hardly have been less propitious. The most recently acquired information, from newly discovered ancient sources, was interesting and valuable, but on the whole very discouraging— Ptolemy's land-locked Indian Ocean, for example. What other factors operated, to make this unpropitious half-century the beginning of a movement of world-wide exploration?

The initial steps in expansion were modest indeed: the rash seizure by a Portuguese force of a fortress in Morocco; the tentative extension of fishing and, a little later, trading, along the Atlantic coast of North Africa; the prosaic settlement by vine and sugar cultivators, by log-cutters and sheep-farmers, of certain islands in the eastern Atlantic. There was little, in these early- and mid-fifteenth-century ventures, to suggest world-wide expansion. In the later fifteenth century, however, new advances in the arts of navigation and cartography, made by a new combination of academic knowledge and nautical experience, enabled the explorers for the first time to observe and record the position —or at least the latitude—of a point on an unknown coast; and even, in favourable circumstances, of a ship at sea. New methods in the design of ships, consequent upon a marriage of European with oriental traditions, made it possible for sailors not only to make long voyages of discovery, but to repeat them, and so to establish regular communication with newly discovered lands. New developments in gunnery and the making of guns, particularly in ship-borne artillery, gave European explorers a great advantage over the inhabitants of even the most civilized countries to which they sailed; enabled them to defend themselves, upon arrival, sometimes against overwhelming numbers; and encouraged them to establish trading posts even in places where they were clearly unwelcome. This vital technical superiority in ships and guns ensured the continuous development of the Reconnaissance and the permanence of its results. By the end of our period European explorers had not only sketched the rough outlines of most of the continents of the world; they had established, in every continent except Australasia and Antarctica, European outposts—trading factories, settlements, or lordships, according to the nature of the area—small, scattered, diverse, but permanent. In so doing, they not only derived help from physical scientists and stimulated the further development of physical science—though tentatively and indirectly at first, as we have seen; they also called attention to new and far-reaching problems in the social sciences, in economics, in anthropology, and in the arts of government. In these fields also there was a tentative but widespread Reconnaissance, a wide but uneven series of additions to knowledge, with momentous consequences for Europe and the world as a whole. In all branches of science, as the Reconnaissance proceeded and became less tentative, as the European picture of the world became fuller and more detailed, so the idea of continually expanding knowledge became more familiar and the links between science and practical life became closer. A technological attitude to knowledge, an extreme readiness to apply science in immediately practical ways, eventually became one of the principal characteristics which distinguish western civilization, the civilization originally of Europe, from other great civilized societies. The unprecedented power which it produced eventually led Europe from Reconnaissance to world-wide conquest, and so created the world of yesterday, much of which was governed by Europeans, and the world of today, almost all of which has accepted European technology and European techniques of government, even if only to escape from actual European rule.

Part I

THE CONDITIONS FOR DISCOVERY

CHAPTER 1
ATTITUDES AND MOTIVES

AMONG the many and complex motives which impelled Europeans, and especially the peoples of the Iberian peninsula, to venture oversea in the fifteenth and sixteenth centuries, two were obvious, universal, and admitted: acquisitiveness and religious zeal. Many of the great explorers and conquerors proclaimed these two purposes in unequivocal terms. Vasco da Gama, on arrival at Calicut, explained to his reluctant Indian hosts that he had come in search of Christians and spices. Bernal Díaz, frankest of *conquistadores*, wrote that he and his like went to the Indies 'to serve God and His Majesty, to give light to those who were in darkness, and to grow rich, as all men desire to do.'[1]

Land, and the labour of those who worked it, were the principal sources of wealth. The quickest, most obvious, and socially most attractive way of becoming rich was to seize, and to hold as a fief, land already occupied by a diligent and docile peasantry. Spanish knights and noblemen in particular had long been accustomed to this process, for which successful war against the Muslim states in Spain had offered occasion and excuse. In most parts of Europe, during the constant disorders of the fourteenth and early fifteenth centuries, such acquisitions of land had also often been made by means of private war. In the later fifteenth century, however, rulers were again becoming strong enough to discourage private war; and even in Spain, the territory still open to acquisition by lawful force of arms was narrowly limited, and protected by its feudal relations with the Crown of Castile. Further opportunities were unlikely to arise unless the rulers of Granada denounced their vassalage, and so gave the Castilians occasion for a formal campaign of conquest. Even if that campaign were successful, kings and great noblemen would get the lion's share of the booty. For lesser men, the best chances of acquiring land by fighting for it lay outside Europe.

A second possibility was the seizure and exploitation of new land—land either unoccupied, or occupied by useless or intractable peoples who could be killed or driven away. New land could be colonized by adventurous farmers or by small owners of flocks and herds. Such men often wished to be their own masters, to avoid the increasingly irksome obligations imposed by feudal tenure and by the corporate privileges of transhumant graziers, particularly in Castile. This was a less attractive, but still promising alternative, which also could most readily be pursued outside Europe. Madeira and parts of the Canaries were occupied in this way in the fifteenth century, respectively by Portuguese and Spanish settlers, comparatively humble people, who borrowed capital from princely or noble promoters in return for relatively light obligations. The settlements were economically successful. They brought in revenue to the princes and noblemen—notably Prince Henry of Portugal—who financed them; and set a fashion for islands which lasted more than two hundred years. Rumours of further islands and mainlands to be discovered in the Atlantic all helped to encourage interest in this type of oversea adventure.

A less sure, and in most places socially less attractive way to wealth, was by investment in trade, especially long-distance trade. The most sought-after trades were in commodities of high value and small bulk, most of them either of eastern origin—spices, silk, ivory, precious stones and the like—or Mediterranean in origin but in demand in the East, such as coral and some high-quality textiles. These rich trades almost all passed through the Mediterranean and were conducted chiefly by the merchants of the Italian maritime cities, in particular Venetians and Genoese. Some Atlantic maritime peoples were already looking enviously at the rich trades. Portugal in particular possessed a long ocean seaboard, good harbours, a considerable fishing and seafaring population and a commercial class largely emancipated from feudal interference. Portuguese shippers were able and eager to graduate from an Atlantic coastal trade in wine, fish and salt, to more widespread and lucrative ventures in gold, spices and sugar. They had little hope of breaking into the Mediterranean trades, which were guarded by the Italian monopolists with formidable naval force; with unrivalled knowledge of the East derived from many generations of merchants and travellers; and with an assiduous diplomacy which reached across the ancient dividing line between Christendom and Islam. Merchant capitalists in Portugal and western Spain therefore had strong motives for seeking by sea alternative sources of gold, ivory and pepper; and according to information current in Morocco, such sources existed. It is highly likely that in undertaking West African voyages, the Portuguese were encouraged by information about the gold mines of the Guinea kingdoms, obtained through their conquest at Ceuta and not available to the rest of Europe. At least, the voyages quickly demonstrated that sailing in the Tropics was easier and less dangerous than pessimists had supposed. If, as was hinted in some of the travel literature of the time, it were even possible to penetrate by sea to the oriental sources of silk and spice, that would provide a still stronger incentive for sea-borne exploration.

Failing the rich trades, there was one commodity which the Portuguese thoroughly understood and which always commanded a sale everywhere in Europe: fish. Long before Columbus reached America, or the sea route to India became a possibility, the demands of the salt-fish trade were encouraging Portuguese deep-sea fishermen to venture further and further into the Atlantic. Fishing took them to Icelandic waters, well on the way to America; and fishing was one of the principal reasons for their interest in the north-west coast of Africa.

Precious commodities—indeed, most marketable commodities— might be secured not only by trade, but by more direct methods; by plunder, if they should be found in the possession of people whose religion, or lack of religion, could be made an excuse for attacking them; or by direct exploitation, if sources of supply were discovered in lands either uninhabited, or inhabited only by ignorant savages. Here again, rumour and imaginative travel literature suggested the possibility of hitherto unknown mines, gold-bearing streams, or pearl fisheries. Casual unforeseen treasures also occasionally came the way of adventurous sailors: the unexpected lump of ambergris upon a deserted beach, or the narwhal's potent horn.

All these economic considerations, these imaginative dreams of quick adventurous gain, were heavily reinforced by the promptings of religious zeal. The discoverers and *conquistadores* were devout men for the most part, whose devotion took forms at once orthodox and practical. Of the many possible forms of religious zeal, two in particular appealed to them, and to the rulers and investors who sent them out. One was the desire to convert—to appeal to the minds and hearts of individual unbelievers by preaching, reasoning, or force of example, by any means of persuasion short of force or threat, and so to bring unbelievers into the community of belief. The other was the more simple-minded desire to ensure by military and political means the safety and independence of one's own religious community and, better still, its predominance over others; to defend the believer against interference and attack; to kill, humiliate, or subdue the unbeliever. Of course, these two possible lines of action might be confused or combined. It might appear politic, for example, to subdue unbelievers in order to convert them. In general, however, two expressions of religious devotion in action were kept distinct in men's minds. The first called for intense effort, with little likelihood of immediate material gain. The second, the politico-military expression, provided an excuse for conquest and plunder on a grand scale. It was an aspect of religious zeal with which Europe had long been familiar, since for several centuries it had supplied one of the principal motives for the crusades.

The fifteenth-century voyages of discovery have often been described as a continuation of the crusades. Certainly the menacing proximity of Islam was always in the minds of fifteenth-century kings, especially in eastern and southern Europe. Nevertheless, those kings were realists enough, for the most part, to see that a crusade of the traditional pattern—a direct campaign against Muslim rulers in the eastern Mediterranean lands, with the object of capturing the Holy Places and establishing Christian principalities on the shores of the Levant—was no longer even a remote possibility. Crusades of this type in earlier centuries had been, in the long run, costly failures. The wide mixture of motives among the crusaders—religious zeal, personal love of adventure, hope of gain, desire for reputation—and jealousy and suspicion among the rulers concerned, had always been powerful factors preventing effective unity. The European nations had never embarked on crusades as organized States. Even those armies led by kings or by the Emperor in person had been bound together only by feudal and personal ties. No medieval European kingdom had possessed an organization capable of administering distant possessions; only the knightly Orders had the organization, and their resources were inadequate. Conquests, such as the Latin States established after the first crusade, were made possible only by disunity among the local Arab principalities, and could not survive the counter-attack of a capable and unifying Muslim ruler. In the long run, the political effect of the crusades was to reduce the Byzantine Empire, the leading Christian State of eastern Europe, to a fragment of Greek territory, and to enable the Venetians to extort commercial privileges in Constantinople. From the thirteenth century onwards the great feudal monarchies of northern Europe lost interest in crusading, and left the war against Islam to those who had Muslim neighbours: to the Byzantine emperors and the neighbouring Balkan kings, and to the Christian kings of the Iberian peninsula.

These war-hardened rulers, left to themselves, achieved considerable successes. The Greek Empire, employing a supple diplomacy as well as military tenacity, showed a remarkable capacity for survival. It was still a formidable naval power. It recovered much territory in the fourteenth century. Weakened though it was, it could normally hold its own, in stable conditions, against a variety of settled and relatively orderly Muslim states, who had no more unity among themselves than had the Christian kingdoms. The chief danger to the empire came from newly-Islamized barbarian hordes who from time to time migrated from their homes in central Asia, broke into the lands of the 'fertile crescent', overthrew the established Muslim States, created new and unified military sultanates and embarked on holy war against the Christian unbeliever. If successfully resisted, a horde might settle down and become, in its turn, an organized and stationary kingdom; but the Greek power of resistance, under successive blows, was becoming less and less reliable. The most dangerous of these invasions, from a European point of view, was that of the Ottoman Turks in the fourteenth century.

At the other end of the Mediterranean these great waves of assault were felt at first only as attenuated ripples. The aggression of the Iberian kingdoms against Islam was a long-term, ding-dong local affair which in the later Middle Ages had steadily gained ground. At the beginning of the fifteenth century the only Muslim State surviving in Europe was the ancient and highly civilized kingdom of Granada; and, rich and powerful though this kingdom had been, it now paid tribute to Castile, and the rulers of Castile could look forward, with good hope of success, to its eventual incorporation in their own dominions. The rulers of Portugal no longer had a land frontier with Muslim neighbours and were beginning to contemplate a sea-borne assault on the rich Arab-Berber principalities of North Africa.

The end of the fourteenth and beginning of the fifteenth centuries brought a brief respite to the beleaguered Greeks. Two great Muslim States confronted one another in the Levant. One was the Mamluk kingdom of Egypt and Syria, firmly established a century and a quarter before by that great Sultan Baybars who had chased the remaining Franks out of Syria and had also defeated the grandson of Chingis Khan. The other was the more recently founded Ottoman kingdom in Asia Minor, which was restless, aggressive, and a constant danger to its neighbours, both Christian and Muslim. The Turks had crossed the Dardanelles in 1353 and in 1357 occupied Adrianople, so almost surrounding the Byzantine Empire. To some extent, Byzantine survival depended on Mamluk power in the Ottomans' rear. At the very end of the fourteenth century, both these Muslim States were over-run by the cavalry of the last great nomad Mongol Khan, Timur the Lame. In 1400 Timur sacked both Aleppo and Damascus; in 1402, he defeated the Ottoman army at Ankara, sacked Smyrna, and took the Sultan Bayezid I prisoner. The Christian rulers naturally regarded this most savage of conquerors as a deliverer. The Byzantine Emperor offered him tribute. Even the Castilians sent him an embassy, which, however, arrived in Samarcand to find him already dead. The Christian respite was thus very brief. Timur died in 1405. His heirs fell to quarrelling and his exploits were never repeated. In the long run, and indirectly, the Mongol incursion worked to the disadvantage of Byzantium and so of Christian Europe. The Ottomans had been less severely mauled, and recovered more quickly from their defeat, than their Mamluk rivals. Their military organization and equipment was by far the best among the Muslim states. Their civil administration bore comparatively lightly upon conquered subjects, and made them not entirely un-welcome conquerors to an over-taxed peasantry. The immediate question was where their formidable strength would first be exerted: against the Mamluks, against the heretic Safawid kingdom in Persia, or against the Byzantine Empire. All three were overthrown eventually; but the Byzantine Empire, the weakest of the three, received the first blows. Constantinople was besieged in 1422. Rebellions in Asia Minor and counter-attacks from Hungary against the Turks prolonged Greek resistance; but the great city finally fell to Muhammad II in 1453.

The fall of Constantinople had been so long expected, and so long delayed, that much of its psychological effect in Europe was dissipated. In Italy, it is true, the news of the fall provided a powerful motive for a general, if uneasy, pacification among the major states—the Most Holy League; but there was no effective call to arms, and despite much talk, no general crusade.[2] If Europe was a beleaguered fortress, its garrison was not so small nor so closely invested that its members felt any special need for unity among themselves. Nevertheless, the event clearly marked the emergence of the Ottoman Empire as the most powerful State of the Near East, a State beside which most European kingdoms were petty principalities; a State, moreover, bent on military expansion. The kingdoms of the Balkans and the Danube basin immediately received the impact of Turkish aggression. They were thrown upon a desperate defensive, retreating step by step, until the middle of the sixteenth century, when Sulaiman the Magnificent unsuccessfully besieged Vienna. Even more serious from a European point of view, the Turks became almost overnight the most formidable of the Medi-terranean powers. They had hitherto been horsemen rather than sailors. In Muhammad I's day they had been decisively defeated at sea by the Venetians. The capture of Constantinople, however, made them the heirs to the naval power of Byzantium. The Venetians, fearing for their trading privileges, hastened to make their peace, and succeeded in retaining most of their business contacts and some of their colonies, notably Crete. They could not, however, prevent the loss of the Morea and other territorial possessions, or deter the Turks from further Mediterranean aggression. In 1480, Muhammad II actually invaded Italy, took Otranto and established there a flourishing market in Christian slaves. Possibly a sustained campaign of conquest was pre-vented only by the Sultan's death in the following year. Naval power made the eventual defeat of the Mamluks and the extension of Turkish rule round the shores of the Levant certain. It also rendered any direct seaborne attack by a western force against the centres of Muslim power in the Levant quite out of the question. By the middle of the fifteenth century the mantle of the crusaders had fallen upon the Iberian kingdoms. Alone among European States, they were still in a position to inflict damage upon Islam. Their activities were necessarily, in the circumstances, local and limited; but the effects even of local successes might be widely felt throughout Islam, if vigorously exploited. It is against the background of disastrous European defeats in the Levant that Castilian campaigns against Granada and Portuguese expeditions to north-west Africa must be considered.

Both in Castile and in Portugal the idea of a crusade still had power to fire the imagination of men of gentle birth and adventurous impulses; though Iberian crusading fervour in the later Middle Ages was more sophisticated and more complex than the headstrong ransom-gambling adventurousness of the earlier crusades. Nor had it much in common with the Christian apostolate which had converted northern Europe in still older times. Nobody supposed that any serious impression could be made upon Islam by preaching or by rational disputation. Muslims were not only powerful and well-organized; they were also—though diabolically misguided—clever, self-confident and civilized. A missionary friar would have had no more chance of making converts in Granada or Damascus than would a mullah in Rome or Burgos. He would have been considered at best an interesting curiosity, at worst a spy or a dangerous lunatic. A duty to attempt conversion was recognized, of course. Individual captives, especially if captured in youth, were brought up in the faith of their captors. Naturally, also, considerable numbers of Muslims under Christian rule—or Christians under Muslim rule—adopted the religion of their rulers, either from conviction or as a matter of political or commercial prudence. Christian conquerors might sometimes attempt the forcible mass conversion of entire Muslim populations; but conversions achieved in this way were generally understood to be insincere and often temporary. No Christian ruler possessed, or attempted to create, any body of men comparable with the Turkish Janissaries. Genuine conversion on a wide scale was generally assumed to be an impracticable ideal. It might, moreover, be financially unprofitable, since both Christian and Muslim rulers often levied special taxes from subjects of different religion from their own; a practice which encouraged wars of conquest but discouraged attempts to convert the conquered. Nor—despite loud talk about smiting the infidel—was a crude policy of extermination ever seriously considered as either practicable or desirable.

Contact with the Arab world in the Middle Ages had formed part of the education of a rough and primitive Europe. European art and industry owe much to the Arabs. Greek science and learning found their way to medieval Europe—in so far as they were known at all—largely through Arabic translations. Even the elaborate conventions of late medieval chivalry were to some extent imitated from Arab customs and Arab romances. The Iberian peninsula was the principal channel of contact between the two cultures; and the more intelligent among the Christian rulers there understood the value and the importance of their intermediary function. Archbishop Raymond of Toledo in the twelfth century had founded schools where Arab, Jewish and Christian scholars collaborated in a series of works which, when communicated to the learned centres in Europe, opened a new era in medieval science. Alfonso X of Castile also gathered into his court the learned of three religions, for he was as eager to sift the wisdom of the East as of the West. He was the first European king to show a systematic interest in secularizing culture. His oriental works were translated into French, and influenced Dante. His astronomical tables were studied in Europe for centuries, and were read and annotated by Copernicus himself. Though exceptional, he was by no means unique in tolerance and wisdom. The greatest of all the monarchs of the Reconquest, Fernando III, King and Saint, is proclaimed by his epitaph to have been a king who tolerated infidel cults in mosque and synagogue.[3]

Within the Iberian peninsula, then, Christian and Muslim kingdoms had existed side by side for centuries and had perforce, when not actually fighting one another, maintained some kind of relations, however perfunctory. Occasionally, Christian rulers had allied with Muslims against Christians, and vice versa. Similarly, within particular kingdoms, Christian and Muslim populations had lived side by side, and while often feeling for one another little respect and no affection, had grown accustomed to one another's ways. Where conversions occurred, there were mixed marriages and mixed blood. Inevitably, Spanish culture, except in the very north, was profoundly affected. Arab influence made itself evident in the immense and varied vocabulary of the Spanish language, in social habits such as the seclusion of women, in architecture and the lay-out of towns, in commercial practices, and in a great range of practical devices: irrigation and water-lifting appliances; the design and rig of boats and ships; saddlery and harness. Moorish influence was less obvious in Portugal than in Spain. By the fifteenth century crusading in Portuguese territory was little more than a distant memory; hence the somewhat bookish and romantic crusading notions of, for example, Prince Henry 'the Navigator', contrasted with the much more practical attitude of his Spanish contemporaries.[4] In their varying degrees, however, both Spain and Portugal were homes of mixed societies, and probably that very fact equipped Spaniards and Portuguese, better than other Europeans, to understand and to deal with the still more exotic cultures they were to encounter when they embarked upon a career of oversea adventure.[5]

By the fifteenth century, European civilization had developed to a point where it no longer depended upon the Arab world for inspiration and instruction, and in Spain Africanizing fashions tended to become a somewhat sterile affectation. At the hedonistic and disorderly court of Henry IV of Castile, this affectation was pushed to extremes in which the Christian religion was derided, Moorish customs openly adopted, and the war against Islam forgotten or deliberately postponed. The Succession War and the accession of Isabella brought a sharp reversal. Isabella, inspired not only by intense religious conviction, but also by apprehension of the danger threatening from the East, was determined to press ahead immediately with preparations against Granada (whose rulers, emboldened by the Succession War, had withheld tribute in 1476) and if possible eventually to carry the war into the enemy's territory in Africa, as the Portuguese had already done at Ceuta in 1415. Systematic operations for the conquest of the Moorish kingdom, village by village, began in 1482. Spaniards embarked on this last European crusade with a complex mixture of attitudes towards the Muslim enemy. The mixture included intense religious exaltation; abhorrence of unbelief, modified (on the part of feudal superiors) by concessions to economic expediency; acquisitiveness, in the sense not only of hope of plunder, but of determination to exploit the Moors as vassals; social dislike, modified by long familiarity; economic envy (for the Moors were usually better farmers and craftsmen, and often sharper traders, than their Spanish rivals); and finally acute political fear—fear not of Granada, but of the powerful support which might reach Granada if that kingdom were not brought under Christian control. As for Granada, isolated and divided within itself, the issue was never in serious doubt. The capital city fell in 1492. All Spain, for the first time in many centuries, was ruled by Christian sovereigns. The territory of Granada was duly divided in fiefs among the leaders in the campaign.

The conquest did not relieve Spain of the fear of Islam; nor did the Spanish invasion of North Africa, which began with the capture of Melilla in 1492, prevent the advance of the Turks. Early in the sixteenth century they conquered Syria and Egypt and extended their suzerainty along the whole north African coast. The immense power of the Ottoman Empire could then be summoned to defend the Muslim rulers of the coast, and possibly even to support rebellion among disaffected Moors in Spain. It was a power too strong to be challenged, as yet, by the forces of the Spanish kingdoms. Meanwhile, the enthusiasms and ambitions generated by the war against Granada persisted, only partially satisfied by victory. An outlet for this pent-up martial energy was suggested, only a year after the fall of Granada, by Columbus' report of islands in the western Atlantic, and by his insistence that those islands might be used as stepping-stones to China. Within a generation, the feelings which had rallied Spaniards against Granada developed into a bold and methodical imperialism which, casting about for new provinces to conquer, found its opportunity overseas. While Portuguese imperialism in West Africa sought, among other objects, a back door through which to attack the Arab and the Turk, Spanish imperialism, by chance discovery, was led to operate in a new world.

Granada was to the Spaniards what Constantinople, in its last enfeebled years, had been to the Turks: the culmination of one series of conquests, and the beginning of another. There was a curious parallel between the role of the Turks in the Byzantine Empire and that of the Castilians in Muslim Spain. The Turks had been nomads; they had entered the Near East as highly mobile mounted bands operating against a long-established agricultural or city-dwelling society. They settled down as overlords, living by the labour of a conquered peasantry, and recruiting their subordinate officials and their technical experts from the literate among their new subjects; but never themselves entirely losing their character as horsemen. The Castilians had never been parasitic upon the horse in the same degree as the Turks, but they too, in Andalusia and elsewhere, employed mobile and largely mounted forces against sedentary communities. Among them, in the arid uplands of Castile, pastoral pursuits, the grazing of semi-nomadic flocks and herds, had long been preferred to arable farming. The preference was social and military as well as economic; it was the legacy of centuries of intermittent fighting, of constantly shifting frontiers. The man on horseback, the master of flocks and herds, was best adapted to such conditions; the peasant, conversely, was economically vulnerable and socially despised. As the work of conquest proceeded, the Castilians, or the upper classes, the fighting classes, among them, retained their pastoral interests and possessions, their mobility and military effectiveness, and their respect for the man on horseback. Like the Turks, as far as possible they lived by the labour and employed the skill of vassal peoples as well as of their own peasants and craftsmen. These social habits produced a class of fighting men well fitted for the conquest, and the subsequent organization, of the settled peoples of the New World, who were prosperous arable farmers or docile town-dwellers, and who had never before even seen horses and horned cattle. Small bands of mounted Spaniards could achieve remarkable victories, and could then settle as quasi-feudal overlords, retaining their own pastoral interests and avocations, relying on conquered peasants to grow grain for them, as both they and the Turks had done in the Old World; their mobility as horsemen enabling them to suppress revolts with a minimum of effort. In this respect also, reconquest in Spain was an appropriate training for imperial expansion in America.

Isabella, however, advised by the uncompromising ecclesiastics who surrounded her, was little disposed to allow the Moors of Granada to settle down peacefully as Muslim vassals of Christian overlords. Religious zeal, for her, must find expression not only in conquest and suzerainty, but in conversion. After the capture of Granada she inaugurated a new policy of vigorous proselytizing. This policy, initially confined to preaching and persuasion, met with very limited success, despite the devotion of the Observant Franciscans to whom it was entrusted. The impatience of the Queen and her minister Cisneros soon insisted upon sterner measures: systematic persecution and a drastic stiffening of ecclesiastical discipline. The expulsion of the Jews, the violent baptism of the Moors of Granada, the extraordinary powers entrusted to the new Inquisition, were all radical departures from medieval tradition in Spain. All three were, on the whole, publicly approved, as they would not have been a hundred years before; and in Castile (though not in Aragon) they were vigorously enforced. They represented both a reaction against the intensified Muslim pressure on Christendom since the fall of Constantinople, and an intensification of religious fervour, and so of religious intolerance, in Spain. This intensification of zeal, this new enthusiasm for conversion, quickly travelled to the New World, where it was to find new and more effective forms of expression.

Humanist learning, apostolic fervour, and discipline, were the principal features of the reform of the Church in Spain undertaken by Cardinal Ximénez de Cisneros in the late fifteenth and early sixteenth centuries.[6] The regular Orders included in their ranks many men who were exalted by a spiritual unrest closely akin to that which was to break out in Reformation in northern Europe. Cisneros' reforms appealed to this unrest, and rendered it effective. He sought above all to purify the clergy by strengthening the austerity and the preaching mission of the mendicant Orders. Among the Orders he favoured his own Franciscans, and among Franciscans the strict Observants, who in Spain and Portugal elected to preach their simple and austere Christianity among poor and neglected rural folk, and among infidels, as their papal privileges expressly commanded them to do. Internal reform movements similar to the Franciscan Observance occurred about the turn of the century in other Orders also, particularly among Dominicans and Jeronymites. A remarkable increase in the reformed mendicant population occurred in Cisneros' lifetime. From it emerged a spiritual *élite* of evangelical tendency, which was to sympathize with Erasmus and to come under suspicion of Lutheranism later in the century. From it emerged, also, a spiritual militia, recruited from disciplined, highly-trained religious radicals, available for employment in the New World. The Amerindian peoples encountered by Spaniards in Cisneros' own day were weak, primitive, and few in number; but from the second decade of the sixteenth century Spaniards came into contact with the settled city-building peoples of Mexico and Central America, and in dealing with them, missionary policy became an issue of burning importance. They were numerous and well-organized. They possessed a material culture which, despite crucial technical weaknesses, impressed and attracted the Spanish invaders. They had no knowledge of Christianity, a deficiency for which they clearly could not be blamed or punished; and on the credit side they were uncontaminated by Islam. Their own religion included rites of horrifying savagery; but individually they appeared to be gentle and docile people for the most part; and their agrarian collectivism seemed to provide an ideal basis on which to build Christian communities. Neither Crown nor Church in Spain could ignore the opportunity and the duty of bringing such people into the Christian fold, or could contemplate leaving matters to the consciences of the *conquistadores*. The Crown early decided to entrust the American mission to the mendicant Orders. For a time, at least, it gave masterful support to the mendicant vows of renunciation, the Christian doctrine of a compassionate deity, and the institutional authority of the sacraments. Such a missionary policy, with its logical consequences in terms of control over the native population, inevitably conflicted with the economic interests of the leading colonists, and led to long and acrimonious disputes; but the friars commanded the respect and sympathy of many of the *conquistadores*, including Cortés, who himself petitioned for a Franciscan mission to Mexico. The feeling of 'bringing light to those who were in darkness' was general even among the humbler soldiers, and helps to explain their conviction that, however unsanctified their own lives might be, the Saints fought on their side. This is not to suggest an unsophisticated credulity. The stories of the actual appearance of St James in battle were invented by chroniclers, not by *conquistadores*; Bernal Díaz treats these 'miracles' with ironic contempt.[7] Nevertheless, the *conquistadores* prayed to St Peter and St James before their battles, and the feeling of divine support was strong among them. In somewhat lesser degree, and in very different circumstances, the same was true of the Portuguese in India. Missionary zeal, the desire to bring genuine conversion to millions of pagan souls, must be placed high among the motives of the Reconnaissance.

Acquisitiveness and religious zeal, however, even taken together, are not the whole story. The unprecedented harshness with which Isabella treated the Moors of Granada was more than an expression of religious intolerance and political hostility. It represented a deliberate rejection on the Queen's part of the African element in Spanish culture. It was accompanied by an equally deliberate affirmation of Spain's community with the rest of Christian Europe. The Queen's iron will and keen intelligence worked to end the intellectual isolation of Spain, not by a timid and defensive obscurantism, but by a vigorous and self-confident encouragement of European learning. Her reign was a golden age for universities. The famous foundations of Alcalá, Salamanca and Valladolid date from this time. (The founding impulse was soon carried to the New World, for both Mexico and Peru were to have universities within a generation or so of their conquest.) Many printing presses were set up in Spain in Isabella's reign. Foreign scholars and foreign books, Italian, French, German and Flemish, were welcomed and encouraged. Ideas and literary conventions characteristic of the Italian Renaissance spread throughout Spain, albeit in forms modified by Spanish sobriety and conservatism, and without the superficial paganism of much Italian writing. Classical scholars such as Alfonso de Palencia and Antonio de Lebrija (who had been educated in Italy) worked in the direct tradition of Lorenzo Valla. The great Polyglot Bible is one of the chief glories of Renaissance scholarship. In more popular literary forms also, Italian influence pervaded Spain. The *Orlando Furioso* of Ariosto was quickly translated and widely read in Spanish. Epics and romances of all kinds enjoyed a great vogue in Spain in the early sixteenth century. Bernal Díaz, writing of his first breathtaking sight of the city of Mexico, remarked quite naturally that it put him in mind of the Amadis romances.

With Renaissance literary conventions, Spaniards absorbed Renaissance attitudes of mind: the cult of the individual, the passion for personal reputation. This passion was vital in the mental make-up of the *conquistadores*, and goes far to explain their prickly pride, their dislike of discipline and regimentation, their insistence on being consulted about every decision. On the other hand, it also helps to explain their extravagant daring and their indifference to wounds and fatigue. They conducted themselves, and their chroniclers wrote, with the high seriousness of men conscious of taking part in great deeds; men who saw themselves not as imitators, but as rivals, of the heroes of antiquity and of romance. Cortés—most eloquent of *conquistadores*, one most sensitive to the mood of his men, and himself a product of Renaissance Salamanca—returned again and again in his speeches and letters to this theme. He alluded sometimes to the riches that lay ahead, and sometimes to the glory of winning pagan souls; but most frequently to the

31

prospect of human fame. In endeavouring, for example, to persuade his men on the beach at Vera Cruz to scuttle the boats in which they had come from Cuba, he gave them 'many comparisons with brave deeds done by heroes among the Romans'.[8] When his more cautious companions complained that Alexander had attempted nothing so foolhardy as the taking of Mexico with four hundred men, he told them that history would relate greater things of them than of the ancient captains. There were darker comparisons, of course. Cortés could not have missed the analogy between Cuauhtémoc and Vercingetorix; *vae victis*. But Cortés, like Caesar, cultivated in general a reputation for gallant and politic clemency, and he ran considerable risks to stop his Indian allies butchering the defeated Aztecs. Bernal Díaz—every historian of the *conquista* must return to that garrulous old soldier—boasted no nobility save that of having fought in a hundred and nineteen battles—more than twice those of Julius Caesar; and like the great Roman he wished—as he explains—to record his own deeds, along with those of Cortés, 'in the manner of the writings and reports of . . . illustrious men who served in wars in time past; in order that my children, grandchildren and descendants can say "my father came to discover and conquer these lands . . . and was one of the foremost in the conquest".'[9] This passionate care for reputation was not, of course, confined to Spaniards. It was common to most of the pioneers of the Reconnaissance, of whatever nation. Sir Humphrey Gilbert's serene (and avoidable) death on board the *Squirrel* was a late instance of it. Such men sought not only riches 'such as all men desire', not only merit in the eyes of God, but also fame among their own people and in posterity.

With a new attitude towards the individual, the Renaissance fostered a new attitude towards the State, also Italian in origin. A sensitive alertness, a studied, objective attention to the most effective and most elegant means of achieving desired ends, tended to supplant the older notion of the State as a network of fixed, traditional rights and duties, over which the monarch presided as a judge of disputes. It was becoming recognized that a government might use force, whether against subjects or against neighbouring princes, in pursuit of rational interests as well as in support of legal claims. Like many Italian rulers, Isabella of Castile owed her throne to a mixture of war and diplomacy. A masterful restoration of public order and discipline was one of her major achievements, and contributed greatly to the growth of authoritarian feeling in Castile. Machiavelli's principles of statecraft had no more successful exemplars than Ferdinand of Aragon and John II of Portugal. It is true that this more flexible attitude towards sovereignty and statecraft, this cult of governmental expediency, was restrained, particularly in Spain, by legalistic conservatism as well as by individual obstinacy.

Nevertheless, it helped to prepare men's minds for the immense task of political and administrative improvisation which was to confront Spanish government in the New World.

The fifteenth century was remarkable for the spontaneous growth, among a few gifted and highly-placed men, of a genuine disinterested curiosity. Like the passion for classical learning (and, of course, associated with it) this spirit of curiosity was among the leading characteristics of the Renaissance. It can hardly, at first, be called scientific, for it was undisciplined and quite unsystematic. The men of the Renaissance were concerned to absorb knowledge rather than to digest it, to amass rather than to select. Their curiosity was far stronger in inquiry than in arrangement; but it was omnivorous, lively, uninhibited; and while it corroded and gradually weakened the accepted medieval systems of knowledge, it collected, with avid and apparently random enthusiasm, the materials of which new systems would eventually be constructed. It was shared not only by scholars, but by princes and by men of action in their *entourage*, especially in Italy, but also in Portugal and Spain. Geography and cosmography were prominent among the objects upon which it seized, but it had many others. The attention paid to medical research at the time, especially to anatomy, is well known. Less obvious, but also important in the growth of the idea of discovery, is a new and more observant attitude towards natural history. How far explorers and promoters of exploration were directly and consciously moved by scientific curiosity, is impossible to say on the scanty evidence which remains; but the explorers' attitude towards what they saw, and the reception of their reports by the public at home, were both profoundly affected by the new spirit. Bernal Díaz, for example, was greatly impressed, but not particularly surprised, by the extensive collections of plants and wild animals kept in Montezuma's compound; botanical gardens and menageries were common among the hobbies of Renaissance princes,[10] and it seemed to him perfectly natural for Montezuma to have similar interests. Diego de Ordaz, who climbed to the crater of Popocatépetl, partly to get sulphur to make gunpowder, partly out of bravado, but also partly out of curiosity, was emulating—consciously or not—the celebrated exploit of Petrarch on Mont Ventoux in an age when mountain climbing was unheard of.[11] One of the earliest books about America, written by an eye-witness—Oviedo's *General History of the Indies*[12]—admirably illustrates this Renaissance interest by the clarity and detail of its account of animals and plants. Of geographical curiosity—the disinterested desire to know what lay beyond the horizon—the outstanding fifteenth-century expression was the *De Orbe Novo* of Peter Martyr,[13] significantly written by a cultivated Italian who found a congenial home in Spain.

Technical inventions in the fifteenth century, not immediately connected with the use of the sea, served to widen and popularize this growing curiosity. The most important of these was, of course, printing. Printing not only made possible a far wider diffusion of sailing directions, navigational manuals, and other aids to literate sailors, and not only spread the news of discoveries far more quickly than manuscripts could do; it contributed to a rapid increase in the numbers of the reading public, and in so doing created a great demand for comparatively light reading—reading intended for literate, educated people who were not professional scholars. This demand was met partly by romances, but also very largely by accounts of travels, both real and fictitious. Mandeville's *Travels*, for example, circulated widely in manuscript in the fifteenth century, among people who could not be sure whether or not the voyages it described were genuine; but it circulated more widely still later, in printed editions, and enjoyed its greatest vogue in the second half of the sixteenth century, when it was already suspected of being a fraud and was read mainly for entertainment. Many serious books—Peter Martyr's *De Orbe Novo*, Montalboddo's *Paesi novamente retrovati*,[14] Sebastian Münster's *Cosmographia universalis*,[15] all 'bestsellers' through many editions—were widely read in the same spirit; and later still, no gentleman's library was complete without the stately folios of De Bry's *Grands Voyages*.[16] These are but a few of the most famous among hundreds of well-known titles. The popularity of travel books, and of references to remote lands in plays and allegories, was a striking feature of the literary life of the sixteenth century, and contributed greatly to the steady growth of interest in exploration and discovery.

The explorers, the promoters who sent them out, the public who applauded their deeds and profited by their discoveries, were impelled, then, by a complex mixture of motives and feelings. Generations of historians have endeavoured to sort out the mixture, to identify the elements in it which can be labelled 'medieval', 'Renaissance', 'modern', and so forth; but the mixture remains. The Renaissance, in the most commonly accepted use of the term, was primarily a Mediterranean achievement, the Reconnaissance primarily an Atlantic one. It is tempting to describe the Iberian peninsula, from which most of the early discoverers sailed, as the meeting ground where Mediterranean knowledge, curiosity and inventiveness met, and inspired, Atlantic courage and skill. The thesis has much truth in it; but it is not a complete explanation, and in linking Renaissance and Reconnaissance we must take care not to anticipate. Portuguese captains were sailing on tentative voyages of Atlantic discovery long before the Italian Renaissance had seriously affected Iberian culture. Most of these early voyages—at least those of which record remains—were undertaken by the command, or with the encouragement, of Prince Henry of Portugal, the 'Navigator', most famous of the precursors and inspirers of the Reconnaissance. The waters between Cape St Vincent, the Canaries, and the north-west coast of Morocco, were already known in his day to adventurous Portuguese fishermen. Prince Henry placed gentlemen of his own household in command of the ships, and set them definite geographical objects to be reached and passed. Thus from the habit of making fishing and casual trading voyages along a relatively short stretch of coast, there developed a programme of progressive, though intermittent, exploration much further south. Prince Henry did not, of course, go to sea himself, except as a military commander against the Moorish kingdom of Fez; late medieval conventions of propriety would have prevented a royal prince from participating—even had he wished —in long voyages of discovery in small vessels ill-provided for his state. His function was to provide the ships, the backing, the organization and the encouragement; and it may be presumed that his personal wishes dictated at least the official aims. Zurara, the contemporary chronicler of Prince Henry's achievements,[17] lists the motives which impelled the Prince to undertake the exploration of the West African coast, and states that the first was a desire to know what lay beyond the Canaries and Cape Bojador. There is no suggestion, however, of a scientific or disinterested curiosity; the purpose was practical. Diogo Gomes, one of Prince Henry's captains, was specific on this point. In his account of his own voyages of 1444 and 1463, he states that the Prince desired to find the countries whence came the gold which reached Morocco by the desert routes, 'in order to trade with them and so maintain the gentlemen of his household'.[18] Again the familiar formula: serve God and grow rich. Zurara gives as Prince Henry's second reason a desire to open profitable new trades, but insists that trade must only be with Christian peoples, whom the explorers hoped to encounter beyond the country of the Moors. This was standard medieval doctrine. Although some purists considered *all* trade to be incompatible with knighthood, it was thought legitimate by many to deprive the infidel of resources for making war by indirect means if direct means failed. The third, fourth and fifth objects mentioned by Zurara were all conventional crusading aims: to investigate the extent of Moorish power, to convert pagans to Christianity, and to seek alliance with any Christian rulers who might be found. The long-lived Prester John legend, fed no doubt by rumours of the Coptic kingdom of Abyssinia, was by this time localized in Africa; and the hope of contact with some such ruler connected African exploration with the older Mediterranean crusade.

The sixth, and according to Zurara the strongest motive, was the

35

Prince's desire to fulfil the predictions of his horoscope, which bound him 'to engage in great and noble conquests, and above all . . . to attempt the discovery of things which were hidden from other men'. This, too, was a conventional late medieval attitude, and a reminder that in Prince Henry's day astronomical knowledge was still more commonly applied to fortune-telling than to navigation. Prince Henry's own personality remains an enigma for the historian; but the picture which emerges from the chronicle is that of a conservative, staunchly medieval figure. The characteristics most stressed by contemporaries who knew him—by Zurara, by Diogo Gomes, and by the Venetian merchant venturer Cadamosto[19]—were his rigid piety, his personal asceticism, and his obsession with the idea of the Crusade. Zurara, it is true, wrote as a panegyrist in Henry's lifetime; but that is all the more reason for supposing that he emphasized traits in which Henry himself took pride. As for Cadamosto, he clearly admired the Prince, but was not his dependent and had no reason to be other than truthful. About Henry's crusading obsession there can be no doubt. Despite his perpetual need of money—a need which the revenues of the Order of Christ only partly relieved—he reconciled himself only late in his career, and then reluctantly, to the trade which his captains initiated—for lack of Christian princes in West Africa—with pagan peoples. He was always ready to drop the indirect crusade of the African voyage in favour of direct military assaults upon Morocco, whenever his royal relatives could be persuaded to mount these costly and fruitless adventures. The memorial which he wrote in 1436 urging an attack on Tangier,[20] and his own gallant but inflexible conduct in command of the enterprise, both recall the pages of Froissart. All this was far from the Renaissance, with its bright, lively curiosity, its clear, hard sense of expediency, its passion for human fame, its love of learning and the arts. The evidence of Henry's support of learning is far from clear. He was not particularly learned himself, and unlike his royal brothers, left no writings. Though he was a generous patron of sailors and cartographers, the story of a school of astronomy and mathematics at Sagres is pure invention. Certainly this pious and chivalrous ascetic was no Renaissance humanist.

The concept of Renaissance itself is elusive and hard to define. An eminent scholar has recently reminded us that the Renaissance, in some of its aspects, was more 'medieval' than many historians have supposed.[21] However Renaissance be defined, the Reconnaissance, the early process of discovery, began independently, with medieval motives and assumptions. Prince Henry and his captains were, in the main, men of the Middle Ages. Even Columbus, as we shall see, embarked on his famous enterprise with an intellectual equipment which was mainly medieval and traditional. In the course of the later fifteenth century, the movement gained speed and power from a series of vital technical improvements and inventions. Towards the end of the fifteenth, and in the early sixteenth century, it was further accelerated and profoundly modified by ideas associated with the Renaissance in Italy and imported from there into the Iberian peninsula. An attempt to define these ideas has been made. It remains to describe the more technical aspects of the matter: the finance, the organization and the tools.

CHAPTER 2

COMMERCIAL EXPERIENCE AND FINANCIAL BACKING

THROUGHOUT the fifteenth century—and indeed throughout most of the sixteenth—the Mediterranean and its sea-borne trade remained the most important single element in the active commercial and maritime life of western Europe. The mid-fifteenth-century Mediterranean was still very much a world of its own. It was a large world, not yet dwarfed by comparison with the world of great oceans beyond Suez and Gibraltar. A ship—an ordinary merchant ship, with reasonable weather —might take up to two months to make the passage, say, from Barcelona to Alexandria; perhaps two or three weeks from Messina to Tripoli of Barbary; ten or twelve days from Genoa to Tunis. There was plenty of space, plenty of elbow-room; and the area as a whole was almost self-supporting. The sixty million or so people[1] who inhabited the countries bordering the inland sea produced between them most of the food, many of the raw materials and almost all of the manufactured goods which they consumed. They built their own ships and carried their own trade. The richest, liveliest and most varied economic activity of the region was concentrated in the relatively small area of northern Italy comprising Milan, Florence, Genoa, Venice, and their smaller neighbours and satellites. Milan and Florence were primarily manufacturing centres, with flourishing export trades. Venice and Genoa, both great industrial centres, were also major naval powers and bases of great merchant fleets.

Most of the shipping of north Italy and of the western Mediterranean generally—like most shipping everywhere—was engaged in the carriage of humdrum bulky necessities. Of these, grain was probably the most important. Most of the larger cities were obliged to import part of their requirements by sea and river over considerable distances, and in times of local failure to increase their imports at short notice. In the East, Constantinople—an immense city by European standards—was a great maw engulfing all the grain that came its way; but Constantinople could draw upon the fertile regions on the shores of the Black Sea. Cairo, the other urban colossus, was even better placed. The Nile valley could always feed Cairo and Alexandria, with plenty to spare. Similarly the thriving commercial cities of Syria had supplies of grain at their very doors. In the West, more populous and less productive, the situation was more difficult. Florence, Genoa, Venice, Ragusa, Naples, the cities of the east coast of Spain—these last mostly set in country producing wine, or oil, or wool—all were importers of grain by sea, since their local supplies were inadequate or unreliable, and local land transport was costly. The principal western sources were Apulia and Sicily, both controlled politically by the rulers of Aragon, who were regular importers; but the western Mediterranean as a whole was rarely self-sufficient in grain, and the importing cities also had constant recourse to the cheap and plentiful grain of the Levant. Venice, particularly, relied upon eastern grain; its Aegean colonies were a useful source of supply, and the republic also regularly imported grain from Egypt. There existed in the western Mediterranean, therefore, a specialized, complicated, and necessarily flexible sea-borne trade in grain. The ships, Venetian, Genoese, Ragusan, were large, were designed to carry their bulky cargo, and usually carried nothing else.

Though by far the most essential, grain was by no means the only bulky article of food to be carried by sea in the Mediterranean. Salt, and food preserved in salt, were both considerable articles of trade. The Venetians were the principal carriers of salt, Istria and Sicily the chief exporting sources. Fishing was universal; the tunny fisheries of the Straits of Messina and the coastal waters of Provence were the richest sources of fish for salting. Mediterranean supplies of salt fish, however, never fully met the demand, and the cities of Italy and Spain also imported fish caught and salted in Atlantic waters. Throughout the fifteenth century the Portuguese brought in tunny from their own waters; and at the very end of the century they found an eager Mediterranean market for salt cod from the Newfoundland Banks.

The other chief articles of food which went by sea in quantity were oil, wine and cheese. Cheese travelled by complex, criss-crossing routes, in many different varieties, from Auvergne, from Parma, from Milan, above all from Sardinia, whence whole shiploads were carried to Italy, France and Spain. Southern Italy and southern Spain were the principal sources of oil; both, but especially Italy, exported it in exchange for grain, even as far as to Egypt. Towards the end of the century, however, exports of oil from Andalusia began to be directed to the Canaries, and later to the West Indies, where it commanded very high prices. The Mediterranean wine trade—since viticulture was spread throughout the region—could not compare with the great fleets which left the Gironde, and later the Guadalquivir, for Atlantic destinations; but Naples supplied by sea the needs of Rome and of cities further north. Neapolitan wines were for daily use. More highly prized as luxuries were the sweet heavy wines of Cyprus and of Crete—home of the famous Malvoisie grape—which were sold at high prices all over the Mediterranean from Constantinople to Genoa, and beyond Gibraltar to England. With these rarer wines went a trade in dried grapes—Spanish raisins and Greek 'currants', almonds and oranges—by the same routes, in Venetian and Genoese ships. Sugar, even in the Mediterranean, was still an expensive luxury in the fifteenth century. Crete and Cyprus were the chief sources of supply, but in the later fifteenth century Sicily and some parts of eastern Spain produced small quantities. Sugar was shipped to Venice from Messina; to Genoa from Alicante, Cartagena, and (after the capture of Granada) Malaga.

A busy and, by the standards of the time, densely populated urban concentration such as that of northern Italy, had to import not only food but many of the raw materials of industry, in particular of textile manufacture. The cloth industry, the principal foundation of the wealth of Florence, no longer depended heavily on English wool, which, indeed, was no longer available in sufficient quantity. Most of its wool came from Spain, shipped through Alicante and Cartagena, more rarely Barcelona and Valencia. The big ships of Ragusa, as well as those of Venice and Genoa, were prominent in this trade. Alum, essential as a mordant and cleansing agent, was also imported in very large quantities, and probably occupied a greater tonnage of shipping than any other commodity, except perhaps grain. The great alum deposits of Tolfa, near Civitavecchia, were not extensively developed until the early sixteenth century. In the fifteenth, most of the alum used in northern Italy came from Asia Minor. Its transport was virtually monopolized by Genoese shippers, who carried it not only to Italy but also to England and the Netherlands. The very large size of many Genoese merchant ships was a consequence of the need to carry this bulky and relatively cheap commodity.

Woollen cloth was not the only textile manufactured in quantity in northern Italy. The Lombard towns, especially Cremona, specialized in light and cheap fustians—linens—which were widely exported: to Germany over the passes, to North Africa, and to the Levant. More important still was silk. The extravagant Renaissance taste in clothes made silk a serious rival to woollens; and although the import of raw silk from China and Turkestan became more and more difficult in the fifteenth century, the Italians tried to overcome the difficulty by developing sericulture at home. Upper Italy, today the biggest raw-silk producer in Europe, then produced very little. Sicily and Calabria were the main producing areas, and the silk was shipped to north Italy from Messina.

While Florence was the chief textile centre of the Mediterranean world, Milan was the centre of metallurgical industry, particularly the manufacture of arms and armour. Iron deposits were so widespread that most Mediterranean iron-working towns could use ore found near their doors; but copper, tin and lead were valuable objects of long-haul trade. Copper came largely from south Germany overland, and much of it was re-exported to the eastern Mediterranean in Venetian ships. England was—as it had been for centuries—a chief source of lead and tin, both brought into the Mediterranean in Venetian and Genoese ships.

These trades in food, raw materials and manufactured goods were the day-to-day basis of Mediterranean prosperity. More famous, more sought after, and, for a few fortunate merchants and capitalists, more profitable, were the trades in luxury goods of eastern origin: Chinese and Persian silks, greatly superior to Italian; Indian cotton cloth; rhubarb, grown in China and much prized as a medicine; precious stones—emeralds from India, rubies from Burma, sapphires from Ceylon; above all, spices. The general term 'spices' included in the later Middle Ages not only condiments for preserving and seasoning food, but drugs, dyes, perfumes, unguents, cosmetics, and sundry expensive articles of food. Pegolotti, whose fourteenth-century merchants' hand-book has already been mentioned,[2] lists two hundred and eighty-eight different 'spices', including eleven kinds of sugar, many waxes and gums and, surprisingly, glue. The most important spices, however, at least in terms of value, were those to which the name would nowadays be confined—aromatic condiments and preservatives, almost all grown in the East. Pepper was the most widespread. Species of *capsicum*, red pepper, grew in many parts of the Tropics including (as Portuguese and Spaniards were to discover) Africa and the New World; but the prized white and black peppers of medieval commerce came from the fruits of *piper nigrum*, which was confined to the East and had been used as a condiment there from very early times. Much of the pepper brought to Europe in the fifteenth century came from western India, but the best originated in Sumatra. Cinnamon was then, and is now, almost con-fined to Ceylon. Nutmegs and their by-product mace were grown chiefly in the Banda islands. Cloves, the most sought-after of the spices, grew only in a few small islands in the Moluccas group. These varied and valuable commodities were the objects of insatiable demand in the Near East and all over Europe. They could all be bought in the spice marts of western India. In the Mediterranean they were handled mainly by Venetians and Genoese; but the Italians supplied only the last links in long, well-established chains of intermediaries.

In the great days of the Mongol Khans much Chinese merchandise destined for Europe had travelled overland on the backs of camels and donkeys by many different caravan routes, to termini in the ports of the Levant and the Black Sea; and European merchants, not infrequently, had themselves travelled with their goods by these routes. Flourishing Italian merchant colonies had grown up at the principal termini, at Constantinople and Pera, its commercial suburb; at Tana (Azof); at Caffa in the Crimea and at other Black Sea ports. In the fourteenth century, Pegolotti's safe route to Peking became exceedingly unsafe and European travel to the East came to an end. The overland routes in general declined in importance, not only because of political disturbance, but from the same physical causes which kept predatory nomads on the move. Progressive desiccation in the lands of central Asia made pasture unreliable. The flow of merchandise overland diminished, and the ancient towns through which the caravans passed became impoverished. In the fifteenth century, though Persian silks still came by way of Tabriz to Trebizond, and thence to Constantinople, the main trade in luxury goods between Europe and the Far East was carried over most of its stages by sea. At its eastern end it was handled by Chinese, whose junks collected the cloves and nutmeg of the East Indies and delivered them for sale in the great Malayan port of Malacca. From Malacca across the Bay of Bengal to India the trade was in the hands of Muslim merchants, whether Indian, Malay or Arab. In India, the far-eastern cargoes, together with the cinnamon of Ceylon and the pepper of India itself, were sold in the spice ports of the Malabar coast—Calicut, Cochin, Cananore, Goa—and further north in the ports of Gujerat. The trade of these ports with the rest of the Indian Ocean littoral was largely in the hands of Arabs. From Malabar their teak-built ocean-going *baghlas* cleared with their precious cargoes for the harbours of Persia, Arabia and East Africa, maintaining sailings whose regularity derived from the regular alternation of the north-east and south-west monsoons. There were two alternative routes from the Indian Ocean to the Mediterranean, and two principal ports of transhipment: Aden and Ormuz. From Aden, the way up the Red Sea, that heated funnel of reef-bound water, was slow and hazardous, and the big *baghlas* rarely ventured beyond the Bab-el-Mandeb. Red Sea trade was carried in a great number of small coasting vessels, *zaruqs*, *sambuqs*, and many other lateen types, mostly Egyptian, plying from one port to another up to Suez, the Red Sea harbour for Cairo and the Nile valley. In the Persian Gulf the large double-ended *boums*, still characteristic of the region, carried eastern spices, and East African goods such as ivory, from Ormuz into the Shatt-al-Arab. From there, shipments were conveyed by river boat and camel caravan by way of the Euphrates to Aleppo, by way of Baghdad to Damascus, or even across Asia Minor to Constantinople, according to political circumstance and prevailing demand.

From Constantinople, from Alexandria, and from Antioch, Tripoli and Beirut, outlet harbours for Aleppo and Damascus, Italian ships carried silk and spice cargoes to Venice and Genoa. The costs of the trade, and the imposts upon it, were enormous; but so were the profits. It was said that a merchant could ship six cargoes, and lose five, but still make a profit when the sixth was sold.

In Constantinople the Italians—the Venetians especially—were a dominant and privileged group, at least until 1453. In the Aegean, the Venetian colonies were colonies in the modern sense of the word, with actual territorial administration. In the Black Sea, the more strictly commercial colonies—self-governing communities of businessmen—survived the decline of the overland silk trade. Caffa, the most important, though no longer the terminus of a route to China, remained a great commercial capital, frequented by Turks and Tatars of the Kipchak as well as by Russians, Poles, and various Balkan peoples. Here, and at many smaller Black Sea markets, the Italians had learned to do business with comparatively primitive nomadic groups, to whom they sold salt, coarse cloth, and even ready-made garments, and from whom they bought caviar and slaves. In Aleppo, Damascus, Alexandria, on the other hand, the Italians were strangers in cities ruled by powerful, civilized, but often capricious Muslim rulers. Their manner of residence, the terms on which they might do business, indeed their right to do business at all, depended upon agreements negotiated with the rulers, which might be reviewed or even in extremity revoked. The major trading groups occupied *fondaci* (from the Arabic *funduq*), factory compounds where the merchants lived and stored their goods. The Venetians held two such compounds in Alexandria. Within its compound, each merchant community was in most respects self-governing; but the officials of the *fondaco* might be held corporately liable for debts contracted or crimes committed by its members outside. This pattern of extra-territorial factories—some open, some fortified, depending on the effectiveness of the local government—was to become a familiar feature of European commercial expansion in the East. In short, all the types of settlement which Portuguese and other Europeans were to establish in the East in the sixteenth and seventeenth centuries had their precedents in Italian settlements in the later Middle Ages in the Mediterranean and the Black Sea.

In their manner of conducting and financing their business, also, the Italians demonstrated the methods which were later to be used by others in the East. To pay for their valuable eastern imports, they exported woollen and linen textiles, arms and armour, all products of northern Italy, and re-exported metals—copper, lead and tin—from northern Europe. Their trade balance with their eastern correspondents, however, was usually unfavourable, so that they also exported bullion. To cover the unfavourable balance, they developed a considerable local trade designed—in anticipation of the 'country trades' in the East in the succeeding century or two—to support the main long-haul trade in luxury goods. Caucasian slaves bought at Caffa were sold by Genoese dealers in Alexandria, where they commanded high prices. From the North African ports, Italian merchants shipped coral, prized almost as a precious stone in East Africa and sent there through Alexandria. Italians participated in the inland trade of the Maghreb with the south Saharan kingdoms—at least one enterprising Florentine sold Lombard cloth in Timbuktu[3]—and derived from that trade part of the bullion with which they paid for even more precious spices.

Venice and Genoa—Venice especially—were throughout the fifteenth century the centres from which Eastern luxury goods were distributed to western and northern Europe. The goods went by river or pack train throughout Italy; across the Alpine passes to south Germany (which in this respect, as in many others, formed part of the hinterland of Venice); by sea to Marseilles and up the Rhône to central France; by sea to Alicante, Malaga, Barcelona, and thence by pack train to the great fairs of central Spain; through the Straits in annual convoys of Italian galleys to England, the Low Countries and the North. These annual convoys, the Flanders galleys, began their sailings in 1314 and continued for more than two hundred years. They were one of the best-known features of late medieval trade, and provided a striking example of co-operation between government and private enterprise. The government provided the organization and usually some of the armament; though the armed vessels of the Republic also carried merchandise, and the majority of the ships in company were privately owned.[4]

Italian seaborne trade to the Levant and to western and northern Europe, with its possibilities of heavy loss as well as of high profit, was backed by great accumulations of capital. If Venice (having outstripped Genoa) was the leading seaport of the western world, Florence was the greatest banking centre, and the Medici bank, throughout the fifteenth century, the biggest financial organization. Its activities reached every region of Europe, the Levant and North Africa; they included not only banking operations and a vast trade in luxury goods, but also staple trades, especially in grain, control of many units of textile production, and the exploitation of alum mines. Many other banks in Florence and in other northern and central Italian cities had huge capital and widespread business interests, maintained by agents in all major centres. The size and efficiency of Italian commercial and financial organization; the superiority of Italian manufactured products; the Italian monopoly of trade in eastern goods; all combined to tie the whole of Europe, in greater or less degree, commercially to northern Italy.

Italian commerce increased steadily in volume throughout the century. As Italy had been the nursery of commercial growth, before the Black Death and the fourteenth-century depression, so Italy led the way in fifteenth-century recovery. By the middle of the century, however, competitors were beginning to appear; and changes, economic, technological and political, were to favour these competitors, and to drive the Italians to more and more ingenious shifts in order to maintain their leadership. Northern Europe, like the Mediterranean, possessed a thriving and well-developed industrial—chiefly cloth-working—area in the southern Netherlands, which imported most of its raw material. As the supply of English wool dried up, the Flemings turned more and more to Spain, and competed with Italian buyers for the supply of high-grade Spanish wool. After the turn of the century, the political connection between Spain and the Netherlands gave the Flemings an advantage in this competition. Even more serious was the competition of the south German towns in the production of cheap linens, and in metal-working, particularly in the manufacture of weapons. South Germany was a mining area, having good supplies both of silver and of copper. Wars and the unfavourable balance of trade with the Levant constantly increased the Italian need for both precious and non-precious metals; but the growing demand for fire-arms in the late fifteenth century encouraged the gunsmiths of Nuremberg, instead of exporting copper to Italy, to import tin by way of the Rhine, and to cast and export bronze guns, as well as armour and weapons of iron and steel. German arms and armour, and metal work generally, were perhaps inferior to Italian, but they were also cheaper.

Italian shipping began in the late fifteenth century to suffer from the relative scarcity, and so the high price, of shipbuilding timber in the Mediterranean area. In 1520 the Arsenal at Venice secured legislation reserving the entire oak supply of Istria for naval use; an ominous sign for the future of the merchant fleet. The concentration of the Venetians and the Genoese upon big ships and upon long-distance trade had always left a great volume of local coastal trade to auxiliary shipping, Catalan, French, Greek. The coastal trades, and even to some extent the less lucrative of the long-distance trades of the Mediterranean, were invaded in the last decades of the fifteenth century by cheaply constructed, relatively small Atlantic ships, Basque, Galician, Portuguese. They came into the Mediterranean originally with supplies of salt fish; but large numbers of them came to be employed, under charter to Italian capitalists, in the grain and alum trades.[5]

45

None of these elements of competition or shortages of raw materials seriously affected Italian predominance in the luxury trades; but they were accompanied by a steady deterioration, from the Italian point of view, in the political situation. The fall of Constantinople was a serious blow. It isolated the Italian colonies in the Black Sea and threatened those in the Aegean. It did not stop trade. The Venetians found ways of doing business with, or through, the Turks; but they lost their special privileges, and were obliged to pay much heavier imposts on a diminished volume of trade. Wars between the Turkish and Persian rulers, moreover, intermittently interrupted the supply of silk from Persia and spices coming through Hormuz. Alexandria, towards the end of the century, was the most reliable channel of supply; but the Mamluk rulers, threatened by the Turks, conscious of their decaying power and wealth, constantly raised the exactions which they levied upon foreign merchants in Cairo and Alexandria. In 1480, the Venetian factors resisted a particularly steep rise, and the Sultan confined them for three days to their *fondaco*, until an agreement was reached. Such high-handed measures were rare, for the Mamluks and the Venetians needed one another's business; and Venice, if pushed too far, could take severe naval reprisals, as the Mamluks knew from experience. Early in the sixteenth century, however, the Turkish conquest of Egypt and Syria was to place the Italian *fondaci* at the mercy of rulers less commercially-minded and much less easily intimidated than their Mamluk predecessors. From 1484, moreover, Italy itself suffered a series of invasions from the North, and war and disorganization at home were added to the difficulties in the way of trade.

The Italians were able, so long as they enjoyed a monopoly, to pass on to their European customers the cost of these successive obstacles to a steady trade in luxury goods. To the customers, high prices emphasized the desirability, either of finding alternative sources of supply, or else of finding alternative routes to the same sources. Portuguese sailors, and Spaniards from the Atlantic ports, were well placed to attempt the search. The Portuguese especially possessed a large fleet of small ships, and a seafaring population trained in the ocean fisheries. Their captains were gaining experience and knowledge of the Mediterranean trades. They had a fairly well organized, though small-scale, system of marine investment and insurance; and they had the encouragement and backing of the royal family. Quite early in the fifteenth century, both Portuguese and Spaniards made use of their island settlements in the Atlantic for producing Mediterranean luxuries. The agents of Prince Henry of Portugal introduced sugar canes and Malvoisie vines into Madeira, and before the Prince's death sugar and Malmsey wine were being produced there in exportable quantity. A little later, the trading possibilities of the Guinea coast began to be exploited, and Malagueta pepper—admittedly a coarse and cheap substitute for the Indian kinds —became an important article of trade, along with slaves, gold dust, ivory and gum-arabic. These were useful additions to European imports; and a few Italians, of whom Cadamosto was one of the first, showed an interest in the island and Guinea trade. The trade never compared, however, in volume or value with that of the Levant, and the big Italian houses ignored it.

In the fourteen-seventies, the all-sea route to India began to appear a practical possibility. At the end of the century a Portuguese fleet reached Calicut and returned to Lisbon with a cargo of spices, the first of many. In 1501 the first consignment of eastern spices from Lisbon reached the Portuguese factory of Antwerp, which quickly became a major centre for the distribution of Portuguese spices to north-western Europe. The Italians were surprisingly undismayed by these events, unwelcome though they must have found them. They could not prevent the sea-borne trade between India and Portugal, and between Portugal and the Netherlands; nor could they participate in it, without risking an oceanic war for which their ships were not designed nor their seamen trained. So they stuck to their own business. The great merchant houses of Venice—accustomed to business vicissitudes, experienced in commercial diplomacy, and disposing of great capital resources—retained their faith in the future of the Levant trade, and events in the sixteenth century proved their faith to be justified. It is true that the annual galley fleets to England and the Low Countries ceased to be profitable, and that organized sailings ceased in 1532. It is true also that in the early years of the sixteenth century spices were scarce in the Levant markets—a shortage caused partly by Portuguese depredations against Arab trade in the Indian Ocean, but prolonged and accentuated by the Turkish conquest of Egypt. On several occasions between 1512 and 1519, Venetian merchants were reduced to buying spices from Lisbon to fulfil the orders of their own regular customers in south Germany and elsewhere. The Italians showed a remarkable resilience, however, in the face of mounting difficulties. By 1519 Venice had come to terms with the Turkish authorities in Cairo and Alexandria, and had imposed a stiff import duty against spices entering the Republic from the West. The spice trade, or a large part of it, soon re-entered its old channels. In the middle years of the sixteenth century, the volume of the Levant trade was as great as it had ever been, and at least as great as that which the Portuguese carried round the Cape.[6] The European demand for spices in the sixteenth century seemed insatiable. In straight competition over price and quality, the advantages were by no means all on the side of the ocean trade. The costs and risks of the Cape route were very great, and tended to increase; and the Portuguese had no goods to offer which could make a profitable outward freight. They bought spices with bullion, and the proceeds of the homeward passage had to cover the costs of the outward passage also. There was little, if any, difference between the price of pepper brought from the Levant and pepper carried by the Cape route, once it reached western Europe. There may have been a difference in quality. Arabs and Venetians were probably more discriminating buyers than the Portuguese. It was widely believed, moreover, that spices tended to spoil and to lose their aroma on the long sea voyage. This, no doubt, was a story put about by the Venetians, but it probably had some foundation in fact, since the Portuguese cargoes were carried in bags, in leaky ships, through latitudes where the weather could be very violent. The Venetians, therefore, far from being put out of business by the Portuguese discovery of the Ocean route, competed successfully with the Portuguese throughout the sixteenth century as purveyors of spices, at least to part of Europe, and continued to get their spices by the old routes. Moreover, the export trade to northern Europe in goods of Mediterranean origin—cottons, silks, glass, wine, almonds, fruit—continued to expand, and remained largely in Italian hands until late in the century. For a hundred years after Vasco da Gama, the trade of the Mediterranean was still of greater significance than that of the outer world, the Atlantic and the Indian Oceans. It was not the sixteenth century, but the seventeenth, which saw the eclipse of the Mediterranean. The heirs of Italian mercantile predominance were not the Portuguese, but the English and the Dutch.

These circumstances help to explain the commercial peculiarities of the beginnings of the Reconnaissance. The Italian City-states, accustomed to the monopoly of a number of lucrative trades, concentrated their energies mainly upon retaining and expanding that monopoly. Their ships were designed, and their seamen trained, to that end, and were mostly unsuited to oceanic work. Although they possessed the most up-to-date geographical knowledge and the most advanced cartographical skill in Europe, Italians took an active part in voyages of oceanic discovery only as individual experts in the employ of other governments. Portugal and Castile had the ships, the seamen, the motives and the opportunity for oceanic exploration; the major voyages of discovery started from Iberian harbours and the ships were manned mostly by Spaniards or Portuguese. The Spaniards and the Portuguese, however, lacked the capital, the commercial experience and the financial organization to exploit commercially the discoveries which they made. The Catalans, it is true, had relatively advanced credit systems and business methods, but their capital was limited, and for the most part they took little interest in oceanic trade. Only in northern Italy and southern Germany were there commercial and financial houses big enough and well enough organized to supply the facilities which the Portuguese and Spaniards lacked. Only by drawing upon the experience and borrowing the capital accumulated in Italy and south Germany, could the Spaniards and the Portuguese exploit the wealth of the Indies, East or West.

A great variety of trading and shipping associations of capital had existed in the Italian cities since the thirteenth century at least. Medieval corporations—merchant guilds, craft guilds, regulated companies—were for the most part official organizations regulating the trade of their members, forcing those members to accept uniform standards; they were not usually trading concerns themselves. Partnerships for conducting commercial enterprises, on the other hand, were usually not corporations, but rather *ad hoc* devices for uniting either a number of capitalists, each contributing a share, and jointly employing the labour of others; or a number of partners, of whom some risked only their capital and some only their skill or labour, and all shared in the profits on a prearranged scale; or a number of active participants in an enterprise who all contributed both capital and labour and lived and worked together. All these types of association, under various names—*commenda, societas, compagnia,* and so forth, were employed in seaborne trade.

In addition to guilds and trading partnerships, a small number of associations grew up in northern Italy in the later Middle Ages which combined some of the characteristics of both—which combined incorporation with financial and commercial enterprise. Most of these bodies began as associations of public creditors. The unpredictable shifts and complexities of public finance obliged the Italian City-states to grant their creditors guarantees for interest payments either in the form of claims on definite state revenues, or in the form of special commercial or administrative privileges. Other and larger states, in succeeding centuries, were to resort to similar devices. In Italy, such grants had created, by the fifteenth century, corporative organizations of creditors carrying out economic functions. There were two principal types. *Compere* were financial corporations administering particular state revenues. Such was the famous Genoese Casa di San Giorgio, whose bank established by special privilege in 1408 came to occupy a central position in the financial affairs of the city. The second group, the *maone,* were associations of individuals formed to undertake particular enterprises—military expeditions, for example—on behalf of the State. The most celebrated of the *maone,* that of the Giustiniani family, was also Genoese. It was a colonizing concern which, among other activities, administered the island of Chios.[7]

49

Outside Italy, large associations of capital were commonest in the cities of south Germany. The famous family trading houses which grew up there in the fifteenth century—Fuggers, Welsers, Höchstetters, and others—resembled the great Italian concerns in the diversity of their business. They dealt in cloth, fustians and silks; they were concerned in the import and distribution of spices, in the export of silver and copper to Italy and the Netherlands, and in mining. Mining, with its fixed and controllable collateral, was then regarded as a particularly safe investment. The system of credit known as *Verlag* enabled miners, and workmen employed by them, to obtain advances in money or in kind for tools and subsistence. The investors drew their returns in the form of products raised. Trading and mining together enabled the German houses to enter the more dangerous fields of banking and international finance; and like the Italians, they maintained a network of agencies in all the principal trading and financial centres of Western Europe. Both the example of their business methods, and their great resources of capital for investment, were available, at a price, to the Spaniards and the Portuguese in the development of the discoveries.

The Iberian governments showed at first an understandable reluctance to allow foreign participation. In their pursuit of West African and Brazilian trade in the fifteenth and sixteenth centuries, the Portuguese rulers frequently leased part of the business to partnerships very like the Genoese *maone*.[8] These partnerships were native, and their capital was small, as was the volume of their trade. This tendency to form overseas trading companies of a relatively advanced type, however, failed to develop further in Portugal, partly through lack of capital, partly through government hostility. It was not the Portuguese but, much later, the Dutch and the English who were to emerge as the Italians' aptest pupils in this respect. The Portuguese Crown thought the India trade, which became possible after 1499, too valuable to be left to individuals or private corporations. It was retained from the first as a Crown monopoly, undertaken on the King's account, at his own risk and in his own ships. Licences to private merchants were given only in very exceptional cases. The government, however, itself lacked the capital to equip the necessary fleets and to purchase the spice cargoes which they brought back. In 1505, foreign investment was openly permitted. The great fleet which sailed from Lisbon in that year was largely financed by foreigners; the Genoese and Florentine investments together amounted to about 30,000 florins, that of the Welsers to 20,000, and that of the Fuggers and Höchstetters to 4,000 each. The profits of this voyage were very great—over 175 per cent per year[9]—but the experiment was not repeated, because of Portuguese bad faith and delay in making the division. The Crown undertook all subsequent voyages, but sold the entire cargoes in Lisbon to merchant syndicates, mostly Italian and German, who shipped the goods to Antwerp and distributed them from there. Frequently, the Crown sold cargoes in advance, while they were still at sea, or borrowed on the security of future cargoes, so that in effect the foreigners provided most of the capital, and both as creditors and as middlemen absorbed most of the profit.

Trade to the Spanish Indies of America developed on different lines. After an ineffectual early experiment with royal trade, the Castilian Crown handed the business over to a private monopoly in the hands of the exporting merchants of Seville, who were naturally willing to pay heavily for the privilege. The trade was carried on under complicated and irksome rules. From about 1526 it was organized in convoys modelled—whether consciously or not—upon the galley fleets which, at that date, still carried Venetian trade with England and the Netherlands. Outside investment was slow and tentative at first, since the trade was small, and concerned chiefly with supplying tools and foodstuffs— flour, oil and wine—to poor and struggling colonies. Most of these products came from Andalusia, and could easily be supplied by the Seville shippers, who were experienced in similar trade to the Canary Islands. The return cargoes in this early stage were hides, a little sugar, and a little gold. As the colonies grew in size, however, and exported more and more precious metals and valuable tropical products, so they demanded more manufactured goods, and more capital was required to finance a rapidly growing trade. The somewhat rigid and predominantly pastoral economy of Castile could not expand quickly enough, on its industrial side, to meet the demand. More and more, the Seville merchants exported goods which were not their own, and not necessarily Spanish. The trade goods carried by Magellan's famous expedition were supplied by the Fuggers, through the Spanish house of de Haro who were their agents. Even after their formal incorporation in 1543 in the famous *Consulado*—the merchant guild formed for the protection of their monopoly—the Seville merchants continued to operate not as a corporate body but as individuals. As shipowners, they traded on commission, exporting in their own name goods belonging to foreign firms; or took foreign merchants and financiers into informal partnership, to raise capital for the purchase of ships and goods.[10] Through their agency, a great part of the sixteenth-century trade to the Spanish Indies came effectively into the hands of Genoese and south German trading houses.

During part of the sixteenth century, in Charles V's time, Germans were even allowed an open and active part in the development of the colonies themselves. The Fuggers, who for many years held a lease of the Almadén mercury mines and the Guadalcanal silver mines in Spain, also operated mines in Santo Domingo and New Spain. So did the Welsers; and they also undertook in 1527 an ambitious and ill-fated settlement enterprise in Venezuela.

Open concessions such as these were rare and unpopular, and ceased with the death of Charles V; but the international financiers retained their grip upon the trade and products of the Indies, because of the insistent financial needs of the Iberian governments.[12] Perpetually borrowing to meet the costs of war, of public display, even of the ordinary work of administration, the sixteenth-century kings were perpetually in disorderly debt. The spices of India, the silver of America, flowed through Portugal and Spain, into the hands of the Italian and German bankers who were the governments' creditors, and thence throughout Europe. Sometimes, through war or bad faith, the flow ceased, and one or other group of creditors was ruined; but while they could, the creditors took advantage of the embarrassment of governments to extract commercial privileges of every kind, from mining leases to slave trade contracts. The beginnings of the Reconnaissance, the first great moves in oceanic discovery, were the work, for the most part, of adventurous Portuguese and Spaniards; but the development of discovery, the foundations of settlement, trade and empire were paid for by capitalists whose bases were in the older commercial centres of the Mediterranean and south Germany. To those centres, the profits mostly returned. International finance made the Reconnaissance the concern of all Europe.

CHAPTER 3

SHIPS AND SHIPBUILDERS

THE ships employed in the great voyages of discovery were not specially designed for their task, nor were they usually outstanding examples of their class and time. The fleet in which Vasco da Gama sailed for India in 1497, it is true, was equipped with great care and at considerable expense, under the experienced direction of Bartolomeu Dias; and two of the ships were built expressly for the voyage. This expedition was a major royal enterprise, undertaken—since Dias had already revealed the route into the Indian Ocean—with high hopes of profitable success. Even so, the *San Gabriel* and the *San Raphael*, though strongly built and well armed, did not apparently differ in design from ordinary merchant ships. The other two ships in the fleet were a store-ship and a caravel. Dias' own voyage of 1487, in which he discovered the Cape of Good Hope, had been made in small caravels of a type commonly used by Portuguese merchants for coastwise trading. Columbus' fleet of 1492 was fitted out in economical fashion by the agents of an impecunious government. Two of his ships were small trading caravels from the Rio Tinto. They were commandeered from their owners by the municipality of Palos, which had been ordered by the Crown to provide two vessels for the voyage, as a fine for some municipal misdemeanour. The flagship was almost certainly a *nao*, a tubby ship-rigged cargo carrier, larger than the caravels but comparatively small for her class.[1] She was built in Galicia, but chartered in Palos by Columbus for the voyage. She proved unsuitable for the intricate pilotage of the West Indian channels, and was wrecked off Hispaniola. Magellan's five ships were bought by the Crown in Cadiz in 1518. They, too, were ordinary merchant ships, and at least one contemporary thought them so old and rotten as to be unsafe. Neither governments nor investors, in the early years of the Reconnaissance, necessarily shared the optimism of the sea-going explorers whom they employed. They were often understandably reluctant to risk first-class ships, or very large capital sums, in speculative enterprises in which whole fleets might be lost; or in which, even if men and ships survived, the discoveries made might prove profitless. Only later, when routes had been explored and the opportunities of profit demonstrated, was capital freely subscribed for oceanic trade; and only then were ships deliberately built for long passages to India or the New World.

This is not to say that the discoverers' ships were unsuitable for their purpose. Their successes prove the contrary. In the late fifteenth century there was no adequate fund of oceanic experience upon which the design of explorers' ships could have been based. The warships of the time, had any been available, would certainly have been less suitable than the merchantmen. Centuries later, with vastly greater accumulated experience at his command and with the resources of the Admiralty behind him, Captain Cook was to choose a north-country collier barque for long voyages of exploration. One of the most striking features of the whole story of the Reconnaissance is precisely the fact that the early voyages, with their immensely long passages through unknown oceans, could be made, and once made could be regularly repeated, by ships built for the everyday trades of western Europe. A hundred years before, such achievements would have been unthinkable. A fourteenth-century ship, with lucky winds and other favouring circumstances, might conceivably have reached America by a direct passage; but by no stretch of imagination could such a chance discovery have led to repeated voyages for settlement and trade. The fifteenth century was, in fact, a period of very rapid change and development in the design of European sea-going ships; a development comparatively little influenced by the particular needs of oceanic discovery, but which nevertheless was a necessary condition for successful oceanic voyages.

The Mediterranean area in the later Middle Ages possessed not only the busiest and most lucrative trades of Europe, but also the oldest and strongest shipbuilding tradition. The tradition had been shaped partly by physical conditions—the absence of tides, the relative freedom of the inland sea from long periods of heavy weather—and partly by the special naval and commercial requirements of the Roman Empire. Two major characteristics of Mediterranean shipping, inherited from imperial times, persisted throughout the Middle Ages: the use of very large, heavily timbered, slow and unwieldy sailing ships for the carriage of bulky cargoes, such as grain; and reliance upon oared vessels for work requiring manœuvrability and speed.

The oared galley was the traditional warship of the Mediterranean, and remained the principal component of fighting fleets there until the seventeenth century. Galley fleets could be manœuvred, in calm weather, with something of the purpose and precision of modern powered squadrons; but, being built for speed, they were deficient both in operating range and in seaworthiness. Most fighting galleys were of light construction. Those laid down in Mediterranean shipyards in the fifteenth century had a length of 120 feet or more, with only about fifteen feet of beam and five or six of freeboard.[2] They had usually only one mast, stepped well forward, and its single sail served, with a following wind, either to increase speed or to rest the oarsmen. Such ships were helpless in heavy seas, and were totally unsuitable for Atlantic conditions; though the Spaniards used light galleys successfully in the late sixteenth century against pirates in the Caribbean, where conditions somewhat resembled those of the Mediterranean.

In the late thirteenth and early fourteenth centuries a major advance was made in the development of galley design. About that time, the Mediterranean maritime states—Venice especially—began to build, in addition to the traditional light galleys, smaller numbers of great galleys, larger vessels, of much stouter construction, with relatively more freeboard, and with a length-to-beam ratio not exceeding six to one.[3] They could be employed in war, and were so used with great effect in the sixteenth century, notably at Lepanto; but in the fifteenth century —the period of their most rapid development and most fruitful use— their usual employment was commercial. About twenty great galleys put to sea from Venice each year. Most of them were built in the naval Arsenal and were bought, or more commonly chartered, from the state by the shipping firms who operated them. They provided regular services from Venice to Constantinople and Alexandria, and intervening ports; and conveyed pilgrims to the Holy Land when political conditions permitted. They could and did operate in the Atlantic, at least in summer. The famous fleets which for two hundred years and more sailed to Cadiz, Lisbon, Bruges and Southampton were made up of great galleys. They were capable of remarkable performances. On one famous occasion in 1509, upon a sudden threat of war, the Flanders galleys were ordered directly home, and sailed from Southampton to Otranto, about 2,500 miles, in thirty-one days.[4] They were three-masted vessels, and when at sea relied chiefly upon their sails. Because of their size and weight, they could proceed under oars only for short distances, and used oars only for entering and leaving harbour, save in flat calms, or in emergencies. This practice had the advantage of enabling them to keep nearer to a time-table than ordinary sailing ships could do, and made them faster and more dependable over a long voyage. Even when not fitted out for war, they were powerful vessels, capable of vigorous self-defence, especially since their oar crews (unlike those in most war-galleys) were paid men who could be entrusted with arms. Reliability was the characteristic which chiefly attracted both passengers and freight to the great galleys. Their chief disadvantages were the difficulty and expense of manning them, and the limitation of cargo space. A galley stowing only 200 or 250 tons of merchandise needed a crew of

200 men. Insurance rates were lower than in sailing ships, but freight rates were very much higher, and only goods of high value and small bulk could be carried economically. The Republic required its citizens by law to ship all spices and similar goods in the galleys, partly to ensure the safety of the cargoes, and partly to protect the state-built galleys against sailing-ship competition. Such protection became ineffective when the Venetian monopoly of the spice trade was broken, and when designers and seamen together produced a sailing ship which rivalled the great galley in reliability and strength, yet required a much smaller crew.

The large crew needed to handle a galley not only raised its operating costs, but limited its operating range. A galley could not carry, in addition to merchandise, the stores necessary to feed large numbers of men for a long voyage out of sight of land. For this reason the great galleys—in their fifteenth-century hey-day probably the most reliable and most efficient vessels afloat in European waters—played no significant part in the Reconnaissance. Seamen could cross great oceans only when they had acquired sufficient confidence in sailing ships to leave their oars behind.

The Mediterranean sailing ship of the Middle Ages was at first sight even less suited than the great galley to ocean work; but it was more adaptable than the galley, and more readily influenced by inventions from outside, whether from the Indian Ocean or the Atlantic. In the early Middle Ages, Mediterranean ships were still built in the Roman fashion, with flush planking set edge to edge, the planks joined one to another along their entire length by joints and dowels. This strong, rigid shell construction made heavy demands on skilled labour. From the eleventh century, it was gradually replaced by a more flexible, less labour-intensive method of building on a pre-constructed frame. In the western Mediterranean, by the fifteenth century, carvel building on a preconstructed frame had become normal for all big ships. It was a more sophisticated operation than clinker building, or than any form of edge-joined construction, because the ship had to be designed, rather than built-up step by step by eye. Lighter planking could be used, and shorter sections of plank; an important consideration in a region where big trees were scarce. Finally, carvel ships on preconstructed frames could safely be built bigger than clinker or edge-joined ships.

Mediaeval Mediterranean ships, of whatever size, usually had little or no superstructure forward, but the stern was high and full, and supported a staged superstructure containing the cabin accommodation. Many ships—especially during the crusades—had large stern ports near the water-line for loading horses; evidence of the stout construction of these Mediterranean ships. Steering was by side rud-

ders. Stem and stern posts and keel were all curved, a most characteristic feature distinguishing all southern European ships. Even when,
in the later Middle Ages, the single rudder hung on the stern post
was adopted in the Mediterranean, it was at first shaped like a scimitar
to fit the curve of the post. In a sea without tides, this shape had important advantages, since it enabled a ship grounded by accident to
be refloated by shifting weight forward or aft. On the other hand, a
ship with a curved keel could not sew ashore. If hauled out, she had to
be shored up on the beach, a major operation with a big and heavy
ship. Bottom-scraping, re-caulking and other under-water maintenance
jobs were usually done with the ship careened in shallow water and
hove down by tackles on the masts. This unsatisfactory method—
unsatisfactory both because it strained the masts and because it never
allowed the planking to dry out before caulking—came to be known
among Iberian sailors as the *querena italiana*. It was to persist for centuries
after the reason for it had disappeared, and was to give ocean-going
sailors a great deal of trouble.[6]

Two distinct outside influences affected the development of Mediterranean shipping in the Middle Ages, that of the Arabs of the western
Indian Ocean and that of the Atlantic coast shipbuilders of north-
western Europe. In modern times, large Arab craft have usually been
built with a frame of ribs and timbers, the planking fastened to the ribs
by spikes or trunnells. Some, especially the big *baghlas* which regularly
trade between East Africa and the Persian Gulf, and still sometimes
cross the Indian Ocean, have massive transom sterns, often carved and
gilded. All these features have been imitated from European examples
since the Portuguese invasion of the Indian Ocean. In the Middle Ages
Arab ships were double-ended, as some, notably the Persian Gulf *boums*,
still are. Planking was sewn edge to edge with coir fibre, and such
framework as was needed for strengthening the hull was inserted after
completion of the shell.[7] The retention of this primitive method of
fastening down to about 1500 is hard to explain. The Arabs were
thoroughly familiar with iron and could obtain it in India or Egypt.
Teak, moreover, the commonest shipbuilding timber in the Indian
Ocean, is an oily wood which preserves iron, unlike oak, which corrodes
it; teak-built ships, therefore, are not subject to iron-sickness, as oak
ships are. Iron-fastened teak ships later proved strong and durable.
Probably cost was the decisive reason; iron was expensive, coir cheap
and plentiful. Sewn planking, also, is flexible, and so suitable for use in
surf. It was quite unsuitable for ships as large as those common in the
Mediterranean, even had coir been available there. Today, even in the
Indian Ocean, it survives only in very remote places.[8] The Arabs,
therefore, contributed little or nothing to the development of Mediterranean hull construction; in this respect, they were imitators. Their

major contribution was to the development of rig; and in this respect their vessels have changed little in the last thousand years.

The lateen sail, the only type ever seen in Arab craft, is a triangular or nearly triangular sail, laced to a long yard hoisted obliquely to the mast. The mast itself has usually a pronounced forward rake. The lateen is as characteristic of Islam as the crescent itself. It is also a very efficient general-purpose sail for small and medium-sized vessels. The place and date of origin of the lateen rig is uncertain. A case can be made for the Levant in Byzantine times; but on the whole, the weight of evidence is in favour of the Indian Ocean, and an earlier date.[9] Whether or not the Arabs invented lateen rig, it certainly spread through the Mediterranean in the wake of the Arab invasions. Until then, most Mediterranean ships had retained the ancient square rig of Roman times: one or two masts, each carrying a single square sail, with a single rope on each side to serve in turn as tack or sheet. Although the small sail of the *artemon*, forerunner of the modern bowsprit, must have given some manœuvrability, the Roman square rig served only for running with the wind well abaft the beam. A ship so rigged, if the wind were unfavourable, must either creep out under oars if its size and design permitted; or else remain in harbour. Similarly, a change of wind while at sea could create serious difficulty. The lateen offered many advantages, of which improved manœuvrability was the most important. Once introduced, it soon superseded the square sail in the Levant, and by the eleventh century it had become the normal rig, not only throughout the Mediterranean, but also on those Atlantic coasts where Arab influence was strong: in Andalusia and in Portugal.

The lateen sail as it has developed in the Mediterranean differs in several respects from its counterpart or forerunner in the Indian Ocean. The Arab lateen is extremely baggy, and is usually cut settee-fashion with the fore part of the sail cut off, leaving a short luff. The modern Mediterranean lateen is triangular, with a flatter set, and with the yard held more snugly to the mast by means of a multiple parrel. These improvements all emphasize the superiority of the lateen over the rudimentary square rig which it replaced. The lateen sail performs much better on a wind than the square, because its yard makes a long and stiff leading edge. It is more versatile, and by varied if somewhat laborious adjustments of brace, tack and sheet, can be set for a great variety of wind conditions. It requires only the simplest standing rigging; indeed in many lateen craft shrouds are set up only on the weather side. This simplicity of rigging made it particularly suitable in the Middle Ages for vessels which also used oars. Its high peak gives it an advantage in light airs, and in sailing along enclosed canals and estuaries, as can be seen from the performance of the *ghaiassas* of the

Nile delta to this day. It is at its best when reaching with a stiff breeze on the beam, and in these conditions lateen craft, especially small ones, have a remarkable turn of speed. It is somewhat less satisfactory when running. The huge mainsail, carried well forward, tends to bury the bows; the vessel will yaw unpredictably with a following sea or with slight changes of wind; and with such a rig an unexpected gybe can be very dangerous.

Beautiful and efficient though it is, the lateen sail has several drawbacks. A vessel so rigged cannot easily be put about. Some of the smaller Mediterranean craft—the *feluccas* of Alexandria, for example—can tack to windward, and for short tacks will keep the yard on the weather side of the mast; but larger vessels cannot do this without risk and without serious loss of efficiency. The masts are not stayed forward, and the strain caused by setting the great sails aback could be dangerous. For this reason, lateen-rigged vessels of any size almost always wear round. The sail is brailed up, the tack-tackle and shrouds slacked off, and the heel of the yard drawn in to the foot of the mast; the sheet is carried round forward outside everything, the yard is hauled over as the stern swings across the wind, and shrouds and tack-tackle are set up on the new weather side; the sail is then sheeted home on the new tack. The sail cannot be reefed. Most lateen vessels carry two or three suits of sails of different sizes, which can be bent on for different weather conditions. Sails cannot easily be furled aloft; the yards are lowered on entering harbour and hoisted again on making sail. All these are laborious operations, especially since each mast carries only one sail, the sails are necessarily large, and the spars needed to carry them are long, heavy and awkward to handle. The length of the main yard is usually about equal to the overall length of the ship. It consists of several lengths fished or scarphed together, tapering towards the peak. An additional length can be lashed on to the peak in good weather or removed in bad. There is a limit to the size of yard which can be handled, and this in turn limits the size of the ship. The Arabs, masters of lateen sailing, never solved this problem. Mediterranean sailors in the later Middle Ages found a partial solution by stepping three masts, instead of the two which were usual in the Indian Ocean; even so, their biggest merchant sailing ships, under lateen rig, were under-canvassed and therefore slow. The number of masts could not be increased indefinitely. Lateen-rigged vessels cannot, in fact, be built beyond a relatively modest size without loss of efficiency, and they always require large crews, relative to their size, in order to handle the heavy spars. A Venetian great galley, with its three big lateens, carried when fully manned, in addition to oar crews and fighting men, fifty seamen. Even without oars, lateen-rigged vessels were expensive in labour costs.

The steady growth, in the later Middle Ages, of extensive trades in bulky and comparatively cheap commodities such as grain, salt and alum, created a demand for big sailing ships which could be run cheaply. With such cargoes, shippers could accept a vessel less manœuvrable than a lateener, less dependable than a galley, provided that its running costs—which chiefly meant its wage bill—were small. To meet this demand, Mediterranean builders again imitated and adapted designs from outside; this time from the Atlantic shipping of north-western Europe.

Seamen of the Atlantic coasts, from the Baltic to Galicia, had developed conventions of ship design independent of the Mediterranean tradition, and differing from it in many ways. Their ships had straight keels, and so could take the ground without strain at ebb tide. Their stern-posts were straight, and from a fairly early date had a stern rudder hung on the post by means of pintles. The ships were clinker-built, with overlapping planks, strengthened internally by frames which, in some instances at least, were inserted after the completion of the shell.[10] Externally, the clinker planking was protected and strengthened by projecting fender-cleats, nailed to the ends of the beams, and by vertical fenders or skids crossing the planks at intervals, in some instances along the whole length of the ship, in others only at the places where additional strength was most needed, beneath the fore and after castles. The castles, and the skids which helped to support them, were distinctively northern features. Northern ships, built for rough and unpredictable waters, lacked the fine lines of some Mediterranean vessels; they were buoyant and tubby; they made very little use of oars, for the same reason; and their relatively primitive rig gave them poor manœuvrability. Their protection against enemies, therefore, was chiefly defensive, and their builders sought to give them—as in fortresses ashore—the advantages of fortified height. Originally the battlemented wooden towers at bow and stern, built for the accommodation of bowmen, were temporary structures; and many northern ports had guilds of castle-wrights, specialized craftsmen employed to add castles to ships intended to sail in dangerous waters, or to remove them when they were no longer needed. In the fourteenth century, however, the castles tended more and more to be permanent features of the superstructure. By the early fifteenth century, instead of both castles being flimsy square towers, unrelated to the design of the hull, the aftercastle had become a raised deckhouse, and the forecastle a high triangular platform resting on the knee of the stem. Both castles long retained their crenellated defensive bulwarks. Both were of lighter planking than the hull proper, and were built above a principal deck which ran unbroken from end to end of the ship.[11]

Most northern merchant ships in the fourteenth century had only one mast, with a crossed yard consisting of a single massive spar, on which was bent a large square sail. Square sails, however, having been in continuous use in the north, uninterrupted by Arab influence, had developed beyond the primitive rig of earlier times in several important respects. The sail was normally furled on the yard, and access was provided by ratlines in the shrouds, a distinctively northern feature. Tacks and sheets were separate ropes, allowing the ship to tack without brailing up the sail. Bowlines were regularly employed to hold the weather-leech stiff against the wind; and reefing was used to reduce sail, rows of reef-points crossing the whole sail at equal intervals. Square-rig, therefore, as it was reintroduced in the Mediterranean, was in many ways superior to the Roman square-rig which during the Dark Ages had yielded there to the lateen of the Saracens.

Northern merchant ships of the build and rig just described, and generally known as cogs, came into the Mediterranean in the wake of the crusaders, and traded there in increasing numbers in the fourteenth century. Many of these were from the Basque coast, and to Basques and other Iberian seamen must be ascribed much of the initiative for the complex hybridization which followed. The cogs, clumsy and slow though they must have been, attracted attention because of their capacious holds, the simplicity of their rig, and the small crews needed to handle them. A lateen-rigged ship carrying, say, 250 tons of cargo in the fourteenth-century Mediterranean required a crew of fifty seamen; a square-rigged ship of the same cargo capacity needed only about twenty, with perhaps half a dozen apprentices in addition. Square rig did not drive out the lateen from the Mediterranean in the wholesale fashion in which lateen rig had ousted the square sail four or five centuries earlier. Lateen rig remained in use in small coasting vessels, in all oared vessels, and in general in ships which required manœuvrability and speed. Square rig, however, by 1400 had been generally adopted for large, slow and capacious merchant ships throughout most of the Mediterranean area.

In making a partial return to square rig, Mediterranean sailors did not rest content with it as they had it from the north. With characteristic lively inventiveness they proceeded to adapt it in ways suggested by their own lateen tradition. To the ties which supported the northern square yard they added lifts at the yard-arms, so making possible the use of longer, more slender yards, which (like lateen yards and unlike northern ones) consisted usually of two spars lashed together and over-lapping at the bunt. Accustomed as they were to tackles at the foot and peak of the lateen yard, they soon replaced the single northern yard-ropes by more powerful braces and brace-pendants; and fitted tackles also to the bowlines. The sails were gored to produce separate wind-bags on either side of the middle line. To give a flatter set when sailing on a wind, bowges were used in addition to bowlines. These were lines made fast to a thimble in the centre of the foot of the sail; they passed round the mast, through the thimble, and down to the deck, so flattening in the middle of the sail while the bowline stiffened the weather-leech. These adaptations were all obvious improvements, and soon spread to northern Europe. Against them must be set two useful northern devices which Mediterranean sailors refused for many years to adopt: ratlines and reef-points. Instead of ratlines in the shrouds, they still used, for access to yards and tops, jacob's-ladders up the masts. This restricted and inconvenient access reflected a curious piece of conservatism; Mediterranean sailors, used to lateen sails, did not immediately adopt the northern practice of furling sails on the yards, but continued for some years to lower the yards, as they had always done. Defence may also have been a consideration, since without rat-lines hostile boarders could not easily swarm up into the tops. The absence of ratlines served, until after the end of the fifteenth century, to distinguish southern square-rigged ships from northern ones of otherwise similar rig and build. Instead of reef-points, the southerners used bon-nets, additional strips of canvas which could be laced on to the foot of the main course in fair weather and removed in foul. The use of bonnets, far from being superseded by reef-points, spread to northern Europe along with the other Mediterranean modifications of square rig; and although reef-points remained common in northern sails until about 1450, after that date the southern device became general.

The northern cog, as we have seen, usually had only one mast. Mediterranean sailors were accustomed to two- or three-masted ships, and in adopting and modifying the cog design they naturally added additional masts to the single mainmast. This was done initially in one of two ways: either by stepping a short foremast, usually with a square sail, giving a rudimentary brig rig; or by stepping a mizen mast, usually with a lateen sail, giving a kind of ketch rig. Both devices, but especially the second, greatly improved the handling qualities of the basic square-rigged cog, and its performance when sailing on a wind. The second device was probably the commoner, but both were wide-spread by about 1430. The two could be combined in one ship: square-rigged on fore and main with lateen mizen. Such hybrid three-masters appeared about 1450; and for more than two hundred years thereafter lateens were the aftersails in all European three-masted ships. By 1450, also, Mediterranean sailors discovered another vital advantage of square rig, the ease with which it enables a large area of canvas to be divided into units convenient for handling. The first step in this direction was the addition of a main topsail, at first of pocket-handkerchief size, and sheeted not to the yard-arms—that came later—but to the top-rim. Other additions followed in the later fifteenth century: a spritsail, bent on a yard carried below the bowsprit, chiefly useful for swinging the ship's head when getting under way; in some big ships, a foretopsail; and in some an additional mizen, also lateen; though this bonaventure mizen had disappeared by the middle of the sixteenth century. The real revolution, the vital marriage between square-rig and lateen, between Atlantic and Mediterranean, occurred in the short space of about twenty years in the middle of the fifteenth century. The marriage produced the basic barque, the direct ancestor of all the square-riggers of the Reconnaissance and the later great age of sail. A new and fertile cross-breed, it quickly spread not only throughout the Mediterranean, but, with only minor local differences, round all the coasts of Europe.

To apply these technical terms—barque, brig, brigantine, ketch—to fifteenth-century ships is, of course, an anachronism. The ships of that time were classified not according to their rig, but according to the design and purpose of their hulls and according to their size. In adapting the Mediterranean hull to Atlantic square-rig, the changes made were fully as drastic as those caused by the adaptation of square sails to Mediterranean spars and rigging. The quarter-rudders were soon discarded in favour of the stern rudder; and although the curved keel and stern-post lingered on for some years, by 1450 the mechanical advantages of a straight stern-post were generally recognized. The keel was then straightened to meet the post and the resulting angle filled in with deadwood. The northern castles, both fore and aft, were adopted for big ships in the south; open arches beneath them giving access from the deck to fire-box and cables in the bows, to cabin accommodation in the stern. The poop, upon which the aftercastle stood, was brought down, so that in southern as in northern ships the castles were of approximately equal height; the forecastle even having an advantage of height in some ships, so reversing the older Mediterranean tradition of low bows and high stern. Conversely, however, some obviously superior features of southern construction remained in the south and spread to the north; particularly the pre-constructed frame of ribs and beams, and carvel planking nailed to the ribs. Clinker-work never found favour in the south, except occasionally in the castles, and in the light planking below the forecastle; even in the north, it disappeared from most big ships in the later fifteenth century. Certain external features such as fender-cleats and skids, originally associated with clinker planking, survived the transition for a time; but by the middle of the sixteenth century these vestigial relics of clinker build were also fast disappearing.

All these developments in build and rig can be traced with the help of contemporary drawings, paintings and seals. Developments in size are more difficult to follow, because of the lack of reliable figures. We do not know a single dimension of any of Columbus' ships. Contemporary references to ships often mention tonnage figures; but the ton as a unit of ship measurement was imprecise, and varied from country to country, often from port to port.[12] In the late fifteenth century and throughout most of the sixteenth, in most European countries the unit used for the computation of freight charges and port dues was presumed to represent the dead-weight capacity of the vessel, if loaded with some standard commodity regularly carried in the area. The commodities most commonly taken as standards were wine, oil, grain or salt. At Seville, and on the Atlantic coast of Spain and Portugal generally, the standard commodity was wine and the standard unit the *tonelada* of two pipes. Two pipes of wine in cask weighed about 2,000 English pounds and held approximately 40 cubic feet of liquid; but the average space which they occupied in hold, allowing for the bilges of the casks and for waste space at the ends of the ship, was considerably more. The English ton, derived from the *tonneau* of the Bordeaux wine trade, was larger by about one-tenth; the *botta* of the Venetian wine trade smaller by about two-fifths.[13] In expressing the size of the ships of the early Reconnaissance, the Spanish *tonelada* was the commonest and most convenient unit. Tonnages were determined empirically by direct experience in loading; not until the mid-sixteenth century were tables of equivalents of various classes of goods commonly kept at the ports. Serious attempts to devise formulae for calculating tonnage from the dimensions of the ship came later still.[14] Experienced seamen or port officials could estimate fairly accurately by eye the capacity of ships of average size; but the tonnage of very large ships was the subject of widely varying and probably wildly exaggerated guesses.

The complex interaction of northern and southern ideas produced, towards the end of the fifteenth century, a wide range of mongrel types, varying greatly in size, and differing from one another in design according to the proportion of northern and southern features which they embodied. In all this confusion of combinations, two extreme types stood out—despite many local variations—as recognizably definite. The vessels known in most European countries as carracks were merchant ships of the largest size. Carracks of six hundred tons were not uncommon in southern Europe, and some were said to exceed a thousand tons. They were broad and bluff like the old northern cogs, heavily built, with carvel planking, with large and well-developed castles, three-masted, square-rigged on fore and main with lateen mizens. The castle structures were tending more and more to be incorporated in the

64

structure of the hull, with the external wales running parallel to the sheer, but with breaks in the internal deck levels to make the best use of headroom. The aftercastle, especially in the sixteenth century, was increasingly elaborated, with projecting counters, one over the other, as shown in the high-charged, waisted vessels painted by the elder Pieter Breughel. Such massive ships might seem unsuitable for the task of exploration, and so they were; but their size and carrying capacity, and their solid construction, commended them to the Portuguese government for the eastern trade, so that they played a special and characteristic part in the work of the Reconnaissance.

At the other end of the scale were the coastal traders generally known as caravels. The name caravel described a variety of types; but all were relatively small, usually not more than sixty or seventy tons, perhaps, and seventy or eighty feet overall. There was very little of the north in them; their ancestry was mixed Mediterranean and Arab. The most famous caravels were those built on the coasts of Portugal and Andalusia plying from the harbours of the Tagus, the Rio Tinto and the Guadalquivir. Cadamosto, an experienced and shrewd maritime traveller, considered the Portuguese caravels the handiest and best-found vessels afloat in his day; and their reputation in African and trans-Atlantic exploration bears out his opinion. They seem to have been carvel built, but lighter and with finer lines than most sailing ships of the time. They had only one deck, and some may even have been open or half-decked. There was no forward superstructure, but a modest raised poop and transom stern. Probably the nearest modern similarity is with the *sambuqs* of Aden and other Red Sea ports. The caravels which Prince Henry dispatched to explore and trade along the West African coast were probably two-masted lateen-rigged vessels, but later in the century three-masted caravels became common, and might carry square sails when circumstances required. Drawings on contemporary maps, and elsewhere, show a variety of combinations. One was the familiar barque rig, square on fore and main, lateen mizen, like a diminutive ship or carrack. Other drawings, about the end of the century, show lateens on main and mizen with a square-rigged foremast stepped very far forward, suggesting that the foremast had been added to a vessel which originally had only two masts. Occasionally there were four masts of which one, sometimes two, might be square-rigged. The variations indicate the versatility of these small vessels. Spanish and Portuguese masters in the later fifteenth century quite commonly altered the rig of their caravels according to the work they had to do. They found lateen rig convenient for nosing in and out of estuaries, in the pursuit of ordinary coasting trade, or for coastal exploration; but for long passages in areas of stable wind conditions—running down to the Cape Verde Islands, for example, or to the Canaries in summer before the north-east trades—square rig was preferable; so they crossed the yards on one or more masts, always retaining at least the lateen mizen for reasons of balance and manœuvrability. Running with square sails set and mizen furled, they could make better time with far less trouble. Of course, such a conversion involved re-rigging shrouds and lifts, changing all running rigging, and some re-sparring; but the labour cannot have been excessive. Columbus on his first voyage had with him, besides the ship *Santa María*, two caravels of which one, the *Niña*, was lateen-rigged; but he had the *Niña* converted into a *caravela redonda* during his stay in the Canaries, outward bound. The work was completed within a week or so, and must have been satisfactory, for the *Niña* never gave any trouble, and was employed again on the second voyage.

Caravels were uncommonly small vessels for long ocean passages, and few of the sea commanders of the Reconnaissance, at least after Bartolomeu Dias' time, relied on caravels alone. This was not a question of safety, for the caravels were better found and more reliable than many larger ships. Size in itself made relatively little difference to safety, in a time when ships were comparatively slow and were built to ride over the seas rather than to knife through them. Columbus probably never experienced a swept deck. Caravels, however, must have been very uncomfortable. They had little cabin accommodation, usually only one room in the poop; and more serious, they could not carry the men, the stores, the goods and the armament required for long voyages, to destinations where trade as well as exploration was intended, and where a hostile reception might await a European fleet. Between the caravel and the unwieldy carrack stretched a whole range of intermediate types; and most of the leaders of the Reconnaissance preferred vessels between 100 and 300 tons, ship-rigged, with relatively modest, but adequate, superstructures fore and aft. Shipbuilders of the Atlantic ports of Spain and Portugal, intermediaries throughout the fifteenth century between the Mediterranean and the north European traditions, built many such ships. Columbus' *Santa María*, Magellan's ships, and most of Vasco da Gama's and Cabral's were of this class. When they could, the explorers sailed in balanced fleets including—as Vasco da Gama's and Cabral's both did—one or two caravels, which they employed for dispatch-carrying, inshore reconnaissance, and other odd jobs which later admirals would entrust to frigates. Such ships and such fleets first became available, through a strenuous process of experiment and change, to Europeans in the late fifteenth century. This was the development which made the Reconnaissance physically possible.

Compared with the fifteenth century, the sixteenth was a period of steady and orderly development, without any major revolution in ship design. The average size of ocean-going ships increased throughout the century. A tendency to employ larger and larger ships was most marked in the Portuguese *Carreira da India*, where—being associated with an equally marked conservatism in matters of design—it was carried to dangerous excess towards the end of the century. The *Madre de Deus* carrack, taken by Burroughs in 1592, was rated by Hakluyt at 1,600 tons, and she was by no means the only colossus in the trade. The *Carreira* was exceptional, however, in its reliance on small numbers of very large ships. Elsewhere, marine monsters of this kind found little favour for ocean work, and the tendency was to employ more and more medium-sized cargo carriers, in place of small vessels of the caravel type. This tendency, especially after 1550, is clearly shown in the records of the Spanish Indies trade, which employed a far greater volume of shipping than did the Portuguese *Carreira*. The lawful minimum size for merchant ships in this trade was 80 tons, the lawful maximum 550. Towards the end of the century more and more ships approached the maximum, and some exceeded it.[15]

Increasing size demanded a larger spread of canvas, and encouraged greater ingenuity in the balance and subdivision of the sails. Shortly after the middle of the century, topmasts, with caps and fids, made their appearance, introduced first by the Dutch, but quickly adopted by others. The fitting of upper masts which could readily be struck or sent up, made it safe to carry much larger topsails, and in big ships to add topgallants above them.

The most important sixteenth-century improvements, however, were in hull design; and in this connection two advances, which affected the Reconnaissance in different ways, call for particular mention. One was the development by the Dutch of a highly specialized cargo-carrier, the *fluyt* or flyboat. *Fluyts* were little more than floating holds. They had a very full section and almost flat bottom; a high proportion of keel length to length over-all—that is, a much reduced overhang fore and aft; bluff bows, and a full round tuck to the stern, instead of the massive transom usual elsewhere. They had a length from four to six times their beam.[16] To minimize longitudinal weakness, their superstructures fore and aft were reduced to the barest necessities of cabin accommodation. Their masts were stepped well apart to allow room for a capacious main hatch. Their rigging was simple, working through winches or tackles as far as possible in order to save labour. Most important of all, for keeping down crew and operating costs, they carried few or no guns. They were launched in considerable numbers in the last two decades of the sixteenth century. Even in the records of the Spanish Indies trade, references to *felibotes* are fairly frequent. In the late sixteenth century and throughout much of the seventeenth, the possession of large numbers of these very economical freighters allowed the Dutch to secure a major share of the carrying trade of the Atlantic, both in Europe and in the Americas.

The other major advance was in the opposite direction, towards the development of a specialized fighting ship. Mediterranean navies clung tenaciously and long to the galleys to which they had so long been accustomed. Some Mediterranean builders, particularly in Venice, while recognizing that in ships intended for deep-sea work oars would have to be discarded, made serious attempts to incorporate in sailing warships some of the valuable features of galley design. The result of these attempts was the development of the galleon, built longer and narrower than the lofty carrack and its smaller relatives, with more moderate superstructures, and especially differing in the form of the bow. The early galleon had, by contemporary standards, an unusually fine entry; it carried a forecastle with little or no projection and, low down, a beak like that of a galley. This original spur beak, proving less useful than had been expected, soon disappeared; but the fine entry remained, and a decorative compromise between galley beak and carrack forecastle eventually became the characteristic galleon beak-head. The first galleon built by the Venetian state for service on the high seas was designed in the Arsenal by the foreman shipwright Matteo Bressan between 1526 and 1530. It was highly successful and widely imitated throughout Western Europe, particularly in Spain. In the second half of the sixteenth century, the duty of convoy escort in the Spanish West Indian fleets was mainly entrusted to ships of this kind. They were always fair-sized vessels, usually between 250 and 500 tons, and their size tended to increase. In the fifteen-seventies both the Spaniards and the English brought into service a number of highly effective 600-ton galleons; and towards the end of the century the trans-Atlantic escorts often included galleons of over 800 tons. Some of the largest were probably too large for easy manœuvrability; but they were all powerful and specialized warships, with relatively severe lines, built to carry heavy guns. The only cargo they carried—except for the private and illicit ventures of their officers—was bullion. With them, the Spaniards long maintained the lifelines of their American kingdoms against heavy and sustained attack. All the naval powers of western Europe built some galleons; and although such ships were obviously unsuitable for exploration, they played a prominent part in the fighting over the fruits of discovery. From them descended the whole great company of oak-built ships of the Line.

CHAPTER 4

SEAMEN AND SEAMANSHIP

ALTHOUGH no precise description exists of the ships which made up Columbus' fleet in 1492, we have relatively detailed information about the men.[1] The Castilian Crown paid their wages, and characteristically demanded full accounts. Columbus' venture was the earliest of the voyages of discovery for which such information survives; whether because of deliberate secrecy, or because of the subsequent destruction of records, there are no corresponding details about the early Portuguese expeditions. Ninety men sailed with Columbus and, except for one or two clerks and officials, most of them were seamen by trade. A handful were Northerners, probably part of the original crew of the *Santa María*. Most of the rest came from Andalusia; either from the small harbours of the Condado de Niebla—Palos, the home port of the two caravels, Moguer, Huelva and Lepe; or else from the seaboard towns of Cádiz, San Lúcar and Puerto Santa María; or from Seville. None of them, as far as we know, was selected because of any specialized experience in exploring work, but probably many of them already had experience of fairly long passages. The Condado is very close to Portugal, and the precise nationality of seamen was always difficult to establish. Men of Palos and Moguer sailed in Portuguese ships, and took their own very similar ships on trading voyages to the islands or on slave-poaching expeditions down the Guinea coast. Cádiz, San Lúcar and Seville had a flourishing trade with Bristol and other northern ports in wine and fruit; and all these harbours had fishing fleets, some of which went far to sea after tunny. The region was to provide many seamen for subsequent Atlantic expeditions. Columbus' people, as their achievements prove, were a competent and seamenlike company. They seem to have been recruited informally, almost casually, through personal contacts with local seafaring families such as the Pinzón and the Niño, whose members took leading parts in organizing the enterprise. Like the ships, they represented the ordinary maritime activities of the Atlantic coast of Spain. From their qualifications and background, and from the remarks in Columbus' *Journal*[2] about their behaviour on the voyage, it is reasonable to generalize about the kind of seamen and seamanship available for voyages of discovery in the late fifteenth century, when the Reconnaissance was entering upon its oceanic phase.

Of the ninety men in the fleet, about forty sailed in the *Santa María*, the remaining fifty being divided between the two caravels. This was overcrowding by modern standards; though since the fleet carried no soldiers and very little armament or merchandise, the crowding was less severe than in some expeditions of the time. In the sixteenth century, it was not unusual to carry one man for every two tons in heavily armed ships. The commanding officer had his cabin aft. Other officers probably had bunks against the ship's side in the steerage at the after end of the main deck. Hammocks were unknown before 1492; they were one of the chief contributions of the West Indian natives to European civilization. The fo'c'sle had not yet, in the fifteenth century, become the traditional shelter for the crew; and the small fo'c'sles of Columbus' ships must have been full of cables and gear. The crew, therefore, slept on deck. A casual reference in the *Journal* suggests that the hatch cover was a favourite place; since the deck was cambered, to enable water to run into the scuppers, it would be the only level place. In bad weather, the crew would have to sleep below, on the ballast.

The ship's officers in Columbus' time were usually the master and the pilot. In a big ship, especially a ship armed for war or employed on some special service, or a merchantman on a long passage with a valuable cargo, there would usually be a captain in general command, not necessarily a seaman. He might be a soldier or a merchant, according to the work on which the ship was employed. In a small ship, however, and in most ships in ordinary trades, the master served as captain also. The master was necessarily a seaman; he commanded the seamen of the crew and was directly responsible for the handling of the ship and the stowage of cargo and ballast. The pilot was responsible for navigation, and was also the mate. Master and pilot commanded the two watches into which the ship's company was divided. In Columbus' ships they each received the same wage: twice that of an able seaman.

The ratings of petty officers and tradesmen varied to some extent in different parts of Europe, but some of them were probably universal. Each of Columbus' ships carried the two most indispensable: boatswain and steward. The bos'n had charge of anchors and cables, sails and rigging, and gear generally. In Spanish ships it seems also to have been his personal responsibility to see that the galley fire was extinguished every evening[3]—an important point. The steward was responsible for the provisions—food, water, wine and firewood—and certain other stores—lamps, sand-glasses and the like. He also had, at least in some ships, a responsibility for the training of the ships' boys in the rudiments of their traditional duties, such as turning the glasses and shouting the appropriate formulae for the various occasions in the ship's routine. Next in seniority to the petty officers were the tradesmen, somewhat confusingly called *oficiales* in Spanish. Every ship of any size needed to carry a carpenter, a caulker and a cooper. The carpenter was responsible for all repairs to hull and spars. The caulker had charge of everything to do with water-tightness—the caulking and paying of seams, and the graving of the bottom with tallow, whenever the ship could be hove down. Tallow was supposed to protect the hull against ship-worm; various forms of sheathing—horse-hair and tar covered with light boarding in the sixteenth century, lead in the seventeenth—proved unsatisfactory or too expensive for this purpose, and coating with tallow remained normal practice until the introduction of copper sheathing in the eighteenth century. Besides caring for the seams of the hull, the caulker, not the carpenter, maintained the pumps. A ship's pump consisted of a wooden pipe, usually bored out from a straight log, with a wooden piston and leather valves, worked by a handle in the waist. Not all ships had pumps; some relied on buckets and a windlass. The cooper was responsible for heading-up, broaching and maintaining all casks and barricoes; a vital task upon whose proper performance the lives of the entire company might depend.

Many tasks, in later years left to dockyard experts, were at that time carried out as a matter of course by ships' companies. Nothing in the whole story of the Reconnaissance is more impressive than the handiness and undaunted powers of improvisation displayed by tradesmen ratings and by seamen working under their direction. They often carried out major repairs to hulls and spars, using natural timber, in remote anchorages, or when necessary at sea in violent weather. Sometimes in a following sea, for example, a rudder would jump out of its gudgeons and be broken or lost; the ship's tradesmen would make and ship a new one, even forging new straps and pintles. On occasion they made rope from cactus fibres, pitch from resinous trees, oil from the blubber of whales or seals. Sometimes when ships were lost upon lonely coasts, their people built new ships, or at least substantial boats. The ship's carpenter, Martín López, who marched in Cortés' army, directed the building and the launching on Lake Texcoco of a whole fleet of *bergantines* big enough to carry cannon mounted in their bows. For success in voyages of discovery the workmanship, the inventiveness and the large-scale organization of civic arsenals and royal dockyards had always to be supplemented by the empirical shipwrightry of men from many small Atlantic harbours who sailed in ships they helped to build and maintain.

Columbus' fleet carried no sailmaker. Probably any competent bos'n and many able seamen knew how to cut and rope sails. When the *Niña* was re-rigged at Las Palmas, her lateens must have been re-cut as square sails, and this tricky job apparently presented no difficulty.

Another tradesman rating surprisingly absent from Columbus' companies was the cook. We do not know who did the cooking in fifteenth- and sixteenth-century ships. Commanding officers had their personal servants, who may have cooked as well as serving meals. Perhaps the gromets—ordinary seamen or ships' boys—cooked for their messmates. How cooked meals could have been prepared for so many men in such cramped conditions is a minor mystery. The only facility for cooking was the fire box, a stout iron tray or shallow box filled with sand, upon which an open wood fire could be made. It usually stood in the fo'c'sle, which was the safest place for it or (especially if passengers were carried) in the waist. It always constituted a hazard, and in bad weather must have been unusable. Permanent hearths built of stone did not become general until the eighteenth century. The food itself, in a well-found fleet such as that of Columbus, was reasonably varied, and probably not worse than that of labourers and peasants ashore in the winter months. Beef or pork pickled in brine was the traditional meat, and many ships also carried barrelled salt fish, sardines and anchovies in the south, herrings in the north. Fresh fish was expected to supplement the salted supplies, especially in calms; fishing lines and hooks are sometimes mentioned—once by Columbus—as an item of ship's stores. Ship's biscuit was the normal bread. In Lisbon the Crown itself organized the manufacture of this vital supply, and the extensive naval biscuit ovens were only a stone's throw from the royal palace. In addition, ships usually carried barrels of flour, heavily salted to discourage rats and weevils. Presumably the seamen made this into bannocks which they cooked in the ashes, as Arab sailors still do. Other items which regularly occur in stores lists included cheese, onions, garlic, dried peas and beans and chick-peas. Dried fruit was a luxury of the officers' mess. Sir John Hawkins, before his time in this as in several other respects, shipped large quantities of oranges on his trans-Atlantic voyages. The progress of discovery made possible several useful additions to ships' stores in the early sixteenth century. For ships provisioning abroad, yams in the East, cassava in the West Indies, were favoured for their keeping qualities. Cassava flour can be made into tough, hard loaves which will keep for months. Their usefulness in storing ships explains the rapid spread of these dreary vegetables round the world in the tropic zone. Supplies of salt were sometimes difficult in the Tropics, and after the introduction of European animals into the New World, some of the West Indian islands developed a regular trade in sun-dried or smoked beef and bacon for provisioning ships. The practice of carrying livestock for slaughter at sea—except for occasional chickens—did not become general until much later. Drinking water was a constant problem. Some of the big Portuguese ships in the *Carreira* were fitted with wooden tanks, which could readily be topped up with rain water in wet weather. The Portuguese learned the idea of fitting these permanent tanks from Arabs in the Indian Ocean. Most European ships, however, relied on casks for storing their water supply. Water in cask quickly becomes foul, and large quantities of wine were also carried. The normal daily allowance of wine in Spanish and Portuguese ships was about one and a half litres per man. Wine and water casks provided part at least of the ballast, and when emptied were often filled up with sea water for this reason.

Overcrowding and rough fare had always been the lot of seamen while at sea. So was exposure to cold and wet, often with inadequate clothing, for 'slops' issues were unknown. All these discomforts, together with the perils of the sea and the violence of the enemy, were accepted as unavoidable hazards, to be forgotten when ashore. In the late fifteenth century, however, ships began to make much longer passages in the open sea, and as a result a hazard of a different kind became dangerously frequent. This was scurvy, the deficiency disease chiefly responsible for the high mortality in ocean-going ships in the Age of Reconnaissance. Columbus, in his 1492 voyage at least, was unusually fortunate in this respect; the health of his ships' companies was good throughout. Each of his ships carried, surprisingly, a man described as a surgeon; though whether these were really qualified practitioners is difficult to say. They might have been seamen who had gone ashore to take up the apothecaries' or surgeon-barbers' trades. In so small an expedition, they must have kept watches and helped to work the ships. Whatever their qualifications, they had little to do in their medical capacity. Columbus, however, did not on this voyage spend very long periods at sea, and in the West Indies he could obtain fresh provisions. Vasco da Gama's experience, on a far longer voyage, was far worse and much more typical. Of Magellan's fleet only fifteen men got back to Spain, and many more died of scurvy than of wounds or drowning. Passages of many months' duration in the Indian Ocean or the Pacific, with only dried or salted food and inadequate water, reduced many ships to floating cemeteries. The efficacy of fresh food in preventing or curing scurvy was generally known. Not until the eighteenth century, however, was any real progress made in dealing with the connected problems of health and of food preservation on long voyages. Throughout the Age of Reconnaissance the horrors of scurvy were accepted by ocean-going sailors, with all the other perils, as normal hazards of their trade. The only improvements came from the common-sense determination of commanders such as Sir John Hawkins to carry fewer men and to keep them fitter, by feeding them as well as possible.

Disease confronted sea commanders with baffling and contradictory problems. Mosquito-borne diseases, such as yellow fever and malaria, attacked men in tropical harbours; and although their nature was not understood, it was soon discovered that they could be avoided by remaining at sea. On the other hand, the many diseases encouraged by insanitary conditions had a cumulative effect at sea among crowded ships' companies on long voyages. The rigorous cleanliness associated in modern times with well-run ships is comparatively recent. European seamen in the Age of Reconnaissance were no cleaner in their habits than were their contemporaries ashore. They had few facilities for washing either their clothes or themselves. Elementary sanitary precautions could be enforced only in well-disciplined ships' companies. A few big ships, towards the end of the sixteenth century, had stern or quarter galleries, presumably for the officers' use. Apart from these, the only sanitary arrangements, even in big ships, consisted of open boxes slung over the rail, such as may still be seen in sailing ships in the Indian Ocean. Accounts of sixteenth- and seventeenth-century voyages often mention the reluctance of passengers, even sometimes of seamen, to make use of these precarious perches, especially in bad weather. Ships of the Portuguese *Carreira*, which carried large numbers of soldiers and other passengers, had a particularly bad reputation for dirt and squalor. The connection between disease and dirt was dimly recognized by intelligent contemporaries; or rather, a connection was suspected between disease and the bad smells caused by dirt; but few captains succeeded in enforcing discipline in the matter. Those who did are sometimes mentioned as notable exceptions.[4] Garbage and filth of all kinds remained inboard, was washed down into the bilges, and collected among the ballast. This was one of the reasons why prudent captains preferred stone ballast. Spanish trans-Atlantic ships outward bound often carried bricks or cut stone as ballast, to be unloaded and used for building in the New World. Generally, however, ships were ballasted with sand or shingle dredged up from harbour bars or dug from a convenient beach, and carried loose in the ships' bottoms. Sand was obviously insanitary, holding sewage like a sponge. In a semi-liquid state it shifted with the roll of the ship; and it tended to get into the pumps and clog their action. It was easiest to obtain and handle, however, and was regularly used despite the protests of careful captains. When the bilges became too foul to be endured, the only remedy was to 'rummage' the ship: shovel out the ballast, scrub the bilges, sprinkle with vinegar, and take in fresh sand or stones. Naturally such laborious work would be done only when absolutely necessary, and could not be undertaken at sea.

The large crew of a fifteenth- or early sixteenth-century ship was needed not only to fight the ship in case of trouble, but also to handle running gear which, by modern standards, was coarse and clumsy. The two most laborious routine operations were hoisting the main yard and weighing anchor. The main yard was usually lowered in harbour; and at sea, also, the yard would be lowered to the deck in order to take in a course, or partially lowered to increase or reduce sail by lacing on or removing a bonnet. Yards were long and heavy spars. In some big ships, by the early sixteenth century they were handled with the help of jeers and a secondary windlass or capstan. More commonly, they would be hoisted by men hauling directly on stout single halliards of hemp, working through massive blocks at the mast-head. The blocks themselves were solid pieces of hardwood, hollowed out to take the sheaves and with the pendant rove through a hole at one end. Blocks of this comparatively primitive kind can still be seen in Arab ships. Except for the pumps, and the capstan or windlass which worked the cables, blocks were almost the only mechanical labour-saving appliances in the ship. Attempts to reduce crew numbers in relation to tonnage—essential both for economical operation and for health—depended largely on the intelligent use of tackles.

For ground tackle, ships of the period used anchors similar in design to the modern Admiralty pattern: a shank with two curved arms at the crown, terminating in flukes. Some anchors, especially in southern Europe, were stockless; but on the Atlantic coasts, the anchor usually had a stock fitted to the shank at right-angles to the arms, to ensure that when the anchor struck bottom one or other of the flukes would take the ground. The stock was often of wood, permanently fixed on the shank. The shank and arms were of iron, welded together at the crown. The iron was impure and brittle, and anchors were sometimes lost by arms snapping off at the weld. Ships on long voyages often lost one or two anchors; small and medium-sized ships carried from two to five, big ships seven or more. Cables were of tarred hemp. One of the dreaded hazards of Magellan's Strait was the sharp-ridged rock forming the bottom in places, which chafed through the hempen cables and caused the loss of anchors. Anchors were light by modern standards, and cables short, so that their holding qualities were poor. This was one of many ways in which, during the Age of Reconnaissance, the size and weight of ships tended to out-run the efficiency of the tackle with which they were handled; a strong reason for using relatively small ships for voyages of exploration. Large ships at anchor were usually depicted with at least two bower anchors out and often a stern anchor as well. In the course of the sixteenth century, tackle for handling anchors improved; and anchors themselves increased in weight and cables in length, relative to the size of ships. Raleigh's *Ark Royal* of 800 tons had three bower anchors, each of 20 cwt., and a sheet anchor of 22 cwt. Her cables were 15 inches and 17 inches in circumference and 100 fathoms in length. The veering propensities of storms in the northern hemisphere were well understood and ships carried their best bowers on the starboard side.

Many pictures of fifteenth-century ships show a massive cross-beam or *catena* passing through the ship below the forecastle and projecting on either side. Probably the cables were bitted to this beam when the ship rode at anchor. About 1500, however, the *catena* disappeared and was replaced by stout upright bitts with cross-pieces, round which turns could more conveniently be taken with the cables. In weighing anchor, the cable in small ships could be hauled in directly by hand; but even quite small vessels often had a windlass set athwartships in the bows. Ships of any size would have a main capstan and big ships one or more auxiliary or jeer-capstans. The main capstan was no more than an upright wooden spindle passing through two or more decks, its rounded foot set in a bearing socket, its head square, with holes through which two or three bars could be passed one above the other, to provide leverage. The drumhead capstan, with all its bars set in slots at the same optimum height, was not invented until the late seventeenth century. Automatic racks and pawls, to prevent the capstan walking back, were late sixteenth- or early seventeenth-century introductions. The fifteenth-century capstan, however, already had whelps set round the spindle to give an adequate working diameter and grip. It was set in the waist, so that cables could be led to it either from the hawse-holes in the bows, or from the cat-holes in the stern if a stern anchor was to be weighed. To hold the cable, while turns were taken off the bitts and the cable brought to the main capstan, some sort of stopper would be necessary, and by the late sixteenth century at latest an appliance known as a voyol had been evolved. Basically this was a length of stout hawser into which seven or eight nippers were spliced at intervals; a nipper being a short piece of rope with a truck at the end, serving to take hold of the cable. In ships of moderate size the first few fathoms of cable could be brought in by hand with the voyol; but in larger ships the voyol itself would have to be taken to an auxiliary or jeer-capstan. The cable would be taken on the main capstan after passing off the voyol, and the anchor then brought in by men shoving on the capstan bars.

Bower anchors were secured outboard at sea. When up to the hawse-hole the anchor would be catted and fished; that is, hauled into a horizontal position by tackles hooked to the ring and crown respectively, and then secured to the ship's side in some way by lashings. In the fifteenth century, one fluke was often hooked over the gunwale, and the shank suspended by a sling, possibly from the projecting end of the *catena*. In the sixteenth century, bower anchors became too heavy to be secured in this untidy fashion. Various experiments with movable beams and davits, tackles and slings, led by the middle of the century to the introduction of permanent cat-heads and fish-davits, embodying their own purchases, as standard fittings to which, in most sailing ships, bower anchors were hoisted and secured for the next three hundred years.[5] All other anchors were hoisted in and stowed below while at sea. When a stern anchor was used, it was usually sent away slung under the ship's boat, and subsequently weighed from the boat, using a buoy-rope. Big ships' boats were fitted with windlasses for this purpose. The boats themselves were heavy and clumsy, and on short passages in fair weather were often towed astern. Hoisting in the boat was probably a far more troublesome operation than weighing anchor.

Once at sea, the fifteenth-century ship's company seems to have worked, as a rule, in two watches, under the command of the master and the pilot respectively, and to have changed watch, then as now, every four hours. Time-keeping was troublesome and difficult. The hour of noon could be checked roughly by setting a gnomon or pin in the centre of the compass card and observing the moment at which it crossed the meridian; but with a magnetic compass this method was necessarily approximate. At night, since the 'guards' of the Pole Star describe a complete circle round the Pole in every twenty-four hours of sidereal time, it was possible to tell the time from the relative position of Kochab, the brightest of the guards. A simple instrument, the nocturnal, could be used for this purpose. It consisted of a circular disk, with a central hole for sighting Polaris and a swivelling pointer to be aligned on Kochab. Marks round the edge of the disk indicated the angle for midnight on various dates in the year; and by extrapolation the time could be worked out for the observed angle at any hour on any date. Apart from the crudity of the instruments, the difference between solar and sidereal time was an unavoidable source of error; but without chronometers no better method was possible. Both methods were well known to ocean-going navigators in the late fifteenth century. Apart from these occasional rough astronomical checks, the passage of time could only be measured by the use of sand-glasses. A half-hour glass was turned eight times in each watch, the moment of turning being announced by a chant sung by the boy of the watch. These accurately blown glasses were manufactured in Venice, and thousands were sold annually to ship-chandlers in all the ports of Europe. They were fragile, and ships carried spares; Magellan's flagship had eighteen of them.

The ordinary work of the watch would include pumping out, since all wooden ships leak to some extent; sweeping, washing and scraping of woodwork; and adjustments to the lanyards or tackles with which the standing rigging was set up. This last required constant attention, since all rigging was of hemp, which stretched continually when new, hung slack when dry, and tightened with every shower of rain. On the other hand, fifteenth- and early sixteenth-century sailors, unlike their modern descendants, spent little time in painting. Paintwork then was usually confined to rails and counters and to an occasional display of armorial bearings; the upper works were treated instead with some dark substance, probably train oil or pitch or a mixture of the two. Apart from routine jobs of cleaning or maintenance, the chief tasks of the watch were maintaining look-outs, trimming the sails as required by changes of course or of wind, increasing or reducing sail, and steering the ship.

Look-outs call for no comment; the usual stations were the main-top and the eyes of the ship. The details of the handling of sails in late fifteenth- and early sixteenth-century ships can only be deduced from contemporary pictures; the earliest detailed descriptions are in seventeenth-century seamen's manuals. In the absence of reef points, the usual way of increasing sail was by lacing bonnets to the foot of the courses; the usual way of reducing, by removing the bonnets. Topsails were furled aloft, either on the yard, or in an upright bundle in the top. In really heavy weather the courses themselves might have to be taken in, and in smallish ships this operation, since it involved lowering the yards, would probably require all hands. The precise manner in which the clues were handled, and the lowered sail gathered in by its martnets, can only be guessed at. The set of the sails was controlled by tacks, sheets and bowlines; the trim of the yards by their braces. Although the performance of square-rigged ships when on a wind had improved greatly in the fifteenth century, it was still poor by modern standards, and a long beat to windward was a tedious and difficult business, to be avoided whenever possible. The lateen mizen obviously performed a vital function in beating, and early in the sixteenth century its handling was made easier by the introduction of the crow-footed lifts so prominent in Breughel's paintings. A lateen yard so fitted could be swung across abaft, instead of before, the mast. Even with this improvement, putting the ship about when tacking must have been extremely difficult, and in a fresh wind impossible. In a short beamy ship, with the relatively huge main course aback, the risk of losing all steerage way and getting the ship in irons must have been very great. Masters must have preferred, as a rule, to wear ship, accepting the consequent loss to leeward. Probably the very beaminess of such ships made them quick on their helm, and so minimized the loss in wearing; but many ships, then and later, have been lost through want of sea-room to wear, when embayed on a lee shore in weather too rough for tacking with square rig.

Steering presented difficult problems in the rapidly developing ships of the Age of Reconnaissance; and in this respect also the size and complexity of ships tended to outrun mechanical efficiency. A ship was steered by means of a long tiller, morticed to the head of the rudder, and working through an open port cut in the stern. The helmsman stood in the steerage at the after end of the main deck, and steered by his compass. He was prevented by the quarter-deck above his head from seeing either sails or sky. His steering was conned by the officer of the watch above, who presumably shouted his orders through an open hatch in the quarter-deck. Ships of caravel size could be handled in this way without much difficulty; but in bigger ships, communication between officer and helmsman became more difficult, and the sheer size and weight of the rudder presented a formidable problem, especially in a beam or following sea. Ships of this period, with their relatively clumsy rig, could not easily be hove-to with head just off the wind, as a modern sailing ship can. In a gale of dangerous force, the practice was to run before the wind under reduced canvas or even bare poles. The high stern served to save the ship from being pooped; but a good deal of water must have been shipped through the tiller-port with every follow-ing sea, and great strength and skill would be needed to hold the tiller steady and prevent the ship from broaching-to. In big ships, relieving tackles were fitted to the tiller and secured to eyebolts on either side of the steerage, in order to reduce the physical labour of steering. Even so, it was reported of the *Madre de Deus*, Burrough's prize of 1592, that twelve to fourteen men were needed to control her tiller in a heavy sea. In the early seventeenth century a device was introduced whereby a ship could be steered from the quarter-deck. This was the whipstaff, a long lever working in a fulcrum set in the quarter-deck. The lower end was attached by a ring to the tiller. The upper end projected above the quarter-deck and was grasped by the helmsman. By pushing the upper end to port or starboard he could move the tiller below. The whipstaff had the advantage of enabling the helmsman to watch the sails, but it allowed only a very limited movement of the helm and was useless in rough weather. Another seventeenth-century improvement resulted from the development of overhanging counters, which enabled the head of the rudder to be carried up into the counter through a small vertical rudder-port and did away with the necessity for a large horizontal tiller-port. This of course greatly improved the watertightness of the stern. The eventual solution of all these steering problems in sailing ships was to fit a yoke to the head of the rudder, and to lead the lines through a series of leading blocks to a horizontal drum, mounted on the quarter-deck, which could be rotated by means of a wheel; but the ship's wheel did not appear until the eighteenth century.

The compass by which late fifteenth-century ships were steered had long developed beyond its primitive form of a needle, magnetized by a lodestone, floating on a chip in a bowl of water.[6] Its manufacture had been taken over by the professional instrument-maker. A magnetized iron wire was bent double and glued beneath a circular card or fly, mounted on a central pin, on which it could pivot freely, and enclosed in a circular box. Being made of soft iron, the needle tended to lose its magnetism, and from time to time had to be lifted from its box and 'fed' with the lodestone which every pilot included in his outfit. The fly was marked with the eight principal 'winds' and their subdivisions, to the total number of thirty-two, sometimes sixty-four points. It was possible, therefore, to read bearings to within five or six degrees, though degrees as a measure of compass-bearing were not used then or for long afterwards, and one of the first lessons of an apprentice seaman was to learn to 'say' or box his compass by the names of the points. Curiously, there is no known mention of a lubber's line, marking the fore-and-aft line of the ship on the compass box, until late in the sixteenth century. Presumably the helmsman took his line from the masts or the ship's head. Ships of any size must have possessed two compasses, one for the helmsman and one for the officer who conned the steering, apart from spares. When in use at sea, a compass would have to be protected from the weather, and mounted at a height convenient for the helmsman's vision. At night a lamp would be placed near it. Many fifteenth- and sixteenth-century ships' inventories mention chests for housing lamps and compasses; though no precise details are known of these fore-runners of the modern binnacle.[7] Gimbals, pivoted rings to hold the compass level against the roll of the ship, were used at least from the early sixteenth century. Deviation was not a serious problem in ships which contained a negligible quantity of iron; but that its existence was known in the sixteenth century is shown by frequent insistence that binnacles should be fastened with wooden pins and that the metal fittings of compasses—pins and gimbals—should be of brass.

The compass came to Atlantic Europe from the more civilized Mediterranean. Tradition associates its origin with the port of Amalfi. The other essential instrument upon which the safety of ships depended was simpler and still more ancient, and may well have originated independently on the Atlantic coasts; certainly it was more constantly in use there than in the Mediterranean. This was the lead and line. In most parts of the Mediterranean basin the coast plunges steeply down to considerable depths; the sea is clear, so that in shallow water the bottom can be seen; and fog is comparatively rare. Sounding, therefore, is rarely necessary. Off the Atlantic coasts, on the other hand, the sea-bed slopes from the shore-line—here steeply, as off Spain and western

Ireland, there gently, as to the west of the English Channel—to a depth of about 100 fathoms, before plunging precipitately to great depths. The outer edge of the continental shelf, the line where the continental slope thrusts steeply up towards the surface of the sea, is clearly defined by the hundred-fathom line. By using a deep-sea lead and line, the seaman could get his first and timely warning of his proximity to the coast; twenty miles or so if it were the coast of Spain or Portugal, over a hundred if it were Brittany or south-west England. Within soundings off most of the Atlantic coasts, fog is frequent, the water is opaque, and depth off shore varies constantly with the ebb and flow of the tides. A seaman in these waters must have—even before a means of determining direction—some means of finding at frequent intervals exactly how much water he has under his ship and of detecting the presence of hidden rocks and shoals. For this he used—and in small vessels uses still —a sounding lead and line.

The earliest surviving detailed descriptions of leads and lines are from the late sixteenth and early seventeenth centuries.[8] The instruments have changed little since that time; probably they were much the same a hundred years earlier. The dipsie lead weighed about fourteen pounds and was attached to a two-hundred-fathom line, marked first at twenty and then at every ten fathoms with so many knots in little strings fixed to each mark. The precise marks varied from place to place, but the principle was universal. To use the dipsie line, the ship was hove-to; the sounding might be taken from a boat; alternatively, the lead was taken forward to the eyes of the ship, and the line coiled down at intervals all along the weather side of the deck to the poop, with a man standing by each coil. When the lead was hove over side, each man as his coil ran out called out to the next man aft; and as the line came up and down and ceased to run, the depth was taken, either so many fathoms or 'no bottom', under the eye of the master.

Backing the yards and heaving-to in order to use the dipsie lead was a troublesome business. In shoal water, twenty fathoms or less, it was necessary to take frequent and repeated soundings while the ship was under way. The sounding lead used in shoal water weighed about seven pounds, and was attached to a shorter, thicker line marked at two, three, five, seven, ten, fifteen and twenty fathoms. The thirteen and seventeen fathom marks are more modern. The leadsman hove his lead in the direction of the ship's movement, and called out the depth as the ship passed the lead and the line came up and down. Sounding was—and, with mechanical devices, still is—an essential and elementary pre-caution in any ship approaching land. Many ships were, and still are, lost through neglect of this precaution, or through delay in appreciating the warning which it gives. Most of the famous voyages of the Age of

81

Reconnaissance were made by Atlantic coast seamen to whom sounding in pilotage waters was so habitual as to be almost second nature. The lead not only gave warning of the approach of danger; it also helped the master of a ship to fix his position. Off a well-known coast the sequence of soundings would fall into a familiar and identifiable pattern. Corroborative evidence was obtained by sampling the nature of the bottom. The lead was provided with a hollow at its lower end, which could be armed or filled with tallow; and fragments of sand, mud or shell sticking to the arming could be examined and identified. This use of the lead was well known off the Atlantic coasts in the fifteenth century and probably long before. Its consideration takes us over the indistinct borderline—more indistinct then than now—between seamanship and pilotage.

CHAPTER 5

PILOTAGE AND NAVIGATION

NAVIGATION, roughly defined, is the art of taking ships from one place to another out of sight of land; pilotage, the art of taking ships from one place to another when land or navigational marks are in sight. In the late fifteenth and early sixteenth centuries navigation, so defined, was in its early infancy and was not regarded as a distinct technique. John Dee, perhaps the most original of the mid-sixteenth-century pioneers of mathematical navigation, defined navigation simply as the art which 'demonstrateth how by the shortest way, and in the shortest time, a sufficient ship . . . be conducted'. Dee was a mathematician rather than a seaman, little interested in pilotage; but he made no clear distinction. Nor did any of his contemporaries or predecessors. Martín Cortés, the Spaniard who published, in 1551, the most famous and most comprehensive sixteenth-century manual of navigation,[1] dealt extensively with pilotage as well as with navigation and cosmography, but lumped them all together under one general head. The first manual to make a clear and explicit distinction—though without using the word pilotage —was that of the Fleming, Michiel Coignet, published in 1581.[2] After defining navigation generally, more or less in Dee's terms, Coignet adds: 'This art is divided into two, namely common navigation and grand navigation. . . . The whole science of common navigation is nothing more than knowing perfectly by sight all capes, ports and rivers, how they appear from the sea, what distance lies between them, and what is the course from one to another; also in knowing the bearing of the moon on which high and low tides occur, the ebb and flow of the waters, the depth, and the nature of the bottom. . . . Grand navigation, on the other hand, employs, besides the above-mentioned practices, several other very ingenious rules and instruments derived from the art of Astronomy and Cosmography.' In the later sixteenth century, pilotage was the stock-in-trade of all competent ship-masters, as it had been for centuries. Navigation, in the narrow sense, was the preserve of a relatively small aristocracy of experts whose business took them across great oceans. These men were still expected to possess the traditional skills of ship-handling and pilotage (though in some difficult harbours they were beginning already to seek the help of specialized port pilots) ; they possessed, in addition, a rough knowledge of astronomy, and knew how to apply mathematical rules to astronomical observations in order to find a ship's position, at least approximately. This special knowledge had come to be recognized as a study in its own right. It could only come from books, and so could only be acquired by literate seamen.

A hundred years earlier, almost the whole art of 'conducting' a ship had lain in pilotage, together with certain extensions of pilotage technique to enable a master to keep track of a ship which passed out of sight of land for relatively short passages. The masters and pilots who sailed with Columbus, and who received twice the wages of able seamen, were men trained in extended pilotage, not in oceanic navigation. Such men need not be, and often were not, literate. They and others like them had to be persuaded, against all caution and experience, that when far from land in strange waters, they could put faith in the observations and calculations of navigational specialists. The leap from extended pilotage to true navigation, like the development of 'sufficient' ships, was the achievement of south-western Europe in the late fifteenth and early sixteenth centuries.

The principal qualifications of the late medieval navigator were experience, detailed knowledge of the coasts where his business lay, and acute powers of observation. To assist him in applying his knowledge he had the simple instruments already described: the magnetic compass and the lead. When within sight of land he could fix his position by taking compass bearings of prominent marks. When out of sight of land but within soundings, he could still get a rough idea of his position by taking frequent soundings for depth and by sampling the bottom. With these aids he sailed from one position identifiable by prominent marks to another; among northern European seamen, indeed, the ship's course was often referred to as the 'caping' of the ship; and for purposes of coastal sailing distances were reckoned in 'kennings', a kenning being the distance—twenty miles or so—at which a coast should be visible from a ship's mast-head. It was not a matter of keeping close inshore— no prudent seaman cares to do that—but of sighting capes and head-lands often enough to be sure of the ship's position. If his business required him to sail for any considerable distance out of sight of land, the ship's master, knowing the course from his point of departure to the point at which he hoped to sight land again, would wait, if he could, for a wind sufficiently favourable to give him a direct passage, and would then steer by his compass. His dipsie lead would give him advance warning of his approach to the coast unless—as usually happened in the clear air and deep water of the Mediterranean—he sighted it first.

Chaucer's shipman, if he was illiterate, as many late medieval ship-masters were, would have needed a capacious memory to retain all the details of 'tydes', 'herberewe' and 'lodemenage' from the Humber to North Africa;[3] and learning the features of an unfamiliar coast must have been a slow business. A literate seaman, already in the fifteenth century, had many advantages. In particular, instead of relying on memory or hearsay, he could use written sailing directions. In the comparatively sophisticated maritime world of the Mediterranean, *portolani*—directions for coastwise passages from place to place—had been in use for centuries. Originating, no doubt, in private notebooks kept by pilots for their own reference, and then passed on to others, they represented a great accumulation of experience in local pilotage. By the late thirteenth century, directions contained in many different *portolani* had been collected together into a comprehensive pilot book, the *Compasso da Navigare*,[4] covering the whole of the Mediterranean and the Black Sea. The directions in the *Compasso* go from port to port clockwise round the Mediterranean from Cape St Vincent to Safi in Morocco. They include bearings, distances in miles (the short 'geometrical' mile), descriptions of landmarks and dangers, instructions for entering harbours, and information about depths and anchorages, often in considerable detail. Besides coastwise passages, the *Compasso* includes directions, with courses and distances, for a number of long-distance crossings between easily recognizable points, usually capes or islands. Some of these open-sea crossings were seven or eight hundred miles in length.

Pilot-books came into use considerably later in northern Europe, and there were known as 'routiers' or 'rutters'. The earliest surviving English rutter is from the early fifteenth century.[5] It gives sailing directions for the English coasts, and for a passage between the Strait of Gibraltar and the Channel. For this last voyage it recommends a direct course across the Bay of Biscay, and gives the bearings from Cape Finisterre of a number of points in Brittany, England and Ireland. Northern rutters differed from southern *portolani* in ways which reflected the different methods of pilotage in shallow and deep seas. Their information on bearings and courses is less full and less precise; their estimates of distance—when given at all—are usually very rough, and in fifteenth-century examples are expressed in kennings. Only in the sixteenth century, with the spread of the use of traverse boards, did the compilers of rutters abandon this vague and ancient measure in favour of leagues or miles. On the other hand, most rutters gave remarkably full and detailed accounts of soundings, both depths and bottoms, not only in the immediate approaches to harbours, but along whole stretches of coast. They also devoted a good deal of space to information about tides. In the Mediterranean area tides mattered little, except in the approaches to riverine ports such as Seville. The only tidal race dangerous to ship-ping was that in the Strait of Messina. On the Atlantic coasts, however, and especially in northern Europe, the rise and fall of the tides and changes in direction of the flow of tidal streams were important con-siderations for the ship-master. On a coasting voyage, he needed to know the times of high and low water at each port of call, the depth of water at those ports at those times, and the direction of flow of the tidal streams likely to be encountered between them. Many theories were propounded in the later Middle Ages about the causes of tides; but the tidal information collected for the use of seamen ignored theory. It was based on two obvious and recognized facts: the daily retardation of the times of high water, and the association between these times and the position of the moon. From these it was possible to calculate, for any particular place, the times of high water on each day of the moon's age. Such information, however, would be of little convenience to seamen who could not read, possessed no clocks or watches, and could reckon time only very roughly with the magnetic compass and the sand-glass. For simplicity and ease of memory, therefore, sailors recorded not the time but the age and compass bearing of the moon at the moment of high water. The moon's reflection on the surface of the sea was a dramatic and obvious track, whose bearing was simple to observe; and since the highest high waters, or spring tides, were seen to occur on days of full and new moon—at 'full and change'—the bearing of the moon at these times became the tidal establishment of the port. The establish-ment of Dieppe, for example, was expressed: 'Dieppe, moon north-north-west and south-south-east, full sea', which meant 'high water occurs at Dieppe on days of full and new moon when the moon bears north-north-west or south-south-east'. Knowing the establishment of a port, the seaman could work out the time of high water on any particu-lar day by remembering the age of the moon—or taking it from an almanac if he carried one—and adding the daily retardation. Portu-guese tide tables used the accurate but arithmetically inconvenient retardation of 48 minutes; in northern waters a rough approximation of 45 minutes was usual. This was conveniently equivalent to one point of the magnetic compass. The seaman marked the fly of his compass in hours as well as in points. To the establishment of the port, expressed as a compass bearing, he added one point for every day of the moon's age.

Rutters usually included the establishment of various ports in the course of sailing directions; and when, in the sixteenth century, such aids to pilotage came to be printed in large numbers,[6] they were supplemented by almanacs, and by ingenious diagrammatic tide tables and tide charts, which enabled the establishment of a port to be picked out at a glance. Most of these diagrams came from Brittany, where tidal conditions are notoriously complex and difficult. Some of them used symbols instead of names, as an assistance to the illiterate.[7] References to tidal streams, on the other hand, were sketchy in sixteenth-century sailing directions, and no reliable information on the strength of such streams was published until the eighteenth century. Ignorance of the strength of tidal streams was a common source of error, one which could only be avoided by long experience of ship-handling in the waters concerned. In general, tidal knowledge throughout the Age of Reconnaissance was rough by modern standards, but in European waters good enough for ordinary purposes; though it was not uncommon for ships to run aground 'from mistaking of the tide' even in well-known harbours.

Such, then, was the pilotage information available to the late fifteenth-century ship-master 'caping' his way about the sea with frequent sightings of the land. When out of sight of land, however, for any considerable time—on long passages in the Mediterranean, for example, or crossing the Bay of Biscay, or sailing to the Atlantic islands —his sailing directions merely gave him a course to steer, a rough estimate of distance, and a description of the land he hoped to reach. In order to know his position day by day while at sea, he had to take the first step from pilotage towards navigation; he had to keep a dead-reckoning. If he were making a direct passage with a following wind, this was a relatively simple matter. All he needed was an estimate of his ship's speed; so many watches sailed, each of so many glasses, gave him the distance covered from his point of departure. In the fifteenth century, however, there was no means of measuring speed. The earliest type of log was a piece of wood made fast to a long line knotted at regular intervals. The log was flanged to resist the tow of the ship, and later fitted with a tripping device to facilitate recovery. When the log was streamed, the speed at which the knots ran out over the stern was timed with a diminutive sand-glass. This rough log was a late sixteenth-century invention. The fifteenth-century sailor studied the behaviour of his ship along known stretches of coast, and learned to estimate his speed by watching bits of wood or other flotsam floating by. Columbus always over-estimated the speed of his ships; probably many masters did so. The likelihood of error was further increased by ignorance of ocean currents and by the difficulty of keeping an accurate account of time.

A passage in the open sea might not be made on a single direct course. A ship might be caught by a gale and blown off its course; or the master might deliberately sail far out into the Atlantic—on passage, for example, from Lisbon to the Channel, or to West Africa—in order to find a favourable wind for his destination. Again, he might decide, rather than wait for a favourable wind, to beat against an unfavourable one. In the late fifteenth century, with the steady improvement in the sailing qualities of ocean-going ships, tacking became much more practicable and much commoner than formerly; and the problems of dead-reckoning became more complicated in consequence. A method of keeping track of a ship's progress in such circumstances was provided by the traverse board. This was a wooden board on which was drawn a large compass rose, with thirty-two radii corresponding to the thirty-two compass points. Along each radius of the rose was bored a row of eight holes, for the eight half-hours of the watch; and attached by strings to the centre of the board hung eight wooden pegs. The traverse board was stowed in the binnacle, beside the compass; and it was the helmsman's duty, at the end of each glass or half-hour of his watch, to insert a peg in one of the holes along the radius corresponding to the ship's course. At the end of the watch, the account so kept on the board was transferred to a slate, and the board cleared for the next watch. From the record on the slate the master, knowing or guessing his ship's speed, translated glasses into terms of distance, and applied such corrections as his experience suggested for the action of waves and currents and for the ship's leeway. Leeway—a serious matter when sailing on a wind—could be measured roughly by streaming a line astern with some kind of buoy attached, and observing the angle of leeway with a compass on the poop; but there are no records of the use of such a method before the middle of the sixteenth century. The fifteenth-century navigator probably estimated his leeway as he did his speed, purely by experience. By these means he arrived at an estimate of his course and distance made good. For convenience of calculation he generally used leagues as his units of distance; a league being originally the distance an average ship would sail in an hour in average conditions. Its conventional value varied to some extent from one locality to another, but usually it seems to have been four Roman miles; that is, about three modern nautical miles, or a little less. In the sixteenth century, a degree a day was regarded as an average run on ocean passages.[8] The whole process of estimation based on the traverse board was thus a rough-and-ready affair; but in northern Atlantic waters it remained the commonest method of dead-reckoning until well into the seventeenth century. Until the middle of the sixteenth century it was, for most northern shipmasters, the only method.

Mediterranean sailors were better provided. At least from the late thirteenth century, Italian and Catalan sailors had used written traverse tables—the *Toleta de Marteloio*. The *Toleta* set out in tabular form the solution of a series of right-angled triangles, the hypotenuse of each triangle representing the course steered and distance sailed. In tacking, a ship-master entering the tables with the series of courses he had sailed and the distances he had covered on each tack, could discover for each tack the distance made good on the course to his destination, the extent to which he had deviated from the desired track, and the course and distance he must sail in order to regain it. Out in the open sea, it is true, he suffered from the same difficulties as his northern European contemporary: ignorance of ocean currents and the lack of a means of measuring speed. These were but two among many instances of the ways in which, throughout the Age of Reconnaissance, mathematical theory outstripped the development of instruments and methods of precise observation. Assuming, however, that his experience enabled him to estimate his speed with reasonable accuracy, the Mediterranean seaman could proceed to calculate and not merely to estimate his course and distance made good. Traverse tables must have been drawn up by men with a knowledge of elementary plane trigonometry; probably first by Jewish mathematicians in Italy, Cataluña or Majorca, in this as in many other ways the intermediaries between the Greek-Arab scientific tradition and the maritime world of western Europe. The Catalan Atlas includes a traverse table, and similar tables were often drawn on marine charts, so that the pilot, having worked out his dead-reckoning, could mark it visually on his chart.

This was the most important of all the navigational advantages possessed by the fifteenth-century Mediterranean seaman. In northern Europe, the marine chart was almost unknown until the middle of the sixteenth century; a plausible tradition attributes to Sebastian Cabot its introduction into England. In the Mediterranean area the use of charts went back at least to the thirteenth century and their development shows a close parallel with that of tables and of sailing directions. All three sprang from the invention of the mariner's compass; and the very word *compasso* was used to describe not only pilot-books, as we have seen, but charts also. Like the *Compasso da Navigare*, the late medieval marine chart of the Mediterranean was based on a series of coastwise compass bearings and distances between ports and prominent landmarks; from each of these principal reference points radiating lines were drawn across the chart, representing compass bearings. The whole surface of the chart was thus crossed by a network of intersecting direction lines. At one side of the chart a distance scale was drawn. The navigator using the chart needed a straight-edge—forerunner of the parallel ruler, which was not invented until the end of the sixteenth century and came only slowly into use—and a pair of dividers. He aligned his straight-edge between his point of departure and destination; if no direction line was drawn along the intended course, he found with the help of his dividers the line most nearly parallel; and set his course accordingly. He did not work out his dead-reckoning, as a modern navigator does, by actual drawing on the chart; he calculated, by the methods outlined above, the distances made good along his chosen course, measured with his dividers the appropriate length on the distance scale, and marked his approximate position by pricking the parchment with the point of the dividers. He used the written *portolano* for coastwise pilotage, the chart for passages in the open sea.

The seamen of the Atlantic coasts of Spain and Portugal in the fifteenth century were the heirs to two distinct traditions of finding a way through the sea. From the southern, the Mediterranean, tradition they inherited relatively sophisticated methods based upon the compass; detailed written sailing directions; traverse tables; the marine chart; and the habit of keeping a regular and careful dead-reckoning. The northern, the Atlantic, tradition was more primitive, with rougher sailing directions, no charts, and limited skill in rule-of-thumb dead-reckoning; but from it they inherited a great store of rough-weather experience off fog-bound coasts; knowledge of tides and tide-tables; perhaps most important of all, the habit of careful and constant sounding in pilotage waters, especially off unfamiliar coasts. Such was the combination of skill and knowledge available to men setting out on voyages to West Africa and to the Atlantic islands, on the long series of explorations which would take them eventually to the Americas and the Far East. Sailing in the open sea had no particular terrors for them, when they knew the course to their destination, roughly the length of time they might expect to be at sea, and the general appearance of the land they hoped to reach. The problem of finding a way through totally unknown oceans, however, demanded new skill and knowledge. Quite early in the course of West African exploration, the Portuguese took the first, decisive step from extended pilotage—if dead-reckoning navigation may be so described—towards navigation proper, the 'grand navigation' of Coignet's definition.

A navigator sailing in unknown seas could clearly expect no help from charts and sailing directions. If he were literate and well-read he might at best get from the cosmographers a general, and in many ways misleading, notion of what to look for. If he were fortunate enough to find some hitherto unknown land which appeared to be of interest or value, his chief need would be a means of fixing its position so that he or his successors on subsequent voyages could find the place again with a minimum of trouble, in order to open a trade or otherwise exploit the discovery. He would, of course, have kept a dead-reckoning account; but the further he had sailed from his home port the greater the likelihood of error, and at best his dead-reckoning could only give him a position relative to his point of departure. On a subsequent voyage he, or his successors, sailing perhaps at a different time of year and in different wind conditions, might be quite unable to follow the exact track of the original discovery. He needed, therefore, a means of fixing the position of newly-discovered places relative to fixed observable objects. The only possible objects were heavenly bodies, and the most easily observable heavenly body was the Pole Star, already familiar to seamen because of its constant northerly bearing and its use in telling the time. The altitude of the Pole Star—its angle above the horizon— grew less as a ship sailed further south, and so gave an indication of how far south she had sailed. Altitude could be estimated by eye in many rough ways—so many spans, so many hand-breadths, 'the height of a man', and so forth. The Venetian Cadamosto, who sailed in a Portuguese trading expedition to West Africa in 1454, reported that after leaving the Canaries the ships ran south before the trade-wind for 200 miles, then stood in to the land and coasted south, sounding constantly and anchoring at night. Off the mouth of the Gambia, he wrote, the Pole Star appeared 'about the third of a lance above the horizon'.[9] This kind of rough eye-estimate was soon found inadequate for recording the systematic exploration of the African coast, and by 1456 was already giving way to measurement with instruments. For this purpose, navigators took to sea greatly simplified versions of appliances —astrolabe and quadrant—which had long been used for celestial observations by astronomers ashore.

The seaman's quadrant was a very simple device: a quarter of a circle, with a scale from 1° to 90° marked on the curved edge, and with two pin-hole sights along one of the straight edges. A plumb-line hung from the apex. The sights were aligned on the star and the reading taken from the point where the plumb-line cut the scale. Polar altitude in degrees gave the observer's latitude—as every astronomer who had read his Ptolemy well knew—provided that the right correction was applied to allow for the small circle which *Polaris* describes about the true pole. This correction could be ascertained from the position of the Guards. Some years elapsed, however, before seamen learned to apply the correction, or to think in terms of latitude measured in degrees. At first, the navigator used his quadrant simply as a means of measuring his linear distance south (or north) of his port of departure, usually Lisbon. He observed the altitude of the Pole Star at his port of departure when the Guards were in a given position. Subsequently during the voyage he observed the polar altitude of each place he came to, with the Guards in the same position, landing for the purpose if possible. He marked the names of important places against the appropriate point on his quadrant scale. He was taught that each degree division represented a fixed distance (16⅔ leagues was the usual reckoning in the third quarter of the fifteenth century, a considerable under-estimate traceable to the influence of Ptolemy[10]; and so he built up his knowledge of the polar altitudes and the distances south (or north) of his base, of all the places he had visited. Conversely, if he wished to find a place whose polar altitude he already knew—say in West Africa or in one of the islands— he would sail south, or as near south as the wind would allow, until he found the right altitude. He would then sail due east or due west until he fell in with the land.

The quadrant was an unsatisfactory device for taking observations at sea, because the least roll of the ship set the plumb-bob swinging and made accurate reading impossible. As navigators gradually acquired the habit of translating the polar altitudes of particular places into the more convenient terms of latitude, measured in degrees, which could be marked on a chart, so the primitive quadrant gave way at sea to more sophisticated devices, astrolabe, cross-staff and their derivatives. The medieval astrolabe was a complicated and often very beautiful instrument. It consisted of a brass disk engraved with a stereographic projection of the heavens and a rotatable grill, by means of which the movements of the more conspicuous heavenly bodies could be followed. It was principally intended as a calculating device for the use of astronomers; but on its reverse side it was graduated in degrees round the perimeter and fitted with a rotating sight bar or alidade for observing altitudes. Only the reverse side of the instrument was useful—or indeed comprehensible—to seamen; and so the simplified type of astrolabe used at sea retained only the peripheral degree scale and the alidade. Most astrolabes were small, from six to ten inches in diameter; but some navigators, including Vasco da Gama, used a specially large type for making more accurate observations ashore. The mariner's astrolabe was slightly more convenient than the quadrant for use at sea; it had no plumb-bob; and it did not have to be held in the hand. It was fitted with a suspension ring at its top edge, and so could be hung independently at a height convenient for taking sights.

Both quadrant and astrolabe used an artificial horizon; they depended, that is, upon perpendicularity. Balancing himself on a heaving deck, a navigator can take more accurate sights with an instrument designed, as most modern instruments are, to measure altitudes from the visual horizon. A rough device of this kind was employed by some medieval Arab seamen. This was the *kamal*, which consisted of a series of small wooden boards, each representing a definite altitude, strung on a cord of fixed length. The navigator gripped the end of the cord between his teeth, and holding the cord taut, selected the board which most exactly fitted between the horizon and the heavenly body he was observing. Vasco da Gama's people found the *kamal* in use in the Indian

Ocean; and possibly their descriptions of it inspired the adaptation to nautical use, in the early sixteenth century, of the cross-staff, another device with a long history of astronomical use ashore. The mariner's cross-staff was a straight rod, usually of box-wood, about three feet long and ¾ inch in cross-section, four-square, graduated along one side in degrees and minutes. A cross-piece was fitted to the staff so as to slide evenly along it. The end of the staff was held to the eye, the cross-piece moved until it corresponded exactly to the distance from the horizon to the heavenly body observed, and the altitude read off from the scale. Such an instrument was cheaper and easier to make than an astrolabe. Being made of wood, it did not require engraving, and a handy seaman, properly instructed, could make one for himself. Martín Cortés' manual contained detailed instructions for the graduation of a cross-staff. The instrument called for considerable skill in use; for accurate readings it had to be held steady and exactly upright, and aligned carefully with the centre of the eye to avoid errors of parallax. Its use was limited; the altitudes of stars could only be observed at dawn and dusk, when both stars and horizon were visible at once; and altitudes less than 20° or greater than 60° could not be observed at all. Despite those limitations, however, the relative simplicity and accuracy of the cross-staff made it the favourite instrument for its purpose, at least in middle latitudes, throughout the sixteenth century.

In northern latitudes, throughout our period, the Pole Star was the heavenly body most commonly observed, because of its constant bearing, because of the ease with which it could be identified, and because of the simplicity of the rules and the relative insignificance of the corrections governing the calculation of latitude from observed polar altitudes. Portuguese seamen, however, sailing south along the West African coast, saw the Pole Star sink lower in the sky night by night until in about latitude 9°N they lost sight of it entirely. Other conspicuous stars, whose distance from the Pole had been tabulated, could be used; a rule for determining latitude by the Southern Cross, analogous to the Rule of the Pole Star, was worked out early in the sixteenth century. Observations of other stars, however, could only be used, with the limited mathematical knowledge of the time, if made at the moment of meridian transit. That moment was difficult to determine, and might occur at a time when neither star nor horizon was conveniently observable. The most obvious substitute for Pole Star altitude was the meridian altitude of the sun. Like the Pole Star, the sun's altitude had long been used for giving the seaman a rough idea of his distance north or south of a point of departure. The measurement of solar altitude by instruments, however, presented practical difficulties; and when these had been overcome, the determination of latitude involved a calculation considerably more complicated than the Rule of the North Star. The navigator wanted to know his angular distance in degrees north or south of the equator, which is equivalent to the zenith distance of the celestial equator; but unlike the Pole Star, the celestial equator cannot be observed directly. The sun does not follow the celestial equator, and the angular distance between the celestial equator and the ecliptic, the track which the sun does follow in relation to the earth, changes from day to day, and from year to year. The navigator needed, therefore, to know this angular distance north or south of the celestial equator—the sun's declination—for any day of any year at midday. This was an astronomical and mathematical problem which no amount of rule-of-thumb experience could solve.

The exact processes whereby late medieval science was made available to seamen are, in general, little known. Chroniclers often stated that princes—Prince Henry of Portugal was not unique in this—invited astronomers to their courts in order to pick their brains; but they very rarely explained precisely what the learned men taught, to whom, and with what result. The Rule of the Sun is an exception: a clear and rare instance of a group of scientists, deliberately employed by the State, applying theoretical knowledge to the solution of a particular and urgent practical problem. John II of Portugal in 1484 convened a commission of mathematical experts to work out a method of finding latitude by solar observation. Declination had long been studied by astronomers, and tables of declination existed in a variety of forms. Among the most accurate and detailed were those worked out for the years 1473-78 by the Jewish astronomer Abraham Zacuto of Salamanca. King John's commission drew up a greatly simplified version of Zacuto's tables, brought them up to date, and devised a fixed procedure to enable an intelligent and literate seaman to use them. The navigator was taught first to find the altitude of the sun by observation of its meridian transit. Without adequate timekeepers, this in itself was a lengthy business. It was done by starting well before the expected moment, and taking a series of observations, which increased in value as the sun approached the meridian and decreased after it had passed. The maximum reading was taken as the meridian altitude. Observations could be made either with cross-staff or astrolabe; to 'shoot' the centre of the sun by squinting at it through the pin-holes of a quadrant was almost impossible. The cross-staff was more practical, but involved maintaining an arm-aching, eye-blinding posture for minutes on end. The more refined back-staff or Davis' quadrant, which enabled the navigator to read solar altitude with his back to the sun by observing the fall of a shadow on a graduated scale, was not invented until late in the sixteenth century; it was, indeed, the last great advance towards accurate observations at sea in our period; for it was not until the eighteenth century that the sciences of optics and mechanics enabled Hadley to produce the reflecting quadrant with Vernier's scale adjustment. The only way in which the fifteenth-century navigator could observe solar altitude without peering at the sun was by suspending his astrolabe independently, and by swivelling the alidade until the point of light shining through the upper sight-hole fell exactly on the lower sight.

Having found his meridian altitude, the navigator wrote it on his slate. He next turned to his tables, looked up the sun's declination for the day, and wrote that down too. He had then to select the appropriate rule for applying the declination to the altitude, according to whether he was north or south of the equator, whether the declination was north or south, and whether the declination was greater or less than the latitude if both had the same name. Application of the correct rule gave him the altitude of the celestial equator above his own horizon; this he subtracted from 90° to obtain his latitude. He might have avoided one stage in the calculation by observing the sun's zenith distance instead of its altitude in the first place; but this would have required an instrument graduated in the reverse direction, and no one in the fifteenth century seems to have thought of it.

The work of John II's commission was summarized for the benefit of practical navigators in a manual compiled in Portugal under the title *Regimento do astrolabio e do quadrante*.[11] This was the first European manual of navigation and nautical almanac. The earliest known copy was printed in 1509, but there were probably earlier editions, and the work seems to have been circulated in manuscript from the fourteen-eighties. It contained, as a theoretical basis, a Portuguese translation of Sacrobosco's well-known treatise *De Sphaera Mundi*; a list of latitudes from Lisbon to the equator, most of them correct to within half a degree, some to within ten minutes; a calendar; and a table of the sun's declination for a leap year (later almanacs were to give tables for each year of a four-year cycle; but in the fifteenth century the crude instruments in use made this degree of accuracy superfluous). In addition the *Regimento* gave the Rule of the North Star and the Rule of the Sun, setting out the instructions summarized above for finding the latitude. These rules were the essential content of the book, and their laborious detail well illustrates the difficulty of making practical seamen understand the elements of mathematics and astronomy; learning had perforce to be by rote and not by reason. Finally, the *Regimento* contained a Rule for Raising the Pole. This was in essence a traverse table; but, unlike the old *Marteloio*, which had been in terms of relative direction only, the new tables were in terms of northing and easting. They told the navigator how far he would have to sail on any course in order to raise or lay a degree of latitude, and how much easting or westing he would make in the process. This aid in working out the course made good was clearly a valuable assistance to the new technique of latitude sailing; though being based on plane right-angled, not on spherical, triangles, it was reasonably accurate only for comparatively short distances, and its use still depended on the navigator's ability to estimate his speed. The Rule gave a value of 17½ Portuguese leagues, of four Italian miles to the league, to a degree of latitude, in place of the older approximation of 16⅔. This was still an under-estimate, soon recognized to be so; but at least in north-south sailing, distance could be checked by observation, and an under-estimate made for safety. Most navigators preferred, in the sixteenth-century English phrase, to have 'their reckoning before their ship' and so 'to sight land, after they sought it'.

The *Regimento* represented the best navigational knowledge of the late fifteenth century; the knowledge and practice which was to take Vasco da Gama to India and (more significantly, since on the return passage he had no local pilot to guide him) to bring him back. It cannot be supposed, even in Portugal, that any save the ablest and most up-to-date navigators then used or understood the *Regimento*; and outside Portugal, some of its rules were quite unknown. Even Columbus, who learned most of his navigation in Portugal, who understood the principle of latitude sailing and who certainly used Pole Star observations, never, so far as we know, took a sun sight, and probably could not have worked one out. Celestial navigation presented an immense task, not only of research and invention, but also of education. Both in Portugal and in Spain schools of navigation were established in the early sixteenth century, one in connection with the *Casa da India* at Lisbon, the other in the *Casa de la Contratación* at Seville, to train and license navigators for the East and West Indies trades, respectively. The Spanish school became especially famous and was much admired abroad. Amerigo Vespucci and Sebastian Cabot served in turn as Pilot Major or head of the Seville school; and Cabot's subsequent service in England did much to spread Spanish ideas in northern Europe. Although many fuller, more accurate and more up-to-date manuals appeared in the course of the century, the rules set out in the *Regimento* supplied for many years the basis of the navigator's training. Conversely, the problems which the *Regimento* left unsolved continued to plague navigators throughout the sixteenth—in some instances throughout the seventeenth—century. Of these problems, two in particular were obvious and urgent: the problem of how to relate celestial observations to the magnetic compass; and the problem of how to fix the position of a ship or a new discovery in terms of longitude as well as of latitude.

Compass variation, the angle between the direction of the magnetic and geographical poles, had mattered little in practice so long as all navigation was by distance and magnetic course or bearing; but the use of celestial observations and the practice of latitude sailing required the navigator to relate his course to the true, not the magnetic north, and so to know the exact allowance to make for variation. Fifteenth-century navigators knew of the existence of variation, and Columbus in crossing the Atlantic had attempted observations of its value. It was generally believed to be symmetrically disposed, and directly and consistently related to longitude. A meridian of no variation was long supposed to run through the Azores. The likelihood of error was increased by the attempts of instrument-makers to manufacture 'corrected' compasses, in which the needle was offset against the north point of the fly, to allow for the variation of some particular area. Such compasses were, of course, worse than useless outside the area for which they were made, and a serious danger on ocean passages. In the course of the sixteenth century, however, experience both in Atlantic and Indian Ocean crossings gradually disproved the early assumptions and revealed the complexity and apparent inconsistency of the variation pattern. The best navigators recognized by the middle of the century that this problem could only be solved by empirical observation. Eschewing mechanical 'corrections' and using a meridian compass, they made systematic observations of variation in all parts of the ocean through which they passed. The chief pioneers in this work were João de Castro, chief pilot of the *Carreira da India* in the fifteen-thirties, a practical navigator of experimental turn of mind far in advance of his time; and the Jew, Pedro Nunes, cosmographer to the Portuguese Crown, who wrote in 1537 one of the ablest and most original navigational treatises of the century.[12] Nunes devised a compass fitting, which Castro used, for observing variation by comparison of the sun's true azimuth, as shown by a shadow, with the azimuth determined by the magnetic needle. By such means, in the course of the sixteenth century navigators built up knowledge of variation in different parts of the world and so learned to apply the appropriate correction to their compass courses and bearings wherever they happened to be.

The other major problem, that of longitude, was more intractable. The Portuguese seamen who explored the West African coast were little troubled by their inability to find their longitude; the problem first took on a practical urgency when Columbus crossed the Atlantic and Vasco da Gama the Indian Ocean; and when, from 1494, the Spanish and Portuguese Crowns tried to agree on a longitudinal division of their respective spheres of oceanic exploration and trade. Sixteenth-century attempts to relate longitude to magnetic variation, or to determine longitude by simultaneous observations from different places of an

97

eclipse or of the occultation of a planet by the moon, have now only an academic interest. The problem of longitude is bound up with that of time. Longitude cannot be measured without a reliable sea-going chronometer, and no such instrument was devised until the eighteenth century. Throughout our period, longitude in practice had to be calculated from east-west distance or *departure*, usually measured from the meridian passing through Cape St Vincent. Because of the convergence of the meridians, the value of a degree of longitude in terms of distance varies with the latitude. At the poles it is zero, on the equator it is approximately equal to a degree of latitude. If the latter were known, the intermediate values could be worked out mathematically. Pedro Nunes suggested a design for a quadrant which should give the length of a degree of longitude along any given parallel of latitude. The *Arte de Navegar* of Martín Cortés—not a particularly original manual, but a very influential one—included a serviceable table showing the length of a degree at each different latitude, expressing it as a proportion of an equatorial degree. The equatorial degree, as we have seen, was reckoned by some to be of $16\frac{2}{3}$ leagues, by others of $17\frac{1}{2}$. Cortés rightly preferred the higher value. This table was, for many years, taken as good enough for practical purposes. Not until the end of the sixteenth century did spherical trigonometry reach a point where a reliable formula could be devised for converting departure into difference of longitude on an oblique course. Even then, the accuracy of the result still depended on measurement of distance sailed. No doubt these difficulties stimulated attempts to devise a more accurate log and line; for no estimate of longitude at sea in our period could be more accurate than the means used to measure a ship's speed.

Throughout the Age of Reconnaissance, then, navigation out of sight of land was a matter of dead-reckoning checked and supplemented by observed latitude. Martín Cortés is explicit on this point. The navigator must keep a careful 'account'; but since on long voyages the errors of dead-reckoning are cumulative, he must check his account by daily observations of latitude. In seeking a destination whose latitude was known, he must steer as directly as possible for that parallel, making of course the best use of the wind, and then alter course east or west until he made the land. Cabral, in the sailing directions supplied by Vasco da Gama in 1500, was told to steer south through the South Atlantic until he reached the latitude of the Cape of Good Hope, then east. Magellan's survivors steered south-west from Banda until they were in the latitude of the Cape, and then beat as best they could to the west. Later, from St Helena they steered north-west until they reached the latitude of the Azores, then east to the islands. Frobisher in 1577, returning from the north-west, sailed south to the latitude of Scilly, then east. On Gilbert's voyage to Newfoundland in 1583 the expedition was instructed 'to keep in the height of 46°', the latitude of their destination; and on return to stand to the north until in the 'height' or latitude of Scilly. Similarly, the Dutch in the Indian Ocean ran their easting down in 40°S before turning north for the Sunda Strait. Of course, the navigator had to compromise, as experience taught him, between sticking to his latitude and making the best use of the winds; but where he could he stuck to his latitude. In good weather, with open-sight instruments, he could observe altitudes to within half a degree, and could hope to sight land within thirty miles north or south of his destination. In the seventeenth century, improved instruments gave him improved accuracy. His east-west reckoning, however, on a long voyage might be hundreds of miles out. For that there was no remedy but a good look-out and the leadsman in the chains.

CHAPTER 6

CHARTS AND MAPS

'I HAVE knowen within this 20 years, that them that wer auncient masters of shippes hath derided and mocked them that have occupied their cardes and plattes . . . saying: that they care not for their sheepes skins, for he could keep a better account upon a boord . . .' So William Bourne, who published in 1574 the first English book on navigation.[1] Ignorance and suspicion of charts was not confined to England; Michiel Coignet's comprehensive definition of the navigator's art, which has already been noticed,[2] does not mention the use of the marine chart. Nor were the 'auncient masters', about whom Bourne grumbled, moved merely by conservative prejudice. The plain chart used by European seamen in Bourne's day—though certainly better than no chart at all—was nevertheless a fruitful source of error. In the late fifteenth century, as we have seen, the arts both of ship design and of navigation took notable leaps forward. The needs of oceanic exploration demanded a corresponding leap in the science of cartography; a radical change, from charts based on simple bearings and distances to charts based on a grid of latitudes and longitudes and representing the earth's curved surface on a plane sheet by a mathematically consistent projection. Such a change, however, was not successfully achieved until late in the sixteenth century, and then did not immediately affect the design of charts for use at sea. Throughout the fifteenth century and most of the sixteenth, the only marine charts available to seamen were of the traditional medieval pattern, extended to cover an ever-increasing area, and only tentatively modified to suit the new techniques of navigation.

To say this is not to belittle medieval hydrography; on the contrary. The drawing of marine charts stands high among the achievements of late medieval art and skill, at least in the Mediterranean area.[3] The charts, moreover, incorporated a wealth of practical experience, and were adequate for their purpose: the conduct of regular trade, largely coasting trade, in the Mediterranean and adjacent waters. The entrenched excellence of the portolan chart in itself, as well as the inadequacy of mathematical knowledge for devising other kinds of chart, hindered change. Most of the navigators in the early years of oceanic exploration were men trained in the Mediterranean tradition; habitual chart users. It was natural for them, and the cartographers who served them, to use the cartographical techniques with which they were familiar, in charting new discoveries. Only gradually, through the experience of repeated long oceanic voyages, did the cumulative errors of the plain chart become apparent. Significantly, perhaps, the first successful method of avoiding those errors was devised in northern Europe, where the practice of using charts was adopted late and with reluctance.

The term *portolano* should strictly be confined to written sailing directions. The extension of its meaning to include marine charts is confusing, but logical, since the marine charts of the Mediterranean in the later Middle Ages were essentially sailing directions drawn in chart form. They were constructed on a base of the known courses and distances between major harbours and principal landmarks; distances were measured in miles, not in degrees, and courses shown in the points or winds of the magnetic compass. The coastline between the base-points was drawn in free-hand, with a detailed accuracy clearly derived from familiarity and experience. All the charts of this type which have survived show a remarkable family likeness. They are drawn on single skins of parchment, usually retaining the natural outline, ranging in length from three to five feet and in depth from eighteen to thirty inches. The coastlines are in black ink, their outline emphasized by the long series of names of ports and coastal features written perpendicularly to the coast. Most names are in black; but important harbours are in red, often with coloured banners to show their political allegiance, a highly decorative as well as useful embellishment. Little inland detail is shown: a few major rivers, conspicuous mountain ranges, vignettes, beautifully drawn, of large cities. Navigational hazards off-shore—rocks and shoals —are shown by dots or crosses. There is no indication of soundings, currents or tide races.

From the late thirteenth century—the date to which the earliest surviving portolan chart is ascribed—to the late fifteenth, the charts changed very little in outline or style and not at all in construction. Being drawn on a base of distances, the charts were provided with distance scales, but none showed parallels or meridians. No account was taken, in their construction, of the sphericity of the earth. The area covered was treated as a plane surface and the convergence of the meridians was ignored. All charts were drawn to bring the lines indicating magnetic north into the vertical; these lines being parallel in all the compass roses on each chart. The errors arising from this in the Mediterranean area were unimportant, because the range of latitude was small and the convergence of meridians within that range was relatively slight. The direction lines which radiated across the charts from all the principal points of reference therefore approximated fairly closely to loxodromes or rhumb-lines, lines of constant bearing. The slight divergence, over the relatively short distances involved, mattered little. The navigator could, with reasonable confidence, read off his course from a ruler laid across the chart, and could steer that course by his compass knowing that it would bring him within a few miles of his destination.

Most of the surviving medieval charts are highly decorated examples which probably were never used at sea, but graced the offices of shipping firms or the libraries of great men. That, no doubt, is why they have survived. They differ from working charts, however, only in their wealth of decorative detail. In general, portolan charts were designed as working tools for the masters of sea-going ships. The cartographers who drew them worked in the ports of North Italy or (a little later) in Barcelona or Majorca. As might be expected, the charts covered the coasts regularly visited by the trading vessels of the Italian and Catalan cities. They showed in considerable detail the Mediterranean and the Black Sea; in less detail, and often on a smaller scale, the coasts of Spain, Portugal, the Bay of Biscay and a hundred miles or so of the Moroccan coast west and south from the Straits. Some charts included, in very rough outline, the British Isles and the North Sea coasts; and very occasionally, sketchily and by hearsay, the Baltic. Little reliance, as we have seen, was placed on charts in these northern waters.

From the middle of the fifteenth century, as Portuguese explorers extended their knowledge of the West African coast and of the Atlantic islands, a demand grew up for charts which might assist merchant vessels to find places of commercial interest recently discovered. The earliest charts embodying the required information were drawn by Italians. Early examples are Andrea Bianco's chart of 1448; a chart drawn in Genoa in 1455 by Bartolomeo Pareto, showing the Atlantic islands and indicating conventionally the probable position of the legendary Antilla; and Grazioso Benincasa's famous chart of 1468, which shows the African coast to a point a little south of Sierra Leone. They were mostly derived from Portuguese sources and give Portuguese place-names. They show, by inconsistencies of scale and other defects, the evidence of second-hand compilation.[4] Similarly, the chart drawn by Soligo and entitled *Ginea Portugalexe* was copied at Venice about 1490 from a lost Portuguese original. John II attempted—probably not very effectively—to prohibit this supply of cartographical information to foreigners. In his reign a chart-making industry grew up in Lisbon itself, partly originated by Genoese settled there—Christopher Columbus' brother Bartholomew was one of these Genoese cartographers who for a time plied his trade in Portugal—but carried on also by native Portuguese. Little is known of the early work of the Lisbon chart-makers. Charts were in high demand; apart from official injunctions of secrecy, they quickly became worn out or were lost at sea; and many old charts must have been destroyed in the Lisbon earthquake of 1755. No original marine chart of any kind has survived from the period 1487-1500. From their later work, however, it is clear that the Portuguese cartographers continued, on the whole, the tradition of their Italian masters. They drew charts, covering an ever-increasing area, in the well-established portolan style; but with one highly significant innovation. Early in the sixteenth century, in addition to the familiar network of direction lines, they drew in a single meridian, usually that of Cape St Vincent, extending across the chart from top to bottom and marked in degrees of latitude. This new device not only provided a consistent north-south distance scale; it also supplied a ready base of reference for up-to-date navigators practising the new methods of celestial observation and latitude sailing. Since, however, charts in the portolan tradition were drawn in relation to magnetic north, the central meridian was a magnetic and not a true meridian. For purposes of latitude sailing the navigator therefore required on his chart an indication of the allowance to be made for magnetic variation, especially in waters such as those off North America where the variation was considerable. This was probably the purpose of the second, geographical, meridian, also graduated in degrees of latitude, which appears on some charts of the period, drawn obliquely on the chart, at an angle relative to the central meridian corresponding to the variation in the area indicated. The earliest surviving chart incorporating these innovations is a chart of the north Atlantic signed by Pedro Reinel and drawn about 1502.[5]

Regional charts of newly-discovered areas must have been drawn in large numbers in the early sixteenth century. A glimpse of the kind of information on which they were based is provided by the Caribbean sketch maps, ascribed to Columbus and his brother, in the archives of the Duke of Alba. Very few of these early regional charts have survived. A chart of the north and south Atlantic of about 1506 (generally referred to as Kunstmann III) has a latitude scale giving, according to the scale of leagues, the relatively accurate value of 75 miles to a degree. Very few of the surviving regional marine charts of this period attempt to show the recent American discoveries; but West Africa, as might be expected, was by this time being charted in considerable detail. Portuguese exploration in the East also produced a number of charts of the Indian Ocean and the Indonesian archipelago. The earliest surviving, drawn about 1510, has the (by then) familiar scales of leagues and of latitude, as well as the net of direction lines, and places the major

Indonesian islands in more or less their correct latitudes; though the coasts of the Bay of Bengal, being then unknown, are left blank and the Malay Peninsula is greatly elongated. A series of more detailed and accurate charts, embodying very recent first-hand information and including the Moluccas, the long-sought Spice Islands, was made by the pilot Francisco Rodrigues about 1513;[6] and these vital islands were drawn in relation to the Indian Ocean in an important chart of about 1518 ascribed to Pedro Reinel.[7] Reinel, 'master of charts and of navigation compasses' by Crown appointment, and his son Jorge, were the leading Portuguese cartographers of their time. They both visited Seville, possibly in connection with diplomatic discussion about the longitude of the Moluccas, shortly before the departure of Magellan's expedition, and provided the expedition with maps and a globe. An attempt by Charles V to attract them into his service failed; they both returned to Portugal and continued there to draw charts of fine quality. Pedro was pensioned by the Crown in 1528. Jorge was described in 1551 as 'examiner in the science and art of navigation'. He was still alive in 1572.

Sectional charts of the kind described, and doubtless many others now lost, were from an early date incorporated in world charts, made either to the order of the governments of Portugal or Spain, for foreign rulers, or for private patrons. For the governments, such charts served as records of the progress of discovery, and also as weapons in the diplomatic contest, waged intermittently between Spain and Portugal from 1493 until 1529, over the longitudinal demarcation of their respective hemispheres of exploration. Italian rulers also, concerned about the future of the spice trade, sought eagerly to obtain reliable world charts embodying recent Portuguese and Spanish information. Probably the earliest world chart to include both old and new worlds is the famous Spanish one bearing the date 1500 and drawn by the Biscayan cartographer and pilot Juan de la Cosa, who accompanied Columbus on his second voyage,[8] and was subsequently concerned in the exploration of the Main. The chart is a somewhat crudely drawn compilation, in the older portolan style, with compass roses but no latitude scale. As might be expected, the part of this chart showing the New World is based on first-hand, though naturally very slight, information; the representation of West Africa is reasonably accurate by the standards of the time, but everything east of the Cape of Good Hope seems to be based either on older academic sources influenced by Ptolemy, or on hearsay. The two halves, moreover, differ considerably in scale.

Only a little later than de la Cosa's chart—if the ascribed dates are correct—is the Portuguese compilation of 1502 known as the Cantino chart, because it was smuggled out of Portugal by a man of that name, for the Duke of Ferrara, Ercole d'Este.[9] This is a more sophisticated work, though it also has no latitude scale. The chart shows the whole coast of Africa, roughly in its correct outline, and has details on the west coast of India clearly drawn from accounts of Vasco da Gama's voyage. Ptolemaic influence is very slight, even in regions where no Europeans had penetrated. A special interest in the New World is indicated by the title: 'Chart for the navigation of the islands lately discovered in the parts of India'. Asia, on the other hand, is bounded on the east by a definite coastline, and its longitudinal extent is greatly reduced, to something near the correct proportion. This estimate, it is true, may have been adopted, not because there was as yet any evidence for it, but because it suited the Asiatic ambitions of the Portuguese; a few years later it was to become a cardinal point in Portuguese diplomacy. Portuguese policy and geographical fact happened to coincide. In a sense, the Cantino chart may be said to anticipate the discovery of the Pacific.

The most important and influential of the world charts was the Spanish *Padrón Real*, the official record of discoveries, which was first drawn by royal order in 1508, kept in the *Casa de la Contratación* in Seville, and revised and amended by the cartographical experts of the *Casa* as exploration progressed. Despite royal prohibitions, men with skill and knowledge to sell passed easily over political frontiers in the Age of Reconnaissance; and Portuguese as well as Spanish cartographers worked on the *Padrón Real*. The most celebrated of these Portuguese was Diogo Ribeiro, who was in Seville, and in contact with Pedro and Jorge Reinel, in 1519, during the preparations for Magellan's voyage. Unlike the Reinels, he remained in Spanish service, and was later described officially as 'Our cosmographer and master maker of charts, astrolabes and other navigation instruments'. Ribeiro drew several charts based on the *Padrón Real*; and since no authenticated copy of the *Padrón* itself now exists, Ribeiro's charts are the principal source of information about it, as well as being splendid productions in themselves. Of those which survive, the most informative is one dated 1529, now in the Vatican.[10] It covers the whole circuit of the globe between the polar circles, and shows the East Indian archipelago in both the eastern and western margins. It reduces the size of the Mediterranean, in relation to the rest of the world, to approximately its correct proportions. It places the continents, both in latitude and longitude, more accurately than any preceding chart, with one major exception: it retains (unlike the Cantino chart) the Ptolemaic exaggeration of the longitudinal extent of Asia. Since the longitude of the Moluccas was in 1529 the subject of intense diplomatic activity, this archaic estimate of Asia may well have been retained deliberately, in order to bring the islands within the Spanish hemisphere. Nothing else about the chart is archaic. Its drawing of the Pacific, for example, incorporates all the discoveries of Magellan and of the Spanish explorers of the coasts of South and Central America. Ribeiro's chart represents a major landmark in the development of knowledge of the world.

All these marine charts, world charts and sectional charts alike, were designed to serve, directly or indirectly, a practical end: to assist navigators to find their way about the world by sea; in particular, to help them to find places recently discovered, or to discover places unvisited by Europeans but believed, on the evidence of reliable reports, to exist in the positions shown. They represent a steady progression, from a blend of ascertained fact and native report, towards the completion of relatively accurate charting. Marine cartographers rarely indulged in conjecture about what was unknown to themselves, or set down merely traditional outlines. The charts combine first-hand knowledge with a restrained use of native information. They are almost wholly empirical, and owe little to academic knowledge or a priori reasoning. Their empirical character, however, had grave defects as well as practical advantages. Charts in the portolan style—plain charts —based on magnetic bearings and recorded distances, checked by reference to a latitude scale, were good enough—or nearly good enough—for navigating in relatively small areas: in the Mediterranean, in the Caribbean, or among the Indonesian islands. They might serve for navigating down the west coast of Africa, since the coast ran roughly north and south; the only place where it did not, in the Bight of Benin, was so near the equator that a degree of longitude was almost equal in length to a degree of latitude, so that sailing by the traverse table was simplified and charting errors were minimized. In crossing great oceans, however, through many degrees both of latitude and longitude—in finding the relative positions, for example, of places on opposite sides of the Atlantic—the plain chart was dangerously misleading. As a device for correcting for magnetic variation the oblique meridian was so crude as to be almost useless. Some cartographers (including Ribeiro) corrected whole charts for variation, as best they could on the basis of limited observations. Others made no such attempt. Some navigators preferred to ignore variation, or even stoutly denied its existence,[11] Apart from variation, in sailing over big distances a chart which ignored the sphericity of the earth and the convergence of the meridians could produce enormous errors, since the proportional relation of northing (latitude) to easting (longitude) was everywhere falsified. A table, such as that of Martín Cortés, giving reductions in the length of a degree of longitude proportional to the latitude, could help an intelligent navigator to calculate courses and distances, but not to plot them. A ruler laid across the chart, unless it were along a parallel, gave a course which might diverge by hundreds of miles from a true compass course. Great circle sailing, of course, was still far in the future. Even over relatively short distances, the plain chart at best could only give a course to steer. It was useless, or almost useless, for the accurate plotting, by celestial observation, of a ship's position when at sea.

The solution of these problems required the help of the academic cosmographer and mathematician. In order to trace the stages in the development of projected charts and maps, of charts on which a compass course extending over great distances could actually be drawn and a ship's, or an island's, position, in terms of latitude and longitude, could actually be plotted, we must return to the world of academic geography, to the world of the students of Ptolemy. We must turn briefly from world marine charts to globes and world maps; maps drawn not to assist practical navigators, but to satisfy curiosity, whether the academic curiosity of scholars and scientists, the political curiosity of rulers, or the more general curiosity of their more educated subjects. Such maps, it is true, showed not only continents and islands which had really been discovered, but also places believed, on traditional, literary, or *a priori* grounds, to exist and to await discovery. In so doing, they might at times be fanciful or absurd; but at the same time they excited curiosity and encouraged adventure; above all they encouraged intelligent speculation about the shape of the world as a whole.

The medieval convention of the *mappa-mundi*, biblically inspired, with its central Jerusalem, its terrestrial paradise, and its symmetrically disposed continents, had become modified almost beyond recognition by the middle of the fifteenth century. It had been influenced, first by the simple and successful style of contemporary marine charts; this influence was most obvious in the great Catalan Atlas of 1375, which treats at least the Mediterranean and adjacent lands in portolan style, and by later Catalan maps in the same tradition. It had been enriched by incorporating information reported by travellers, especially Marco Polo, and Nicolo Conti, the Venetian who travelled to India and the Indonesian islands, who possibly touched the coast of south China, and whose narrative was recorded by Poggio Bracciolini in about 1448. Above all, it had been modified by the recovery of classical writing on the geography of the world outside Europe, in particular the *Geography* of Ptolemy. The famous world map of Fra Mauro, drawn at Murano near Venice in 1459, shows all these influences clearly. Fra Mauro enjoyed a great reputation as a cartographer in his day, and his map was commissioned by the Portuguese Crown. The original is lost; but the copy which survives and is preserved in the Marciana at Venice, was made by Fra Mauro himself in the same year, for the Signory.

The coastlines in Fra Mauro's map are drawn in portolan style; though, since this is a *mappa-mundi* and not a marine chart, there are no compass roses or loxodromes. The south, moreover, is at the head of the map. Jerusalem, though latitudinally central, is displaced longitudinally to the west in order to show the relative extent of Europe and Asia; though the cartographer felt bound to apologize, in a note, for this departure from orthodox practice. The outlines of Europe are of the normal portolan shape. The outline of Africa resembles that in the later Catalan maps. There is some information about the interior of Africa, which may have come to Venice through Cairo or Jerusalem from Coptic Abyssinian sources. The East African coastline bears a number of Arabic place-names. The detail of West Africa is disappointing, considering that the map was drawn for Portuguese patrons, and that the Portuguese had already reached Sierra Leone; but the Portuguese presumably were not interested in Fra Mauro's views on West Africa, an area about which they were themselves better informed. What they wanted was the best information on the East. Fra Mauro included a good deal of information, based on Marco Polo's *Travels*, in the interior of Asia, and drew the Indonesian archipelago in considerable, though muddled, detail, with notes on the sources of spices, all drawn chiefly from Conti. For the general shape and size of Asia and of the world as a whole he relied on Ptolemy, but not uncritically, for the map shows a continuous ocean to the south of Africa and Asia. Fra Mauro was aware that in departing from Ptolemy in a major feature of the map he invited criticism; and in another apologetic but confident note he explained his reasons for doing so. The whole map is of splendid workmanship. Though unscientific, it is not uncritical. Taken as a whole, it must have given great encouragement to the Portuguese to persevere in the quest for a sea route to the East.

Fra Mauro's map is generally regarded as the culmination of medieval academic cartography. In the next fifty years, classical influence steadily gained ground. It may be seen at work in the map of Henricus Martellus of 1489, which in its delineation of Asia and the Indian Ocean follows Ptolemy closely, except that, like Fra Mauro, but now with knowledge of Dias' voyage, its compiler leaves the sea-ways into that Ocean open. Classical influence spread widely and rapidly through the distribution of successive printed editions of Ptolemy's *Geography*, and the construction of new maps, many of them designed to accompany and illustrate these editions, others printed independently but influenced by Ptolemy in varying degrees. The maps all reveal the conflict in the minds of the cartographers between Ptolemy's own geographical beliefs, and the new knowledge, gained from successive exploring expeditions and laid out in the world charts already described. The major issues were the overall size of the globe; the shape and longitudinal extent of Asia, and the proportion of the globe which it occupied; and the extent and nature of the vast *terra incognita* which, according to Ptolemy, filled a great part of the southern hemisphere. The most important surviving maps illustrating the conflict and attempting to resolve it are the Contarini map of 1506,[12] the earliest printed map to include Columbus' discoveries, drawn on a conical projection with Ptolemy's prime meridian as its central meridian; the Ruysh map of 1508, on a projection similar to that of Contarini, but embodying later information; and the famous world map made by Martin Waldseemüller in 1507. This is a very large woodcut in twelve sheets drawn on a single cordiform projection. Its title accurately describes it as 'according to the tradition of Ptolemy and the voyages of Amerigo Vespucci and others'; it is the first map to use the name America to describe the New World. It nevertheless retains from its Ptolemaic basis an enormous exaggeration of the eastward extent of Asia; the Old World land mass in this map extends through 230° of longitude.

Waldseemüller was one of the few eminent cartographers of his time who was neither an Italian nor an Iberian. He came from St Dié in Lorraine, and was one of a gifted circle of scholars and scientists patronized by the Duke, René II. He acquired a European reputation as a result of the wide sale of his 1507 map, which indeed became, and for some thirty years remained, the popularly accepted world type. Waldseemüller was soon afterwards engaged in making woodcut maps for the splendid edition of Ptolemy published at Strasburg in 1513. This edition marked the peak of Ptolemy's influence upon cartography; though Waldseemüller himself appears to have changed his mind about this time, on at least one important Ptolemaic notion. His last major work, the *Carta marina navigatoria Portugallen*, abandoning Ptolemy and following the Cantino chart or a compilation similar to it, reduced the longitudinal extent of Asia to something near the correct figure. Waldseemüller, therefore, is an important transitional figure in the history of cartography. He was not an original scientist but an encyclopaedic and intelligent interpreter. His maps, his globe and his *Cosmographiae Introductio* form an impressive body of old and new geography which to some extent anticipated the equally popular and still more fruitful work of Mercator.

Dias and Vasco da Gama, by sailing round the southern tip of Africa, dealt one blow against Ptolemaic geography. Magellan and del Cano, by sailing round the world, by revealing the immense size of the Pacific, and by setting limits to the easterly extent of Asia, dealt another. After

1529 not even Spaniards had any interest in perpetuating Ptolemy's estimate of the size of Asia. The *Geography* did not, for many years, lose all its authority. Serious editions, with maps, were prepared by Sebastian Münster (Basel 1540) by Jacopo Gastaldi (Venice 1548) and by Mercator (1578). *Terra australis incognita* in particular survived on most world maps for many years; but, in general, in the second half of the sixteenth century, Ptolemy became, for most serious geographers, a revered antiquarian curiosity.

Though many of Ptolemy's specific geographical statements were one by one modified or disproved by exploration, however, the methods of map construction associated with him remained a fruitful source of inspiration. The map-makers who worked under Ptolemy's influence had all tried, in various ways, to relate the continents to a graticule of latitudes and longitudes and to indicate the sphericity of the earth. The marine charts did not do this, and their accuracy suffered in consequence. It was a matter of practical necessity, as well as of scientific interest, to bridge the gap between the theoretical constructions of academic cartographers and the simple empiricism of the makers of marine charts. To some extent the gap could be filled by the construction of globes. On the curved surface of a globe it was possible to plot the meridians and parallels geometrically; to draw land masses in their true shape and in their correct latitude and longitude (in so far as this was known); and to indicate true courses and distances between them. The earliest known terrestrial globe is that of Martin Behaim of 1492.[13] It has scales both of latitude and longitude, but no graticule. Behaim was not a particularly original or a particularly distinguished geographer. The chief interest of his globe—apart from its early date—lies in the similarity of the geographical ideas it displays to those of Columbus. It is an extreme example of a 'wide' Asia (234°), the eastern extremity of which is drawn within easy sailing distance of western Europe. Much better globes were to follow. Waldseemüller made one. Gemma Phrysius, the celebrated professor of Louvain, made several globes, both celestial and terrestrial. His pupil Mercator in 1541 constructed a globe of beautiful workmanship and remarkable accuracy, ruled not only with parallels (at 10° intervals) and meridians, but also with compass roses and rhumb-lines. To enable courses to be laid or read off, it was fitted with a flexible and adjustable quarter-circle. Globes such as this, with their celestial counterparts, were used in training navigators. Smaller and cheaper models were made and widely sold, and some navigators used them at sea in the sixteenth century. The very elaborate instrumental equipment carried on Frobisher's expedition of 1576 included a blank globe, presumably intended for plotting new discoveries.

The use of a globe must have sharpened a navigator's geographical perceptions; though to turn from the globe to the plain chart for practical plotting must have required considerable mental agility. It was extremely difficult to plot on the surface of a globe, and in any case the scale of a globe small enough to be carried conveniently at sea was too small for practical navigation. The navigator needed to have the true proportions of the globe represented on a plane sheet by a projection. All projections involve distortion in one direction or another. The navigator required a chart in which the projection was mathematically consistent, so that he could know what allowance to make for distortion at any particular place. Above all he needed a chart on which he could plot his course accurately over long distances with the simple instruments, rulers and dividers, at his disposal. A compass course, corrected for variation, is a rhumb-line; that is, a line which intersects all meridians at a constant angle. Since the meridians converge towards the Pole, a rhumb-line plotted on the surface of the globe—unless along a meridian or a parallel—is a heliacal curve; a spiral approaching the Pole. The navigator needed a chart on which this spiral, or a relevant part of it, could be plotted as a straight line, by a ruler laid across the chart, without incurring the errors inherent in such plotting on the traditional plain chart. He needed a chart on which a ship's position, ascertained by observations, could be shown in terms of latitude and longitude, without thereby falsifying its position in terms of the nearest lee shore.

The Portuguese mathematician and cosmographer Pedro Nunes was the first to investigate seriously the problem of rhumb-lines, to demonstrate their spiral form by ingenious mathematical figures, and to experiment with methods of drawing them on the surface of a globe. Nunes never reached the point of projecting a chart on which rhumb-lines could be drawn as straight lines; though in view of the close relations between Portugal and Flanders in the middle sixteenth century, it is possible that his work was known to the Fleming, Gerhard Kremer or Mercator, who eventually succeeded.

Mercator possessed an unusual combination of theoretical and practical qualities. He was in turn land surveyor, engraver, maker of mathematical and astronomical instruments, and cartographer. He had been, at the University of Louvain, the pupil of Gemma Phrysius the cosmographer, and himself acquired a profound knowledge of cosmography as well as of cartographical technique. While at Louvain, and subsequently as a lecturer at Duisburg, he enjoyed the patronage of the Emperor, and was in a good position to pick the brains of Spanish and Portuguese navigators and cartographers. In time, he himself became generally recognized as the most learned geographer of his day. His principal achievements were the globe which has been mentioned; a large-scale map of Europe; world maps; an edition of Ptolemy; and an atlas of the world, which was still in course of publication at his death in 1594. All were works of great originality and distinction, but it is on the world map, published at Duisburg in 1569, that Mercator's fame chiefly rests. Only four copies of this map now survive. It was an ambitious project, very large, made up in twenty-four sheets, beautifully engraved. Its title, *Nova et aucta orbis terrae descriptio ad usum navigantium emendate accomodata*, indicates its character. It was an attempt to combine world map and world chart; to show land surfaces as accurately as possible, as well as serving the practical purposes of the navigator by sea. It was the first map to be drawn on the new projection which, though considerably modified, still bears Mercator's name.

The basic principle of Mercator's projection is comparatively simple. It is constructed upon a graticule of latitude and longitude in which the meridians, like the parallels, are drawn as parallel straight lines. The effect of this upon the map (since the meridians in fact converge) is an exaggeration of the length of the degree of longitude increasing progressively towards the Poles in exact proportion (though Mercator did not say so in so many words) to the secant of the latitude. In itself, this would produce progressive distortion of east-west distances, and so of direction and area at any given point. Mercator's answer to this difficulty was to increase the length of the degree of latitude on his map, progressively towards the Poles, in the same proportion. In the contemporary phrase, maps on Mercator's projection have 'waxing latitudes'. By this means, the correct relationships of angles, and so correct direction, are preserved. Rhumb-lines can, therefore, be plotted accurately as straight lines. Similarly, since at any point the angles are correct, the shape of small areas is truly shown; the projection is conformal, and so valuable and accurate for the construction of local charts. On the other hand, areas in high latitudes are greatly exaggerated, and since the exaggeration is progressive, the shape of large areas is distorted. Mercator charts are, in fact, unsuitable for navigation in high latitudes. The scale of 'waxing latitudes' also made the measurement of distance an intricate operation. A modern navigator, using charts on a projection essentially based on that of Mercator, also uses as his unit of distance a nautical mile equivalent to a minute of latitude; he can read off distances readily from the latitude scale opposite his position. A note on Mercator's map explains how to work out the relation of distance to the latitude scale by the principle of similar triangles; but it is unlikely that contemporary navigators understood the process.

Mercator's map, though drawn *ad usum navigantium*, was not a marine chart, but a scholar's map. Many of its outlines were still traditional and vague; some still derived from Ptolemy. The revolution which he achieved, though real, was a delayed revolution. Not until the very end of the sixteenth century were marine charts for practical use drawn on his projection. Edward Wright was the first to explain, in 1599, the theoretical construction of Mercator's projection.[14] Wright drew up a table of meridional parts for the correct spacing of lines of latitude by the continuous addition of secants at one-minute intervals (where Mercator had worked only in intervals of one degree) and in other ways refined and improved the projection. On the Wright-Mercator projection the navigator, for the first time, could draw a 'nautical triangle' which showed latitude and longitude, course and distance in their correct relation; and could measure distance with a close approximation to accuracy at the mid-latitude point.

The true chart, invented by Mercator and made practical by Wright, was perhaps the most important advance in both navigational and cartographic technique since the Portuguese astronomers had first taught the use of solar declination. In 1646, Dudley produced the first comprehensive collection of sectional charts on the new projection.[15] But sailors were still conservative and suspicious of innovation. At the end of the seventeenth century up-to-date navigators were still complaining that the majority of their calling refused to use Mercator charts, and insisted on sticking to the plain chart and the traditional methods. New islands, even unknown stretches of mainland, were still being discovered by men who did not know how to plot their discoveries accurately upon a chart. Even the best navigators, using the best charts, were, of course, still unable to observe their longitude. Throughout the Age of Reconnaissance most sailors groped their way about the world. They could find their way well enough by experience and rule-of-thumb (though many of them were wrecked in the process); but they could not explain to others exactly how they did it or show the precise record of their track. It was not until the eighteenth century that reconnaissance gave way to accurate charting and precise knowledge.

CHAPTER 7

THE FIGHTING CAPACITY OF MEN
AND OF SHIPS

THE early voyages of discovery were not made by fighting ships. The only specialized warships of the time—galleys—were obviously useless for such service; and there were good reasons, especially where coastal exploration was intended, for preferring caravels to larger ships which could carry heavier armament. Dias, Columbus, Cabot, went in search of India, or Cipango, or Cathay, in small ships designed for coastwise trade, with few arms beyond the personal weapons of the ships' companies. To enter the harbours of great and rich kingdoms with so little armed force would require—in men who knew the violent and lawless nature of life at sea in European waters—a remarkably self-confident courage; yet the explorers apparently did intend to enter those harbours if they could find them. They were to sail, it is true, through waters where danger from European pirates or rivals was negligible; and they carried formal greetings from their own sovereign to present to any civilized princes whom they might encounter. Probably the phrases in their instructions, authorizing them to find and acquire islands and mainlands not occupied by Christian princes, were merely formal, not intended to be taken literally at first contact. It is true also that, apart from the permanent enemy, the Muslims of the Levant, their only experience of non-European peoples was derived from voyages to the Canaries and to West Africa; though men who had read Marco Polo could hardly have supposed that the principalities of India and China would be as small and as ill-armed as the chiefdoms of the Guinea coast. Possibly they assumed that they would be peaceably received, as the Polos had been; that oriental princes, even if not Christian, would share the Christians' antipathy to Islam, and welcome them both as peaceful emissaries and as potential allies. Possibly the commanders' minds were so full of the problems of exploration and of the hazards of the voyages that they gave no thought to the possible hazards of fighting when they reached their destination. Whatever the frame of mind in which they set out, their expeditions were not equipped for any aggressive purpose; their armament was no more than that required for elementary self-defence.

In the West Indies Columbus' confident optimism proved, in this respect, to be justified. The Tainos were a weak and peaceful people, and the Spaniards had few encounters with the fiercer, though equally primitive Caribs. Until other Europeans disputed their monopoly they had no need, in the New World, of heavily armed ships. In the East, however, any illusions the Portuguese may have had about a peaceful and profitable welcome were quickly dispelled. The reports of Covilhã and other travellers revealed that the great Khanate, of which Marco Polo wrote, had long disappeared; that 'Prester John' was a remote and hard-pressed Christian—but heretic—ruler in the hinterland of East Africa; and that the menacing influence of Islam was growing and spreading rapidly round the shores of the Indian Ocean. Vasco da Gama's first voyage confirmed the hostile presence of Muslim rulers or traders in all the harbours which he visited. Da Gama's first fleet carried twenty guns in three ships; enough for defence and for ceremonial display. His second expedition, and the expedition of Cabral which preceded it, were made in powerful fleets carrying large numbers of men and formidable armament. The Portuguese used their armed strength not only in self-defence, but in reprisals for real or fancied injuries, in demonstrations to force their Indian hosts to trade, and soon in outright aggression. They were not always and everywhere successful; they received a severe mauling, for instance, from an Egyptian and Gujerati fleet off Chaul in 1508; but in general, when competently led they could defeat at sea any fleet which the eastern rulers could send against them. They owed their success chiefly to the stout construction of their ships, to the physical and moral effect of the fire-arms which they carried, and to an intelligent tactical use of these advantages. Guns and gunpowder, it is true, were not European monopolies, nor, in the fifteenth century, were they more highly developed in Europe than in some parts of the East, particularly in the Ottoman Empire, as the defenders of Constantinople had found. The use of guns as a major part of the armament of ships, however, was first developed by western Europeans, and gave them a naval superiority in the East which lasted until recent times.

Sea-fighting in the later Middle Ages was chiefly a matter of boarding and entering. The attacker sought to bring his ship into direct contact with the enemy, and to seize and hold fast with grappling hooks and lines, in such a position that his men could leap over the side at its lowest point, in the waist, and overpower resistance by hand-to-hand fighting. From platforms—fighting-tops—at the mast-heads, and from the fo'c'sle, his bowmen and arquebusiers, during the last stages of the approach, shot at the defenders, in order to keep them scattered and under cover. With the weapons at his disposal, he could do little damage to the enemy's ship, save by fire. In naval battles fire was sometimes employed, especially in the Levant, by slinging wads of flaming tow or other inflammable projectiles on board the enemy. Alternatively, on laying alongside, the enemy's rigging could be cut with sickles wielded from the yard-arms. In most sea-fighting, however, the attacker's object was to capture rather than to destroy; and if his superiority in armed men was enough for this purpose, it was to his interest to keep the enemy's ship intact, at least until it had been overpowered and looted.

Fighting galleys represented an extension and a modification of these ideas. They were usually fitted with rams; a galley commander tried to catch the enemy broadside on, with the ram to cripple his motive power, the oars, and if possible to hole his hull. His men-at-arms, massed on the raised fighting platform in the bows, would then leap into the enemy's waist, using the ram or beak as a bridge. Galley tactics—the only naval tactics known—were based, like tactics in land-fighting, on an advance in line abreast. The oars rowed blade to blade and each ship protected his neighbour's vulnerable flank. Sailing ships often co-operated with galleys in naval war, either as transports intended to land men for fighting ashore, or as armed merchant auxiliaries, slightly modified for war and with soldiers on board, a body distinct from the sailors who worked the ship. In fighting at sea, they operated on the flanks and individually seized any opportunity which offered, in the free-for-all following the initial attack. These tactical arrangements were common to Christian and Muslim fleets in the Mediterranean. When they reached the Indian Ocean the Portuguese, operating without galleys, had to find means of countering Muslim attacks on much the same lines.

Outside the Mediterranean, pitched battles at sea were rare in the later Middle Ages; but any merchant ship of any size, in whatever trade engaged, might have to defend itself on occasion. Caravels and similar small vessels, before the general introduction of artillery, were necessarily unwarlike craft. Lying low in the water, lacking castles and fighting tops, they were easily boarded, and if surprised when at anchor were relatively helpless. At sea they could avoid contact with superior force by means of their manœuvrability and speed. Larger, slower and less manœuvrable ships—like towns on land—found their best defence in heavy manning and in fortification. Stout planking and thick projecting wales could deflect the thrust of a galley's ram. High topsides made boarding more difficult. Above all, the castles at the ends of the ship gave defensive strength. As the enemy approached, his arrow fire could be returned by bowmen in the tops and on poop and fo'c'sle. If the ship were entered at the waist, access ladders could be taken in, hatches shut and barricaded, and the castles used as defensive keeps by the ship's company. Penned in the waist, the boarders could break out goods from the hold, but they could not gain control of the ship, and would be subjected to constant shooting from above. Sheer defensive strength often enabled large merchantmen in the later Middle Ages to beat off repeated attacks by considerable numbers of well-armed, more mobile, lighter adversaries.

It is difficult to say who first introduced ship-borne artillery, and when. Probably the Venetians first used it in the fourteenth century in their incessant quarrels with the Genoese. By the middle of the fifteenth century most big European fighting ships carried guns. Artillery, of course, revolutionized sea-fighting; but the revolution was relatively slow. Throughout the fifteenth century guns were merely an additional weapon to be fitted into an existing tactical pattern. They were confined to this modest rôle because of their small size. All guns used in ships in the fifteenth century were of the forged or built-up type. In making such a gun, a number of long, thin bars of wrought iron were bound round a cylindrical core, heated in a forge and hammered into a tube open at both ends. Over the barrel so made, hoops of iron were slipped at white heat, and contracted on to the barrel by cooling, thus clamping the barrel more firmly together. The gun might be lashed into a groove cut in a massive block of wood and fixed to the deck. Alternatively, one of the hoops, approximately at the point of balance, might have welded to it a stout spike, which served as a mounting for the gun. Sockets were drilled at appropriate points round the ship's upper works to receive these spikes, so that each gun could be trained by swivelling it in its socket. The gun was a breech loader. Its breech-block, containing a chamber for the charge, was a separate forging, which fitted into a bracket welded on to the breech end of the barrel. In loading, the shot was placed in the breech and the charge in the chamber; the breech-block was dropped into its bracket, and wedges were hammered in to press the chamber hard against the breech. The gun was fired by inserting a smouldering match into the touch-hole drilled in the upper side of the chamber.

This method of manufacture and mounting could obviously be used only for small guns. The shot, usually of stone, probably weighed ounces rather than pounds; the effective range was perhaps two hundred yards. Even with the weak and impure 'serpentine' powder of the time, a heavy charge might either burst the barrel, or break the breech bracket and send the chamber flying backwards. The recoil also, with a heavy charge, would have posed a difficult problem on board ship. The charge, therefore, was small even in relation to the size of the gun, and the muzzle velocity very low. The pebbles fired by weak charges from small guns obviously had little penetrating power, even at point-blank range. The fifteenth-century ship's gun, like its small relative the arquebus, and like the crossbow which preceded them both and for many years shared their work, was intended to kill the enemy's men rather than to sink or damage his ships.

Small breech-loading swivel-guns could be mounted on the gunwales of caravels; the term 'gunwale', indeed, derives from this practice. Handy small vessels of this type, so armed, could defend themselves without coming to very close quarters, and could become effective commerce raiders, in waters such as the Indian Ocean where most ships were relatively small and flimsy. More powerfully, however, the widespread use of these guns reinforced the arguments in favour of using, in distant and dangerous trades, massive high-charged ships of carrack type. The guns were mounted in the castle structures fore and aft, firing through loop-holes, not only outboard, but also inboard into the waist, which could thus be made a death-trap for hostile boarders. The enormous exaggeration of the castles in big ships in the late fifteenth and early sixteenth centuries reflected the need to house more and more guns. Henry VII's *Regent* mounted over 200 small guns. The preference of the Portuguese for massive high-charged carracks in the *Carreira da India*, though difficult to defend on grounds of seamanship, was understandable on military grounds, since the commonest danger these ships had to face—apart from shipwreck—was a boarding attack when in harbour by large numbers of small local craft. Against such an attack the design and armament of the carracks was extremely effective; they were virtually impregnable.

The difficulty of attacking a stoutly-built floating fortress by conventional means led to attempts by aggressive naval powers in Europe to arm their ships with larger guns which could batter the enemy's hulls, just as siege pieces were used to breach fortifications ashore. Of the two main disadvantages of the fifteenth-century ship-borne gun—the weakness of the barrel and the insecurity of the detachable breech-block, which together kept the gun small—the first could be overcome by casting the barrel in one piece instead of forging it from many pieces. On land, some very large guns were made and used in the fifteenth century; not only the primitive bell-shaped mortars which lobbed showers of stones into beleaguered towns, but great siege guns such as the Turks employed to batter the walls of Constantinople. These were cast guns, but like all such guns at that time they were enormously heavy in relation to their power. They could not have been hoisted into a ship, much less mounted and fired. In the first two decades of the sixteenth century, a growing metallurgical industry, chiefly in Flanders and Germany, later in England, found an answer to this difficulty. Experimenting gun-founders discovered ways of casting guns which were more manageable but of equal or greater force. The overall length was cut down, in the early stone-throwers or 'perriers' to as little as eight calibres (though eighteen or twenty was a more usual proportion for cannon, and long-ranged English culverins were of thirty-two calibres). The outer circumference of the barrel was tapered, the metal being cast thick at the breech to withstand the explosion of the charge, but much thinner towards the muzzle. By these means a gun was produced which could be moved about on land on horse- or ox-drawn carriages and which could also be mounted—though with some difficulty—in a ship. It could fire a polished round stone—or, a little later, a cast-iron ball—heavy enough to damage, at short range—say 200 to 300 yards—the hull of another ship. To make such a gun safe for the user, however, the advantage of breech loading had to be sacrificed. The difficulties of the detachable breech-block proved insurmountable in big guns. Attempts to overcome them, by making the breech-block screw into the breech, failed because the heat of each explosion expanded the thread, so that for several hours, until it cooled, the breech could not be unscrewed for reloading. The cast cannon, as used in ships, was therefore necessarily a muzzle loader. It was cast in one piece, by pouring molten metal into the space between a mould and a cylindrical clay core. The casting included not only barrel, chamber and breech-block, but also the trunnions by which the gun was to be suspended in its mounting and the breech-ring by which it was to be secured to the ship's side. Sixteenth-century furnaces could not easily produce big enough quantities of iron, in a sufficiently liquid state, for so large a casting; so after much experiment iron—exclusively used for forged guns—was abandoned in making big cast guns. After about 1520, for a century or more most large guns, and all the best guns, were made of gun-metal or brass—a somewhat vague term which usually meant an alloy of copper, tin and zinc.[1]

It was the cast guns of the sixteenth century, not the built-up guns of the fifteenth, which wrought a revolution in the design of fighting ships and in the tactics of their employment. Such guns might be any-thing from five to twelve feet or more in length, throwing balls weighing from five to as much as sixty pounds, with a formidable recoil. The larger ones weighed several tons. They could not safely be mounted in the castle structures of a ship. They could be ranged along the upper deck in the waist, firing through embrasures in the gunwales—in caravels, guns of moderate size usually were mounted in this way—but the best and safest place for the heaviest pieces was between decks. The idea of cutting ports in a ship's side was not new; big transports had used them, in the crusades for example, for loading horses. In the first years of the sixteenth century, shipwrights had begun to cut small ports for guns at regular intervals along the ship's side. At first these were small round holes, allowing little traverse for the guns, but adequate for the small built-up pieces of the time. With the advent of the cast great gun, the holes were enlarged, and in the course of the sixteenth century they developed into big square ports, with hinged scuttles which could be secured against the sea in bad weather. The cannon were then mounted on wheeled carriages to absorb the recoil, and fitted with wedges for laying and tackles for training. These devices—and indeed the whole design and use of heavy guns on board ship—were to change very little from the late sixteenth century to the early nineteenth.

The introduction of heavy guns necessitated major changes in tactics; not immediately, it is true, but gradually as the power of the guns and the quality of the ammunition improved and gained recognition. Boarding and entering a well-armed ship became a hazardous operation, not to be attempted until resistance had first been weakened by superior gunfire. If, on the other hand, the fire was so far superior that the enemy could be sunk or crippled by it, then boarding became unnecessary, unless it were for the purpose of looting. Off-fighting, therefore, became commoner and boarding rarer, at least in formal naval war. A warship's captain sought usually to keep to windward of the enemy, in order to have the initiative and the choice of range. He tried to keep the enemy abeam, so as to bring his whole broadside to bear. In fleet actions, approach in line abreast, followed by a general mêlée, gradually gave way to manœuvring in line ahead. As in tactics, so in ship design; in the new conditions a sailing warship must possess manœuvrability and speed as well as massive strength. The principal purpose of castle structures disappeared, save in special cases such as the Portuguese Indiamen; and the castles dwindled to the minimum needed for good visibility and adequate cabin accommodation. Guns between decks competed with cargo for space, and so encouraged a growing distinction between warship and merchantman and the gradual development of a specialized sailing warship of galleon type, designed expressly to carry guns. Guns along the ships' sides placed a heavy strain on the timbers; the desire to counteract this strain, among other reasons, produced the 'tumble-home' of the sides, the inward slope from waterline to gunwale, which became a characteristic feature of fighting ships in the late sixteenth and throughout the seventeenth centuries. In extreme cases, especially in big Spanish ships, the width of the upper deck was only about half the water-line width, which still further increased the difficulty of boarding and entering. As for the old warship, the galley, the introduction of heavy artillery hastened its obsolescence for most purposes. The light galley was obviously unsuitable for carrying heavy guns. Even great galleys, which more and more tended to replace *galeas sotiles* in Mediterranean warfare in the sixteenth century, could only mount one big gun, or at most two or three, firing forward over the bows. Drake's *Golden Hind*, by contrast—not a large ship, and not exclusively or even primarily a warship—probably mounted eighteen battery pieces, seven in each broadside and four in the bows. A true sailing warship such as the *Revenge* mounted thirty or forty. This difference in fire-power was naturally a serious handicap to the Mediterranean powers, including both the Ottoman Empire and Spain, whose navies throughout the sixteenth century included large numbers of galleys. The Spaniards indeed, compelled to fight simultaneously in the Mediterranean and the Atlantic, maintained two distinct navies of different types. This was one reason why, in the Atlantic, they tended to fall behind the English and the Dutch in technical development, in ship design, in gun-founding, and in gunnery skill and experience.

In considering the gunnery revolution of the sixteenth century, as in considering any revolution, we must take care not to exaggerate or to anticipate. The great gun gained recognition slowly, and at no time during the century was it efficient enough to preclude the possibility of hand-to-hand fighting. The fighting galley died hard; not until Drake's exploit in Cadiz harbour in 1587 was its weakness fully recognized. Oared vessels did good service in patrolling the Caribbean in the late sixteenth century, and lingered on in the Mediterranean for more than a century after that. Of the two most famous sea battles in which Spanish fleets were engaged in the sixteenth century, one, Lepanto, was an action on traditional lines between two opposing fleets of galleys—almost the last major action of this kind. The other, the Armada battle, was an action—or rather a series of actions—between two opposing fleets of sailing ships. Both fleets were heavily armed and their fire-power was roughly comparable. The Spaniards had a greater total fire-power and a superiority in short-range, heavy-shotted guns. The English were superior in longer-range, lighter-shotted pieces—culverins—and superior also in manœuvrability.[2] The English, therefore, chose to fight at a range where the Spanish heavy shot could not reach them and where their own culverin shot, though reaching its mark, made little impression. In the early actions in the Channel, hundreds of broadsides were fired with negligible damage on either side. Only later, at Gravelines, when the Spaniards had run out of ammunition, were the English able to close the range and inflict really serious damage on the Spanish ships. A late sixteenth-century sea commander could hope to sink or cripple an adversary by gunfire; but only if he possessed a marked superiority of armament.

The seamen of the Reconnaissance did possess a marked superiority of armament. The ships which took part in the early voyages of discovery were lightly armed; but they did carry some guns, and no other ships in the waters they visited mounted guns at all. The fleets of Cabral and of Vasco da Gama on his second voyage, though more heavily armed, carried only the small built-up pieces of the time. The stone shot with which da Gama bombarded Calicut cannot have done much damage to the town, except perhaps to flimsy godowns on the waterfront, and to passers-by; but the moral effect, as subsequent visitors reported, was very great. Eastern rulers hastened to arm their own ships; but they had no vessels designed and built for mounting guns, and before much headway could be made the Portuguese had put heavy cast cannon into their ships. So armed, the ships were unassailable—except by surprise boarding attacks in harbour—until other Europeans, Dutch and English, arrived with better guns and more manœuvrable ships. In the New World and in African waters, of course, European pioneers met no hostile fighting craft larger than dug-out canoes; apart from occasional bombardments of recalcitrant waterside towns, their guns were used mainly to frighten or impress.

The development of nautical gunnery not only made European ships physically more formidable; it made ships' companies more homogeneous, and therefore better fitted for long voyages. Fighting ships in the fifteenth century, and for much of the sixteenth, carried two distinct bodies of men: the seamen, under seamen officers—the master and his mates—who worked the ship; and the soldiers under their own officers, who did the fighting. The captain was usually a soldier, though not necessarily a professional. He might be a gentleman adventurer. The master was a technical expert under the captain's command, and his social inferior, as was natural in a society where social standing still largely corresponded to military function. Local hostility and European rivalry, at an early stage in the Reconnaissance, made it necessary for ships sailing to newly-discovered lands to go well armed; but a large body of soldiers, untrained to the sea, would be an unmitigated nuisance on a long and possibly uneventful voyage, besides overcrowding the ships. The possibility of divided counsels, also, on a voyage in which most decisions would be nautical rather than military in nature, was highly dangerous. To avoid these dangers, gentleman-captains must learn seamanship in order to command intelligently; sailors must learn to fight in disciplined fashion, not as mere freebooters; the handling of ships in battle must acquire a professional standing and a social prestige of its own, comparable to that traditionally connected with the command of armies on land. Heavy artillery made this possible. Its use required a specialized technique of ship handling, and called for commanding officers who understood both gunnery and seamanship. Such officers began to appear in considerable numbers in the second half of the sixteenth century. Some, like Drake, were professional seamen, but most of them were still gentleman-soldiers, who trained themselves in sea-fighting, partly by learning from seamen, partly by experience, partly by reading the available manuals. The theory of gunnery, using the same mathematical principles, had much in common with navigation. William Bourne, for example, wrote treatises on both,[3] and his books were widely read. The handling of the guns themselves, probably because it was at first regarded as a craft or 'mistery' rather than a form of fighting, was from the beginning entrusted at sea to sailors rather than to soldiers. When that essential officer, the gunner, secured recognition on board ship, he was nearly always a seaman. As the importance of boarding in sea warfare declined, fewer and fewer soldiers were carried, even in formally commissioned warships. With well-served guns, a ship could give a formidable account of herself without employing soldiers at all. The more irregular fighting ships, such as those with which Drake raided the Caribbean and sailed round the world, were manned entirely by seamen, except for a few gentleman-volunteers. Some of these volunteers gave trouble, and Drake had to hang one of them on the coast of Patagonia. Drake himself, the very type of the fighting seaman, in proclaiming that he must have the gentleman to pull and haul with the mariner, enunciated an essential principle of sea-fighting. The handling of ships and the handling of the weapons in them were all part of one complex operation. To sail confidently in dangerous waters, a ship must be a fighting unit and not merely a transport for the conveyance of fighting men.

The lessons of homogeneous manning and unified command, like the lessons of the great gun, gained acceptance only gradually. The Spaniards and the Portuguese learned them more slowly than the English and the Dutch. With a more rigid social hierarchy, they were less willing to entrust command to professional seamen and less critical of the sea-going abilities of men entitled to command by birth or military experience. With a more established tradition of land-fighting, they could not easily accept the idea of a fighting unit manned entirely by seamen and relying on its guns. In the *Carreira da India*, the ships had to carry soldiers as reinforcements for the garrisons in the East. The soldiers were useful on occasion, in beating off boarding attacks by pirates and others; but for most of the time at sea they were unpopular and troublesome passengers. In that graphic chronicle of disaster, the *Historia trágico-maritima*,[4] many incidents illustrate these weaknesses. In moments of crisis, in ships near to foundering or shipwreck, quarrels would break out between soldiers and mariners; a captain, in responsible command, would lack the seamanlike knowledge necessary to give the right orders; a sailing master, knowing what ought to be done, would lack the authority to get his orders obeyed. On many occasions the outcome was a chaotic *sauve qui peut*. The contrast between north and south must not, however, be exaggerated. Spain could produce, in the later sixteenth century, sea commanders such as Menéndez de Avilés and Santa Cruz, of great ability and wide oceanic experience. In England, fleets could still be entrusted to gentleman-soldiers such as Grenville, who took to the sea late in life, exercised command without previous experience, and had to learn as they went along. As for discipline, it was never a conspicuous sixteenth-century characteristic, ashore or afloat. Even a Drake had to contend with mutiny on occasion; and so able an explorer as Henry Hudson—a seaman commanding seamen—met his death by it. With all these qualifications and contrasts one generalization is certain: throughout the Age of Reconnaissance, European ships and fleets were greatly superior, as fighting units, to any non-European ships and fleets which they encountered in the Atlantic, the Indian Ocean or the Pacific. Despite their small numbers, no non-European power on those ocean shores was strong enough to dispute their passage on the high seas. Few powers were strong enough to deny them the trading privileges and the territorial harbour bases which they demanded.

The Reconnaissance was principally a maritime movement, and most of the fighting which accompanied it was maritime or amphibious. Europeans who went overseas, however, had to go ashore, whether to negotiate, to trade or to settle. When ashore they frequently had to fight. Seamen, of course, were not averse to fighting; even when on board ship, their guns did not always save them from the necessity of hand-to-hand encounter. As a fighting man, however, the sailor had peculiarities of his own. He was unaccustomed to wearing armour; officers habitually used it, since it was a symbol of social standing as well as a protection, but the men did not, very sensibly, since boarding affrays called for agility and speed. He rarely had much training in the use of hand fire-arms; this was one of the disadvantages of doing without soldiers, and helps to explain why the crossbow remained in use at sea long after the arquebus and, a little later, the musket had rendered it obsolete ashore. He was expert with knife and cutlass; but in handling the basic infantry weapon of the time, the pike, he lacked the disciplined steadiness of the trained soldier—naturally enough, since he was never drilled as soldiers were. In affrays ashore, these characteristics could be a serious disadvantage. In order to secure a foothold in the countries which they discovered by sea, the pioneers of the Reconnaissance soon found that they could not dispense entirely with soldiers for fighting on land.

The Portuguese, when they established commercial bases overseas, fortified them and manned them partly with trained soldiers shipped out from Portugal, partly with local levies, mostly Nestorian Christian natives under Portuguese officers. These troops came in time to be supplemented by recruits from among the half-caste offspring of Portuguese soldiers who settled on the coast. The garrisons were often besieged and sometimes very hard pressed. Their main difficulties were small numbers and, on occasion, indiscipline. They owed their successes to courage of a desperate back-to-the-wall kind; to generalship; to command of the sea at their backs; and to the lack of unity among their adversaries. In this warfare the Portuguese fought as one among many warring territorial powers. On land, they were a minor power. In West Africa, it is true, they had the advantage of superior weapons; but in India they enjoyed no great superiority, either in arms or in tactics, and they were always deficient in cavalry. For these reasons they were rarely able, even when they wished, to take the initiative outside the tiny fortress areas under their control. Occasionally they fought on land as the mercenary allies of eastern princes. They supported Krishna Raya, the Hindu ruler of Vijayanagar, in south India—though not very consistently or effectively—against his Muslim adversaries. They intervened—more decisively, because of their possession of up-to-date fire-arms—in the defence of the Coptic kingdom of Abyssinia, against Muslim attacks which otherwise might have overwhelmed it.[5] These operations, however, were all on a relatively small scale. For the most part, the Portuguese land-fighting of the Reconnaissance was confined to the minimum needed to defend the harbour bases of a predominantly maritime and commercial empire.

The one phase of the Reconnaissance in which the pioneers left the support of their ships, and embarked on extended campaigns on land, was the Spanish conquest in America. The dramatic and rapid success of these campaigns, all of which were fought against immensely superior numbers, calls for some explanation. Unlike the inoffensive Tainos of the Caribbean—unlike even the much less inoffensive Caribs—the settled Amerindians of the highlands were familiar with organized large-scale war. Some of them, the Aztecs in particular, made a cult of it. They had specialized war-chiefs, clans or orders of professed warriors, and a well-organized system of territorial levy whereby large numbers of armed men could be assembled under their local chiefs at comparatively short notice. They had also systems of runners, by means of which messages could be conveyed over long distances at least as rapidly as in contemporary Europe. Their weapons were primitive by European standards, being made chiefly of wood or stone, but formidable nevertheless. Their *maquauhuitl*, a battle-axe made of a stout staff with obsidian blades, could cut off a horse's head. For throwing missiles they had efficient slings, spear-throwers, and in some places long-bows. Their body armour, made of quilted cotton, was light and effective; some Spaniards, in the tropical heat, abandoned their own armour of leather and steel and took to wearing native armour instead. Their tactical conventions were comparatively primitive, and their habit of fighting in dense masses in the open made them vulnerable to fire-arms; but they learned quickly, and sometimes showed considerable adaptability in making use of cover, in preparing ambushes and stratagems, and in selecting positions on rough ground where cavalry could not manœuvre.

The Spanish preparations for the American campaigns, in a period when warfare both at sea and on land was developing and changing rapidly, had a haphazard and curiously old-fashioned quality, recalling the earlier crusades or the romances of late medieval chivalry. The ships were not fighting vessels, but small coasters bought or hired for use as transports. This did not matter, since there was no resistance by sea and little on the coasts. The fighting forces were not organized armies in the European sense, but motley groups of adventurers, each arming himself as best he could, or attaching himself to a leader who would provide him with arms. There were men among them, professional or semi-professional soldiers, who had served under the Great Captain; there were also blacksmiths, bakers, silversmiths, carpenters; men who lived by their wits; men of no occupation at all, whose only experience of fighting had been gained in pot-house brawls. They came, however, from a harsh country and were accustomed to a hard and frugal life; they made extremely formidable fighting material. The leaders were mostly poor gentlemen, bred to arms as was the custom of the time, but not professional soldiers; a few—Francisco Pizarro, for example—were cut-throats of undiscoverable origin. Both discipline and tactics were informal, largely improvised; this was just as well, since the *conquistadores* found themselves in novel situations which no drill book could have foreseen. The arms and equipment were as heterogeneous as the men; they included surprisingly few weapons which in Europe would have been considered modern, and certainly did not, in themselves, confer an overwhelming superiority upon the Spanish forces. The possession of fire-arms was naturally an important, but probably not a decisive, factor. A ship carries its armament wherever it goes; but on land, cannon had to be dragged over mountains and through swamps by human strength. The army with which Cortés invaded Mexico had a few cannon, taken out of the ships at Vera Cruz and carried along with the army. They were hauled first by sailors, then by Indian auxiliaries, and finally mounted in boats on Lake Texcoco for the siege of Tenochtitlán. They must have been very small and probably not very effective pieces, though no doubt their noise and smoke made a great impression. Apart from the cannon, Cortés had thirteen muskets. Horses were perhaps more important than fire-arms. The rapid success of the Reconnaissance in bridging the Atlantic owed much to experience, gained through several centuries of crusading, in transporting horses by sea. Bernal Díaz on several occasions attributed victory 'under God, to the horses'; but Cortés had only sixteen horses when he landed, and some of these were soon killed in battle. For the most part his men fought on foot with sword, pike and crossbow. They had the advantage of steel over stone; but they were not a well-equipped European army fighting a horde of helpless savages.

The opposition, of course, was not united; the invaders were usually able to form alliances, and encourage one Indian tribe to take arms against another. Then the small numbers of the Spanish forces was, in some situations, an advantage. In a region where there were no carts or beasts of burden and all supplies had to be carried on the backs of porters, the large Indian armies could only keep the field for a few days at a time. When they had eaten the food they carried with them, they had to return home. The Spaniards could move much more swiftly and live off the country as they went. On one critical occasion, after the first disastrous flight from Tenochtitlán, Cortés' army in retreat seemed at the mercy of the Aztecs; but it was not pursued, and after a few days' hurried march, was able to re-form in friendly territory. The conventional formalism of the Aztecs in war, and their preoccupation with capturing prisoners for sacrifice, also put them at a disadvantage in fighting tough and desperate men who took no prisoners.

Moral factors counted for much. The Spaniards were able to exploit some of the legends and superstitions of their adversaries in such a way as to paralyse opposition, at least temporarily. The horses and the guns could be represented, while they were still new and unfamiliar, as trappings of divinity. Finally, the Spaniards had the advantage of their truculent missionary faith. In the old world, this, though a stimulus to aggression, had not been a military advantage, because the enemy, usually Muslim, also possessed an optimistic faith, whose attitudes towards war, victory and death were similarly encouraging. Amerindian religion, by contrast, was profoundly pessimistic, the sad, acquiescent faith of the last great Stone Age culture, past the height of its glory and already entering upon its decline. The Indian believed that his religion required him to fight and if need be to die bravely. The Spaniard believed that his religion enabled him to win.

Part II

THE STORY OF DISCOVERY

CHAPTER 8

AFRICA AND THE INDIAN OCEAN

THE far-reaching plans and hopes attributed by the chroniclers to Prince Henry of Portugal have attracted more attention than his actual achievements. The exploration of the West African coast appears as a mere preliminary, a rehearsal for the opening of the India trade forty years after the Prince's death. Yet the two enterprises were separate and distinct. The Gulf of Guinea is not on the way to India; not, certainly, for a sailing ship. The Guinea trades had a value of their own, independent of the lure of India. The discovery of a coast where gold could be obtained from the same sources which supplied, by desert caravan, the cities of Morocco, was a geographical and commercial achievement of great significance in its own right.

The chroniclers, after the manner of their calling, concentrated their attention on voyages sponsored by the Prince and recorded the achievements of his captains: of Gil Eannes who in 1434 first rounded Cape Bojador with its dangerous shoals stretching far out to sea; Nuno Tristão, who sighted Cape Branco in 1442, who two years later landed on Arguim island, within the curve of the cape, which was to become the first European slaving-station in Africa, and who in 1444 discovered the mouth of the Senegal; Dinis Dias who, also in 1444, reached Cape Verde with its high, rounded hill visible far to seaward, and explored Palmas island where the great slave barracoons of Gorée were later to be established; Nuno Tristão again, who explored the wide mouth of the Gambia where (probably) he was killed in 1446; Cadamosto, the Venetian, whose expedition in 1455 was probably the first to visit the Cape Verde Islands; Diogo Gomes, who disputed Cadamosto's claim and who certainly in the following year found the mouths of the Geba and the Casamance rivers; and Pedro da Sintra, who about 1460 sighted the mountains of Sierra Leone and gave them their name because—it was said—of the thunderstorms that growled and roared, as they still do, about Mount Auriol. These, however, were only the most famous among many fishing, sealing and trading voyages of which no record now remains. The fisheries off the Mauretanian coast were valuable enough in themselves to have attracted Portuguese and

131

Andalusian skippers. Prince Henry and his brother Prince Pedro, by placing gentlemen of their households in command of some of the ships and demanding from them longer voyages, more detailed reports, more captives to be converted or enslaved, and higher returns, gave energy and direction to a movement of maritime expansion which probably would have taken place in any event, but which might for many years have been confined to fishing and casual slaving.

The Mauretanian coast was and is sandy, monotonous and sparsely inhabited. This was the kind of Africa which Horace described, *leonum arida nutrix*, inhospitable and dry. Apart from fish, sealskins and seal oil, either taken directly or bought from the coastal people, and a few slaves, the country had little of commercial value to offer. Beyond 17° of north latitude, the coastline is broken by several big rivers, of which the Senegal and the Gambia are the chief, descending from the Futa Jallon mountains. Villages at the mouths of these rivers were to become in time major centres for the trans-Atlantic slave trade, and ivory, gums and a little gold dust were to be had. Cadamosto describes the country vividly; its inhabitants—Muslims in their white gowns, and naked pagans; its animals—elephant, hippopotamus, monkeys; its markets, where one could buy, besides the ordinary commodities of the trade, ostrich eggs and skins of baboon, marmot and civet; its tree-lined estuaries. From just south of Gambia, however, to just south of Free-town—the coasts of Portuguese and French Guinea and Sierra Leone—the shallows are full of islands, rocks and shoals, and the whole stretch from Iles de Rhos to Cape St Ann is marked on modern Admiralty charts 'all approach dangerous'. Beyond Freetown the shore trends south-east to Cape Palmas, then east: the coasts of modern Liberia and Côte d'Ivoire, flat, lined with lagoons and mangrove creeks. The coast of Liberia has many inlets, and produced a coarse and inferior pepper, *malagueta*, which gave it for a time the trade name of the Grain Coast. Côte d'Ivoire had no harbours—the approach to Abidjan is recent and man-made. About Cape Three Points, however, there is a change, to an open sandy coast with occasional rocky headlands. The coast is readily approachable, except for a heavy surf. This was the Mina de Ouro, the Gold Coast which in recent times has appropriated the name of Ghana, an unconnected medieval empire far inland. The *Mina* was not, of course, a gold mine (though some envious Spaniards seem to have thought so) but a stretch of coast where gold was traded in considerable quantities, some worked into ornaments, but most in the form of dust washed from streams inland. East of the Volta there is another long stretch of low-lying coast, with a few good harbours, particularly Lagos, with lagoons and mangrove creeks stretching as far as the Niger delta. This, the largest mangrove swamp in the world, is a vast sodden sponge into which the waters of the Niger pour, to seep out to the Gulf through tortuous innumerable creeks. At the western edge of the delta is the Benin river, which gave access to the most powerful and most developed of the coast kingdoms, the kingdom of Benin. Benin, besides numerous slaves captured in its constant wars, produced—and still produces— pepper of a ferocious and lasting pungency, comparable in quality with pepper imported into Europe overland from India.

Prince Henry's death in 1460 removed an incentive to explore. The explorers had reached a difficult and dangerous stretch of coast, with no evident prospect of improvement; and some of them were alarmed by the probability that their friend the North Star, barely visible above the horizon at Sierra Leone, would disappear if they went further. The merchants were content to develop their modest but prospering trade at the mouths of the Senegal and the Gambia. The Crown, to which Prince Henry's African rights reverted, was willing enough to encourage discovery, but unwilling to incur expense, especially since Henry had left a load of debt. One voyage at this time may have been made on the direct order of the Crown: a second voyage commanded by Pedro da Sintra, which reached Cape Mensurado in 1462. But Afonso V was more interested in a straightforward crusade in Morocco, in particular in plans for seizing Arzila and Tangier and so securing control of the Straits, than in the exploration of Guinea. No official action was taken on Guinea until 1469, when Afonso agreed to lease the whole enterprise, excepting only Arguim and the Cape Verde Islands (where Portuguese residents had already settled) to a private individual. The lessee, Fernão Gomes, convenanted to pay an annual rent and to explore 100 leagues of coast annually during the five-year period of his lease. Little is known of Gomes as a person; but he was clearly a man of energy, a good organizer and a good judge of men, and his story is one of success. He carried out his obligations, and more; he made a fortune from his highly speculative investment; spent much of it serving his king in arms in Morocco; and was knighted for his pains.

In 1471 Gomes' captains reached Sama, near Cape Three Points, the first village of the Mina de Ouro, and in the next four years the coast was explored as far as Benin. Whether Gomes' people investigated the Cameroons coast is uncertain. The coastal current in the Bight of Biafra sets strongly from east to west and winds are notoriously unreliable; but certainly during this period Fernando Po discovered the fertile island which bears his name. Mount Cameroon is only ninety miles to the north, and clearly visible in good weather. Probably the discoverer followed the coast from there on his return passage, past the many mouths of the Niger delta. Finally, probably in 1474, Lopo Gonçalves and Rui de Sequeira discovered the southerly trend of the coast beyond

Malimba, and followed it south to Cape López and then to Cape St Catherine, which is in 2 °S. About that time, Gomes' lease expired. He did not seek to renew it, probably because of the increase in the cost and danger of the trade after the outbreak of war with Castile in 1475. During the years of his concession nearly two thousand miles of coastline had been roughly explored, the Guinea trade had assumed roughly the form which it was to retain for more than a century, and its commercial value had been clearly demonstrated. No doubt with that value in mind, the King, after the expiry of the lease, entrusted responsibility for the affairs of Guinea to his son, the future John II.

The immediate cause of the Succession War between Portugal and Castile was the determination of the Castilian nobility to exclude from the throne Juana, the daughter and heiress of Henry IV, and to install Isabella 'the Catholic' in her place. Juana was Afonso V's niece; he espoused her cause, married her, and laid claim through her to the throne of Castile. The sequel was nearly four years of bitter and destructive fighting, which quickly spread to Guinea and to the islands. The Portuguese Crown claimed a monopoly of the Guinea trade, on the grounds both of prior discovery, and of papal bulls of 1454 and 1456 granting to Prince Henry and the Order of Christ the sole right and duty of converting the natives of the region. Despite the claim and despite the bulls (the binding force of which was disputable), ships from the Andalusian ports were already trading in Upper Guinea before the war. The Andalusians had even hit on the ingenious idea of collecting sea-shells in their settlements in the Canaries and shipping them to the Coast, where they were used as coin.[1] In 1475 Isabella issued a formal authorization to her subjects to engage in the African trade, and in 1476 and 1477 privateering fleets were fitted out in the Río Tinto to intercept Portuguese ships homeward bound from Mina. On the Portuguese side, an armed fleet under Fernão Gomes—as commanding officer, not as lessee—was sent out in 1477 to bring Guinea produce home, and made a successful passage out and back. The fighting throughout the war was extremely savage, prisoners usually being hanged or thrown over the side. The last big Spanish expedition of the war, consisting of thirty-five sail, went out in 1478; it was out-manœuvred and out-fought, and many of the ships were taken by the Portuguese. In general, in sea and island fighting the Portuguese more than held their own everywhere except in the Canaries, where there were established Spanish settlements. Consequently, although at home the Portuguese were heavily defeated and withdrew all their claims in Castile, the Treaty of Alcaçovas, which ended the war in 1479, contained clauses dealing with oversea trade and settlement highly favourable to Portugal. Castile retained only the Canaries. The Castilians, according to Pulgar, were extremely reluctant to abandon their claim to trade with Mina; but many of their ships were still in African waters, and in danger of interception. Eventually, after very tenacious bargaining, Castile accepted the Portuguese monopoly of fishing, trade and navigation along the whole West African coast, and the Portuguese gave safe-conduct to Spanish ships returning from the coast at the end of the war. The Treaty of Alcaçovas was the first of a long series of European treaties regulating colonial spheres of influence, and in this respect was a signal diplomatic triumph for the Portuguese.

The treaty was followed in Portugal by a remarkable burst of enthusiasm for discovery and oversea trade, vigorously encouraged by John II, who succeeded his father in 1481. The new king immediately turned his attention to the problems of regulating and defending the Guinea trade. Spanish adherence to treaty obligations was not entirely to be trusted. Clandestine fishing continued off the Mauretanian coast. A proposed English expedition to Mina in 1481 was believed to have been instigated by the Duke of Medina Sidonia; and the treasonable correspondence of the Duke of Braganza, discovered in 1481, had included proposals for Spanish trade to Guinea. Legislation by itself could do little; though decrees were issued prohibiting the trade in shells from the Canaries and prescribing savage penalties for any foreigners caught in African waters. Serious attempts were made also, for the first time, to prevent the export of information about new discoveries. Probably they were not very effective. Genoese sailors went everywhere and peddled everyone's secrets; there were many Portuguese, from the Duke of Braganza downwards, whose national allegiance sat lightly upon them; and there was a regular trade in smuggled charts. The lack of documentary information about Portuguese voyages is probably due more to slovenly record-keeping and to the destroying hand of time than to a formal policy of secrecy. But these were relatively minor matters. Adequate defence was the most urgent need; and this was provided in 1482 by the construction of the factory-fort of São Jorge da Mina. This famous fortress—its successor still stands on the same site—was built by Diogo d'Azambuja, diplomat, engineer and soldier, of dressed stone shipped from Portugal, on a site acquired by negotiation with the local chiefs. It had a garrison of sixty soldiers—not always up to strength—and soon gathered round it a native village inhabited by labourers and fighting auxiliaries. Its provisioning was difficult: the water supply was poor, and food, other than local fish, and fruit and vegetables brought from the island of São Thomé, came out from Portugal; but interlopers kept away from it, and it served its purpose well for a hundred and fifty years.

The trade which Elmina Castle defended was chiefly in gold, slaves and pepper, with minor dealing in ivory, gum, wax, palm oil, occasional ostrich eggs and similar curiosities. The principal exports were cloth and hardware. The trade was carried on chiefly by firms and private individuals operating under licence from the legal monopolist, the Crown; and the Crown reserved the right of the sole purchase of some commodities on arrival in Portugal. Ivory was so reserved under the Gomes lease, but not subsequently. Dealing in pepper was always a royal monopoly in Portugal, and high-quality Benin pepper was an important source of revenue; but after the turn of the century its import was prohibited, in order to protect the price of Indian pepper imported by the Crown itself. Malagueta continued to be used as a cheap substitute. Slaves were valuable, though not very numerous; perhaps 500 a year at the end of the century.[2] There was a 'country' trade on the Coast. The Portuguese factory at Gató on the Benin river exported slaves not only to Portugal, but also to Mina, where the local up-country traders needed carriers and would pay for them in gold. Gató was provisioned from São Thomé Island, which served as an *entrepôt* for the Gulf, as Santiago in the Cape Verde Islands did for Upper Guinea. Both exported food—rice, meat, sugar, and in the sixteenth century maize—to places along the Coast. All in all, some twelve or fifteen Portuguese ships annually traded on the Coast at the end of the century; as Vasco da Gama, according to Barros,[3] informed the ruler of Calicut. In the early decades of the sixteenth century the trade, especially the slave trade, steadily increased.

The discoveries of Lopo Gonçalves and Rui de Sequeira, by revealing the southerly trend of the Gaboon coast, disillusioned those who hoped for an easy passage to India. John II prudently developed the Guinea trade which he already possessed, while simultaneously but separately pursuing coastal exploration. He sent out a series of expeditions at Crown expense, in caravels equipped for discovery, not for trade, commanded by extremely capable professional navigators. Among their equipment they carried stone columns, which they were to erect at prominent points on newly-discovered land; several of these *padrões* have been found, and brought back, two to the Lisbon Geographical Society, one to Germany, the most solid possible evidence of the achievements of the discoverers. In 1483 Diogo Cão set up his first *padrão* at São Antonio do Zaira at the mouth of the *rio poderoso*, the Congo; explored the river for some distance; and pushed on down the coast as far as Cape Santa María in 13°S, where he erected a second *padrão*. He returned to Portugal in 1484, bringing several Congolese natives with him to be instructed in the Christian faith and taught to wear clothes. Cão's reception was more than usually enthusiastic; his Congolese were fêted in Lisbon and taken into the King's household for education; and Cão was knighted. A curious story circulated both in Rome and in Lisbon in the following year, to the effect that the King of Portugal's men had actually reached the Indian Ocean and that the King had so informed the Pope. Immediately south of Cape Santa María is a large bay, the Lucira Grande; it is just possible—though, with so thorough an explorer, unlikely—that Cão took the Lucira Grande for the Indian Ocean, and so informed the King. If so, Cão's second voyage in 1485-7 was a severe disappointment: he sailed on south nearly to the Tropic of Capricorn and set up his last *padrão* on Cape Cross, in 22 °S, just north of Walfisch Bay. On the return passage he again entered the Congo, returned his Congolese passengers to their homes, was warmly welcomed by the local people, and took his ships up as far as the Yelala Falls, a most difficult and dangerous passage. Nothing is certainly known of his return or of his later life. Perhaps he was disgraced because of the King's disappointment, for John II had none of Prince Henry's patience; perhaps he died on the return voyage. He had explored 1,450 miles of unknown tropical coast, much of it against the Benguela current and the south-east trades.

The increasing length of the African voyages posed difficult problems in victualling the small caravels employed in the work. Wood and water could be taken in here and there on the coasts of Angola and South-West Africa, but no food was to be had there. Cão's successor, the equally capable and still more famous Bartolomeu Dias, took a store-ship in addition to his two caravels on the expedition which left Lisbon in 1487. He provisioned the caravels from the store-ship in Angra Pequeña, probably Luderitz Bay, and left the store-ship there with a small party on board, about Christmas. From there they beat against wind and current until, about Cape Voltas, with the south-east wind freshening against them, the caravels stood out from the coast to seek a better wind. They sailed south-west or sou'-sou'-west for many days until, about latitude 40 °S, they at last picked up the prevailing westerly wind. They ran east for some days, hoping to regain the coast, until well east of the longitude of Cape Voltas, then stood to the north, and eventually fell in with the land about Mossel Bay. They had doubled the Cape without sighting it. They coasted on east and north-east past Algoa Bay and on as far as the Great Fish River. The current there sets to the south-west and the water is warm, corroborative evidence that the way to India lay open; but Dias' people, tired and anxious about their provisions, persuaded him to turn back. There was no mutiny; the habit of submitting major decisions to a general meeting was deeply ingrained in all seamen during the Age of Reconnaissance, and few commanders far from home ventured to override if they could not over-persuade. It was on the return passage that Dias sighted the great cape he had been seeking. He was a fortunate as well as a brave and skilful navigator; the southernmost point of Africa is not the Cape of Good Hope, but Cape Agulhas, further east. The Agulhas current sets strongly to the north-west, and a sailing ship rounding the Cape of Good Hope too closely ran the risk of being embayed in False Bay or running foul of Danger Point. Dias had discovered not only the way to India but one of the most important rules on how to get there under sail. At Angra Pequeña he found his store-ship, with only three of the ship-keepers still alive. He set up a *padrão* at the point now known as Point Dias, put in briefly at Elmina on his passage home, and finally reached Lisbon in December 1488.

During the period covered by Cão's and Dias' voyages, John II had been collecting information about the countries which the navigators hoped to reach. If a trade with India was to be opened, it was clearly important to know something of the geography of the Indian coast and of the political and commercial situation there; and if possible to estab-lish preliminary contacts. Even if (as seemed possible from Cão's reports) Africa could not be circumnavigated, India might still be reached by sailing up the African rivers or by travelling across the con-tinent overland; but for this powerful friends in Africa would be needed. Hence the persistent interest in 'Prester John', the semi-legendary priest-king whom increasingly circumstantial reports identified as the ruler of a Christian Ethiopia, somewhere in the African interior. At Benin and elsewhere on the Guinea Coast the Portuguese heard stories of powerful rulers inland. The stories might have referred to any one of the numerous emirates of the western Sudan, but they naturally became associated in the minds of the hearers with the Prester John legend. Random exploration of the West African rivers produced no results. There remained a possibility of establishing preliminary contact from the east side of Africa. In the fourteen-eighties a number of explorer-ambassadors were sent from Portugal to various places in the Near and Middle East, both to discover what they could about India, and, if possible, to establish relations with Prester John. The most successful of these Portuguese travellers was Pedro da Covilhã, who left Lisbon in 1487, the same year that Dias sailed for the Cape.[4] Covilhã was a picaresque individual who had formerly been employed as a spy in Spain and Morocco. He travelled ostensibly as a Muslim merchant—he spoke Arabic—*via* Cairo and Suakin to Aden, where he shipped in an Arab dhow to Calicut. There he made a reconnaissance of the ports of the Malabar coast, including Goa, the terminus of the Arabian horse trade to India. From Malabar he sailed to Ormuz, the great commercial entrepôt of the Persian Gulf; and from there to Sofala, where he carried out a corresponding survey of the Arab trade along the East African coast. He then returned to Cairo, arriving there late in 1490. Up to that point it would still be possible—just possible—to follow in Covilhã's tracks today, substituting Kuwait for Ormuz and Cochin or Colombo for Calicut, for the sailing-ship routes he described are those still followed by the few surviving *baghlas* and their kind; but only the boldest and hardiest of men would attempt it. After 1490, however, Covilhã's story, bold already, becomes fantastic. Having spent some months in Cairo he set off for Mecca, dressed as a pilgrim—a most dangerous proceeding, and quite outside his instructions. Eventually, in 1493, after further adventures, he reached Abyssinia, and there spent the remaining thirty years of his life as a powerful and trusted (but probably captive) servant of the Emperor. During his stay in Cairo in 1490, however, he had found a messenger to take a report of his travels to John II. If this letter reached the King—and though positive evidence is lacking, there is reason to believe it did—then the King had before him not only Dias' report of the sea route into the Indian Ocean, but an eyewitness account of the trade route of the Ocean itself. The commander of an expedition could be told what harbours to make for and broadly what to expect on his arrival.

Barros says that Dias called his cape the Cape of Storms and that it was the King who changed its name to the Cape of Good Hope. It was to be for some years the Cape of hope deferred. The delay of ten years between Dias' return and Vasco da Gama's departure calls for explanation. Naturally voyages to India were not to be undertaken by small European kingdoms without due thought. There were political troubles at home and succession disputes to distract the King's attention. To confuse the situation, in March 1493, Columbus' *Niña* put into the Tagus, having returned—so her company said—across the Atlantic from easternmost Asia. Columbus' claims at least called for investigation, and the resulting diplomatic situation required careful handling. In 1495 John II, the far-sighted planner, died; and although his successor Manoel the Fortunate was enthusiastic over the India enterprise, a demise of the Crown necessarily added to delay. Apart from these political difficulties, delay was probably necessary, or at least desirable, for purely technical reasons. Dias' account of coasting many hundreds of miles in the teeth of the south-east trades was, from a seaman's point of view, discouraging. An explorer may have to battle with such conditions, but merchants cannot afford to do so regularly. Vasco da Gama did not follow Dias' track, and from the instructions he received it is not unreasonable to surmise—though positive evidence is lacking—that the ten years' interval had been used to collect information about the wind system of the central and south Atlantic; information which could only have come from voyages of which no record survives.

139

Vasco da Gama's expedition[5] was well planned, and planned to all appearance with a confidence which could have come only from reliable intelligence. He himself, though by no means ignorant of navigation, was not a professional seaman, but a nobleman, a soldier, and a diplomat. His ships, except for the *Berrio*, were not caravels, but *naos*, square-rigged ships, mounting twenty guns between them and carrying trade goods. This was not, then, a voyage of discovery, but an armed commercial embassy. Da Gama had 170 men with him, some of whom had been with Dias. They were all well armed. The fleet was fitted out under Dias' supervision; and the type of ships employed in itself suggests the expectation, based on knowledge, of finding favourable winds. The suggestion is strengthened by da Gama's track, which in the Atlantic was close to that subsequently followed by generations of Indiamen. Leaving Lisbon in July 1497, with Dias in company in a caravel, he sailed between the Canaries and the coast and ran before the familiar north-east trades to the Cape Verde Islands. He watered at Santiago, and worked his way through the tropical calms first by a long board to the SE (during which Dias parted company for Mina), then south until he encountered the SE trades and altered course SW across them. In reaching south-west across the trade wind, the main danger is that of getting too far west too soon, and fetching up to leeward of Cape São Roque. For this reason modern sailing ships are advised to cross the equator as nearly as possible on the meridian of Cape Verde. Da Gama did this, and passed well clear of Brazil on his south-westerly course. In the last quarter of the year—the season in which Da Gama was sailing— the trade wind usually shifts to the east in about 20 °S, enabling ships to steer more directly south; and in the zone of the variables of Capricorn they can usually work further to the south-east, until they pick up the steady westerlies which will carry them past the Cape. Da Gama turned east a little too soon (by modern rules) and fell in with the land about St Helena Bay, a hundred miles or so north of the Cape. By the standards of the time his navigation was extraordinarily accurate. He had been at sea for thirteen weeks, by far the longest passage made until then by European seamen out of sight of land.

Da Gama encountered difficulties in rounding the Cape and Cape Agulhas similar to those which Dias had experienced, though in better weather; and eventually anchored in Mossel Bay, where the main fleet provisioned from their store-ship and the store-ship was broken up. They passed the Great Fish River into the unknown; gave the name of Natal to the coast along which they were sailing at Christmas; experienced further difficulty—which was noted for the future—in making headway against the Mozambique current; and reached, at Mozambique, the beginning of the area of Muslim influence on which Covilhã had reported and in which, both as Christians and as commercial interlopers, their arrival must have been unwelcome. They received, and perhaps provoked, an unfriendly reception in most of the harbours where they called, especially Mombasa, where an attempt by the local people to cut-out one of the ships was repelled by gunfire. The exception was Malindi, where at least outwardly civil relations were established, perhaps through fear of the Portuguese guns, or perhaps through a hope of securing support against the suzerainty claimed over all the neighbouring ports by the Sultan of Kilwa.

The Portuguese felt at home in the small neat harbour with its Mediterranean appearance; and there, by a remarkable stroke of luck, da Gama secured the services—by what inducement we do not know—of a competent local pilot. The success of the voyage was due in great measure to this man's skill and experience. Despite the southwest monsoon, which broke during their passage and pushed them along at a great rate, he brought the fleet safely through the scattered atolls of the Laccadive Islands, to anchor in Calicut road in May 1498. Da Gama at once opened negotiations with the local ruler, the Samuri, and applied for permission to trade for spices.

The development of the spice trade in the fifteenth century was closely bound up with the expansion of Islam, both west and eastward, at the expense both of Christian and Hindu. While the Ottoman Turks were terrorizing eastern Europe, other central Asian peoples were pressing into India. A series of foreign Muslim dynasties had long been established at Delhi, and a string of loosely organized Muslim sultanates ruled the west coast as far south as Goa. Only in the south the rich, powerful and highly civilized kingdom of Vijayanagar survived as the principal stronghold of Hindu power. At the same time Islam was expanding by sea. Arab colonists—as Covilhã reported and da Gama confirmed—had long controlled the towns and trade of East Africa as far south as Mozambique. Muslim traders were spreading their religion through the East Indies and establishing principalities. Petty sultans, usually either Arab or Malay in race, Muslim in religion, set up as merchant princes in the principal spice-producing islands. Wherever the European Christians went in the East, they found that the Muslims had gone before them. On the Malabar coast south of Goa, the rulers of the port towns and the main populations were Hindu; but their oversea trade was mostly handled by Arabs and Muslim Gujeratis. These capable sea traders exported spices to the West and paid for them with horses from Mesopotamia and copper from Arabia. The merchant houses of Arabia, Egypt and East Africa maintained warehouses and resident factors in Malabar, and paid the rulers for the privilege. In these circumstances, it is not surprising that da Gama's reception at

Calicut was unenthusiastic. His trade goods—cloth and hardware such as were sold on the Guinea coast—were unsuitable for the Indian market. His ceremonial presents were few and mean. The Samuri, though initially civil, was naturally unwilling to endanger his profitable Arab connections, and the resident Arab merchants put pressure upon him to refuse facilities to the Portuguese. Da Gama, with great difficulty and great persistence, collected a quantity of pepper and cinnamon. With this cargo he cleared for home. The crossing of the Indian Ocean was plagued by storms, head winds and sickness, and took three months; but once round the Cape, da Gama, in relatively familiar waters, again made the best use of his winds, running up before the SE trades directly to the equator, thence to the Cape Verde Islands, then reaching NW and N across the NE trades to the Azores whence he could run before the westerlies of late summer straight to Lisbon. He arrived home in September 1499. The unerring navigation and seamanship of this voyage, especially in the Atlantic, were even more impressive and significant than its immediate economic and political results. Da Gama, in a two-year voyage, had spent three hundred days at sea and lost more than a half of his company. He was well rewarded; and the great church and monastery of the Jerónimos at Belem, which King Manoel built in thanksgiving, is a monument to his success.

Within six months of da Gama's return a second and larger fleet was dispatched from Lisbon under the command of Pero Alvares Cabral[6]— again a soldier-nobleman rather than a sailor—with old Bartolemeu Dias commanding one of the caravels. Cabral, sailing much earlier in the year than da Gama, was able to steer due south from the Cape Verde Islands, and was well past the equator before he entered the SE trades. He made the now standard swing south-west across the trades, but deviated from it in about 17 °S to make the first recorded landing on the coast of Brazil. Leaving the coast on a south-easterly course, the fleet ran into a violent storm in which four ships, including that of Dias, were lost. The remaining six held on their course, duly picked up the westerlies, and passed well to the south of the Cape. Their experiences in East Africa were similar to those of da Gama. Not until Malindi could they trade, refit and obtain pilots. They reached Calicut after a total passage of six months, which was to be the usual time for the run throughout the sixteenth century. Cabral found the Samuri again civil, but unhelpful and evasive; and after a series of quarrels ending in a street fight between Muslims and Christians, he sailed down the coast to the rival port of Cochin where he did a good trade and obtained permission to build a factory.

The third Indies fleet, commanded again by Vasco da Gama, sailed in 1502. It was a powerful and well-armed force, fourteen sail in all, equipped for a demonstration of force. Da Gama exacted as tribute from the Sultan of Kilwa the gold of which the Belem monstrance was later made; he carried out a punitive bombardment of the harbour of Calicut; and fought and won the first naval pitched battle in the struggle for control in the East, against a fleet fitted out against him by the Malabar Arabs. Gunnery decided these encounters; at that time a Portuguese fleet, if well armed and commanded, could defeat any Asiatic fleet in the open sea. Further proof was provided by the decisive victory of Almeida, the first Portuguese governor-general on the coast, over a combined Gujerati and Egyptian fleet off Diu in 1509. Once committed to force, the Portuguese could not renounce it. Their plan in the East was never out of mere commercial competition. They never proposed to undersell Arab and Venetian merchants by flooding Europe with cheap spices; nor could they have done so had they wished. Portuguese goods were crude and unattractive in Eastern eyes; and the local rulers could not be expected to see, in tattered crews and crowded sea-stained ships, the forerunners of a power which was to conquer half the East. Momentarily dangerous the Europeans might be; but in the eyes of a cultivated Hindu they were desperadoes, few in number, barbarous, truculent and dirty. In fair and open trade, therefore, the Portuguese could neither compete with the Arabs nor rely on the good-will of the local rajas. In order to profit fully by their monopoly of the Cape route they would have to destroy the Arab trade in spices by force of arms at sea.

The task of planning this deliberate oceanic war for trade fell to Afonso d'Alboquerque, perhaps the ablest naval strategist of his day. When Alboquerque first went to India the Portuguese settlements consisted simply of warehouses and associated dwellings. The royal factors chaffered for spices in the water-front bazaars and stored their purchases until the next fleet arrived from Lisbon to collect them. The Portuguese appreciated that their foothold was precarious, and saw that it could be made secure only by a permanent fleet in the Indian Ocean. For this they required a naval base, with adequate facilities for provisioning and refitting their ships, and a reserve of seafaring men on the spot to replace the appalling losses caused by disease among their ships' companies. In addition, they needed fortresses, supported by mobile cruiser squadrons, commanding the termini and clearing-houses of the Indian Ocean trade routes. They had to change a seaborne interloping commerce based on Lisbon into a chain of permanent commercial and naval establishments covering the whole of the Middle East. This was the costly and ambitious plan which Alboquerque forced on a parsimonious government when in 1509 he became governor-general in succession to Almeida.

143

The Malabar coast, running straight and flat below the rampart of the Ghats, lacks reliable harbours.[7] Calicut, Cochin, Cananore, all were unsafe during the SW monsoon and difficult of approach in the NE monsoon. The base which Alboquerque selected was Goa, a big and prosperous city built on an island, with a reasonable harbour, one of the centres of the shipbuilding industry of the Malabar coast. In order to take Goa, Alboquerque formed a temporary alliance with a powerful and ambitious bandit named Timoja, ambitious to found a territorial dynasty as many of his kind had done; and selected for the attack a moment when the Muslim suzerain was occupied with a rebellion inland. Even so, the capture of Goa was a bold and difficult operation, and its retention against the armies of the Sultan of Bijapur a lesson in the effects of sea power. The channels which separate Goa from the mainland are shallow and could be forced—were indeed forced several times—by Indian cavalry. Horses will not breed in south India; they had to be imported. Alboquerque's fleet cruising off Goa could deny to his enemies this essential weapon and could confine the supply of horses to princes friendly to the Portuguese.

Goa was taken in 1510. Already before that, Alboquerque had established fortresses off the Arabian coast. One was the island of Socotra off Cape Guardafui, intended as a base for forays into the Red Sea—waters then unknown to European sailors—and for the interception of spice cargoes consigned to Jedda and Suez. Socotra is rocky and almost waterless, and its approaches difficult and dangerous. Aden would have been a better base; but Alboquerque's attempts on Aden were failures, and Socotra also was abandoned after the first few years. The other Arabian fort was in a much more important place—Ormuz, the island market at the mouth of the Persian Gulf. Ormuz occurs constantly in the literature of the sixteenth and seventeenth centuries as a synonym for oriental wealth and splendour. It was the capital of an independent sultan and itself a considerable naval power. The Portuguese took it by a combination of seamanship, gunnery and bluff, with only six ships.

Established at Ormuz and Socotra, the Portuguese commanded the western extremities of the Arab maritime trade routes. With a major base at Goa and minor bases strung along the Malabar coast, they could prey upon the trade of the west coast of India and in due course extend their power to the coast of Ceylon. It only remained for them to capture a base further east, to enable them to stop or control Muslim trade across the Bay of Bengal. The obvious place was Malacca, commanding the strait through which all intercourse with the Far East had to pass. Alboquerque took Malacca in 1511, risking his hold upon Goa in order to do so. All sailing in the archipelago is governed by the monsoons, and the wind which took him to Malacca made it impossible for him to return until five months later. The siege strained his resources in men and ships to the utmost and Goa all but fell in his absence. The gamble succeeded; with Malacca, the western terminus of Chinese trade, in their hands, the way to the Far East lay open to the Portuguese. The first Portuguese ship to reach a Chinese port put into Canton in 1513; this was the first recorded European visit to China for more than a hundred and fifty years. It was not an immediate success, for the Chinese authorities were suspicious of the strangers and contemptuous of the goods they carried; but eventually, in 1556, the Portuguese secured the right to establish a warehouse and settlement at Macao, a little downstream from Canton, and began to take a direct part in the trade from China to Malacca.

More important still, from their own point of view, at about the same time, 1513, the first Portuguese ships reached the Moluccas, the famous spice islands which had been the ultimate goal of almost all their endeavours. The pilot, Francisco Rodrigues, who has already been mentioned as a cartographer, took part in the first expedition to the Moluccas. The explorers were greatly assisted by a large-scale Javanese map which fell into their hands about 1510 or 1511. The original was shortly afterwards lost in a shipwreck, but not before Rodrigues had made a tracing, with transliterated names, which Alboquerque forwarded to the King.[8] In the Moluccas, the Portuguese entered into treaty relations with the Sultan of Ternate, the principal clove-producing island, and built a fortified warehouse there for collecting the cloves. No doubt they intended to turn the place into an outright possession like Goa and Malacca as soon as their strength allowed.

In all this breathtaking story, no single factor is more remarkable than the acuity of Alboquerque's strategic judgements, based, as they must have been, on incomplete and grudging local information.[9] He was perhaps the first sea commander to appreciate fully the complex relation between a fleet and its bases, allowing for the additional complication caused by seasonal changes of wind. He calculated accurately the necessary proportion of escorts to merchant packets, neither wasting cargo space nor leaving valuable cargoes unprotected. In order to assert the Portuguese Crown monopoly of the spice trade, he established a systematic blackmail, whereby only those ships carrying certificates from the captain of a Portuguese port were free from molestation. His depredations against Arab spice shipments raised the prices which the Venetians had to pay at Alexandria; and for a few years, spices and other valuable cargoes destined for Europe by sea were almost confined to Portuguese bottoms and carried via the Cape.

145

CHAPTER 9

THE ATLANTIC AND THE SOUTH SEA

PRINCE HENRY of Portugal was not only the instigator of exploring voyages along the west coast of Africa; he was also a patron of westward exploration into the Atlantic, for related but somewhat different reasons. Throughout the exploration of West Africa, the Portuguese had upon their seaward flank a group of islands, some of which were occupied and all of which were claimed by Castile. These were the Canaries, the Fortunate Isles which in Ptolemy marked the western edge of the inhabitable world. The Portuguese—jealous of their African trade monopoly and vindictively hostile to any foreign shipping they encountered off the Guinea coast—tried repeatedly to establish a counter-claim to the Canaries. In this they were unsuccessful; but they did succeed in forestalling other Europeans in the occupation of the other island groups in the eastern Atlantic. The islands were important in three respects: firstly in themselves, since many of them were fertile and became extremely productive; secondly as bases which, if occupied by foreigners, could be used to mount attacks on Portuguese ocean trade; and thirdly as ports of call.

Four main groups of islands were involved: the Canaries, the Madeira group, the Azores and the Cape Verde Islands. From the early fourteenth century at least, Europeans knew of the existence of all these groups except the last, the Cape Verde Islands, which were first sighted either by Cadamosto or by a Portuguese contemporary. Some of the more ambitious portolan charts of the fourteenth century marked the Canaries and Madeira and even indicated the Azores, vaguely and inaccurately. There were many stories of voyages made to various islands by Catalans, Frenchmen and even one Englishman, Machin by name, who was supposed to have sailed to the Azores accompanied by an abducted bride. Most of these stories were romantic legends. Not until the fifteenth century was any systematic attempt made to occupy or even to explore the islands. The colonization of Madeira and the Azores in Prince Henry's day may fairly be called a rediscovery.

The first settlement of Porto Santo and thence of Madeira began in 1420 under charter from Prince Henry. After the inevitable initial hardships the islands quickly became productive and prosperous, and yielded a handsome profit to the settlers, to those who traded with them, and indirectly to Prince Henry. The earliest important trade—as the name Madeira suggests—was the export to Portugal of high-quality timber for furniture and the beams of houses. Next in time, but financially more rewarding, was the sugar trade. The demand for sugar all over Europe was large and growing. Prince Henry caused canes to be brought from Sicily and planted in Madeira. In 1452 he put up the capital to build the first water-mill for crushing the cane, and from that time Madeira sugar began to be sent, not only to Portugal, but to all the major ports of Europe. To Prince Henry also, Europe owes the introduction to Madeira from Crete of the Malvoisie grape from which Malmsey wine is made. When Brazilian sugar captured the Portuguese market a century or so later, wine became the chief business of Madeira and has remained so ever since.

Prince Henry's claim to Madeira was based on the solid ground of prior occupation backed by papal grants and was never seriously disputed. The settlement of the Canaries was a much more contentious and complicated story. Unlike Madeira, the Canaries—or some of them—were inhabited by a primitive but numerous and warlike people, the Guanches. The conquest and colonization of the islands—there are seven important ones—was a long and arduous business. The Castilian Crown secured some sort of papal title to the Canaries as early as 1344. From the first years of the fifteenth century various adventurers, mostly Normans, planted settlements in Lanzarote, Ferro and Fuerteventura, and did homage for them to the King of Castile. Prince Henry's attempts on the islands began with two expeditions, in 1425 and 1427, to Grand Canary, then unoccupied by Europeans. These expeditions were beaten off by the natives. Next, in 1434, he obtained from the Pope a bull authorizing him to settle those islands not actually occupied; but the King of Castile protested and the bull was withdrawn. In 1448 the Prince purchased rights in Lanzarote from the principal settling family, and sent an expedition which succeeded in occupying the island. A period of intermittent and unofficial local war ensued. It was during an interval of comparative peace that Cadamosto visited the Canaries and touched at both Spanish and Portuguese islands. His account shows the Canaries developing economically along the same lines as Madeira, with sugar, wine and wheat as the principal products.

The local war in the islands became merged in 1475 in the Succession War between Portugal and Castile. In the Treaty of Alcaçovas the Portuguese Crown abandoned all claims in the Canaries, and the Spaniards undertook to respect the Portuguese monopoly in the other three island groups. The Spaniards had occupied Grand Canary during the war. They began the settlement of Palma in 1490 and Tenerife in 1493. The Guanches, like the Moors of Granada, as they were subdued, were divided in *encomienda* among the leading settlers.[1] The Canaries lie near the northern edge of the north-east trade wind zone, and in Spanish hands were a convenient port of call for seamen setting out into the Ocean Sea. Columbus took his departure from Las Palmas. In the sixteenth century the last vanishing sight of Europe, for many Spanish adventurers, must have been the towering cone of Tenerife.

The Portuguese claim to the Cape Verde Islands was never in dispute. Settlement began in the fourteen-sixties. The little harbours of Ribeira Grande and Santiago developed a modest entrepôt trade with Upper Guinea and did a considerable business in ships' stores. The islands were in the direct trade-wind route of ships outward bound from Portugal for the Gulf of Guinea or for India. Ships homeward bound also sometimes put into Santiago but more often passed to seaward of the islands. In order to avoid a long and tedious beat against the NE trades, homeward-bound ships usually made a long reach out into the Atlantic until they found a westerly wind to take them home, and made their last call at the Azores. The systematic exploration of this last group had begun in the fourteen-thirties, and seven of the islands had been discovered by 1439, in which year Prince Henry granted charters to various people to settle the islands. Settlement went on steadily from that time, and considerable numbers of sheep were taken out by Prince Henry's orders. The two westernmost islands, Flores and Corvo, were not discovered until after the middle of the century. The wind-carved cliffs of Corvo, not the peaks of the Fortunate Isles, are the true western extremity of the Old World.

Throughout the fifteenth century sailors were discovering islands in the Atlantic. There was no apparent reason why the discovery of fresh islands should not go on indefinitely. A cloud bank can look very like an island at dusk, and optimistic explorers peppered the Atlantic charts with imaginary islands: Brazil Rock, not removed from Admiralty charts until 1873; St Brendan's Isle, off Ireland; most famous of all, Atlantis or Antilla, the isle of the seven cities, where seven Portuguese bishops were supposed to have migrated with their flocks, during the barbarian invasions, and where their descendants had lived in piety and great prosperity ever since. It was one of the dreams of fifteenth-century sailors to rediscover this mythical country, its Christian people and its gold. Probably in the Atlantic harbours of Portugal and Andalusia there were men who claimed to have sighted Antilla. It was into such a world of sailors' yarns, where anything might happen, that Columbus came peddling the 'enterprise of the Indies' round the courts of Europe.

Columbus came into the circle of Iberian explorers from the outside. That a great explorer should be the son of an obscure weaver in Genoa was not in itself surprising; the Genoese went everywhere in Europe, and nearly all the professional explorers—nearly all professional sailors, indeed—were men of comparatively humble origin. Columbus, however, though he had spent some years at sea and had sailed in Portuguese ships to Guinea, was not a professional seaman. He was a self-taught and extremely persuasive geographical theorist, with some knowledge of hydrography and a grounding in navigation. The precise nature of his theories, their origin, and the practical proposals which he based upon them, have been the subject of much learned controversy. By the agreement under which he sailed in 1492, he was to 'discover and acquire islands and mainland in the ocean sea'. This was a standard formula. In this instance it probably included Antilla, if any such place existed; but almost certainly the phrase 'islands and mainland' was also understood to mean Cipangu and Cathay. There was nothing fantastic, at least in theory, about a proposal to reach Asia by sailing west. It had been suggested by several travel authors, including the popular Mandeville. Since the earth was known to be round and there was no suspicion of an intervening continent, the practical possibility depended on winds, on currents, above all on distance; and on this there were many theories and no certainty. According to Barros and others, Columbus first made his proposal in 1484, to the Portuguese Crown. At that time, enthusiasm for exploration was at its height in Portugal. John II's committee of astronomers was sitting, Vizinho was translating the *Ephemerides*, Diogo Cão had returned from his first voyage and had left, or was about to leave, on his second. Columbus' proposal, which was for an expedition at royal expense, was declined after a careful hearing. In the following year, however, an expedition was planned by an Azorean Portuguese, Fernão Dulmo, with royal approval, 'to seek and find a great island or islands or mainland by its coast, which is presumed to be the isle of the seven cities'. If this expedition ever sailed, the prevailing winds in the latitude of the Azores would have prevented its achieving anything. Had Columbus sailed in a Portuguese ship he too might have taken his departure from the Azores and similarly failed. The disappointment of Diogo Cão's second voyage may have caused second thoughts, for, in 1488, negotiations between Columbus and the Portuguese Crown appear to have been reopened on a hopeful note; but the triumphant return of Dias put an end to them, and Columbus, having tried France and England without success, turned finally to Castile.

In Spain Columbus had fewer vested interests to overcome; and after many importunities he succeeded in enlisting the support of a great

officer of State, Luis de Santángel, keeper of the privy purse to the
King of Aragon and treasurer of the Santa Hermandad. Santángel
himself raised a considerable part of the money needed to finance the
enterprise. Through his good offices the consent and participation of the
Spanish monarchs was secured, and once committed, they agreed to all
Columbus' terms, including the rewards, listed in the agreement, which
he was to receive in the event of success. They provided him, as we have
seen, with well-found ships; and with their money he could man them
with reliable crews and capable and experienced officers. He sailed
from Palos in August 1492. His outward passage, apart from its
terrifying distance out of sight of land, was remarkably prosperous.[2]
Columbus was a careful and accurate, though not very up-to-date,
navigator. To picture him as an unpractical mystic is mere caricature.
His course, due west from the Canaries, passed along the northern
fringe of the north-east trade belt. Apart from the danger of late summer
hurricanes, the trade winds are unreliable in that latitude; Columbus,
discovering this, made his later passages considerably further south,
and this became the normal Spanish practice. In 1492, however, he
was fortunate. He had a fair wind all the way out, and after thirty-three
days of uneventful sailing, with nothing but the floating gulf weed and
the bosun birds to feed their hope, the fleet sighted the outer Cays of
the Bahamas.

Whatever Columbus' original object may have been, there is no
doubt that he regarded San Salvador as an outlying island in the
archipelago of which Japan was supposed to form a part; such an
archipelago as is marked, for instance, on Martin Behaim's 1492 globe.
Columbus apparently reached this conclusion by combining Marco
Polo's estimate of the east-west extent of Asia, which was an over-
estimate; the same traveller's report of the distance of Japan from the
Asian mainland—1,500 miles—a gross over-estimate; and Ptolemy's
estimate of the size of the world, which was an under-estimate. He
assumed the length of an equatorial degree of longitude to be ten per
cent shorter than Ptolemy had taught and twenty-five per cent shorter
than the true figure. This calculation would make the westward distance
from Europe to Japan less than 3,000 nautical miles. The actual great
circle distance is 10,600 nautical miles. According to Columbus'
reasoning, San Salvador was very near to where Japan ought to be, and
the next step was to find Japan itself. The expedition, threading its way
to the south-west between the Cays, found the north-east coast of Cuba
and the north coast of Hispaniola, modern Haiti, clothed to the water-
line in high forest. Here prospects brightened. Hispaniola yielded a little
alluvial gold, and a few gold nose-plugs and bracelets were obtained by
barter from the natives. On the north coast of Hispaniola, however,

Columbus lost his flagship, wrecked by grounding, and decided to return home, leaving some of his men behind with instructions to build houses and search for gold mines.

On his return passage Columbus made one more important discovery: the necessity, on leaving the West Indies, of standing well to the north and out of the trade wind before attempting the Atlantic crossing. He found a westerly wind, as thousands of his successors were to do, in about the latitude of Bermuda, and ran down before it to the Azores. On approaching Europe, however, he ran into foul weather, and was compelled to put in for shelter, first in the Azores and then in the Tagus. Here the Portuguese authorities demanded an explanation of his activities. With previous experience of Italian exaggeration, they were sceptical of his story, contemptuous of his geographical reasoning and unimpressed by his description of the Arawaks of Hispaniola. They had been irritated by a recent revival of Andalusian poaching on the coast of Upper Guinea and, with an expedition to India under discussion, were extremely suspicious of all Spanish maritime activity in the Atlantic. John II decided to lay claim to Columbus' discoveries on the grounds that they came within the provisions of the Treaty of Alcaçovas, that they lay close to the Azores, and might even be regarded as forming part of that group.

From the Spanish point of view, the voyage had been successful, but expensive. It was now essential to follow up the discovery and produce a return on the investment. Immediately on receipt of Columbus' first report, and even before his arrival in their presence, the sovereigns commanded him to begin his preparations for a second voyage. They then took steps to forestall Portuguese objections, by seeking papal support for a monopoly of navigation and settlement in the seas and lands which Columbus had discovered. Support was readily forthcoming. The Pope of the time, Alexander VI, was himself a Spaniard, already under heavy obligations to the Catholic monarchs and looking to them for support in his endeavour to create a principality in Italy for his son. He issued a series of four bulls, each successively strengthening and extending the provisions of the preceding ones, in accordance with successive demands made by Ferdinand and Isabella, upon Columbus' advice. The first two granted to the sovereigns of Castile all lands discovered, or to be discovered, in the regions explored by Columbus. The third, the famous *Inter Caetera*, drew an imaginary boundary line from north to south a hundred leagues west of the Azores and Cape Verde Islands, and provided that the land and sea beyond the line should be a Spanish sphere of exploration. The fourth, *Dudum siquidem*, extended the previous grants to include 'all islands and mainlands whatever, found or to be found . . . in sailing or travelling towards the west and south, whether they be in regions occidental or meridional and oriental and of India'.

Portugal clearly would not go to war over the possession of a few distant islands inhabited by naked savages; but *Dudum siquidem*, with its specific reference to India, gave serious cause for alarm. All the resources of diplomacy and of geographical reasoning were used, therefore, to limit the effect of the bull. Unable to move the Pope, John II opened direct negotiations with Ferdinand and Isabella. Dropping his claim to the islands, he accepted the bull of demarcation, *Inter caetera*, as a basis for discussion, but asked that the boundary line be moved 270 leagues further west, to protect his African interests. The Spanish monarchs, secure in the delusions which Columbus had fostered concerning the western route to Asia, agreed. Both sides must have known that so vague a boundary could not be accurately fixed, and each thought that the other was deceived. Both sides, moreover, were anxious to avoid open conflict. The Treaty of Tordesillas[3] was duly signed in 1494, a diplomatic triumph for Portugal, confirming to the Portuguese not only the true route to India, but most of the south Atlantic with the imaginary land of Antilla and—as shortly afterwards appeared—the real land of Brazil.

Columbus was back in the West Indies long before the treaty was signed. He left Cadiz in September 1493 in command of a large fleet, ships, caravels and pinnaces, seventeen sail in all. The composition of the fleet, no less than the instructions which the admiral carried, indicated the purpose for which it was sent. It contained no heavily armed fighting ships; it carried no trade goods, other than small truck of the kind normally used for barter with the more primitive of the West Africans. Its chief cargo was men—twelve hundred people, priests, gentleman-soldiers, artisans, farmers—and agricultural stock—tools, seeds and animals; a whole society in miniature. The immediate object of the voyage was not to open a new trade or to conquer oriental kingdoms, but to settle the island of Hispaniola, to found a mining and farming colony which should produce its own food, pay the cost of the voyage by remitting gold to Spain, and serve at the same time as a base for further exploration in the direction of Cipangu, Cathay and India. There had been no lack of volunteers, and the fitting-out was done with efficiency and speed. Columbus complained, as sea-going commanders often do, of dilatory and obstructive dockyard administration; but, in fact, five months was a very short time for the preparation of so large an expedition in fifteenth-century Spain. The only serious mistake was failure to provide the colony with enough food for the first year. Over-optimism about the extent to which Europeans could live off the country in the Tropics was a common feature of these early explorations, and was one of the chief causes of the difficulties which Columbus encountered.

The fleet made a prosperous passage and a good landfall at Dominica, the wild Carib island whose sharp volcanic spires were to be, for thousands of travellers, their first glimpse of America; though for many years none settled there. Columbus sailed on along the beautiful arc of the Lesser Antilles, through the Virgin Islands, past Puerto Rico, to the north coast of Hispaniola. There his good fortune ended. Further exploration revealed only the south coast of Cuba, with its harsh xerophytic vegetation, and the beautiful but then profitless island of Jamaica. The original settlement planted on the first voyage had been wiped out. The new colony in Hispaniola was distracted from its beginning by wars with the local 'Indians' and by internal quarrels. It would have taken a leader of commanding genius to maintain discipline among those early Spanish settlers—touchy, adventurous and greedy as they were—to compel them to clear trees, build houses and plant crops, instead of roaming the island in search of gold or of slaves. Columbus, a great explorer and sea-commander and a navigator of native genius, was also, it must be remembered, a foreigner, the son of an artisan tricked out with an empty title and a new coat of arms. With all his pertinacity and indomitable courage, he lacked the experience and the temperament of a successful colonial governor. Little had been achieved by 1496, when he returned to Spain to report. It was Bartholomew Columbus, in his absence, who persuaded some of the settlers to begin the building, on the south coast, of the city of Santo Domingo, which for fifty years was to be the capital of the Spanish Indies.

The sovereigns still trusted Columbus. With their support and at their expense he returned to the Indies in 1498; but this time there were no volunteers and men had to be pressed, or released from prison, to sail with the admiral. Columbus steered to the south of his former courses, to discover the island of Trinidad and the mouths of the Orinoco, by far the largest river then known to Europeans, whose great volume of fresh brown water proved the new-found coast to be part of a great continent. From the Venezuelan coast he sailed north, by a remarkable feat of navigation, to the new city which his brother had founded in Hispaniola. He found half the colonists in open revolt. His own vacillations between conciliation and severity made matters worse. In 1499 he was superseded, and his successor sent him home in irons. The Catholic monarchs, though they confirmed his titles and property and treated him, then and to his death, with punctilious courtesy, soon wearied of his financial importunities. They never again allowed him to exercise his offices of admiral and viceroy, or entrusted him with any administrative responsibility. He made one more voyage, in 1502, which revealed a long stretch of mainland coast in Honduras and Costa Rica and yielded some gold, but which ended ignominiously with his ships, no longer seaworthy, beached in the shallow water of St Ann's Bay. He died in 1506, a disgruntled though still a rich man.

The disappointment of Columbus' second voyage made responsible people in Spain suspect what the Portuguese had already assumed—that the new islands in the West were much further from mainland Asia than Columbus had believed. Already in 1494 Peter Martyr, on hearing the first reports of the voyage, could write 'when treating of this country one must speak of a new world, so distant is it and so devoid of civilization and religion'.[4] Exploration outside the Caribbean increasingly confirmed this suspicion, as other European governments, particularly those of England and Portugal, became interested in western discovery in the north Atlantic. For the English this interest was not new. There had long been talk in west-country ports of islands to the west of Ireland, and attempts had been made to find them. From about 1490, something more than islands seems to have been involved; ships were reported[5] to have left Bristol regularly, two or three each year, for unknown destinations in the western Atlantic. Possibly the Bristol men had found, and were exploiting, the Banks fishery; conceivably they had even reached the mainland coast.[6] Nothing of this, apparently, was known in London. In 1488 Bartholomew Columbus had visited England, had tried to interest Henry VII in his brother's project, and had failed. In 1496, however, with knowledge of Columbus' discovery, Henry granted licence to explore in the western north Atlantic to John Caboto or Cabot, an Italian recently settled in Bristol. Nothing is known certainly about Cabot's intentions. His project was certainly much more than a fishing voyage, and more than a mere search for Atlantic islands. He may have learned, from Bristol seamen in the Iceland trade, something of the Vinland story; he may have heard of Scandinavian maps, or of actual English sightings of a mainland coast; he probably reasoned that such a coast, if it existed, must be a north-easterly extension of Asia, and proposed to follow it to the south-west until he reached mainland China, far to the west of Columbus' deceptive islands. The voyages which he made under the 1496 licence followed approximately the Viking route across the north Atlantic—though somewhat further to the south, since, so far as we know, he sighted neither Iceland nor Greenland—using the easterly winds which are frequent in early summer in those latitudes. Of a probable first, unsuccessful voyage in 1496, nothing certain is known. On the 1497 voyage, Cabot found land, possibly in Newfoundland, and after coasting for some distance returned to report. His last expedition, in 1498, apparently followed up the discovery, sailing past Newfoundland and Nova Scotia, as far as New England, perhaps further.[7] The geographical results, with English banners attached, appear in de la Cosa's map. Cabot's ships brought back no silk or spices; his project was a commercial failure; he himself died on the voyage, and his English backers showed no further interest. His discoveries were followed up and extended by the brothers Corte-Real, Portuguese resident in the Azores, who made a series of voyages under royal commission in the first years of the new century to discover lands in the north-west within the Portuguese demarcation. Gaspar Corte-Real coasted south-east Greenland, and in a second voyage crossed the Davis Strait to Labrador. His brother Miguel in 1502 visited Newfoundland and possibly the Gulf of St Lawrence.[8] Like Cabot, the Corte-Reals found no spices; but to judge from maps of the time, they still thought that Greenland and Labrador might be north-easterly peninsulas of Asia. They also appreciated the value of Newfoundland as a fishing station and as a source of mast timber, and before their deaths—both were lost at sea—they claimed the whole coast for Portugal. Labrador was generally thought at that time to be within the Portuguese demarcation, and was so marked on the Cantino Chart; but naturally, after Vasco da Gama, the Portuguese had little further interest in that quarter, except for the fishery.

Meanwhile the immense extent of the mainland coast of South America was year by year becoming known. In 1499, before the details of Columbus' third voyage were known, Vicente Yáñez Pinzón, formerly captain of the caravel *Niña* and companion of Columbus, visited the north coast and found a great river, which may have been the Amazon (as he later claimed) or was possibly the Orinoco. Alonso de Ojeda, also an old companion of Columbus and a constant source of trouble to him, in the same year followed up the admiral's voyage to the Gulf of Paría and explored the coast of Venezuela. In 1500, as we have seen, Cabral, on his way to India, made the first certainly recorded landing on the coast of Brazil. The most interesting feature of this exploit is that Cabral had taken the best passage through the central Atlantic to avoid the lee shore of Cape São Roque, and made his landfall at Porto Seguro twelve degrees further south. The likelihood of making such a landfall as a result of freak weather or navigational error was remote; and it is highly probable that Cabral had been instructed to investigate a coast whose existence was not merely suspected, but already known. Possibly his purpose was to find a convenient watering-place on the way to the Cape. The Brazilian coast was not much used, in subsequent years, for this purpose; but it lay on the Portuguese side of the Tordesillas line, and its discovery had the immediate effect, in Portuguese opinion at least, of barring the south Atlantic to Spanish shipping.

One result of all this mainland coastal exploration was to reveal that the New World—as it was beginning to be called—had a certain interest and value of its own. Peter Martyr might complain 'What need have we of what is found everywhere in Europe?' thereby voicing the usual attitude of promoters of discovery; but Columbus had found gold in Hispaniola, and from 1511 Cuba, ably settled by Diego de Velázquez was to yield considerable quantities of it. Ojeda in 1499 discovered, on the Venezuelan coast, the Margarita pearl fishery, which quickly became a valuable possession, and the centre of a thriving and very brutal trade in slaves to serve as divers. Cabral's visit to Brazil revealed the presence there of brazil-wood, a commercially valuable red dye, which indeed gave the territory its name. Cabot found no spices, but he found a teeming fishery which the ubiquitous Portuguese, among others, were quick to exploit. Within a few years cod from the Banks was coming into Portugal in large enough quantities to make an import tax on it worth while. Apart from these commercial considerations, public interest in the New World was kept alive by a number of books on discovery published in the early sixteenth century, mostly in Italy and Germany.[9] The earliest and ablest history, the De Orbe Novo of Peter Martyr, was not published in full until 1530, though parts had appeared earlier, and a pirated Italian version of the first Decade, known as the Libretto, was produced at Venice in 1504. All the Decades were circulated in manuscript as they were written; but Peter Martyr wrote in Latin for a small and sophisticated public. A far more influential book was the collection of accounts of voyages published by Fracanzano da Montal-boddo at Vicenza in 1507, under the title Paesi novamente retrovati. The Paesi had six Italian editions, six French, and two German. It was the first great source book of the discoveries. Among the contents of the Paesi were two tracts, originally printed in Florence, which purported to be letters written by Amerigo Vespucci. They described four voyages which Vespucci was said to have made to the New World, and one of them actually bore the significant title, Mundus Novus. The other, and longer letter had no formal title in the Paesi; but it also appeared in a Latin version, entitled Quattuor Navigationes, as part of the Cosmographiae Introductio published in the same year as the Paesi, by Martin Wald-seemüller at St. Dié; a book which rivalled the Paesi in popularity, though by no means in merit. Both tracts are now generally, though not universally, considered by scholars to be forgeries, in the sense that they were not written by Vespucci. They were pirated accounts, partly based on genuine letters by Vespucci, partly invented; but the

156

principal achievements which they described were real.[9] Manuscript letters, subsequently discovered and more certainly attributable to Vespucci, though they contradict the printed tracts in important particulars, and record only two voyages, confirm the central facts. Vespucci was a business man, a man of substance, and indeed of some eminence in his native Florence. He first went to Spain in 1492 as a representative of the Medici, to supervise a number of marine supply contracts. His study of geography and navigation was a pastime, though one which, to judge from his letters, he pursued systematically and seriously. His residence in Seville gave him the opportunity to apply his theoretical knowledge to practical ends, and in early middle age he left his business concerns and became an explorer. Of the two voyages now generally accepted as authentic, the first, made in Spanish ships in 1499, was in the region visited by Ojeda, and for part of the way in company with him. It covered the coast from a point west of Cape Sao Roque, north-west and west to the Maracaibo lagoon. Vespucci's description of the drowned coast lands of Guiana and Venezuela is recognisably accurate. On this voyage, also, he made original and significant trials of a method of calculating longitude from the times of the conjunction of planets with the moon; a method too cumbersome to be of much practical use, though it persisted in manuals of navigational theory until the late eighteenth century. In 1501 Vespucci embarked on a second voyage, under Portuguese auspices and with knowledge of Cabral's sighting of the coast of Brazil. Vespucci reached the same coast in about 5° S. and followed it in a south-westerly direction for more than two thousand miles, beyond the Rio de la Plata, to a point—perhaps San Julián—on the coast of Patagonia; which coast he rightly reckoned to be on the Spanish side of the Line of Demarcation. Vespucci's two voyages, therefore, between them covered the greater part of the Atlantic coast of South America, revealed the continuity and vast size of that continent, and pointed the way which Solís and Magellan were later to take in seeking a western passage round it. The magnitude of these discoveries prompted Waldseemüller's suggestion that Vespucci's name should be given to the continent whose coast he had explored. The suggestion caught the popular fancy, and the name America quickly became attached to the Southern continent. Later in the century, largely through Mercator's use of it, it came to be extended to North America as well.

Vespucci returned to Spain in 1505. He was appointed Pilot-major to the Casa de la Contratación at Seville, the first to hold that important and responsible office, in which he served until his death in 1512. His work was significant not only because of the extent of his discoveries, not only of the publicity—unsought by him—which they received, but even more because of the soundness of his geographical knowledge and judgment. As an interpreter of discoveries he was unsurpassed. After him, all Europe recognized America for what it was, a new continent and a barrier between Europe and Asia. To everyone except the Portuguese it was an unwelcome barrier. No other nation yet cared to dispute with Portugal the monopoly of Vasco da Gama's route; but neither da Gama's success, nor the failures of Columbus and Cabot, nor the increasing evidence of the value of the New World in itself, was enough to kill the hope of reaching Asia by sailing west. The problem, however, was clearly not one of threading a way through an archipelago of islands, but of finding a passage through, or round, a land mass whose dimensions from east to west were unknown.

The strong westerly set of the current flowing into the Caribbean along the north coast of South America had been noticed by Columbus, and encouraged a belief that North and South America were separate land masses. The return current north-east through the Florida Channel for some years escaped notice; and Columbus and others argued that so great a volume of water must find an outlet. The Caribbean seemed to offer the best hope of a seaway westward to Asia. The hope was progressively weakened and eventually extinguished by the reports of Spanish adventurers—Bastidas, Ojeda, Nicuesa, Balboa, Fernandes, Cortés—who, sailing from the islands in search of gold or slaves, coasted the shores of Central America, Yucatán and Mexico between 1500 and 1520. These men, however, discovered the crucial fact of the existence of another ocean beyond America. Balboa, following up an Indian report, crossed the Isthmus of Darien in 1513 and, first of Europeans, sighted the Pacific, its coast running east and west as far as the eye could see, separated from the Caribbean by a neck of land less than a hundred miles across. Balboa's discovery suggested two possibilities. If no strait existed in Central America, tools and materials might be carried across the Isthmus and ships built on the Pacific coast. Alternatively, Atlantic shipping might find a way into the South Sea by following the south-westerly trend of the Atlantic coast of South America, as Vespucci had done, and eventually sailing round the south of Brazil.

Almost every European monarch at one time or another dreamed of finding a western passage. This universal ambition called for a new type of specialist—the professional explorer. The exploring activity of the early sixteenth century was dominated by a small group of men whose national allegiance sat lightly upon them and who were qualified and willing to undertake exploration on behalf of any prince who would employ them. They were the maritime counterparts of the great army of mercenary soldiers who by that time were making a profession of the land-fighting of Europe. Most of them were Italians, such as Vespucci, Verrazano and the two Cabots, father and son, or Portuguese, such as Fernandes, Magellan and Solís. They served in turn the Kings of Spain, Portugal, France and England and the Grand Signory of Venice. Against a background of growing jealousies and diplomatic cross-purposes they changed allegiance at will and carried from court to court information which their employers would have preferred to keep secret; yet such was the value set upon their knowledge that they were welcome wherever they chose to settle. The Portuguese government was more successful than most in employing its own subjects and keeping its own secrets; all Portuguese voyages to the East were organized by the Crown and commanded by its officers; but eventually it was a Portuguese sailor of fortune in the service of Spain who discovered the secret of the passage to the South Sea.

The employment of Magellan by the Spanish Crown was the climax to a long diplomatic contest. In 1494 the Spaniards had made a bad bargain and had unwittingly signed away the right to explore Brazil. The Portuguese pursued their advantage by securing papal confirmation of the treaty in the bull *Ea quae*, issued by Julius II in 1506. This bill prevented any attempt to revive Alexander VI's line of demarcation. By that time the regular arrival of spice cargoes in Lisbon had revealed to the Spaniards that they were being beaten in the race for the spice islands. They sought, therefore, to use the Treaty of Tordesillas to stay Portuguese advance in the Far East, hoping that a western passage would soon be found. According to the Spanish interpretation, the line of demarcation established by the treaty ran right round the world, dividing the world into two halves. In the one half, all unoccupied or heathen lands were to be the prize of Portugal, in the other half the prize of Spain.

The Portuguese, for their part, had no intention of accepting any limitation of their eastward expansion. Even after their arrival in the Moluccas, they had no exact means of determining the longitude of the islands, nor did they know the size of the Pacific. If the Spanish view of the demarcation treaty were accepted, it was by no means certain that the Moluccas would fall on the Portuguese side of the line. The Portuguese therefore required an authoritative pronouncement that the line of demarcation was confined to the Atlantic; that it served simply to determine for each power the route which must be followed to the Indies. Once again they sought the support of the papacy.

The amiable hedonist Leo X was interested in discovery and friendly to Portugal. The papal fancy had recently been pleased by the present of a performing elephant, sent to Rome by Alboquerque. In 1514 Leo acceded to all the Portuguese requests. The bull *Praecelsae devotionis* gave papal blessing to discoveries and conquests which the Portuguese might make, and granted to Portugal all lands which might be seized from heathen people, not only in Africa and India, but in any region which might be reached by sailing east.

Magellan, though a Portuguese, was impelled by circumstances to ignore the ruling of the bull. Before the date of its issue he had been in the East for some years, and had been present at the taking of Malacca. It is not certain whether he had visited the Moluccas, but some of his friends certainly had, and he knew the latitude of the islands. As for their longitude, he believed that the Moluccas lay reasonably near to South America and within what the Spaniards regarded as their sphere of influence. In that, of course, he was wrong. He also believed that a western passage might be found by following up Vespucci's third voyage, to the extreme south of South America. In that he was right. When Solís made his voyage to the Río de la Plata in 1515, Magellan questioned the survivors and calculated from their reports that the south-westerly trend of the coast south of the estuary brought all that southern territory within the Spanish demarcation. In that he was also right. Obviously a successful voyage of discovery based on Magellan's reasoning would benefit nobody but the Spaniards; it was useless to ask the Portuguese government to finance such a voyage. Magellan accordingly turned to Spain, with an offer to discover rich islands in the East, within the Spanish demarcation and reached by an all-Spanish route.

In Magellan's agreement with the Emperor the Moluccas were not specifically mentioned. Magellan knew, though Charles V probably did not, that the Portuguese had already reached the Moluccas and that the bull *Praecelsae devotionis* therefore applied to the islands. Perhaps he hoped to find other equally valuable islands in the same longitude; but the Moluccas were generally assumed to be his destination. His enterprise appeared as an act of aggression against Portugal and an act of defiance against the Pope. The Portuguese government tried by all possible diplomatic means to stop the expedition, but without success, and in September 1519 Magellan sailed from Seville with a fleet of five ships, laden with such goods as Portuguese experience had found suitable for trade in the East.

The events of Magellan's voyage were ably chronicled by Pigafetta, who sailed with him and who paid a moving tribute to his leadership.[11] Like Columbus, Magellan was a foreigner in command of touchy Spaniards, and the first part of his voyage was plagued with quarrels between Portuguese and Spanish officers. The fleet gave the coast of Brazil a diplomatic wide berth, and made its first call on the Patagonian coast, in the cold and treeless harbour of San Julián, inhabited only by a handful of the most primitive people in the world. Here the inevitable mutiny broke out, suppressed with prompt resolution by Magellan and followed by the inevitable hanging of ringleaders. Further south, in the mouth of the Strait which bears his name, Magellan lost two ships, one by wreck and one by desertion. Magellan's Strait is a most dangerous place for sailing ships. The channel runs through a maze of reefs and islands, holding grounds are rocky and insecure, and the abrupt ice-covered mountains on both sides funnel the wind in violent and baffling squalls. Magellan was relatively fortunate in his weather, and made a relatively prosperous passage of the Strait in thirty-eight days. In the Pacific, he was obliged to steer north to find a favouring wind; and when he found it, he struck out across the ocean in a latitude well to the north of the Moluccas, possibly in the hope of finding similar islands out of reach of the Portuguese. The seemingly endless crossing reduced the ships' companies to eating rats and gnawing leather. A brief stay in the Ladrones gave them poor and grudging refreshment. Finally they made landfall at Sebu in the Philippines. Here Magellan—like Columbus a better seaman than diplomat—became involved in a local war, and he and forty of his people were killed.

The skill, the endurance and the achievement of Magellan before his death set him with Columbus and Vasco da Gama among the greatest of explorers; but the voyage was only half completed. Sebastián del Cano, the Spanish navigator upon whom the command devolved, sailed south from the Philippines with only two ships remaining, skirted the north and east coasts of Borneo, and in November 1521 reached the Moluccas. The Spaniards were well received by the Sultan of Tidore, upon whose territory they landed. They traded their merchandise for cargoes of cloves and established a warehouse at Tidore, leaving a small garrison to prepare for future expeditions. Then, since none of his company were willing to face the dangers of Magellan's Strait again, del Cano divided his forces. The *Trinidad* set off across the Pacific for the Isthmus, and was captured by the Portuguese before she was many days out. Del Cano himself eluded the Portuguese and took his battered *Victoria* out through the Banda Sea, between the islands, across the Indian Ocean, round the Cape of Good Hope and back to Spain, with a precious cargo and fifteen men surviving out of a fleet of five sail. It was a prodigious feat of seamanship and del Cano shares with Magellan the honour of this astounding voyage. He was the first captain to sail round the world.

The wealth of information which this voyage supplied can be seen in Ribeiro's chart of 1529. Apart from cartography, del Cano's triumphant return produced two parallel sets of consequences. The first was a state of open war between Spaniards and Portuguese in the islands; the second a fresh series of outwardly amicable negotiations between Spain and Portugal in Europe. The second Spanish expedition to Tidore, in 1524, was a disastrous failure; only one ship of a powerful fleet reached its destination. Another fleet, of Pacific-built ships sent by Cortés from Mexico, fared no better. It became clear that whatever happened in Europe, the Portuguese were in command of the situation in the East and the value of the Spanish claim was beginning to depreciate. The Emperor, at war with France and on the verge of insolvency, in 1527 conceived the ingenious idea of selling or pawning his claim to the Moluccas before it should depreciate further. In 1529, despite the opposition of the Cortes of Castile, the Treaty of Zaragoza was duly signed. By this treaty Charles V pledged all his rights in the Moluccas to Portugal for 350,000 ducats, and an arbitrary line of demarcation was fixed seventeen degrees east of the islands. The little garrison at Tidore, which had held out stubbornly against heavy odds for more than five years, was instructed to hand over to the Portuguese, and the Spaniards were given passage home in Portuguese ships.

The Treaty of Zaragoza marked the end of a chapter in the story of discovery. Magellan's Strait was never used, by Spaniards or anyone else, as a regular channel of trade. Apart from a disputed frontier on the Río de la Plata and the comparatively unimportant question of the Philippines, the colonial questions at issue between Spain and Portugal were for the moment settled. But neither the bulls nor the treaties in this long diplomatic contest could bind third parties, and the search for a western passage was to be carried on by other nations.

CHAPTER 10

THE AMERICAN CONQUESTS

BALBOA and his kind went to Central America to look for gold mines. Even in forcing his way through the steaming forests of the Isthmus to the South Sea, Balboa was not primarily interested in the search for a western passage to India. His discovery naturally gave great encouragement to those who were, and in the next few years a number of Spanish expeditions left the islands to search the mainland coast. These expeditions, however, were not single-minded searches for a sea route to Asia, not maritime explorations financed and ordered to serve the long-term ends of a European government, but private ventures, undertaken, it is true, under Crown licence, but for predominantly private ends. The men who took part in them were adventurers by land, who used ships only as initial means of transport. They were prepared to take their fortune where they found it, and though they failed to find a strait, they founded a great empire. If the first two decades of the sixteenth century may be called the age of the professional explorer, the next three decades, from 1520 to 1550, were the age of the *conquistador*.

Before 1520 most of the larger islands of the West Indies had been explored and a considerable number of Spaniards had settled, especially in Hispaniola and Cuba. These settlers had imported cattle and horses, and negroes from West Africa to replace the dwindling native Arawaks, and had set up as slave-owning ranchers or gold-prospectors. Their settlements were turbulent and unstable. Many of the settlers were soldiers who had served in Moorish or Italian campaigns. There was no congenial work for them in Spain, nor did they propose to work in the Indies. They would settle for a short time, and then desert their holdings to investigate a rumoured gold strike, or because shortage of labour made life arduous, or simply through boredom and restlessness. From their number were recruited the first conquerors and settlers of the mainland.

The shores of the Gulf of Darien had first been visited in 1500 by Rodrigo de Bastidas, accompanied by Columbus' old pilot and cartographer, Juan de la Cosa. In 1504 de la Cosa carried out a more thorough exploration, and on his reports the Crown decided to authorize mainland settlement. Despite the protests of Diego Colón, the admiral's son and heir, two licences were issued, one to Diego de Nicuesa for the settlement of Veragua, the other to Alonso de Ojeda for what is now the north coast of Colombia. The two expeditions, which sailed at the end of 1509, numbered together over a thousand men, but hunger, sickness and poisoned arrows soon killed all but a few score. This was the most serious loss which the Spaniards had suffered in America up to that time, and one of the earliest casualties was Juan de la Cosa, whom Spain could ill spare. Reinforcements eventually arrived from Hispaniola, with a royal official, Martín Fernández de Enciso in command; but the leadership devolved, by common consent, upon the popular desperado, Vasco Núñez de Balboa. Balboa had the advantage of local knowledge, having sailed with Bastidas in 1500. He was decisive, unscrupulous, and no respecter of persons. He shipped Enciso back to Hispaniola (Ojeda had gone already), turned Nicuesa adrift to drown, and assumed command of the whole enterprise. Balboa was the first of the great *conquistadores* of the American mainland, and Oviedo, who knew him well, is a convincing witness of his courage and his ability. Besides leading the famous expedition to the Pacific shore, he founded the town of Darien; he achieved an ascendancy over the Indians of the Isthmus by a combination of force, terror, conciliation and diplomacy; he collected from them large quantities of food and gold; but at the same time he compelled his own people to provide for the future by building houses and planting crops. Both as a discoverer and as an architect of empire Balboa deserved well of his comrades and his king. Like Columbus, however—whom he resembled in no other way—he suffered from the tale-bearing of enemies who returned to Spain. The King was understandably concerned over the loss of Nicuesa and Juan de la Cosa, and resented the affront to his authority in the person of Enciso. The first royal governor of Darien, appointed in 1513, was not Balboa, but Pedro Arias de Avila, the terrible old man whom his contemporaries called *furor Domini*. Pedrarias and his captains ruled, exploited and devastated the Isthmus for sixteen years. He drove on with great energy the work of discovery and settlement, exploring not only the Caribbean coast of Nicaragua and its hinterland, including the lake, but also the Pacific coast, in boats built locally for the purpose. Balboa himself fell victim to Pedrarias' jealousy. He was tried on a charge of treason in 1519, and beheaded.

While Balboa's discovery encouraged exploration westward from the islands, the formidable reputation of Pedrarias ensured that the explorers kept well away to the north of his jurisdiction, to the Gulf of Honduras, the Yucatán coast, and eventually the Gulf of Mexico. There they were to find far greater opportunities of conquest. Scattered through tropical America were a number of distinct peoples who, though lacking iron tools, wheeled vehicles and beasts of burden, had achieved a remarkable skill in some of the arts, in sculpture and building, and in handcraft industries including pottery, weaving and the working of soft metals. Some of them had evolved forms of writing, ranging from the relatively simple, beautifully executed pictograms of central and southern Mexico to the intricate glyphs of the Maya people in Guatemala and Yucatán. Most of them were curiously obsessed by the need to measure the passage of time and to select auspicious dates for major undertakings; the Mayas in particular had a highly elaborated science of astronomical observation and calendric reckoning. The basic crop of most of these peoples was maize, a cereal more sustaining than the cassava of the islands; and they had brought the hoe cultivation of maize, squashes and beans to a high level by means of well-organized systems of communal work and, in places, irrigation. Their principal settlements, adorned with stone or adobe temples and community-houses, were large enough to be called cities; and a primitive form of city-state was their normal political unit. In at least two centres, however, the valley of Mexico and the central plateau of the Andes, warlike tribes had established themselves as overlords, exacting tribute and forced labour from subject peoples over a wide area, and had set up political organizations bearing a superficial resemblance to empires or kingdoms in the old-world sense. Among Spaniards the wealth and power of these peoples lost nothing in the telling; and for pious Christians their religions had a horrible fascination, combining, as in some cases they did, messianic legends of familiar beauty with the practice of human sacrifice and ritual cannibalism. They were not seafaring peoples. Their chief centres were all inland, and for that reason the Spaniards for some years remained unaware of their existence. Even the Maya cities of Yucatán were difficult of access from the sea. The first of the 'empires' to be discovered, attacked and subjugated was that established in central Mexico by the Aztecs, an intrusive and aggressive people whose chief city, Tenochtitlán, was built upon islands in the lake of Texcoco. Overcrowding on these islands had driven the Aztecs to expand; and by a series of wars and alliances in the century before the arrival of the Spaniards they had extended their influence west and south nearly to the Gulf coast.

The isthmus, Castilla del Oro, had been settled from Hispaniola. The men who explored and invaded Mexico came from Cuba, and the leading spirit in the work of preparation was the able and ambitious governor, Diego Velázquez. Velázquez' people had for some time been slave-raiding in the Bay Islands off the Honduras coast, and there perhaps found evidence of trade with the more developed cultures of the mainland. Small expeditions were sent from Cuba in 1517 and 1518 to reconnoitre the north coast of Yucatán, sailing west from Cape Catoche and then following the coast of the Gulf of Mexico. In 1519, as a result of their reports, Velázquez fitted out a much larger fleet with a view to trade and exploration, and appointed as its commander Hernán Cortés, who had been his secretary, and was financially a partner in the enterprise. Cortés' *entrada* is the best-known and best-documented of all the Spanish campaigns in the new world. There are four surviving eye-witness accounts, of which two at least are of unusual literary and historical merit. Cortés' own letters[1] are graphic and detailed, though naturally affected by political considerations and by a tendency to represent all decisions as Cortés' own. The corrective is to be found in the *True History* of Bernal Díaz,[2] which tells the story from the point of view of a loyal and intelligent foot-soldier who happened to possess a remarkable memory. Few tales in classical legend or medieval romance are more arresting than this conquest of a powerful, if semi-barbarous, empire by a handful of down-at-heel swordsmen.

Cortés was personally popular, and the project attracted a force of about 600 volunteers, a large number for a sparsely settled island. Velázquez and Cortés did not trust one another, and probably Cortés from the start contemplated the conquest of an independent kingdom. He left Cuba in clandestine haste, and upon landing near what is now Vera Cruz, lost no time in repudiating Velázquez' authority by two symbolic acts. The first was the destruction of the ships in which he had come; by this he prevented malcontents returning to Cuba, and freed the sailors to march with the army. The second was the ceremonious founding of a municipality. To the magistrates of the 'town' of Vera Cruz—whom his officers elected—he resigned the commission he had received in Cuba; from them, as representatives of the Spanish Crown in Mexico, he received a new commission, and wrote at once to the Emperor for confirmation of it. Having thus legalized as best he could his assumption of an independent command, he led his army up the long and rugged climb from the steamy jungles of Vera Cruz to the high plateau of central Mexico.

To the modern traveller Cortés' route seems almost perversely difficult. It included two high passes, the pine-clad saddle between Orizaba and the Cofre de Perote, and the Paso de Cortés between the twin snow-peaks Popocatépetl and Ixtaccíhuatl. Neither pass carries a usable road today. The route was dictated largely by political considerations, by the need to travel as far as possible through friendly territory. Between Vera Cruz and Tenochtitlán were many *pueblos* which paid tribute unwillingly, and one town, with its surrounding countryside, was still holding out against the Aztecs. One or two early Spanish castaways, who had taken to life among the Indians and spoke local languages, joined Cortés as interpreters. By a mixture of force and diplomacy he was able to quicken the resentment of Cempoala and neighbouring *pueblos* into open defiance, and after sharp fighting he achieved an offensive alliance with the recalcitrant town of Tlaxcala. These friendly towns helped the Spaniards with food, with porters, with fighting auxiliaries and, most important of all, with information. In Cempoala Cortés first heard of Quetzalcoatl, the divine hero of Toltec mythology, god of priesthood and learning and introducer of maize, whose return to earth was expected by Mexican augurers about the time that the Spaniards landed. From the redoubtable warriors of Tlaxcala Cortés learned something of the military strength and weaknesses of the Aztecs. Embassies arrived in the camp, bearing presents whose value and workmanship revealed the wealth of Mexico to the greedy eyes of the waiting Spaniards. They brought also threats, and unconvincing pleas of poverty, in a hopeless attempt to dissuade Cortés from advancing on the capital. Cortés wisely sent the best of the treasure home to the emperor (though some of it was intercepted by French privateers and never reached Spain). From the threats he divined the mixture of defiance and superstitious dread in the mind of the Aztec war-chief and saw the use which could be made of Montezuma's fears. Cortés' genius largely consisted in his power of appreciating the psychological factors in a situation, and in skill in building up his own prestige alike among his allies and his enemies. His chief difficulty at this stage was in restraining the allies, whose notions of war were less subtle and more direct. He succeeded in this delicate task. The advance of the army was orderly and swift, and in due course the Spaniards, escorted by their Aztec hosts, marched along the causeway into Tenochtitlán, making their best attempt at a display of martial pageantry. The Spaniards were lodged in a great community-house, or palace as they called it, in the city, while the allies camped outside on the shore of the lake. It was remarkable evidence of Aztec powers of organization that, in a country where all transport was either by canoe or on the backs of porters, so many extra mouths could be fed at such short notice.

Peace was short-lived. The first interruption was the arrival at Vera Cruz of a powerful force under Pánfilo de Narváez, one of the original conquerors of Cuba, who had been sent by the governor to apprehend Cortés. Cortés rushed down to the coast, out-manœuvred Narváez, and by a mixture of threats, bribes and promises enlisted the men from Cuba under his own command. In his absence, however, the zeal of his lieutenants in destroying heathen temples, and their incessant demands for food, had exasperated the Aztecs to the point of war. Montezuma, a discredited captive in Spanish hands, could do nothing to restrain his people. A new war-chief had been elected, and Cortés' return with reinforcements precipitated the outbreak. His only serious mistake in the whole campaign was his re-entry into Tenochtitlán, trusting to his own prestige and to Montezuma's authority. Montezuma was stoned to death by his own people, and Cortés had to fight his way out of the city along the broken causeways by night, losing in that one night a third of his men and most of his baggage. The auxiliary tribes remained loyal to the alliance, however. The army was able to retire on Tlaxcala and re-form for a more thorough and less spectacular advance. Cortés had boats built for fighting on the lake, and laid siege to the city, cutting off its drinking water and its food supply, systematically looting and destroying it building by building with the help of the Tlaxcalans and shovelling the rubble into the lake as he advanced towards the centre, until at last, in 1521, the surviving inhabitants surrendered. In the magnificent Spanish city which Cortés began to build upon the site, hardly a trace of Indian building remains. The place was built over as completely as the Roman cities of Europe, and the lake floor, drained and eroded, is now a dusty plain. The loot of the conquest proved disappointing. It could hardly have been otherwise, so high were the soldiers' expectations. Cortés was blamed for it, and even accused of hiding treasure for his own profit. His remedies were to appease his followers with grants of *encomienda* and to send the more ambitious of them away on new expeditions. The system of *encomiendas* was not new; it had been used in Granada, in the Canaries and in the West Indian islands; but in Mexico it received more precise definition and far more extended use. An *encomienda* was a native village, or group of villages, 'commended' to the care of an individual Spaniard, an *encomendero*, whose duty was to protect the inhabitants, to appoint and maintain missionary clergy in the villages and to undertake a share in the military defence of the province. The conquering army was thus to be settled as a quasi-feudal militia, residing in towns of Spanish foundation but living on the country. *Encomenderos* were entitled by their grants to support their households by levying tribute from the villages in their care, tribute which in the early days took the forms both of food and cotton clothing and of free forced labour. A grant of *encomienda*, however, involved no cession of land or jurisdiction. *Encomiendas* were not feudal manors; nor were they slave-worked plantations. In theory and in law the Indians remained free men and their rights over the land they occupied were unimpaired. In the valley of Mexico, and in many other places, Indian land custom already made provision for the payment of tribute to overlord peoples and for the support of chieftains and priests, of temples and community houses. The Spanish *encomenderos* stepped into the places of the Aztec rulers and drew the tributes and services formerly paid to them. As a means of initial settlement the *encomienda* was logical, indeed obvious. Without it there would have been no settlement. As a permanent arrangement, however, it had grave disadvantages. Like any system involving forced labour, it lent itself to abuse, especially in view of the Spanish mania for building. Partly for this reason, partly because of the feudal implications of the *encomiendas*, Charles V and his advisers were highly suspicious of the whole system. The permanence of any governmental structure depended, among other things, on royal confirmation. Cortés succeeded in securing confirmation of his initial grants—and prudently reserved a large proportion of the Anáhuac villages to the Crown—but royal second thoughts could be expected to modify these rough and ready arrangements. Moreover, the number of Spaniards who could be supported by *encomiendas* was relatively small, for—in the early days at least—the grants were large. Cortés arrogated to himself a vast *encomienda* in the valley of Oajaca, comprising officially 23,000 tributary heads of households, in fact many more. This was exceptional; but *encomiendas* of 2,000 and more tributaries were common. The humbler soldier who received no *encomienda* had two choices open to him. The conditions of colonial society being at first wholly unsuitable for small-scale farming or the practice of European trades, he could either remain the follower, the *paniaguado*, of a great *encomendero* and live on his bounty; or he could move on to fresh conquests and hope eventually to secure Indians of his own. Society in these circumstances was necessarily restless, factious and disorderly, with dissatisfied adventurers constantly moving out to new frontiers of conquest.

Cortés never forgot that the discovery of New Spain had originated in attempts to find a route to the Pacific and so to the Far East. Mexico occupied and its valley secure, he quickly resumed the search, whether for a strait between the oceans or for harbours which could become bases for Pacific exploration. Of his subsequent expeditions, only those to Pánuco—the first commanded by himself, the second by Sandoval—had a purely Caribbean object; they were undertaken chiefly to counter the slave-raiding activities of the island settlers on the Gulf coast. The other expeditions organized by Cortés were all intended to open exploration to the west and south. Between 1522 and 1524 Michoacán and most of the Pacific coast area as far north as the Santiago river were conquered and granted in *encomienda*. In 1523 Pedro de Alvarado led a well-equipped force through Tehuántepec into the Maya region of Guatemala, and Cristóbal de Olid was sent by sea to the bay of Honduras, to occupy the settled country there and to search for a strait. Both these expeditions encountered not only natural obstacles and stout Indian resistance, but also opposition from an unexpected quarter, from Pedrarias de Avila's men exploring north from Darien. The two great streams of mainland conquest met along the southern borders of what are now the republics of Guatemala and Honduras, and a dangerous armed clash seemed imminent. To complicate the situation still further, Olid repudiated Cortés' authority and set up an independent command. Cortés thought it necessary to deal with mutiny and possible civil war in person. His army marched to Honduras across the base of the Yucatán peninsula, through appallingly difficult country in which abrupt mountain ranges alternated with dense rain-forest. One river and its riparian swamps had to be crossed by means of a floating bridge whose construction required the felling of over a thousand trees. Few horses survived the march, and the men who survived emerged from the forest broken in health and even, for a time, in spirit. Nevertheless, Cortés' presence sufficed to restore order among the Spaniards in Honduras—Olid had been murdered before his arrival—and to make an arrangement with the men from Darien which attached Honduras, for a time, to Mexico. Meanwhile Alvarado had carried out a successful, rapacious and brutal campaign in Guatemala. The Mayas, vigorous, intelligent, with a developed though decaying culture, lacked political unity, and Alvarado profited by the enmity between two principal peoples, Cakchiquel and Quiché, to support one against the other and ultimately to subdue both. The Spanish city of Guatemala, on the first of its three successive sites, was founded in 1524, and *encomiendas* were distributed among its founders in the usual way. Alvarado succeeded in holding his men together and in standing off incursions from Darien. He visited Spain in 1527 and returned to America a knight of Santiago, with his government of Guatemala confirmed.

Cortés was too famous and too powerful to enjoy the same confidence. He travelled to Spain in 1529 and arrived at court with appropriate gifts and a train of Indian acrobats. Charles V greeted him warmly, confirmed his *encomienda*, created him marquis of the valley of Oajaca, but refused to entrust to him the government of New Spain. Already in 1527 an *audiencia*, a court of appeal, had been established in Mexico to safeguard Crown interests and keep an eye on Cortés. It is true that the president of this court, Nuño de Guzmán, soon deserted his post and went off on an independent conquest of his own in New Galicia, to the north-west; but Nuño was replaced by an eminent ecclesiastic, and the *audiencia* system was retained. In 1535 the Emperor appointed a viceroy with civil and military powers: Antonio de Mendoza, soldier, diplomat, cadet of a great noble house. Again Cortés was passed over. He offered to lead troops against Nuño de Guzmán in New Galicia, but the offer was refused. His plans for expeditions in search of rumoured cities to the north were thwarted by Mendoza, who had similar

ambitions. His energies were more and more confined to business activities, to the management of his sugar and cattle properties in Oajaca
and his house property in Mexico City. Finally in 1539 Cortés wearied
of the New World and returned to Spain, where he lived in retirement
on the revenues of his *marquesado*. His reputation as a commander
of expeditions against semi-barbarous tribes was little valued in
Europe. Neither his services nor his advice were sought by the Crown,
even in fields such as North Africa where they might have been of value.
He died at his house of Castilleja de la Cuesta, near Seville, in 1547.

Meanwhile other *conquistadores* had been busy far away, in South
America; and by the time of Mendoza's arrival in Mexico another
equally formidable Amerindian empire had been subdued by Spanish
arms.[3] Ever since the occupation of Darien rumours had been current
among the Spaniards there of civilized and prosperous kingdoms to the
south, but the reality long eluded discovery. The chief political and
religious centres of ancient Peru lay high up on the Andean plateau,
guarded by the gigantic ramparts of the Cordillera. Here, at heights
varying from 9,000 to 13,000 feet, over a period of some four hundred
years the Inca clan and dynasty of the Quechua people had established
a military dominion which, at the time of the Spaniards' arrival,
extended for nearly two thousand miles from north to south and had its
capital at Cuzco. The Inca empire was held together by a tight social
discipline based on communal land-holding and a far-reaching system
of forced labour. Discipline was enjoined by an elaborate and magnificent cult of ruler-worship and enforced by a military organization
which maintained fortresses and stores at strategic points, and a network
of mountain roads and liana-cable bridges all over the empire. The
Inca polity was far more closely organized than that of the Aztecs in
Mexico, and its communications were better, considering the extreme
difficulty of the terrain; but the general temper of the Peruvians was
less bloodthirsty, and human sacrifice had ceased among them before
the Spaniards arrived. Their material culture was largely of the Stone
Age, but they were skilled workers in soft metals, made more use of
copper tools than did the Mexicans, and employed gold and silver
freely for ornament and even for utensils. They were accomplished and
artistic weavers, using cotton near the coast, llama and vicuña wool in
the mountains. They had no writing, but used a kind of abacus of
knotted cords for keeping accounts, such as tribute returns. Their
agriculture was based not on grain crops such as maize, but on roots,
chiefly varieties of potato. Their cities were solidly and skilfully built
of dressed stone. Like the Mexicans, they had no knowledge of the
wheel; but unlike them possessed a beast of burden, though a small
and relatively inefficient one—the llama.

In the century or so before the Spanish invasion the Incas had extended their domination north into modern Ecuador, south into Chile as far as the Maule river, and over the region of the highly individual and well-developed Chimu culture of the coastal plain of Peru. These relatively recent acquisitions were a source of weakness to the empire. It was from the northern regions that rumours of Inca wealth reached the Spaniards in Darien, and their inhabitants, still resentful of Inca rule, received the European invaders with acquiescence, if not with enthusiasm.

The Peruvian enterprise was initiated in Darien by a syndicate comprising two soldiers of fortune from Estremadura, Francisco de Pizarro and Diego de Almagro, and a priest named Luque. All three had settled in Darien, had acquired land and Indians, and had prospected there for gold with modest success. Luque, though he took no active part in the conquest of Peru, provided most of the initial capital. The partners spent four years in voyages of coastal exploration, in which they collected enough evidence to encourage them to approach the emperor for a formal capitulation. Pizarro's journey to Spain coincided with the triumphal appearance of Cortés at the court—a favourable omen; and Pizarro secured appointment as *adelantado* and governor of the kingdom which he undertook to conquer. He returned to Panama with his four half-brothers and other volunteers. Leaving Almagro in Panama to follow later with reinforcements, Pizarro finally set out in 1530 with about 180 men and twenty-seven horses for the conquest of Peru.

The arrival of Pizarro at Túmbez on the northern coast of Peru coincided with the final stage of a succession war in which the reigning Inca, Huáscar, was defeated and dethroned by his usurping half-brother Atahualpa, who chose as his capital not Cuzco but Cajamarca in northern Peru. Reports of this conflict encouraged Pizarro, after establishing himself in the Túmbez region and founding the 'city' of San Miguel, to march inland to Cajamarca. Here, by means of a surprise attack under cover of a formal conference, the Spaniards succeeded in killing most of Atahualpa's immediate retinue and capturing the ruler himself. Aided by surprise, by a favourable political situation, and by a breath-taking boldness that frightened the conquerors themselves, Pizarro and his men decided the fate of the Inca empire in a single afternoon. Almagro, with 200 men, arrived shortly afterwards. The Inca forces, deprived of the authority of their ruler, were unable effectively to resist the conquerors' march, with about 600 men, on Cuzco, which was taken and sacked in November 1533. The gold looted from Cuzco, together with the roomful of gold vessels which Atahualpa collected in the vain hope of buying his freedom, was melted down, the royal fifth subtracted, and the rest distributed; enough to make every man in the army rich for life, though comparatively few lived long to enjoy it.

Despite the hardships, the almost incredible mountain marches, and the fighting that lay behind, Cuzco was the beginning rather than the end of Pizarro's worst difficulties. Hitherto the campaign had followed approximately the same lines as that of Cortés in Mexico, but after the capture of Cuzco the pattern of events diverged. Pizarro, unlike Cortés, did not establish the centre of his power in the ancient capital of the kingdom, but founded in 1535 an entirely new Spanish capital—Lima, the City of the Kings, close to the sea in the Rimac valley. The choice was natural on military grounds, for Cuzco was remote from the harbours on which Spanish Peru depended for reinforcements and supplies from the outside world, and its mountainous surroundings made the use of cavalry, the chief Spanish arm, difficult if not impossible; but by this decision Pizarro emphasized the division between Spanish coast and Indian mountain and lost one means of attaching the Peruvians to a new allegiance. Pizarro was in any case a man of a very different stamp from Cortés. He had the disadvantage of not being, in the conventional social sense, a gentleman. In Spain he was the illegitimate son of obscure peasants, in the Indies a warrior among warriors, owing his leadership to vaulting ambition, boundless courage, and skill in fighting. He was illiterate, and therefore dependent upon secretaries. Shrewd though he was, he lacked Cortés' charm and diplomacy, his sensitive understanding of human situations, his genius for attaching even defeated enemies to himself. The judicial murder of Atahualpa was a blunder, condemned by many Spaniards. Pizarro had, moreover, jealous rivals in his own camp, and serious disputes soon arose among the conquerors. The first news of trouble came from San Miguel, whose governor, Belalcázar, had marched north into the region of Quito at the invitation of some of its inhabitants to rid them of their Inca governors and to establish a conquest of his own. The situation was complicated by the unexpected arrival from Guatemala of the restless and warlike Alvarado who also had designs on Quito. First Almagro and then Pizarro hastened north to avert civil war. Almagro and Belalcázar (who were *compadres*) made common cause against Alvarado, who after an interview with Pizarro agreed to return to his own government. Belalcázar retained his conquest of Quito.

Meanwhile, Hernando Pizarro, the conqueror's half-brother, who had been sent to Spain with news and presents, had returned with dispatches granting to Francisco Pizarro the title of marquis, and to Amalgro that of *adelantado* in a necessarily undefined area to the south of that governed by Pizarro. Almagro promptly claimed Cuzco as part of his grant; Pizarro refused to give up the city; and after a face-saving reconciliation Almagro departed on an expedition to explore and conquer his southern kingdom. He was away for two years, during which his army traversed the bleak *Altiplano* of what is now Bolivia and penetrated far into Chile, returning by way of the coastal desert of Atacama. Almagro's people suffered great hardships from cold and hunger, from heat and thirst; they lost most of their horses and many of their own number; found no more cities and no plunder worth the name; and returned to Cuzco in April 1537 still more bitterly jealous of Pizarro's good fortune.

During Almagro's absence Pizarro had to face a dangerous and widespread Indian rising led by Manco Inca, a successor of Huáscar whom Pizarro tried, unsuccessfully, to use as a puppet ruler. Manco failed to make any impression on Lima, but invested Cuzco closely and cut the city off from reinforcements sent from the coast. Indian armies were too large to keep the field for long periods, with the primitive means of transport available, and after some six months Manco's army began to dwindle; but before Pizarro could take advantage of this weakening, Almagro arrived with his army from Chile, took Manco in the rear and defeated him, marched into Cuzco and seized the government of the city and province. This was the origin of the first of the civil wars of Spanish Peru, the war of Las Salinas.[4] Like many subsequent disturbances in Peru, the war was a quarrel not only between two factions of Spaniards, but between the coast and the mountains, between the cities of Lima and Cuzco. Lima won; Almagro, after many vicissitudes, was defeated in 1538, and strangled by order of Hernando Pizarro, who took him prisoner. He had been an open-handed and popular leader, and his death made many enemies for the Pizarros. Francisco Pizarro's own turn came three years later. In 1541 he was murdered in Lima by a group of the 'men of Chile'.

Manco Inca, who after his defeat lived for ten years as a fugitive ruler, may well have reflected on the ironical fate which befell the conquerors of his people—little bands of armed spoilers seeking one another out and fighting to the death among great mountains, with an empire at their feet awaiting an organizing hand. Francisco Pizarro's death was the signal for a fresh series of civil wars among men who had been his lieutenants.[5] The home government intervened, but made matters more difficult for its officers by its attempt, in 1542–3, to abolish the *encomienda* system. The last recalcitrant chieftain, Gonzalo Pizarro, was captured and beheaded in 1548. Of the five violent and ungovernable brothers who had conquered Peru, only Hernando survived the wars to end his days in a Spanish prison. Gonzalo's death was the end of overt armed defiance; but even then the establishment of an effective royal administration was a slow and difficult process. It was not complete until the time of Francisco de Toledo, the organizing genius who in twelve years of government (1569–81) gave the viceroyalty of Peru its permanent bureaucratic stamp; and who, incidentally, ordered the execution of Túpac Amarú, the last recognized Inca prince.

The area under Spanish influence had greatly expanded during the civil wars. Belalcázar had extended his dominion from Quito through forest country inhabited by primitive tribes, north to Popayán, and beyond into the isolated but settled land of the city-building Chibchas. Here his advance met that of Gonzalo Jiménez de Quesada, who had marched south from the Caribbean up the Magdalena river to the populous savannahs of Bogotá. On this occasion the leaders, approximately equal in strength, agreed on a division of territory. Santa Fe de Bogotá became in time the capital of the Spanish kingdom of New Granada. Belalcázar—who had added a new technique to the methods of conquest by driving a great herd of pigs along with his army, a source of food on the march and an acquisition to the country—became governor of Popayán. Gonzalo Pizarro had also led an extremely arduous expedition from Quito through the vast jungles on the east slope of the Andes. The people of this expedition, lighting on the Napo river at a time when they were lost and starving, built a boat of timber felled on the bank, in order to explore the river in search of villages and food. It was in this boat that Francisco de Orellana and a handful of companions, unable to return against the stream, followed the entire length of the Amazon to its mouth in 1542. Meanwhile, far to the south, Almagro's reconnaissances of Chile had been followed up by Pedro de Valdivia who founded the city of Santiago in 1541. Valdivia's conquest was unusual in two respects. As a result of Pizarro's death he found himself without a master and became one of the few elected governors in the Indies by the choice of the householders of Santiago, much as Cortés had been 'elected' at Vera Cruz. Finding no gold and no settled Indian culture, he succeeded in establishing a modest but soundly based Spanish farming community, in one of the loveliest and most fertile valleys in the world.

The exploits of Cortés, Pizarro, and their like attracted the attention both of their contemporaries and of historians because of their dramatic and breath-taking success. They conquered populous provinces, established cities, found productive silver mines—Potosí was discovered in 1545, Zacatecas in 1548. It should be remembered, however, that by far the greatest part of the Americas at that time was neither populous nor productive. Immense areas were traversed by Spanish explorers who, as *conquistadores*, were failures, in that they found nothing which they considered to be of value. Most sixteenth-century knowledge of what is now the southern United States, for example, was derived from two expeditions, that of Hernando de Soto who in 1539 explored from Tampa Bay in Florida north to the Appalachians and west to the Mississippi, and that of Francisco Vázquez Coronado. Coronado in 1541 set out from New Galicia across the Rio Grande and the Pecos into the great prairies west of the Mississippi, and reported immense herds of 'cows' and primitive people parasitic on them, 'living like Arabs'. These exploits added much to geographical knowledge, but they had no immediate results and added nothing to the wealth or reputation of those who took part in them. The same is true of the men who first explored California, or 'Cíbola'—the *pueblos* of New Mexico—or ascended the rivers of Guiana in search of El Dorado, or discovered the route, later much used by smugglers, up the Río de la Plata and the Paraguay river into Upper Peru. Wounds, sickness, death and disappointment was the lot of the great majority of these eternal optimists.

The rule of the *conquistadores* was quarrelsome and brief. They had gone to America at their own expense, endured great hardships, risked their lives and fortunes, such as they were, without help from their government at home. Most of them looked forward to a pensioned retirement. Left to themselves, they would probably have settled in loose communities, employing the feudal terms which already were anachronisms in Spain, exploiting the Indians as the needs of the moment dictated, and according verbal homage but little else to the Crown. The rulers of Spain never for a moment thought of allowing such a state of affairs to persist. In the late fifteenth and early sixteenth centuries the Crown, with considerable bloodshed and expense, had cut the claws of the great feudal houses, of the knightly orders and of the privileged local corporations. A growing royal absolutism could not tolerate the emergence of a new feudal aristocracy overseas. Private commanders like Cortés, Pizarro, Belalcázar and Nuño de Guzmán, if they escaped the knives of their rivals, were for the most part soon displaced by royal nominees. Lawyers and ecclesiastics took over the direction of the empire; cattle ranchers, mining capitalists and the exporting merchants of Seville exploited its riches. The great age of the *conquistadores* ended when the principal settled areas were deemed secure. There was nothing further for them to do. Forests and empty prairies were not to their taste. Some succeeded in settling down as *encomenderos*, ranchers or miners; some met violent ends; some, like Bernal Díaz, lived on in obscure poverty in America; some, like Cortés, returned to Spain with their winnings and spent their last years in bored and litigious retirement. Very few were trusted by the Crown with any real administrative power. They were not the stuff of which bureaucrats are made.

1
Vasca da Gama's fleet, from a print in the Science Museum, South Kensington.

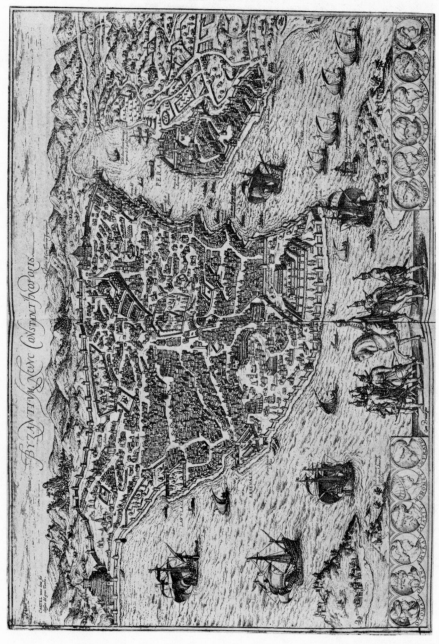

2
Constantinople and
Pera, from G. Braun
and F. Hogenberg,
*Civitates Orbis
Terrarum*, Cologne,
1576.

3
Detail from the
world map of Martin
Waldseemüller,
woodcut, 1507, in
the library of the
Prince of Waldburg,
Wolfegg Castle; from
J. Fischer and F. R.
von Wieser, Die
älteste Karte mit den
Namen Amerika. . . ,
1903.

4
The Venezuela pearl fishery, from de Bry, *Grands Voyages*, Part IV, Frankfurt, 1594.

VERAGVA PARS.

5
Shipbuilding in the New World; adapted from a drawing of
Noah's Ark by Sadeler, to illustrate the misadventures of Nicuesa.
From de Bry, *Grands Voyages*, Part IV, Frankfurt, 1594.

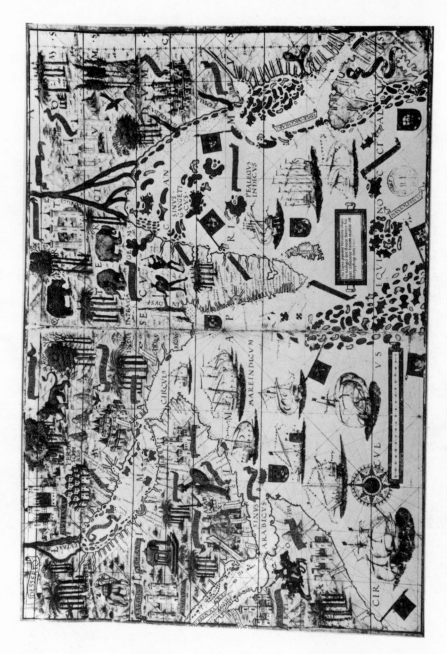

6
Map of the Indian
Ocean, MS, by Lopo
Homem, c. 1519, in
the Bibliothèque
Nationale, Paris,
from *Portugaliae
Monumenta Carto-
graphica*, Lisbon,
1960.

7
Small merchant ship, c. 1532, drawing by Holbein, from a print in the Science Museum.

8
The island of Tidore, from de Bry, *Petits Voyages*, Part VIII.

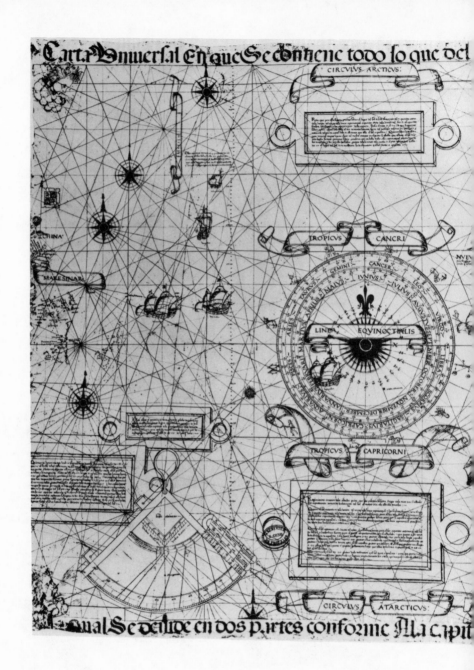

CIRCVLVS ARCTICVS

CHINA

MARE SINARE

TROPICVS CANCRI

NVEV

GEMINI

CANCER

TAVRVS

ARIES

MAIVS

ABRILE

MARÇIO

LINEA

IVNIVS

IVLIVS

EQVINOCTIALIS

AGOSTVS

SEPTEMBER

OCTOBER

LIBRA

NOVEMBER DETIEMBER IANARIO

CAPRICORNI

SAGITARIVS

AQVARIVS

TROPICVS CAPRICORNI

CIRCVLVS ATARCTICVS

9
World chart by Diogo Ribeiro, 1529, in the Vatican, from *Portugaliae Monumenta Cartographica*. (*Continued on following page*)

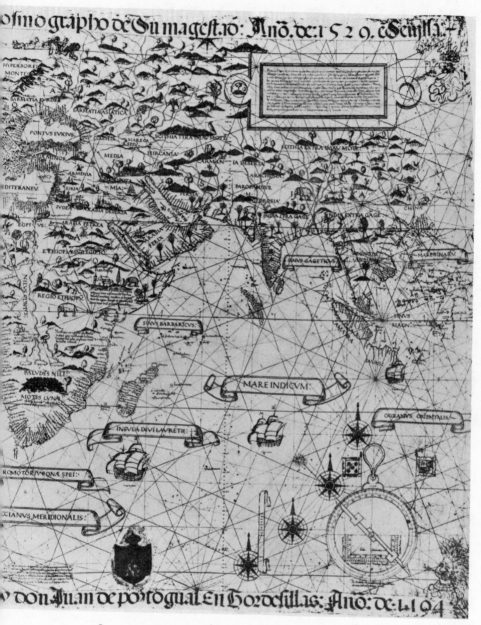

9
(*Continued*) World Chart by Diogo Ribeiro, 1529.

CHAPTER 11

ATLANTIC TRADE AND PIRACY

THE business of discovery in the fifteenth and early sixteenth centuries was cosmopolitan, if not international, in character. Renaissance princes patronized explorers and cartographers much as they patronized painters or goldsmiths, without much concern about their nationality. The explorers, for their part, drew upon a common fund of carto-graphical knowledge, maritime experience and geographical surmise; and the eager market for maps and for books on the subject ensured that knowledge of new discoveries quickly spread throughout Europe. When the discoveries, or some of them, began to offer promise of substantial profit, however, political and economic nationalism soon reasserted itself. Knowledge of discoveries might unavoidably become common property; but the commerce resulting from a discovery was always, as far as was practicable, maintained as a national monopoly, in keeping with the economic theory of the time which linked foreign trade closely with war as an instrument of national policy. Two large-scale oceanic trades, the westward trade of Spain and the eastward trade of Portugal, grew up in the sixteenth century, the one a private monopoly, the other a public monopoly, both national in character, established by governmental regulation and guarded by naval force. Much of the exploring activity of other nations during the century was inspired by the hope of breaking or circumventing one or other of these monopolies.

Of the two monopolies, that of Spain was the larger both in bulk and in value. Trans-Atlantic trade between Spain and Spanish America in the sixteenth century employed far more shipping and moved far more goods than the trade from Portugal to India—paradoxically, since the one served the needs of, at most, a few hundred thousand Spanish settlers, *mestizos* and Hispanicized Indians, while the other connected western Europe directly with the great populations of the East. But precisely because it was a colonial society, Spanish America, much more than the highly-developed societies of the East, was the economic complement of Europe. The settlers imported from Spain the goods they needed to maintain their Spanish mode of life in an American environment. They developed, to pay for these imports, a ranching, planting and mining economy, producing goods for sale in Europe. For their plantations they required slaves, and so created a market for a whole new trade with West Africa. Finally, in the middle of the sixteenth century they stumbled upon the richest silver mines in the world.

The great silver discoveries of the fifteen-forties encouraged a great increase in trans-Atlantic trade. The European population of the Spanish Indies mounted rapidly and its purchasing power increased more rapidly still. The demand for Andalusian wine and oil persisted, but outward cargoes included also a larger and larger proportion of more valuable manufactured goods—clothing, weapons, household utensils, glass, paper, books—which were not products of Andalusia nor even necessarily of Spain. Return cargoes, in addition to hides and sugar, included large and increasing quantities of bullion, chiefly silver, and also sundry luxury goods of American origin such as cacao, cochineal and tobacco, the use of which was spreading in Spain. The average annual tonnage sailing from Seville increased from 7,000 or 8,000 tons in the fifteen-forties to over 20,000 tons in the fifteen-eighties, representing perhaps one-tenth of the total shipping capacity of Spain. The peak year was 1608, with 45,000 tons.[1] The number of ships clearing from Seville varied greatly from year to year, but the annual average decade by decade, remained fairly steady, about 60 or 65, from 1550 to 1610. The average size of the ships, however, increased steadily, dictated by the needs of self-defence as well as by the interest of exporting merchants. Many small ships remained in the trade, including ships from the Canaries, which were allowed to sail to the Indies, and which carried much of the less lucrative trade in agricultural products to the smaller settlements; but on the other hand, the fleets in the later sixteenth century included many ships of over 600 tons, and in the seventeenth century ships of over 1,000 tons occasionally crossed the Atlantic.

The most productive mines and the most insistent markets throughout our period were in the viceroyalty of Peru, whose harbours were all on the Pacific coast, and virtually inaccessible to Atlantic commercial shipping. The passage of Magellan's Strait was slow and dangerous, and Tierra del Fuego was generally believed—at least until Drake's circumnavigation—to be part of a continent bounding the Pacific to the south. The discoverers of Peru had coasted south from Panama, and trade followed the same route. Goods from Europe were unloaded at Nombre de Dios or Puerto Bello on the Isthmus and sold to Peruvian merchants. They were lightered up the Chagres to its headwaters, and thence packed by mule train to Panama; loaded again into ships on the Pacific coast; landed at Callao and other Peruvian or Chilean harbours;

and then, if they were destined for inland towns such as Cuzco or Potosí, packed again over high and difficult mountain passes. There was another route from Europe, up the Río de la Plata and the Paraná into the heart of South America, and by mule train across Tucumán to Potosí. This back-door trade involved fewer transhipments and, being illicit, paid no duties; but it never became the main channel of supply, for good reasons. Official prohibition of the Río de la Plata trade was a minor reason; more important was the poverty of the immediate hinterland of the hamlet which, in 1583, became Buenos Aires; most important of all, for ships sailing from Spain, the difference in distance. In those days of small ships and slow passages, sheer distance mattered much more, portages and transhipments mattered much less than they do today, in all except very bulky trades. The trade in oriental goods via Cairo or Aleppo, as we have seen, survived by a hundred years or more the opening of the all-sea route to India. Similarly, trade via Panama, manufactured goods one way, silver the other, held its own in spite of the competition of the *peruleiros*.

Another reason for the long survival of the Isthmus trade was that it could draw upon the services of a considerable volume of shipping engaged in coastal trade between the two viceroyalties.[2] Both Mexico and Peru produced silver; it was their chief value in Spanish estimation. But Peru produced much more silver than Mexico, and in the sixteenth century produced little else, other than its bare subsistence needs. Civil wars, Indian revolts and the difficulties of the terrain combined to prevent the inter-penetration of Indian and European ways and the acquisition of European crafts by Indian artisans. The *conquistadores* in Peru remained a small Spanish community with a good deal of specie at their disposal and an avid desire for consumers' goods. In Mexico, on the other hand, Spanish and Indian communities quickly began to mingle and to fuse. Mexico was industrious and productive, and was relatively short of specie, because of the efficiency of silver-tax collection and the large private remittances made to Spain. From the fifteen-thirties it became profitable to import goods of Spanish origin from Mexico to Peru, to supplement the trickle of supplies across the Isthmus. With these transhipments went a much larger volume of Mexican products; mules, sugar, preserved fruit; European-type wares made in New Spain by Spanish or Indian craftsmen; and an assortment of Indian wares—polished obsidian mirrors, lacquered gourds, feather-work tapestry, and the like. The return cargoes were almost entirely silver, except for a period in the sixteen-sixties and -seventies when large shipments of quicksilver from the Huancavélica mine were sent to Mexico. The ships in the trade, or at least their hulls and spars, were built at Huatulco and other small ports on the coast of Tehuantepec, a region which produced not only timber but *pita* and *caguya* fibres from which rope could be made. Discarded sails and rigging from the *flotas*, and all necessary iron and brass fittings, were brought across from Vera Cruz. In the second half of the sixteenth century a shipbuilding industry also developed at Guayaquil. Some of the ships were as large as 200 or 250 tons, and a dozen or more might make the Mexico–Peru voyage in a year. Though built in Central America, they were mostly owned in Peru, whence came the capital to build them. From Callao they were sent to Panamá when a trans-Atlantic fleet was expected, at other times to Mexico.

Fed from these diverse sources, Spanish Atlantic trade grew and, to all appearance, prospered. It was, however, always hazardous. The employment of larger ships, beyond a point, gave no improvement in safety; on the contrary, the largest ships—unhandy, heavily armed, often overloaded—were more dangerous than those of moderate size, especially in the open harbours which the Indies fleets had to use. Among the most serious disasters were those of 1563—seven ships driven ashore at Nombre de Dios, fifteen wrecked in Cadiz harbour, five lost in the Gulf of Campeche; 1587—six ships grounded and broken up on the bar at San Lúcar; 1590—fifteen ships driven ashore by a 'norther' in Vera Cruz harbour; 1591—sixteen ships wrecked at Terceira; 1601—fourteen at Vera Cruz, again by a 'norther'; 1614—seven wrecked on Cape Catoche. Navigational errors caused many of these losses; but the frequency of groundings in familiar harbours also provides a significant comment on the handling qualities of the ships. Not all the lost ships were large, it is true, nor were all Spanish; for shipowners in the Indies trade often employed foreign-built ships, Flemish, Dutch or Portuguese, when they could get round the law. Nevertheless, the evidence is clear that in Spanish, as in Portuguese shipbuilding, size outran design.

Ships carrying valuable cargoes, by well-defined and predictable routes through the Caribbean and across the Atlantic, were in danger not only of shipwreck, but of attack by privateers in time of war, and pirates at any time. French privateers were active off the Azores and in the Caribbean from the fifteen-thirties; in 1556 a party of them landed in Cuba and sacked Havana; and down at least to the Treaty of Câteau-Cambrésis they constituted the principal danger to Spanish shipping. Increase in the size of merchant ships, again, was not an adequate answer, when the attackers carried artillery. The first tentative attempts at convoyed sailing were made in the fifteen-twenties. Regular convoys were organized during the war with France which broke out in 1542; and from the fifteen-sixties almost all shipping for the Indies, in peace or war, sailed in convoy. A fleet for New Spain was supposed to leave San Lúcar every May, and usually entered Caribbean waters by the Mona passage. Once inside the Caribbean, ships for Honduras and the Greater Antilles parted company; the main body passed south of Hispaniola and Cuba, through the Yucatán channel, across the Gulf to Vera Cruz. The Isthmus fleet left San Lúcar in August, and set a slightly more southerly course, passing through the Windward Islands. Some ships put into small harbours on the Main, but the main body anchored off Nombre de Dios (later Puerto Bello) where it unloaded goods for Peru and loaded silver. It then retired to the fortified and sheltered harbour of Cartagena. Both fleets normally wintered in the Indies. The Isthmus fleet began its return voyage in January, steering north-west—usually a comfortable reach with the wind on the starboard beam—until it could round Cape San Antonio and put into Havana. Meanwhile, the Mexico *flota* in February made its tedious three- or four-week beat against the trade wind from Vera Cruz, for a rendezvous at Havana in March. Havana guarded the only convenient exit from the Gulf of Mexico for sailing ships. The fleets refitted and victualled there, and endeavoured to sail in company for Spain in the early summer in order to get clear of tropical waters before the hurricane season. The fleets beat out through the Florida Channel—a tedious and dangerous stretch, with headwinds and with pirates lurking among the Bahama cays—and then stood to the north until they could pick up a westerly wind for the Atlantic crossing. Each convoy was escorted by armed galleons, from two to eight according to the international situation and the shipping available. These warships carried the royal silver, and often also carried trade goods on the private account of the captains-general and their staffs. On one occasion a flagship was reported to be so heavily loaded that her lower gun-ports were under water. On the whole, however, the system served its purpose. Reasonably regular sailings were maintained for a century and a half. Though stragglers were often captured, shipping in convoy was protected against mere pirates or individual privateers. Open attacks on convoys or on major harbours could only be undertaken by naval forces; and although during this period Spain was frequently at war with powerful maritime states, only on three occasions were whole convoys intercepted and defeated, once by the English and twice by the Dutch.

The main objection to the system was its expense. The cost of the escorts was met by a heavy additional duty on the goods carried. The unavoidable delays of convoy made the economical use of shipping impossible. The predatory activities of naval officers and fiscal functionaries intensified what a recent French writer aptly calls a 'psychosis of fraud', and added still further to the costs. High transport costs, heavy duties, restrictive regulations, chronic shortage of shipping, and the general failure of Spanish industry to expand in the later sixteenth century, together made it impossible to meet, from Spanish sources, the mounting demand for goods in Spanish America. The Indies formed a classic interlopers' market. The system designed, with considerable success, to deter pirates, offered an irresistible temptation to smugglers.

The earliest and most successful smugglers were Portuguese, who already from the early sixteenth century had a foothold on the South American coast. Portuguese trade to Brazil was comparatively free from restrictive regulation. In the early years, small settlements had been formed by brazil-wood cutters; but apart from the seasonal cutting, they served merely for watering fleets which occasionally called on the way to India, and for victualling slavers with cassava bread; later, a trade conducted through many small ports, scattered along two thousand miles of coast, defied regulation. Sugar, in keen demand in Europe, was the chief object of this trade. In the late sixteenth century and the first half of the seventeenth, the Brazilian plantations supplied most of the sugar consumed in Europe, and imported considerable quantities of manufactured goods, not only for the use of the few thousand Portuguese planters and settlers and their slaves, but also for illicit re-export to Spanish America. The *peruleiros*, the Brazilian smugglers, were well placed to use the back-door route which the Spaniards neglected. Goods were shipped from the southern ports of Brazil up the Río de la Plata, and carried by mules across the uplands of Tucumán to Potosí, even to Cuzco and Lima, where, not having paid Spanish customs or convoy duty, they competed with lawful imports via the Isthmus. These goods consisted chiefly of cloth and hardware which—since Portugal had little industry—came originally from northern Europe; and slaves.

The slave trade formed a commercial link between the Spanish and Portuguese empires long before the union of the Crowns. The Portuguese were the only Europeans in the sixteenth century who possessed barracoons in West Africa and maintained regular contacts with the slave-dealing rulers. Portuguese slavers not only supplied the Brazilian plantations; they were also, unofficially before 1580, openly thereafter, purveyors to the planters of the Spanish Caribbean, to the mines of New Spain, and by way of Buenos Aires to the mines of Potosí. Since slavers, with their perishable cargoes, could not be expected to wait for convoys, Portuguese contractors were licensed, by a series of *asientos* with the Spanish government, to sail directly from Lisbon to Spanish America. Many slavers went a step further, and sailed unlicensed from Guinea. The temptation to evade duties by shipping other, denser, goods along with the slaves was obvious. None of the regulations or *asientos* made by the Spanish Crown succeeded either in stopping smuggling or—because of the shortage of shipping—in ensuring an adequate supply of slaves.

The first foreigner who systematically exploited this opportunity was Sir John Hawkins.[3] During Mary's reign and the early years of Elizabeth the English were in a strong position to make a bid for peaceful trade with America. Relations between England and Spain were friendly. The Spanish government was even capable of using the offer of a share in the Indies trade as a political bargaining-counter. At worst, an English merchant would not be taken for a pirate on sight, as a Frenchman would have been. Of the two commodities most in demand in the Indies—cloth and slaves—the English produced the first and could purchase the second at the risk of a brush with the Portuguese authorities; a risk which they minded less and less as their sea-fighting strength increased. Hawkins had at least a reasonable hope of securing some sort of Spanish trading licence; he was no smuggler; he was prepared to pay all legal dues; in return for a licence he declared himself willing and able to assist the Spaniards in operations against Caribbean pirates, and in particular to destroy a troublesome settlement of French Huguenots which had established itself on the coast of Florida.

Rather than apply to the Spanish court and endure all the delays and prevarications which such an application would have involved, Hawkins proposed to embark on the Indies trade at once, and to prove his good intentions by his good works. In 1562 he set out on his first slaving voyage—a modest venture of three small ships, but brilliantly planned and executed. He called first at Tenerife, where through the good offices of a business acquaintance he signed on a Spanish pilot and sent word to possible purchasers in Hispaniola that he would be arriving later with a cargo of slaves. At Sierra Leone, his next call, he procured three hundred negroes, some kidnapped, some bought from Portuguese factors who subsequently complained to Queen Elizabeth that Hawkins had used force to compel them to sell. With this cargo, he sailed across the Atlantic to Hispaniola. Here, after much negotiation, he obtained from the local officials permission—which they had no authority to grant—to sell his slaves. He paid customs duty and licence fees, and even secured local testimonials to the effect that he had behaved correctly and engaged in peaceful trade. He accepted payment in hides and sugar, and chartered two extra ships in Hispaniola to get his cargoes home. The whole voyage made a handsome profit, and Hawkins at once began to plan a second voyage on a much bigger scale. In this undertaking the Queen and several of her Privy Council were shareholders, though naturally their participation was not made public.

On his second voyage Hawkins took his outward cargoes to the mainland ports of Venezuela and the Isthmus; and though he had some difficulty in persuading, or bullying, the local officials to permit trade, he again made a good profit. On his return to England, however, he heard that the Spaniards were doing for themselves what they would not allow Hawkins to do for them. The able and ruthless admiral, Menéndez de Avilés, had been appointed to the Indies, had destroyed the French settlement in Florida, and was busy tightening up the defence arrangements generally. Prosecutions had been started in Spain against the officials who had connived at Hawkins' visits. The Queen, determined to remain at peace with Spain, forbade Hawkins to return to the Indies; and though he sent out a third voyage under one of his captains, the results were poor. In 1567, Hawkins persuaded the Queen to let him command one last voyage in person; and this voyage ended in disaster. His ships were caught by bad weather, and ran for shelter to San Juan de Ulúa, the harbour of Vera Cruz, where they were trapped by the annual Spanish convoy, arriving several weeks before its expected date, with the new viceroy of New Spain on board. For the first time in his life Hawkins had to deal, not with Spanish colonials who were willing to evade the law in their own interests, but with high officials whose careers depended on maintaining the law. To the viceroy, Hawkins was a heretic pirate with whom no faith need be kept. Entering the harbour under cover of a pretended truce, the Spanish fleet sank or captured three of Hawkins' five ships. The other two, one commanded by Hawkins himself and one by his cousin, Francis Drake, eventually reached England in a sinking condition early in 1569.

The battle of San Juan de Ulúa was an important episode in that steady deterioration of Anglo-Spanish relations which culminated in the Armada. It made clear that there could be no hope of Spanish compromise over trade, much less over settlement in the New World. Smuggling went on, and there is no reason to suppose that the Spanish silver which continued to come to England was all the result of piracy. Open war did not break out until 1585. Nevertheless, from 1570 the Caribbean was the scene of an intermittent privateering war of which Drake was the central figure.[4] His first reprisal voyage of 1571 was a reconnaissance in which he obtained a few small prizes and a good deal of information about the Isthmus of Panama; and in which he established contact with French corsair captains and with communities of maroons, runaway negro slaves and their offspring by Indian women. With these allies he embarked in the following year on an ambitious plan for intercepting a Peruvian silver consignment at its most vulnerable point, on the long haul by mule-train across the Isthmus. Drake's preparations were in startling contrast to those favoured by

Hawkins and other more conservative commanders; his ships, although probably supplied by Hawkins, were small enough to operate close inshore and to be propelled by sweeps when becalmed. His men numbered only seventy-odd, too few, even with his allies, to seize the town of Nombre de Dios; but he ambushed and captured a mule-train laden with silver on the road, and got most of the booty back to his ships and home to England in the summer of 1573.

In 1574 Spain and England patched up a grudging and temporary reconciliation, and Drake's next employment, in 1577, was away from the Caribbean, on an ostensibly peaceful but still provocative mission, the famous voyage of circumnavigation. He was back in the Spanish Indies in 1585, when war with Spain was already certain. This expedition was no mere raid, but a full-scale naval operation by a fleet of more than twenty sail, mounted with the objects of taking and holding Cartagena and Havana and so paralysing the trans-Atlantic trade system of Spain; denying to Spain the silver which provided the means of making war in Europe; and throwing the Indies open to English exploitation. The operation achieved a partial success. Santo Domingo and Cartagena were taken and looted, but not held; Havana was judged too strong to be attacked; and the *flota* escaped interception. The damage to Spanish prestige was probably more lasting than the material damage to Spanish possessions. Philip II, though short of men, ships and money, was capable of learning from misfortune. In the fifteen-nineties the defence forces of the Indies were greatly strengthened both by land and by sea. The Morro at Havana and the walls of Cartagena were extended and a beginning was made by Antoneli, the best military engineer of his day, on the immense fortifications of Puerto Rico. When in 1595 another great armament left England, under the joint command of Drake and Hawkins, it was driven off successively from Puerto Rico, Cartagena and Puerto Bello. Drake and Hawkins both died during this voyage. Their successor in command, Baskerville, was intercepted by a Spanish fleet when homeward bound through the Florida Channel, and had some difficulty in fighting his way out.

The attempts made by the English and the French in the sixteenth century to break the Iberian monopoly of trade and territorial power in the Americas were thus, on the whole, failures; such successes as they achieved were either temporary or clandestine. Surprise raids sometimes yielded rich hauls; and smuggling was usually profitable, though always risky, and only possible at the smaller ports. More permanent results apparently could be achieved, if at all, only by a very formidable concentration of naval strength which could both defeat Spanish fleets and seize and hold Spanish bases; or alternatively—or additionally— the acquisition of territories, outside the immediate range of Spanish power, which might serve both as colonies of settlement producing tropical crops for export, and as naval bases and commercial depots. In 1596, at the Treaty of the Hague, France under Henry of Navarre, England and the Netherlands formed an alliance against Spain which seemed strong enough to dismember the Spanish empire. A joint English and Dutch fleet promptly destroyed a whole American convoy lying in Cadiz harbour, thus stopping communication between Spain and the Indies for nearly two years. The alliance failed to fulfil its promise, however; the French backed out and made their peace separately in the Treaty of Vervins in 1598. According to later accounts, Henry IV tried to secure a share of the American trade in this treaty, as his price for peace. There is no contemporary evidence of these attempts. If made at all, they were unsuccessful.

There remained the possibility of territorial acquisition. In 1604—the pacific James I having succeeded Elizabeth—England, like France, made a separate peace, the Treaty of London. In the negotiations for this treaty a new and important principle was put forward. James announced that he was willing to respect Spanish monopolistic claims in all territories effectively occupied by Spain, but that he recognized no Spanish rights in unoccupied parts of America. The claim that 'prescription without possession availeth nothing' of course contradicted the basic assumption of Spanish imperialism in the Indies, and it was only after considerable haggling that the Spaniards agreed to a silence which their enemies might interpret as consent. In the truce of Antwerp of 1609, which interrupted for twelve years the long war between the Netherlands and Spain, and which recognized the Dutch as an independent nation, the same principle was embodied in a formal, if ambiguous, clause.

The Dutch were more deeply committed than the French or the English to sea-borne commerce as a means of livelihood. They were already becoming the principal sea-carriers of the Atlantic coasts of Europe, and had already incurred in Spain a hostility so relentless that they had nothing to lose by an aggressive policy in America. Their intrusion into American trade had begun later than that of the English, but was on a much larger scale. Dutch smugglers began to appear off Brazil about 1587 selling cloth and slaves and buying sugar. Their share in this trade increased rapidly. They began to visit the harbours of the Greater Antilles about 1595. The first Dutch slaver recorded in the West Indies appeared off Trinidad in 1606. In 1608 their trade in hides and sugar from Cuba and Hispaniola was said to employ twenty ships annually. The commodity which first attracted Dutch shipping in force to the Caribbean, however, was salt. The Dutch used immense quantities of salt in their herring fishery, and were the principal carriers of salt to the rest of northern Europe. Most of the salt came from southern Portugal; and when this trade was interrupted by war, the Dutch salt merchants turned first to the Cape Verde Islands and then to the Caribbean, where they discovered and began to exploit the great salt deposits of Araya, near Cumaná in Venezuela. The Araya salt-pan is an enclosed lagoon, about eight miles long, surrounded by a vast encrustation of salt left by evaporation. It is one of the hottest and most desolate places in the world; but Dutch skippers anchored there for weeks at a time, and employed their own crews in breaking out and loading the hard lumps of salt. This point was noted by William Usselincx, the famous proponent of West Indian settlement, to prove that white men could do hard manual work in tropical conditions. An astonishingly large volume of shipping concentrated on Araya, despite losses inflicted from time to time by Spanish warships. According to the Spanish governor, from 1600 to 1606 his province was visited every year by over a hundred foreign ships, most of which were Dutch salt carriers of an average capacity of some 300 tons.[5] This was a total annual tonnage comparable with that of the combined official fleets from Seville to Mexico and Puerto Bello. The salt belonged to nobody and was never paid for; but the Dutchmen brought out cloth and hardware, which they sold along the Main and in the islands, and besides salt they took home island hides and sugar, Guiana tobacco and Margarita pearls. Many of them carried letters of marque, and were prepared to take goods by force if the owners refused to trade.

In 1609, with the truce, the old Setubal trade was resumed and the special reason for the Araya voyages disappeared. Dutch smugglers continued to operate in Brazil and in the Caribbean, however; and towards the end of the truce a series of events occurred in Europe which was to alter the whole aspect of affairs in those areas. In the United Provinces, Maurice of Nassau and the Orange party triumphed politically over the Republicans. The Grand Pensionary, Oldenbarneveldt, champion of Republican oligarchy and the East India interest, was executed in 1619. The twelve years' truce expired in 1621. The Dutch girded themselves for renewed war with Spain, and the West India Company, which Usselincx had advocated for years, received its formal charter. Here at last was an organization capable of challenging Spain in the West Indies—no mere temporary association of partners in smuggling or raiding, but a great permanent joint-stock corporation with adequate capital, with its own fleet of warships, and with the enthusiastic support of its home government.

The company's objects were plunder, commerce and conquest, and in the first two at least it achieved immediate and overwhelming success. Dutch fleets carried out sweeps in the Caribbean which practically

187

drove Spanish shipping from the sea. In 1628 Piet Heyn, ablest and most celebrated of the company's admirals, in command of a fleet of thirty-one sail, surprised and intercepted the homeward-bound *flota* off Matanzas Bay, and captured the whole sailing almost without firing a shot. This triumph, achieved for the first time and not to be repeated for thirty years, yielded booty worth fifteen million guilders, enough to pay a dividend of fifty per cent to the company's share-holders, and to finance a campaign of conquest in northern Brazil. It ruined Spanish credit in Europe. In the West Indies it paralysed for a time both communications and defence. It was followed by several years of systematic pillaging by smaller fleets. By 1630, except for the armed *flotas*—which by a miracle of determination continued their sailings—and for insignificant small craft, there was no Spanish shipping worthy of mention in the area. By 1640, even the official shipping between Seville and the Indies had shrunk to less than 10,000 tons annually. It continued to shrink throughout the rest of the century. With more efficient shipping, Dutch traders stepped in as carriers of the colonial trade of Spain and Portugal in the New World as they were already in the old, and Amsterdam became a market for logwood, cochineal, cacao and tobacco, for Peruvian silver and Brazilian sugar and gold, as it was for Eastern silk, cloves and pepper.

The Dutch were well aware that raiding would not pay indefinitely, and that a trans-Atlantic carrying trade would be difficult to maintain without permanent bases. The objects of the West India Company included conquest and settlement as well as trade. Between 1630 and 1640 the Dutch seized Curaçao, Saba, St Martin and St Eustatius, all of which were confirmed to them by the Treaty of Münster. These small crumbs of land were of value chiefly as trading and smuggling depots. Curaçao was the centre of Dutch power in the West Indies, and today is enormously prosperous both as a free port and as a refining centre for Venezuelan oil. Outside the Caribbean, the Dutch company settled New Amsterdam, modern New York, which offered easy access by way of the Hudson river to an immense forest area occupied by fur-trapping and trading tribes. New Amsterdam quickly became the centre of a lucrative export trade in beaver fur. The greatest Dutch effort, however, was concentrated on Brazil. Brazil had become, through the enterprise of Portuguese planters, the principal source of sugar for most of Europe. The sugar was produced on slave-worked plantations along the north-east coast. The Dutch proposed to seize for themselves not only the planted area of Brazil, but also the Portuguese slaving-stations in West Africa, without which the plantations were unworkable. Slaving interests, indeed, were prominent among the groups which worked for the establishment of the company and governed its policy.

The fortress at Elmina fell to the Dutch in 1637. In Brazil, the first Dutch assault, on Bahía in 1624, was defeated; but the attack was renewed in 1630, this time against Recife, and for over twenty years a long stretch of the Brazilian coast remained in Dutch hands.[6] Although the Portuguese eventually recovered their possessions in Brazil, the Dutch were able during this time to establish themselves as the principal suppliers of slaves not only to Spanish and Portuguese America, but also to the new English and French plantations which were growing up in the West Indies and on the North American mainland.

The Dutch were not the first northern Europeans to establish settlements in America in defiance of Spain. The English had anticipated them in Virginia and New England, the French and the English in the Caribbean. It was Dutch action in the Caribbean, however, which enabled these other settlements to take root and grow. Dutch victories strained the overtaxed resources of Spain almost to breaking point, and provided a naval screen behind which the English, the French, the Scots and the Danes, without much danger of Spanish interference, could build up their colonies in a long string down the Atlantic coast from Newfoundland to Barbados. These new colonies called new trades into being, by importing manufactures and producing exportable staples. Behind the organized fleets of the Dutch company operated a swarm of private Dutch merchants, more or less tolerated interlopers in the company's official preserve, picking up cargoes wherever they could find them, often in places too insignificant to be worth the company's attention. These enterprising poachers were ready to help settlers of any nationality with capital and with technical skill, to supply them with slaves and manufactured goods on long credit, and to buy their crops as soon as they had crops to sell. Every new colony in the Americas meant more cargoes for Dutch shipping as well as a blow against Spain. Dutch naval and economic strength therefore sheltered and encouraged the infant settlements of France and England, especially in the Caribbean. From envy of the Dutch, and eventually from rivalry with them, English and French governments learned a theory of mercantile imperialism which was to influence their policies of colonial settlement and trade for the next two hundred years.

CHAPTER 12

NEW ROUTES TO THE EAST

THE Portuguese secured fortified bases and a place in eastern commerce in the first two decades of the sixteenth century by the use of naval force; and naval power, particularly the superiority of European ship-borne artillery, enabled them to protect their trade against the attacks of oriental competitors. Goa, their Asian capital, was a naval base of considerable strength. It is an exaggeration, however, to speak of Portuguese 'domination' of eastern trade routes. They dominated the sea route from Europe to India, because for a hundred years they had no competitors; but in Asian waters they soon accepted the position of one among many groups of traders. They preyed on Muslim shipping in time of war, and from their strategic bases at Ormuz and Malacca they exacted duties from it in a somewhat erratic fashion in time of peace; but Arab shipping continued to cross the Indian Ocean, Chinese and Malay shipping to ply in the China and Java Seas. Portuguese merchants sometimes shipped goods in Chinese junks, and vice versa. The commercial success of the Portuguese was due not so much to naval strength—formidable though their ships were by eastern standards—as to the great diversity and geographical range of their activities. From the point of view of the 'grocer king' the Portuguese organization in the East had but one main function: the regular shipment to Lisbon of oriental spices. Of these spices, pepper was by far the most important in volume, but the cargoes also included finer and more expensive condiments and preservatives: cinnamon from Ceylon, nutmeg from the Banda Islands, camphor from Borneo, and, most valuable of all, cloves from Ternate and Tidore in the Moluccas. To pay for these cargoes, since Portugal had little of its own to offer, and little trading capital, a whole network of ancillary trades had to be developed.

The basis of this local commerce was the export trade in cotton textiles from the ports of Gujerat and Coromandel. These textiles found a ready sale in Indonesia, where they were exchanged for spices, and in East Africa where they were bartered for gold and ivory. The populations of all these regions provided as profitable a market for Indian piece-goods in those days as they have done in more modern times for the products of the looms of Manchester and Osaka. Equally profitable to the Portuguese was the acute demand in Japan for Chinese manufactured goods. Direct commerce between the two empires had been permanently forbidden by the Ming Emperor about 1480, because of the depredations of Japanese *Wako* pirates along the China coast. Smuggling no doubt went on; but in official trade the Portuguese, as intermediaries, held an important advantage. Although the annual Macao carracks had a shorter history than their more famous contemporaries, the Manila galleons—sixty years as against two hundred —they were no less profitable. Many of them were built in India of Malabar teak. Sailing from Goa by way of Malacca, they carried assorted European goods to the Portuguese settlement at Macao, where they loaded silk goods, raw silk, and porcelain purchased at Canton. These were sold at Nagasaki, the returns being made, as a rule, in silver bullion. Since the value of silver was higher in China than in Japan, a further profit could be made by exchanging silver for gold on return to Macao. The practice of sending one very large ship to Japan each year was abandoned in 1618, because of the danger of Dutch attack, but numbers of smaller and faster ships continued in the trade down to 1639. Silks were carried also from Macao to Macassar—a source of spices—and to Manila, where they were sold for Mexican silver. There were many other local trades: the sandalwood trade, for instance, between the China coast and the Lesser Sunda Islands; the slave trade, whether in African negroes or in Chinese and Japanese *muitsai*; the import to India of horses from Mesopotamia and copper from Arabia; the export from India to China and Japan of hawks, peacocks and even an occasional tiger. The Portuguese were the first world-wide traders. For over two hundred years Portuguese was the lingua franca of Asiatic maritime trade. Pidgin English had a predecessor in pidgin Portuguese.

The 'country trade' was far more extensive and probably far more profitable than the trade of the royal fleets which it helped to finance. Ironically these fleets, connecting Goa with Lisbon, formed the weakest link in the chain of empire. The Portuguese pioneers, lacking detailed geographical knowledge, had established their chief oriental base on the first coast they came to, the Malabar coast of India, which notoriously is deficient in sheltered harbours. Most of their other stations were on the ancient routes of Arab trade, on the north shores of the Indian Ocean. Their successors rarely entered the southern hemisphere except to round the Cape or to visit Timor or the Moluccas. Even in sailing to the China Sea and the Spice Islands, they took their departure from Goa and used the northern route long used by Malay shipping, through the sheltered waters of the Malacca Strait. Goa was both the economic and administrative centre of their organization and the terminus of the fleets. As at all the Malabar ports, the sailing traffic of Goa was governed by the alternation of north-east and south-west monsoons. For three months every winter ships could not, without some difficulty, approach Goa harbour, and for three months every summer they could not leave it. Malacca and Ormuz, the most important subsidiary stations, were cut off from Goa for long periods every year; the seasons during which spices could be brought to Goa for transhipment were restricted; and the sailing dates of the royal Indies fleets were fixed within narrow limits. They left Lisbon in March for an estimated arrival at Goa in September; they sailed from Goa in January or February for the direct run to the Cape, or in December for the longer but safer passage through the Mozambique Channel, in order to reach Lisbon in August or September. Failure to sail on time meant delays of many months, and might mean disaster on the way. The route had its dangers at all times: frequent heavy weather off the Cape, and corsairs off St Helena, the Cape Verde Islands and the Azores, especially after the union with Spain, when Portuguese shipping became fair game for Spain's enemies. Victualling stations—Brazil or Mozambique outward bound, St Helena or Luanda or the Azores homeward —were many weeks apart, so that the dangers of hunger and thirst, scurvy and dirt-borne infections were always present, health was precarious and mortality high.

The fleets which made these hazardous passages were small, rarely more than five or six sail, sometimes only one or two; but the ships which composed them were very large. They were carracks of Mediterranean type, built for maximum cargo capacity rather than for fighting or sea-keeping qualities. A small fleet of very large ships was cheaper to build than the equivalent tonnage in smaller ships—a major consideration in Portugal, where timber was scarce and construction costs high. In theory, also, such a fleet was more economical to man and operate, on a regular fixed run with predictable cargoes. In practice the *naos da Carreira da India* grew too large for safety, without any corresponding improvement in construction or design. In order to reduce costs, maintenance work on them was scamped. In order to increase profits, they were over-loaded, and over-loading was made worse by the private ventures of officers and men. They were always short of trained seamen; and to make good the shortage of men caused by tropical mortality, untrained hands had to be signed on in Indian ports for the return voyages. In the second half of the sixteenth century about one sailing in every six ended in disaster.[1] At best, the quantity of spices which these ships carried was insufficient to meet the European demand, even when added to the trade which persisted through the Levant. Except for local and temporary gluts, the price of spices remained high. The temptation to the interloper was as great at the end of the sixteenth century as it had been at the end of the fifteenth.

The discovery of a sea route to India, like the discovery of America, caught the imagination of the reading public all over Europe, and books about the East were in keen demand throughout the sixteenth century. In Portugal itself the eastern empire was recognized as a major national achievement. The deeds of the pioneers became a central theme in Portuguese literature, commemorated in a stately series of prose Annals, as well as in the noble verse of Camoens, who himself spent seventeen adventurous years in the East. Outside Portugal, interest concentrated chiefly upon descriptions and narratives of travel. The Portuguese government, as is well known, maintained a policy of official secrecy on eastern trade and navigation, and on the whole succeeded in keeping essential charts and sailing directions out of general circulation; but it could not control the publication of travellers' reminiscences, and these appeared in increasing number and variety. One of the earliest and most interesting was the *Itinerario* of Ludovico di Varthema,[2] a Venetian who travelled to the East by way of the Red Sea in 1502 and returned round the Cape in a Portuguese ship in 1507. Love of adventure and of travel for its own sake appeared to be his principal motive. His exploits included a pilgrimage to Mecca; a sojourn in Persia; visits to the principal cities of south India, including Vijayanagar, near the close of its glory, Goa a few years before the arrival of the Portuguese, and Calicut just after their arrival; and a voyage to Malacca and some of the Indonesian islands. Varthema gives a graphic account of the sharp decline in the trade of Calicut, consequent upon Portuguese depredations. His exciting, and on the whole convincing narrative was published in 1510, enjoyed an immediate success, and went through many editions all over Europe. The more pedestrian and more detailed *Book* of Duarte Barbosa,[3] describing the Portuguese stations in the Indian Ocean and their trade, was completed in 1516, though its first publication was in 1550, in the first volume of Ramusio's *Navigazioni e viaggi*.[4] The extraordinary travels of Fernão Mendes ('Mendax') Pinto, soldier, merchant, doctor, missionary and ambassador, covered Abyssinia, Ormuz, India, Sumatra, China and Japan between the years 1537 and 1558, though his *Peregrinaçam* was not published until 1614, in Lisbon. Pinto's tale has a strong Arabian Nights flavour, and his veracity is suspect, but his adventures caused a great stir at the time. In 1583 an English party led by John Newbery and Ralph Fitch were sent on a commercial reconnaissance overland to the East, bearing letters from Queen Elizabeth to the Emperor of China. Newbery died in the East. Fitch was captured by the Portuguese at Ormuz and spent some time in captivity at Goa. Escaping from there, he visited Akbar's court near Agra, found his way to the capital of the Burmese kingdom at Pegu, thence to Malacca, and back by way of Bengal and Cochin. He returned home in 1591. His account, published in the second edition of Hakluyt's *Principal Navigations*, set all London talking of Portuguese misrule and the wealth of the Indies trade. More important than Fitch was the Dutchman Jan Huyghen van Linschoten, who—though a staunch Calvinist—lived in India from 1583 to 1589 as a dependant of the Archbishop of Goa. Linschoten returned to Holland, and in 1595–6 published his *Itinerario*, a geographical description of the world, including the author's personal observations of the East and a series of sailing directions for reaching America and India.[5] This work contained a series of distinguished charts, especially of Africa, India and the East Indies, based on Portuguese charts drawn by Vaz Dourado and Bartolomeu Lasso. It became a best-seller in several languages and supplied a direct impulse for the foundation of the Dutch and English East India Companies. None of these books, except the last, provided foreigners with detailed practical information on how to get to the East; but their descriptions of the court of the Great Mogul at Agra, of the lavish Burmese metropolis of Pegu with its ten thousand elephants, of the brilliant hybrid Portuguese capital at Goa, all appealed strongly to the Renaissance imagination. Books such as these—for there were many more—served to maintain public interest in attempts to break into the Portuguese monopoly of direct oriental trade by sea.

The first Europeans, other than Portuguese, who succeeded in establishing regular trade with a part of the extreme East were the Spanish adventurers who from 1564 settled in the Philippines. These islands, first discovered by Magellan, lay on the Portuguese side of the arbitrary line established by the Treaty of Zaragoza, but the Portuguese had never shown much interest in them, and made only ineffectual protests when Miguel López de Legazpi sailed from Mexico and, by a well-organized and almost bloodless conquest, established himself first in Cebu, then in Manila. The Portuguese spice trade at that time was in serious difficulties arising from the political situation in the Indian Ocean area, and a new route to the Far East offered even more attractions than usual. The project of opening a spice trade with the Moluccas by way of the Philippines and Mexico, however, produced an immediate and jealous Portuguese reaction, and was dropped. Legazpi himself suggested the alternative of a trade in silk, which could be bought readily from Chinese junks frequenting Manila. Over the next thirty years the jealousy of the Portuguese changed to a willing naval and commercial co-operation. The Spanish settlement at Manila became a principal market for the merchants of Macao, who sold Canton silk for American silver, and soon controlled a large part of the business of the Philippines. When in the seventeenth century the Portuguese lost their access to Japan, and when the Dutch closed the Malacca Strait against them, the Manila trade helped to save Macao from commercial extinction.

The trans-Pacific trade established direct contact between a society in which silver was in high demand and one where it was plentiful and cheap. The Spaniards were able, therefore, to buy silk in Manila at prices which justified an appallingly long and hazardous voyage between two very hot and unhealthy places. Acapulco, the Mexican terminus, like Vera Cruz and Puerto Bello, was only occupied when the galleons were in. For the rest of the year its population moved to higher and healthier ground. From Acapulco to Manila was a trade-wind run of eight or ten weeks. As in the Atlantic, the return passage was the dangerous one. The only safe west–east routes across the Pacific are in middle latitudes. The Manila galleons used the route pioneered by Andrés de Urdaneta in 1565. After leaving Manila they spent about two months struggling north-eastward in a region of normally light and variable winds but subject to frequent typhoons. This was the worst region of shipwreck. In the forties of north latitude a wind could usually be found which would take the ships to the coast of California and thence south-east to Acapulco. The whole return voyage took from four to seven months, and on the longer passages hunger, thirst and scurvy always took a heavy toll of the ships' companies. The ships used in the trade were mostly built in the Philippines, of local teak by European designers and local craftsmen. They had the reputation of the strongest and most durable ships in the world.

In the later sixteenth century much of the silk landed at Acapulco was packed across Mexico and re-exported from Vera Cruz to Spain, so insistent was the European demand for silk and so inadequate the supply. Still larger quantities were transhipped coastwise from Acapulco to Peru, since the Pacific winds prevented direct passage from the Philippines to Peru. In the peak year, 1597, the amount of bullion sent from Acapulco to Manila, 12,000,000 *pesos*, approached the total value of the official trans-Atlantic trade. In the seventeenth century the trade declined sharply. Silk brought to Europe by so long and complex a route could not compete with the increasing quantity, both Chinese and Persian, imported into Europe by the Dutch, and about 1640 shipments from Mexico to Spain ceased. As for the trade to Peru, it had always been disliked in Spanish official circles, because it diverted Peruvian silver to the specie-hungry Orient, and because it flooded Peru with Chinese goods, and spoiled the market for textiles from Spain. Peruvian silver production also was declining. From 1631 trade between the viceroyalties was forbidden. The trans-Pacific trade shrank to the volume which Mexico alone could absorb. The Manila galleons, nevertheless, continued their hazardous but always profitable sailings to the end of the eighteenth century. Manila remained all this time the meeting-ground, half way round the world, of the heirs of Columbus and Vasco da Gama; a triumph of maritime communication in defiance of probability.

One other attempt to open a trans-Pacific route to Asia calls for notice: Drake's voyage of circumnavigation. The original purposes of this famous voyage have remained obscure. They probably did not include a search for *Terra Australis*, a visit to the Moluccas, a circumnavigation; they may have included a search for the "Strait of Anian"; they did include a coastal reconnaissance of southern South America. Like Magellan, Drake sailed with five ships, and like him had to suppress a mutiny in St Julian Bay. He broke up his store-ships there, and made, for the time, a very rapid passage of the Strait—only sixteen days. He then explored the west coast of Tierra del Fuego—or was driven along it by the weather—and found no continent, but only rocky islands and a great expanse of wild sea. He may have sighted Cape Horn; though that Cape was not named or described until 1616, by Schouten and Le Maire. Whatever Drake's intentions about the Moluccas, the wind off Tierra del Fuego must have convinced him that there was no crossing the Pacific from east to west in that latitude. One of his ships foundered off the coast and another, under John Winter, lost company and eventually, after waiting some time in the Strait, returned to England. Drake in the *Pelican* set off on a highly successful privateering cruise up the coast of Chile and Peru. He sailed north at least as far as the Californian coast, careened his ship there, sailed with the trade wind across the Pacific, found the Moluccas, loaded with spices at Ternate, and then followed del Cano's track back to Europe. Like del Cano, he arrived home with one ship surviving out of five; but with her company in good heart and a valuable treasure in her hold.

Drake's discovery of open water south of Cape Horn had no immediate practical results. The Strait was dangerous enough; Cape Horn, for the ships of the time, was worse. They were too leewardly to beat safely against the violent west winds off the Cape, and too small and too heavily manned to carry stores for so long a continuous voyage. The passage of the Strait did at least offer an opportunity to kill and salt sea-birds for victualling ship. Drake's depredations off Peru, however, shook the confidence of the Spaniards in their monopoly of Pacific navigation, and probably discouraged them from further extensions of their Asian trade. Finally, though Drake's voyage established no regular eastern trade with northern Europe, at least it revealed that the Portuguese, far from being masters of the East, were defending immensely long trade routes and widely scattered strongholds against a host of jealous enemies.

While Drake was exploring the south-west passage to Asia, Frobisher was searching for a possible passage to the north-west. All the northern maritime nations in the sixteenth century made attempts to find passages to Asia either round northern Europe or through or round northern America. All the attempts failed in their main purpose, though they had other results to which we shall have to return. In the fifteen-nineties, however, the need for contact with the East acquired a new urgency. The union of the Spanish and Portuguese crowns had included Portugal in the hatred and fear with which the Protestant nations by then regarded Spain. Portugal was a potential enemy at home and a potential victim abroad. The outbreak of war had removed the diplomatic obstacles to an open policy of dismemberment, or at least of intrusion and plunder. Economic events pointed the same way. The revolt in the Low Countries interfered with trade between Portugal and Antwerp and interrupted the supply of spices, of which the Dutch had been the distributors throughout northern Europe. The ships of the English Levant Company, which had been bringing considerable quantities of eastern goods from the Syrian ports by virtue of a treaty with the Ottoman Sultan in 1579, now found that their passage through the Straits of Gibraltar was disputed by Spanish and Portuguese men-of-war. Both politically and economically the time appeared ripe for an attempt on the East Indies trade by the route which the Portuguese used, or by some variant of it, rather than by some doubtful and hazardous Arctic passage.

Queen Elizabeth first gave her consent to a direct intrusion in the Indies trade by the Cape route in 1591. The expedition of Raymond and Lancaster in that year was a costly experiment, since two of the three ships were lost. The third reached Malaya and Ceylon and returned to England, after many buffetings, with a cargo of pepper but only twenty-five survivors.[6] Tip-and-run voyages of this sort, which had achieved considerable success in clandestine trade with the West Indies, were inadequate to capture trade in the East; a more permanent organization, furnished with adequate capital, was required. In 1600 the East India Company of London received its charter, and in 1601 made its first voyage, again under Lancaster. This venture was highly successful. Lancaster bought a full cargo of pepper at Bantam, and captured a Portuguese carrack on the way. The company, however, was a very modest concern, with a separate joint-stock for each voyage. The Dutch, meanwhile, set about capturing eastern trade in a more thorough fashion and on a much larger scale. A number of private partnerships, from 1595, sent out commercial expeditions. In 1602, in order to avoid competition between these groups and to create a buying monopoly, and in order to strengthen the hands of Dutch commanders in treating with local rulers and fighting the Portuguese, the States General in its turn amalgamated the eastern traders into one great national concern, the Dutch East India Company.[7]

The Portuguese, as might be expected, always had difficulty in manning their Indies fleets and took seamen where they could get them—Lascars, Scandinavians, Englishmen, Dutchmen. The Dutch were well informed on Portuguese shipping routes in the East, therefore, not only as distributors of spices and providers of shipbuilding capital in Europe, not only through writings such as Linschoten's *Itinerario*— essential though that book was to them—but also through the personal experience of sailors. The groups of Dutch adventurers who began voyages to the East on their own account in 1595, and who in 1602 coalesced in the East India Company, made a radical and deliberate departure from Portuguese practice by leaving India on their flank and establishing direct contact with the Indonesian sources of spices. It was a fixed principle of Dutch commercial policy to go behind the middleman where possible; and prudence initially suggested that fleets intended for trade should keep well clear of Goa and Malacca. The Dutch, therefore, from an early date used the alternative entrance to the Java Sea, through the Sunda Strait, which lies south of the monsoon latitudes and in the belt of the south-east trade winds, and is difficult of access for a sailing ship approaching from the west or north-west, but readily accessible at all times of year to ships coming from the south. In sailing direct from the Cape to the Sunda Strait they soon discovered the cardinal principle of navigation in the southern Indian Ocean—that of 'running the easting down' in the thirties or forties of south latitude, before shaping north to catch the trade wind for Java or India; a principle which held until the last days of sail. Such a course had its dangers. It demanded seaworthy ships; and in a time when chronometers were unknown and longitude was computed by dead-reckoning and guesswork, a ship might drive too far east. The west coast of Australia, though in lesser degree, became in time a graveyard for Dutch Indiamen, as the shore of Natal was for the Portuguese. The southerly course also posed trading problems. Ships sailing directly to the East Indies, unsupported by a network of local trade, unless they were to export large quantities of bullion, must offer goods of European origin acceptable in the Indonesian market. The Dutch, with industrial towns at their back door in Europe, solved this problem by carrying cargoes of German manufactures—helmets, armour, fire-arms, linen, velvet, glass, and a range of ingenious toys compendiously called *norembergerie*.

In the five years 1598-1602 fifty–one ships left the Netherlands for the East. With the exception of one fleet of nine sail, which attempted the western route by way of Magellan's Strait and by a series of misfortunes became an almost total loss, all these expeditions were successful as navigational experiments, and most were moderately profitable—one very profitable—as trading ventures. The fleet commanded by Jacob van Neck in 1598-9 reached the Moluccas, loaded spices, and returned to its home port in fourteen months, a remarkable turn-round. The United Company, in the first four years of its existence, sent out some fifty ships, all armed for fighting, and although several were destroyed or severely damaged by enemy action, only two were lost in other ways. Like the Portuguese, the Dutch grew more careless as time went on, but the ships which they employed were better suited to their tasks, and more efficiently and economically operated, than Portuguese carracks. The Dutch extended to the East the policy of operating large numbers of medium-sized ships, which had served them well in Europe. As the seventeenth century progressed, the Dutch built bigger Indiamen, but the increase in size was kept well within the bounds of operating efficiency. By 1670 about a hundred ships were regularly employed between the Netherlands and the East Indies, mostly of about 600 tons[8]—much the largest class of merchant ships in Dutch possession, but still smaller than the sluggish leviathans of the *Carreira da India* fifty years earlier.

From its foundation the Dutch company possessed greater resources in money and ships than were commanded by the Portuguese Crown or the English company. In 1619 that far-sighted seaman, Jan Pieterszoon Coen, established at Batavia a fortified base to windward of Goa and Malacca, which gave the Dutch fleets a permanent strategic initiative. He and his successors used their advantage deliberately to eliminate buyers' competition and to establish as nearly as possible a monopoly. They sought first to capture the 'country trade' from the Portuguese by the forcible seizure of their factories, and to stop, by blockade or capture, the long-haul trade between Portugal and India; then to exclude other traders, European or Asian, from the most remunerative trades of the archipelago; and finally to reduce to vassalage the rulers of the chief spice-producing areas, in order to control production and prices in the Dutch interest. What the Dutch left, the English snapped up. Of the chief Portuguese fortresses, Ormuz was taken by Shah Abbas, with the help of an English fleet, in 1623. The trade which it controlled was already drying up, and the place soon became a mere village. Malacca, after many attacks and counter-attacks and eleven years of blockade, was taken by the Dutch in 1641, and similarly left to decay. The trade which it had handled went to Batavia. The Portuguese factories in Ceylon and South India were mostly taken by the Dutch. Goa was never captured, but a Dutch fleet blockaded it for eight successive winters from 1637 to 1645, the monsoon in summer maintaining a natural blockade. Much of its export trade was directed to other ports under Dutch or English control. The chief native centres of Indonesian trade, Atjeh, Macassar and others, suffered a like fate, their rulers undertaking after defeat to restrict their seafaring subjects to trade in rice and similar necessities, except with the company's permission. English traders, the strongest European competitors, were driven from most of their stations in the archipelago in the sixteen-twenties; and many of the spice-producing islands—Amboina, Ternate, the Banda Islands—were brought under direct Dutch control, either by outright conquest or by foreclosure on trading debts.

The naval aggressiveness and commercial enterprise of the Dutch in the seventeenth century worked a major revolution in the trade system of the Indian Ocean and adjacent waters. A great volume of trade deserted the northern half of the ocean for the southern. The Red Sea and the Persian Gulf gradually became commercial backwaters. Their ports, and those of East Africa, cut off from the valuable products of the Far East, subsisted largely on a local trade in slaves and dates. Their decline was accelerated by the depredations of the Sultan of Muscat, who, after the eviction of the Portuguese from Ormuz and Muscat itself, had become the principal naval power on that coast. The only harbour immune from his rapacity was the Dutch trading post at Bandar Abbas. Similarly, the Malacca Strait lost much of its former importance and for a time was almost deserted by European shipping. Trade between south-east Asia and Europe went from Batavia to the Cape south of the equator all the way. In 1652 the Dutch colony at the Cape was established for the convenience of this trade. Even trade with India followed, as far as possible, a southerly route. By mid-century, Indian Ocean trade had become fixed in routes it was to follow for more than two hundred years. The square sail had triumphed over the lateen, the trade wind over the monsoon.

Although the intentions of the Dutch were chiefly commercial, their voyages added greatly to European geographical knowledge. The sixteenth-century world maps of Mercator and Ortelius, still influenced by Ptolemy, had marked a vast continuous land mass separated by straits from South Africa and South America. Drake's voyage reduced the size of this imaginary continent. In the seventeenth century, east-bound Indiamen found thousands of miles of open water in the thirties and forties of south latitude. *Terra Australis* retreated to the southern extremity of some maps and disappeared entirely from others. The real Australia was discovered as an incidental result of Dutch expansion.[9] It was probably unknown to Europeans until a series of captains, mostly Dutch, chanced upon its coasts in the early years of the century. William Janszoon touched the coasts of New Guinea and north-eastern Australia in 1606, but thought them parts of the same land mass. The first navigator to use the Torres Strait between Australia and New Guinea—without, however, appreciating the nature of the discovery—was the Spaniard who gave his name to the strait, also in 1606. Two other Dutchmen, Hartogszoon and Houtman, in 1616 and 1619, discovered and explored part of the coast of south-western Australia. In 1642, under the governorship-general of van Diemen, Abel Tasman sailed from Batavia to Mauritius, thence round Australia, along the north coast of New Guinea and back to Batavia by way of the Macassar Strait. Tasman discovered Tasmania and New Zealand. He never actually sighted the coasts of Australia on this voyage; but his discoveries set limits to the area in which the continent might be found. The coasts discovered by these Dutchmen, however, all appeared unattractive and unpromising to the officials of a trading corporation, and the East India Company was unwilling to finance geographical exploration for its own sake. The systematic exploration of Australian waters was left to Cook and his successors, more than a century later.

The most vivid illustration of the spread of European, and especially Dutch, sea power is to be found in the modifications of native shipping in the Indian Ocean. European ships were not necessarily more efficient than native ones for purposes of local trade, but local owners often found it prudent to make their ships as European as possible in appearance. *Baghla, khotia* and *ganja* acquired high transom sterns, carved and gilded in imitation of seventeenth-century Indiamen. Until very recent years native ships could sometimes still be seen with dummy gun-ports painted along their sides. The Portuguese, the Dutch and the English all established dockyards in the East and introduced European methods of fastening. In rig, the Arabs stuck to their traditional lateen, but other builders began to produce square-rigged types, notably the trim brigs and brigantines of the Maldive Islands, which still regularly make the passage to Colombo. Sailing ships still carry a considerable volume of trade in the Indian Ocean, and some of the smaller ports are living museums, full of small-scale models of the types of ship which fastened the grip of European armed commerce on the eastern seas in the seventeenth century.

We must now turn back a little in time and notice briefly the exploits of the explorers who sought new routes to the East and failed to find them. In the first half of the sixteenth century the great rivers which seemed to offer hope of passages to the Pacific were one by one investigated and—with the partial exception of the insignificant Chagres—found hopeless. Solís found the estuary of the Río de la Plata in 1515, and in 1527 Sebastian Cabot explored the river in some detail as far as the Apipe rapids in the Paraná; but these discoveries brought early profit to no one save the *peruleiros* and their customers in Upper Peru. In 1524 Verrazano, in the service of the King of France, made the first recorded voyage along the eastern seaboard of North America between Florida and Cape Cod, and explored the mouth of the Hudson. He returned with a report of a narrow neck of land between Atlantic and Pacific, which influenced some contemporary maps, but which later exploration proved false. The French government persevered, however, and Cartier's expeditions of 1534 and 1535 were made at royal expense.[10] Cartier was one of the ablest and most thorough, as well as one of the most intrepid of sixteenth-century explorers. In 1534 he sailed from St Malo to Cape Bonavista and made a careful investigation of the north coast of Newfoundland; sailed through the Strait of Belle Isle and, despite constant dangers from ice, examined both the Labrador and Newfoundland shores of the strait; and explored the Gulf of St Lawrence as far as the western shore of Anticosti Island. The following year Cartier sailed boldly up the St Lawrence as far as ships could go, to the Lachine Rapids near where Montreal was later to be built, and diligently collected native information which showed the St Lawrence to be a river and not a strait. He and his people wintered up the river, and suffered the inevitable hardships of cold and scurvy; though they relieved the disease to some extent by drinking an infusion of the leaves of a tree—probably hemlock—which the Indians showed them. The following spring they returned, by way of Anticosti, Cape Breton and Cape Race, to St Malo. The whole voyage was a very notable achievement.

The French was the first northern government to make serious plans for permanent settlement in unoccupied parts of the Americas, both as an end in itself and as a means of furthering future voyages to the East. Cartier, despite his disappointment over the strait and his bitter winter experience, took good note of Indian cultivation and reported the evident fertility of the soil in the lower St Lawrence basin. His third voyage in 1541, again under royal auspices, had colonization as its object. The Huguenot Roberval, was sent out as governor, with instructions to establish a settlement, to convert the natives to Christianity, and to pursue the search for a strait. Several hundred men and women emigrated to the new colony of Charlebourg Royale; but neither French experience nor available French resources were yet adequate for such a venture, and the survivors soon returned to France. This first attempt at settlement in the north parts of America failed as completely—though not as inevitably—as the search for the strait.

If not the St Lawrence, then perhaps further north; to navigators and geographical theorists who habitually used globes, it seemed obvious that there should be a more direct route to China across the Arctic than round the Cape of Good Hope. Most sixteenth-century maps show the Arctic as open sea, with large but widely separated islands. Little was then known of the vast extent of the northern ice cap. Seamen argued that the Tropics had proved passable, contrary to all expectations; why not the Arctic? A considerable number of voyages were planned in England, and financed by special syndicates in the second half of the sixteenth century, to search for passages either to the north-west or the north-east. Of the two, the north-west had the weightier support from both ancient and modern geographers. Sir Humphrey Gilbert's persuasive *Discourse* on the subject gives an impressive list of authorities.[11] The actual search, which began with Frobisher's first voyage in 1576, was another story of heroism, of failure in its main purpose, and, later, of successful results in unexpected directions.[12] Frobisher claimed to have found a strait; in fact the deep inlet now known as Frobisher Bay. He also found quantities of a dense and heavy black rock, which he and others believed to be gold ore. Frobisher made two more voyages to the same region, and his third voyage, like that of Cartier, was intended to establish a colony; but the colony was not planted, the strait was not found, and the gold content of the 'ore' was too small to repay the cost of extraction.

Frobisher's work was continued—unhampered by gold strikes or colonizing plans—by John Davis who was a neighbour and associate of the Gilberts and who made his exploring voyages under a licence granted to Adrian Gilbert. His attention was chiefly concentrated on the sea which separates Greenland from the North American archipelago. Davis was one of the most distinguished seamen of his time, a great experimenter and designer of instruments, the author of one of the best and most original sixteenth-century navigation manuals, *The Seaman's Secrets*. He also wrote a book on the north-west passage, *The Worldes Hydrographical Description*, and his influence can be seen in Hakluyt's 'new map' and in the beautiful Molyneux globes. The development of a characteristically English school of navigators was largely the result of interest in the north-west passage, and Davis largely determined its character. He added greatly to knowledge of Arctic seas, and had the distinction of seeking the passage in the direction where, but for the ice, it might have been found.[13] Next in time was Henry Hudson, who in 1609, on a voyage in the service of the Netherlands government, had explored the river which bears his name as far as modern Albany. On his last voyage in 1610 he penetrated the Hudson Strait. The strait itself was not a new discovery—both Frobisher and Davis had noted its entrance—but Hudson was the first to sail through it and into the great bay beyond. He was spared the disappointment of learning later that this was not the South Sea, because his company, after suffering great hardships through wintering on the shore of the bay, mutinied and set Hudson adrift in a small boat to die of exposure. The mutineers, with difficulty, made their way back to England, and spread about an edited version of their adventures from which the conclusion was generally drawn that Hudson had succeeded in his search. In 1612 the men who had financed his voyage secured incorporation as the 'Company of the Merchants of London Discoverers of the North-West Passage'; and in this capacity sent out a series of expeditions to complete Hudson's work and open trade across the South Sea. For the next twenty years captains employed by the company engaged in fruitless—or apparently fruitless—exploration of the shores of Hudson's Bay and Baffin Bay.[14] All these men—Bylot, Baffin, Button, Foxe, James—are commemorated in the names of capes, bays and islands in Arctic America. Apart from the increase of geographical knowledge, the chief practical result of their work was the discovery, in Hudson's Strait and Bay, of a back door to the richest fur-producing region in the world, a region which otherwise would have been monopolized by the French. In the later seventeenth century this vast and lonely Arctic bay was to carry an adventurous and profitable trade, and to become a hotly contested international waterway.

The search for a north-west passage, except for Cartier, was largely an English enterprise. The corresponding search in the north-east was, in its later stages, the work of Dutchmen and Danes, but it was initiated by an English company and Englishmen played a considerable part in it. 'The company of merchant adventurers for discovery of regions, dominions, islands and places unknown' had as its first Master old Sebastian Cabot who, though born in England, had been pilot-major of Spain, and who survived as a living link between the maritime Renaissance of the Mediterranean and the Elizabethan seamen. Cabot lived in the memory of his father's achievements. After his own disappointments in the north-west and in the Río de la Plata, he was determined in old age to see the north-east explored. In 1553 the company dispatched a fleet of three ships under Sir Hugh Willoughby with the express intention of sailing to China by way of a north-east passage.[15] The names of the ships are worth mentioning for their gallant though misplaced optimism. They were the *Bona Speranza*, the *Bona Confidenza* and the *Edward Bonaventura*. Off the Lofoten Islands the ships were separated by a storm. Two of them, including Willoughby's flagship, put into an inlet somewhere near North Cape. There they were frozen in and all their company died of cold and starvation. The *Edward*, however, commanded by the senior navigator, Richard Chancellor, entered the White Sea and reached Archangel. There Chancellor learned for the first time of the power and wealth of the Russian emperor, and after long haggling with the local people, he and some of his officers set off on an astonishing journey in horse-drawn sleighs, in winter, from Archangel to Moscow.

Russia at that time was almost completely isolated from other civilized countries. It was hemmed in by nomad peoples to the south and east; it was allowed no intercourse with militant Catholic Poland to the west, and its only seaboard, to the north, was ice-bound for much of every year. Within this isolation, Ivan the Terrible and his predecessor had achieved a considerable measure of order and national unity throughout Great Russia. His kingdom had its own channels of supply of oriental goods, by way of the great rivers which flow into the Black Sea and the Caspian, but its only contact with Europe was through the ships of the North German Hanse. As it happened, relations with the Hanse towns had been broken off shortly before Chancellor's arrival for political reasons, and Moscow was suffering from the consequent shortage of imported manufactured goods, in particular woollen cloth, and, above all, arms of all kinds. England produced these things, and was also a steady market for furs, hemp and tallow, which Russia produced. For these reasons the English adventurers were doubly welcome, as civilized strangers and as merchants. Chancellor, who was a competent diplomat as well as a fine seaman, was received with a terrifying royal hospitality. His visit led to an opening of trade and a long series of diplomatic exchanges, extending even to tentative suggestions of alliance and royal marriage.

Commerce between England and Russia never amounted to much in the sixteenth century, despite its fair beginning. The Muscovy Company, formed to exploit it, soon ran into difficulties. The journey to Russia was too long and difficult and the risks were too great. The Dutch, later in the century, profited most by the opening of trade. This does not detract from Chancellor's achievement. His voyage was one of the great English voyages of discovery; but it contributed little to a solution of the problem of the north-east passage. Subsequent attempts to find the passage were made by captains in the service of the company, and later in the century by a series of Dutch explorers, of whom the most prominent were Linschoten—already famous for his knowledge of the East—and William Barents.[16] Barents in 1596 discovered Bear Island and Spitsbergen, and thence sailed east to Novaya Zemlya, where he was obliged to winter in a house built of driftwood. This first winter in complete Arctic darkness was a severe hardship, though Barents' people managed to survive on the meat of bears and foxes, which they caught in traps, and discovered the virtues of 'lepel leaves' (scurvy grass) by means of which they avoided the worst consequences of scurvy. They returned to Amsterdam, with great labour, in the summer of 1597. For many years Novaya Zemlya, Vaigach Island and the outfall of the Ob river into the Kara Sea represented the extreme limit of Arctic knowledge to the east. The ice defeated all further progress. The Dutch continued the search until 1624, but their voyages resulted only in the collection of information about Spitsbergen, Novaya Zemlya and the north coast of Russia. This knowledge was of use, not indeed to spice merchants, but to whaling skippers. Both the English Muscovy Company and various Dutch concerns were interested in whaling. The steady development of the Arctic whale fishery in the late sixteenth and early seventeenth centuries, and the establishment of the prosperous *Traankokery*—the extensive, though primitive, whale-oil factory on the beach at Smeerenberg Bay—were largely inspired by reports brought home by seekers for the north-east passage.

Accurate knowledge of Arctic seas and coastlines has become possible only in comparatively recent times, with the help of aircraft and ice-breakers. The voyages made in the sixteenth and seventeenth centuries in search of a passage, whether north-east or north-west—imaginative, bravely led and increasingly thorough—were all failures; but failures only in an immediate sense. They added greatly to geographical knowledge and to navigational experience and confidence. Those who took part in them—and they included some of the best seamen of their day—found new lands and opened new trades, which their successors were to develop and exploit.

CHAPTER 13

FISHING, FUR-TRADING AND PLANTING

At the end of the sixteenth century, as at the beginning, the only settled colonies in the Americas were those of Spain and of Spain's vassal, Portugal. No other Europeans had achieved anything in the way of permanent settlement. Few had contemplated anything worth achieving. Experience of war with Spain in American waters, however, was driving Dutchmen, Englishmen, Frenchmen—those few among them, at least, who were interested in America—alike to one conclusion: only by permanent settlement could they secure a permanent share in the profits of the New World. There was clearly no hope of inducing the Spanish government to countenance regular trade with the occupied parts of America. In war, open attempts to seize settled American territory from Spain had all failed. In peace, solid investors could not be expected regularly to finance smuggling ventures, much less piracy. The only solution—other than acquiescence in Spain's outrageous and unenforceable claim to monopoly—seemed to be for the northern nations to seize and colonize empty territory in America and mine the silver, cut the timber, and grow the sugar for themselves. Strategic as well as commercial considerations pointed the same way. An escape had to be found from an intolerable situation; a situation in which Spain, by a monopoly of American treasure and oriental trade, was apparently able to finance war anywhere in Europe and to interfere in the internal affairs of any European state. If—as the English hoped— a northern passage to the Orient could be found which would make the old Cape route unprofitable and obsolete, American settlements would be needed as staging points; and if—as most Dutchmen and some Englishmen believed—war with Spain was to be a permanent and inevitable feature of Protestant policy, then American settlements might still be valuable as bases from which a steady pressure could be maintained against the sources of Spanish wealth and against the convoys which carried that wealth to Spain.

Governments, investors, and the public at large in northern Europe accepted these arguments slowly and with reluctance. To governments at war, a long-term constructive policy of settlement appeared unattractive, when compared with the quicker returns and greater dividends to be gained by swift raids upon Spain and the Spanish colonies. Without the directing, protecting, sometimes limiting policy of government, attempts at colonization, then as always, were unlikely to succeed; but in the sixteenth century, governmental support and organization never advanced beyond a primitive urge to oppose Spain wherever she claimed to rule. Colonies and settlements were merely flanking movements in the attack on Spain, of secondary interest, always likely to be abandoned in a crisis. Investors, similarly, failed for the most part to see their interest in oversea colonial ventures, which at best would require large capital and yield slow returns. The West Indies certainly attracted adventurers; but like their governments in wartime, they found scope for their activity in raiding rather than in settling. In peacetime their ventures lapsed either into smuggling or into piracy. The hope of booty was high enough to cause a lack of capital for more constructive attempts, and the outcome was further to handicap the merchant and the would-be settler by making them liable for the depredations of the raiders. Settlement in the Caribbean was certainly, and on the more remote mainlands probably, a dangerous proposition in which investors might lose their capital and settlers their lives or liberty, in one stroke of Spanish retaliation. Men who remembered the fate of the French in Florida would be unlikely to invest in further undertakings of a similar kind. Even if willing investors could be found and government support secured, there still remained the question of where the settlers were to come from. England and the Netherlands, unlike Spain a hundred years earlier, had no surplus of needy and desperate men-at-arms who saw no future at home and were willing to seek their fortune anywhere. It is true that in England a land-labour problem existed and was growing more acute; but homestead emigrants, and their social betters who wanted cheap estates, could both find a field of activity near home in Ireland. Ireland rather than America absorbed most of the colonizing energies of Elizabethan England.

In these circumstances, enthusiasm for projects of settlement overseas was for many years necessarily confined to small groups of private individuals to whom America made an imaginative appeal, and who were more far-sighted, less cautious in the matter than their governments were obliged to be. In France they were mostly Huguenots, men such as Roberval who adventured in Canada, Villegagnon in Brazil, Ribault and Laudonnière in Florida—men who had the strongest possible reasons for hating Spain. Their principal patron and supporter was Coligny, whose death Philip II—for this and many other reasons—most urgently desired. They could not expect—and certainly did not get—consistent and powerful support from the government of France.

The assassination of Coligny and the long misery of internecine religious war put an end, until after the turn of the century, to serious French plans for American settlement.

In England the enthusiasts were a well-defined group, among whom the most famous names were Humphrey and Adrian Gilbert, Frobisher, Grenville and Raleigh. They were a close-knit group, nearly all West Country men, bound together by ties of neighbourhood, blood and marriage as well as by common Protestantism and common interests. They were well educated men, with that lively Renaissance curiosity and inventiveness which came late to England, when it was already losing its first force and excitement in Mediterranean lands. Their circle of acquaintance included the thoughtful and scientific navigator, John Davis, the eccentric but brilliant mathematician and astrologer John Dee, and perhaps most important of all, those masters of persuasive publicity, the elder and younger Richard Hakluyt. Some of them—Humphrey Gilbert especially—had friends among the French Huguenots. Most of them at one time or another had interests in Ireland and experience of Irish affairs. Gilbert's *Discourse* was written, or at least revised, in the intervals of its author's service in Ireland; and probably French example and Irish colonizing experience combined to suggest to him the possibility of organizing settlement further afield. As was natural for West Country men with Irish interests, they were all advocates of the north-west passage project, as against the Londoners of the Muscovy Company who fixed their hopes in the north-east. Their principal supporter in government circles was Walsingham, always the advocate of a 'forward' policy against Spain. From the Queen they had sympathy and lively interest, but necessarily very little in the way of practical support and help.

The Elizabethans were nothing if not fertile in ideas. They produced plans so many-sided and complex that no one project could easily be pursued to a conclusion. Random prospecting for precious metals fell out of fashion after the Frobisher fiasco, but the search for the north-west passage continued. With it went plans for twin settlements, one perhaps in Newfoundland or the St Lawrence basin, one in the neighbourhood of Drake's New Albion, which could be linked by the passage when it should be found. Alternatively, or in addition, settlements might be planted on the Atlantic coast of either North or South America, outside the Caribbean but near enough to serve as bases for naval assaults. There were plans for trading and raiding in the Pacific, where Drake had shown the way, but possibly based on a settlement in an unoccupied part of the coast of Peru. Some bold spirits, including Gilbert and—in a more practical fashion—Drake, advocated a frontal attack for the seizure and settlement of island bases in the Spanish

Caribbean itself. This last proposal was generally felt to be over-bold. Most prudent men, and certainly one prudent woman, thought it desirable at first that new colonies should be situated well out of reach of Spaniards. Even so, with France torn by religious war and the rebel Netherlanders desperately defending themselves against Spanish armies in their own country, English colonizers had a free choice of thousands of miles of Atlantic coastline. Apart from obvious considerations such as safe anchorages, the choice of a site was governed by two principal requirements; a reliable source of food, whether from the natives (if there were any) or from the soil by the colonists' own efforts; and the known presence, in reasonable abundance, of some commodity valuable in Europe, which when exported there could yield an income to the colonists and a return to the promoters on the capital which they invested. Such matters as fertile soil and healthy climate were largely guesswork in the sixteenth century. Some of the sites selected were to prove less fertile and much less healthy than they looked; and in the search for valuable products the Elizabethans often showed themselves as optimistic and as credulous as their Spanish precursors. Sir Humphrey Gilbert, the first of them to plan and lead a serious attempt at settlement, probably obeyed a sound instinct on his last voyage—the only American voyage in which he achieved anything practical—in fixing on Newfoundland. At least, the marvellous abundance of fish in Newfoundland waters was an established fact, ensuring a dependable source of food and an acceptable commodity for export to Europe.

Since the beginning of the century the Banks fisheries had been steadily exploited by Portuguese and Spaniards, Normans and Bretons, Englishmen, Dutchmen and Scandinavians. As the number of ships in the trade increased, its nature had changed from the immediate sale of 'green' fish to the marketing, at longer intervals, of much larger quantities of 'dry' fish. The fishermen set up temporary shelters ashore during the summer months in order to dry and repair nets and smoke and salt the catch. No attention was paid to the territorial claims of Portugal. The beaches of Newfoundland and the Gulf of St Lawrence became the regular seasonal camp-sites of a tough and independent cosmopolitan fishing community. These developments had effects of far-reaching significance, both in Europe itself and in the story of European expansion. One effect was a steady increase in the numbers of ships and men fitted for long and hazardous ocean passages. Fishermen often signed on for voyages of exploration, and must have been very valuable hands. The exploit of a small craft like Gilbert's *Squirrel*, said to be of less than ten tons and carrying only eleven men, which in 1580 crossed the Atlantic unaccompanied and returned safely, is rightly admired as a feat of seamanship; but it should be remembered that fishing vessels, some probably no larger, made the trip regularly every year. Apart from seamanship, the import of great quantities of cod was in itself a significant economic event, in a continent where many people lived near starvation level for part of every year. The fishing camps, also, became centres for barter with the natives, so that the trade in furs grew up as a profitable sideline of the fishery. For half the year, however, the camps were deserted, and one of the motives in plans to replace the seasonal camps by permanent settlements was a desire to increase the effective length of the season. Such plans did not emanate from the fishing community; fishing skippers usually disliked schemes for planting colonies in North America, whose inhabitants might compete with seasonal fishermen by fishing for a greater part of the year. Nevertheless, since the trade was international, the assumption of territorial authority by some one European power might be expected to be welcomed at least by those fishermen who were nationals of that power.

A cargo of fish was a valuable and easily marketable prize. Fishing vessels went armed in order to protect their catch against Dunkirkers and other freebooters, who were to the fishery what the dogfish is to the herring. It was commonly said that the English fishermen, whether by reason of their numbers or their armament, were the dominant group in the camps. Certainly when Gilbert's fleet arrived at St John's in 1583, the unofficial 'admiral' of the harbour was an English skipper and the organization of the camps appeared to be effective and orderly. After some initial hesitation, Gilbert, having produced his patent from the Queen, was welcomed civilly enough by his compatriots, and the other fishermen made no objection; possibly they enjoyed the show, and did not take it seriously. He raised the royal arms, proclaimed himself governor and landlord under the Queen, promulgated a rough code of laws, and issued leases of foreshore land to such as cared to apply. He made no payment, other than promises of future favour, for the food which he requisitioned. This formal taking seizin made little or no practical difference, for some years, to the life of the camps; but nobody seriously disputed it, and Newfoundland became the first English possession in the New World.[1]

Newfoundland was only part of Gilbert's colonizing plan. The patent of 1578 under which his voyages were made was drawn in very general terms, and provided the legal warrant for a complex network of inter-locking schemes. Some rights under the patent were sold to pay for the Newfoundland voyage; but Gilbert and his associates themselves apparently also hoped, among other things, to plant a colony further south, on the long coast between Cape Breton and Cape Hatteras. Gilbert himself, for all his imagination and energy, had neither the capital nor, probably, the temperament needed for success in such a project; but his enthusiasm and his writings had fired others to continue his efforts. He was lost at sea shortly after leaving Newfoundland; but within a year of his death Sir Walter Raleigh had obtained a patent similar to Gilbert's and was actively preparing to plant settlements in the vast coastal area named by Englishmen, with the Queen's approval, Virginia. A voyage of reconnaissance was made in 1584. In 1585 the first colony of a hundred-odd was planted by Grenville, on Raleigh's behalf, on Roanoke Island off the coast of what is now North Carolina.

The Roanoke voyages were the most persistent, best-organized and best-backed attempts by any northern European promoters up to that time to establish settlements in America.[2] They failed, from a complex series of causes. The capital available, though generous by the standards of the time, came chiefly from the private fortunes and borrowings of gentlemen adventurers, and was inadequate to provide the continual supplies and reinforcements needed in the initial years. The settlers, obsessed by the search for precious products, neglected the arduous tasks of clearing and cultivation. The Indians of the area were wild and primitive, and their rudimentary agriculture could not provide a surplus of food enough to supply the settlers' wants, so that relations, good at first, soon became exasperated and hostile. Discipline, except when Grenville himself was present, was bad. In addition, the whole enterprise was conducted in the teeth of Spanish hostility which, though never expressed in an open assault, affected the colony in many indirect ways. Grenville, on his way out in 1585, had still been able to call at minor harbours in Hispaniola and buy livestock for the colony; but, in the same year, Drake sailed on his biggest Caribbean raid. Sharp Spanish retaliation was to be expected, and full-scale war only a matter of time. It was Drake, on his return, who took off the first batch of anxious and disheartened settlers. The imminence of war made it essential, for reasons of security, to keep secret the site, the strength and the precise nature of the colony. The promoters could not publish details or use the resources of printed propaganda—as Gilbert had done earlier—to solicit support. Roanoke itself, lying among dangerous shoals and inlets, lacking a sheltered harbour and limited in extent, was an unsuitable place; but it had the merit of being difficult for the Spaniards to find, which was one reason why the settlers clung to it instead of moving, as the promoters wished, to Chesapeake Bay. A second colony was sent out, still with high hopes, in 1587; but the threatened Armada invasion prevented Grenville from sailing with fresh supplies in the following year, and when an expedition finally reached Roanoke in 1590 the colony had disappeared almost without trace. The enterprise, however, created a tradition. Through the accounts published by

Hakluyt and others—since after 1588 the need for reticence had passed —it provided evidence that Englishmen were fully capable, in favourable circumstances, of establishing permanent settlements. It produced also our most valuable early descriptions of primitive America in John White's drawings of plants, fish and people, and in his maps, the best yet made by any European of any part of North America; above all in Hariot's *Briefe and true report*. No travellers' tales or improbable marvels here, but a detailed, accurate and orderly account of the land, its flora and fauna, and its people, as observed by a good scientific mind.

'It is the sinfullest thing in the world to forsake or destitute a plantation once in forwardness, for besides the dishonour, it is the guiltiness of blood of many commiserable persons.'[3] So Bacon, who hated Raleigh; but in the circumstances it is difficult to see what more could have been done. Hope of the colony's survival lingered on; but in 1592 Raleigh, already disheartened, lost the royal favour, without which he could do little. Throughout the fifteen-nineties the country's energies were largely absorbed in the war, mercantile interests moved strongly over to privateering, enthusiasm for colonial settlement declined. It was in the hope of reviving it that Hakluyt published, in 1601, his greatly enlarged edition of the *Principal Travels*. We owe to Hakluyt the survival of nearly everything we know about the early American voyages. He was the continuing figure linking the two waves of Virginia enterprise, the abortive attempts of the fifteen-eighties and those which gained a permanent footing after the turn of the century. He was dedicated to the project of planting in America, a propagandist of immense persistence, imagination, and force. He had immense knowledge too, and a conscientious accuracy, well above the normal editorial standards of his time. He was a greatly respected figure. Like Raleigh, but more happily, he lived to see the projects for which he had striven take root.

Propaganda was vital to the planting operations of the English and the Dutch in the early seventeenth century; far more vital than it had been to the Spaniards in the early sixteenth. English colonies were almost all planted in places where there was either no native population, or only a sparse and primitive one, numerous enough to be dangerous on occasion, but too wild to be employed as a labour force. This was a matter of necessity, not of choice. The Spaniards already possessed most of the territories where docile native labour existed. English promoters of colonization had therefore to transplant whole communities with a complete labour force of Europeans. These men had somehow to be induced to emigrate. The cost of their emigration had to be paid, and their tools, equipment and initial supplies provided from England, by the promoters. The risk, responsibility and expense—as the Roanoke voyages had shown—were more than private gentlemen could normally undertake. It was clearly essential to bring in the great city merchants with their capital and their connections; above all with their flexible and relatively new mechanism of the joint-stock company, whereby considerable numbers of people might invest their money without necessarily adventuring their persons. More difficult still, it was essential to bring in the Crown. Hakluyt had seen this all along,[4] though the Queen would never have it. A planting company needed a legal title to the soil, authority to govern the settlers, a firm assurance of diplomatic and naval support. For these, a formal royal charter was necessary. The books and pamphlets put out by English promoters of colonization, therefore, had three main purposes: to invite subscriptions, to attract emigrants, and to solicit government support.

The arguments used were religious, social, economic, strategic. Every colonizing company in every European country throughout the Age of Reconnaissance claimed the spreading of the Gospel among its leading motives. John Smith in Virginia told his followers that 'the gaining provinces addeth to the King's Crown; but the reducing heathen people to civility and true religion bringeth honour to the King of Heaven'.[5] Here was the old formula, serve God and grow rich, which any *conquistador* understood; but the North American Indian was a less promising neophyte than his Mexican or Peruvian contemporary, as Hariot's cool descriptions had shown. Moreover, the Protestant communions in northern Europe were too much concerned about their own situation at home to have much energy left for missionary fervour abroad. Convention required the inclusion of religious arguments; the missionary motive was always present, but usually subordinate. Social arguments were more obviously attractive, though specious. The England of James I suffered from widespread unemployment—due chiefly to enclosures and to shifts in the nature and location of industry —and from a rapid growth in the size of the big towns, especially London. Contemporary economists, having no reliable statistics, concluded that the country as a whole was over-populated, and many of them recommended colonies as a vent for the surplus population. To quote one example among many—William Vaughan's *Golden Fleece*,[6] an eccentric but shrewd economic and social allegory published in 1626: 'This main business,' wrote Vaughan, 'is to be promoted in regard of the general populousness of Great Britain'—Vaughan was a Welshman, otherwise he would have said 'England'—'Every man hath enough to do to shift for his own maintenance, so that the greatest part are driven to extremities, and many to getting their living by other men's losses; witness our extortioners, perjurers, pettifoggers at law, coney-catchers, thieves, cottagers, inmates, unnecessary ale-sellers, beggars, burners of hedges to the hindrance of husbandry and such like, which might perhaps prove profitable members in the New Found Land.' Planting, by this reasoning, was commended to the unemployed as a means of getting a free passage to America, a job on arrival, and eventually a piece of land; to government, it was suggested as a means of getting rid of unwanted and troublesome people.

Strategic arguments were of two kinds. There was the anti-Spanish argument. One of the petitions of the Virginia Company suggested 'the inestimable advantage that would be gained to this State of England in case of war, both for the easy assaulting of the Spaniard's West Indies from those parts, and for the relieving and succouring of all ships and men-of-war that should go on reprisals'. This was a familiar suggestion, already becoming, in James I's day, a little old-fashioned. More cogent and more far-sighted—because it looked forward to a time when Spain would no longer be the principal enemy—was the argument about naval stores. England had long been short of fir poles for masts, pitch for caulking seams and hemp for cordage. In the later sixteenth century, oak frames and planking were also becoming scarce. Most of these came from the Baltic, and access to them could be denied by whatever power controlled the shores of the Sound. An alternative supply of naval stores was thus a powerful attraction. The attraction was economic as well as strategic; and, in general, economic arguments were the most compelling. Colonies were to enrich the investors and the realm by producing commodities which were in demand in Europe; to enrich the Crown by means of customs duties; and to enrich the merchants and manufacturers of England by serving as a market for English products. This last argument lost some of its force as the sparseness and poverty of the native population became better known. More compelling was the claim that colonies would be a source, not only of naval stores, not only of fish and furs, but of tropical and sub-tropical luxuries, even of gold, silver and pearls. The most striking feature in all this economic discussion is its optimism, its cheerful assumption that any part of America might yield precious metals, that any warm country such as Virginia might be made to grow vines and mulberry trees, drugs and spices. Mercantilist opinion naturally welcomed the possibility of importing such things from colonies instead of from foreign countries, and of obtaining surplus produce for re-export to Europe.

The times were propitious for this flood of propaganda. The treaty of 1604 was the first sign of the tipping of the balance between Spain and England in North America. The Spaniards would not admit publicly any reduction of their sovereign claims; but their efforts to defend the Caribbean while carrying on aggressive war in Europe had taxed their strength to the limit. They could not hope, in practice, to exert much influence on the Atlantic coasts, and there was even talk in Madrid of abandoning Florida. Conversely, though James I refused to acknowledge Spanish rights in unoccupied places, he insisted that duly occupied possessions should be respected. Armed excursions into Spanish territory were sharply discouraged. Investors who for years had been backing privateers had to find new outlets for their money, and some of them put it into plantations. Similarly, the numbers of potential emigrants steadily increased. In England prices were high, jobs were hard to get, land was dear and encumbered by irksome tenurial restrictions. The movement into Ireland had led only to disillusion, bitterness and war; so the minds of the impoverished, the landless and the discontented turned towards the continent which still, in the reiterated phrase of the time, possessed its maidenhead. The capital needed to exploit the riches of America was still under-estimated, as was the effort which settlers would have to make in clearing and cultivation; but, for the first time, capital, labour, opportunity and organization coincided.

The Virginia Company was incorporated in 1606 and began operations in the following year at Jamestown on the Tidewater. Its principal promoter was Sir Thomas Smythe, that shrewd commercial magnate and indefatigable organizer whose hand lay behind many of the oversea enterprises of the time: the Muscovy Company, the East India Company, and now Virginia. Smythe was trusted both in the City and at Court. He served as treasurer of the company throughout its early years, finding the money year after year to send out shiploads of emigrants and supplies, until 1619 when he was ousted by the intrigues of Sir Edwin Sandys. The successful establishment of Virginia was due more to him than to any other individual. The definitive charter which Smythe negotiated in 1609 was an adaptation of the familiar type of charter granted to joint-stock trading companies. The general government of the company was entrusted to the whole body of shareholders. A man could become a shareholder in two ways: the first, by investing money, by buying shares. A share was valued at £12. 10s., which was the estimated cost of planting one settler. Alternatively, he could become a shareholder by adventuring his person, by emigrating to Virginia at his own expense with his family and servants. One body equalled one share. After an initial period of common labour, land was to be distributed among the shareholders, whether emigrant or not, in proportion to their investment. The emigrant shareholders became planters or free-farmers, paying only a small quit-rent to the company. Below them in the social scale were the indented servants—men who emigrated at the expense of the company or of individual employers, binding themselves in return to work for a fixed term of years, hoping at the expiry of their indentures to set up for themselves as tenants or even freeholders. Most of the labourers and many of the artisans were men of this class.

The directors, and investors generally, hoped to draw their dividends from quit-rents, from trading on their own account, and from duties levied on the trading of other merchants. For some years, however, the colonists had nothing to sell; they were hard put to it to feed, house and defend themselves, even with help from England. Many of them died within a few months of their arrival, probably more of contagious illnesses which they brought with them than directly of hardship and hunger. The mortality among the Indians was equally alarming. It is curious that the early settlements in the fifteen-eighties had been remarkably healthy. The almost contemporary settlement in uninhabited Bermuda, started by the accident of shipwreck on the way to Virginia, also enjoyed good health. For a time, indeed, the settlers in Bermuda outnumbered those in Virginia; though it is true that their early prosperity came from an unexpected piece of luck, in finding an enormous and very valuable lump of ambergris on the beach. In Virginia the settlers had little luck. They might once again have given up in despair had it not been for the buoyant leadership and the Indian connections of John Smith at the beginning, and the character of the early governors, a series of old-soldier martinets who by savage discipline kept their people to clearing and ploughing instead of wandering about the woods hunting and searching for gold mines.

The colony was saved from economic extinction and raised to modest wealth by the cultivation of a single crop, tobacco. The art of growing and curing tobacco had been learned from the Spaniards in the course of voyages to Guiana. The King and conservative opinion in England disliked it as a wasteful, noxious and immoral drug; but there was a great demand for it, hitherto supplied by import from Spain. Admittedly Virginia leaf was then inferior in quality to that grown in the Spanish Indies; but that was the kind of disadvantage which mercantilist theorists expected the consumer to put up with. Tobacco saved Virginia. It did not save the Virginia Company. The company never paid a dividend and by 1623 it was insolvent. The worst feature of its insolvency was its inability to do enough to help the settlers, and their distress was evident from the letters which they sent to the Privy Council. Factious quarrels among the directors made matters worse, and one faction led by Sir Edwin Sandys tried to drag the dispute into Parliament. James I quickly put a stop to discussion, on grounds of prerogative; and in 1624 himself began *quo warranto* proceedings against the company. As a result, the charter was revoked, and Virginia became the first, for many years the only, Crown colony. The cost of royal administration was appropriately defrayed by an export duty on tobacco.

A council for New England had been formed at the same time as the Virginia Company. Its leading spirit was Sir Ferdinando Gorges, a West Country gentleman-soldier of great energy and transparent honesty, dedicated like Raleigh, Hakluyt, Smythe, to the cause of American settlement. He is still commemorated as the founder of Maine. New England, however, had a harsh, stony soil, heavily timbered, and a bitter winter climate. The council failed at first to find either the men or the money to begin planting, and by 1620 were willing to lease part of their grant to anyone who would settle under their auspices. In that year the *Mayflower* arrived in New England waters carrying her little band of Puritan emigrants with their wives, dependants and indented servants. They were humble folk, members of a dissenting congregation who some years before had emigrated to the Netherlands for conscience' sake, and had then, thanks probably to Sir Edwin Sandys' Puritan sympathies, obtained permission to settle in the northern part of the Virginia Company's territory. They sailed for Virginia; but making their first landfall near Cape Cod, they decided to stay there and to found their settlement at New Plymouth. The New England Council, when they heard of it, granted a lease on easy terms. The settlement was small and weak. The Pilgrim Fathers had to struggle not only against the wilderness and the climate, but against a heavy burden of debt, for they had emigrated on borrowed capital. They had, moreover, unsympathetic neighbours. Not all the settlers in New England were Puritans, and some were rogues. The fur trader Thomas Morton and his companions, for example, did very well, trading and carousing with the Indians, living chiefly on fish and wild game. Morton's book, *The New English Canaan*,[7] is full of detail about birds and beasts, and of a sportsman's contempt for the town and village-bred Puritans. This confrontation of the Reformation with the more disreputable aspects of the Renaissance had its amusing side; but the rum and fire-arms which Morton supplied to the Indians were a real danger, and the settlers of New Plymouth had no control over him.

Despite the poverty and weakness of New Plymouth, the initiative in New England remained with the Puritans. Their position in England was growing steadily worse. With the assumption of personal rule by Charles I, all hope of Presbyterianism in the Church or of parliamentary government in the State seemed at an end. At the same time, war in Europe and a series of bad harvests at home made the economic outlook in England very uncertain. Many people of influence, wealth and Puritan sympathies became willing not only to invest in colonization, but themselves to emigrate to places where they could shape Church and Commonwealth more to their own liking. In 1629 a powerful syndicate, consisting largely of prominent Puritans, obtained a grant of land for settlement in New England, and incorporated themselves by royal charter as the Massachusetts Bay Company.

In legal form the new enterprise resembled the Virginia plan. Similar rules governed the rights of shareholders, planters and indented servants; but the charter had one significant peculiarity—it did not specifically require the government of the company to remain in England. That the document passed the seals with this omission is in itself surprising. Puritan lawyers, it is true, were not above sharp practice where they considered the Lord's work to be involved, and they certainly exploited official ignorance of geography in procuring a gross infringement of the rights of the New England Council; but neither inadvertence nor bribery seems adequate as an explanation. Whatever the means employed, a group of shrewd businessmen were in fact empowered by charter to retain property rights in England and the formal status of British subjects, while establishing themselves in self-governing independence in America. Accordingly, those of the promoters who wished to remain in England were induced to sell their holdings, and the remaining stockholders with the whole government of the company, charter, records, capital and everything, left England with about 900 settlers and established their headquarters at Boston in Massachusetts.

Like Virginia, Massachusetts suffered great hardships and heavy mortality in the early years; like Virginia, it overcame them by virtue of stern discipline. This discipline was enforced, however, not by old-soldier governors sent from England, but by a very able elected governor, and magistrates guided by the ministers of an uncompromising and increasingly separatist Church. The governing oligarchy, initially of stockholders, then of freemen who were also accepted Church members, was narrow, sometimes unscrupulous, utterly lacking in humour, but very efficient. It successfully enforced communal labour, unlike the government of Virginia, which had early found private enterprise more efficient. It patronized and bullied the long-suffering people of New Plymouth. It deported Thomas Morton, ostensibly for dancing round the maypole. Maypole-dancing, of course, with its suggestion of fertility cults and witchcraft, was for seventeenth-century Puritans no subject for humour; but the Massachusetts Puritans were ruthless in punishing any kind of opposition or heterodoxy. This was a factor of some importance in the colonizing of New England, for many who quarrelled with the ruling oligarchy in Massachusetts over politics or religion either were expelled, or fled to escape worse punishment. These people founded new settlements—Connecticut, New Haven, Rhode Island—which grew and flourished modestly; though as time went on both Massachusetts and Connecticut began to develop an imperialism of their own and to swallow up the smaller settlements.

Expansion meant encroachment on Indian hunting-grounds. The Massachusetts company, with its customary legalism, was careful to cover its acquisitions by purchase treaties. The Puritans were never enthusiastic missionaries; most of them apparently thought that the Indians were beyond hope. Like the Spaniards, they sometimes enslaved Indians captured in rebellion or frontier war; but unlike the Spaniards they had little feeling of a paternal civilizing duty. The company did, however, enforce those clauses in its charter forbidding the sale of fire-arms and liquor to the Indians. In this matter Christian conscience and common prudence pointed the same way. It is untrue to say that the Puritan settlers had no conscience where Indians were concerned; but their conscience for the most part worked in a negative way. They did not exploit the Indians, nor did they try to absorb them; but as their farms expanded they inexorably pushed the Indians aside.

The Puritans concentrated doggedly upon immediately useful crops and made no attempt to fit into a theoretical scheme formulated in England. They eschewed tobacco; but within twenty years they were producing a surplus of food, which they sold to the Indians in exchange for furs. They fished assiduously, and quarrelled and competed with the seasonal fleets which fished for the English and European markets. Some of the cod caught in New England ships went to Old England, some went direct to the Mediterranean markets; but much was consumed in New England by a population which increased year by year. At the outbreak of the Civil War Massachusetts had some 14,000 inhabitants and exercised most of the attributes of an independent state.

Not all the northern colonies had Puritan connections. The desire for secure bases for the fishery and the fur trade inspired the planting of English settlements in Newfoundland. Vaughan was a prime mover in this enterprise. The settlements were not at first particularly prosperous or particularly important, and they led to perpetual quarrelling over foreshore rights; but they survived, and developed as a permanent British colony. Sir William Alexander's Scottish settlement in Nova Scotia had a more chequered history. It was only just founded in 1627 when war broke out between England and France. Nova Scotia became, and long remained, disputed territory between British and French settlers.

The French entered the colonial field at about the same time as the English and settled in the same sort of places on the Atlantic coast of North America. They could not hope to live on native tribute or to employ native labour on a large scale, and they found no precious metals; they had to live by agriculture, by fishing, or by the fur trade. Like the English, they were keenly alive to the importance of sea power and the possible value of colonies as sources of naval stores; and like the English they made use of joint stock companies of the commercial type for founding colonies. The chronology of the development of French America corresponds closely to the English story. The moves of the two nations suggest either conscious mutual imitation, or the tactical counter-moves of the chess-board; and what a chess-board it was, in size and variety of pieces! The French, like the English, had engaged in exploring and privateering in American waters in the sixteenth century. French fishermen had regularly fished the Banks. Cartier had explored the Bay of Fundy and the St Lawrence, and Roberval had tried, without success, to found a colony. Henry IV, like James I, granted colonizing monopolies in America, and French companies first began to achieve permanent settlements in the early seventeenth century, after the end of the maritime war with Spain. In 1605 a French Huguenot group founded Port Royal in Acadia— their name for what became Nova Scotia. In 1608 the great Champlain —sailor, scientist, cartographer, later famous as the explorer of the Great Lakes—founded the French settlement of Quebec. Acadia became a self-supporting colony of small farmers who, like those of New England, in time enjoyed a modest prosperity. Quebec, on the other hand, was a trading station rather than a colony. Its inhabitants traded with the Indians for furs, which they shipped down the St Lawrence to France. Their capital, their trade goods and most of their food came from France. They were backed by the Company of New France, which was incorporated by Richelieu and which sought to pay its share-holders out of the profits of the fur trade. English and French settlers soon came to blows. In 1613 the Virginia Company organized an expedition which attacked Port Royal and destroyed an incipient French settlement on the coast of Maine. In 1627 the Nova Scotia Scots seized Port Royal, and in 1629 an English squadron intercepted the French food-ships on their way up the St Lawrence and starved Quebec into surrender. The Treaty of St-Germain-en-Laye of 1632 restored both places to France. Charles I and his advisers had no inkling—why should they have?—of the future importance of the St Lawrence. The exploration and development of Canada was left to French fur traders and Jesuit missionaries.

Meanwhile a similar Anglo-French game of chess was being set up in the troubled islands of the Caribbean. There the old fear of Spain gradually gave way in the seventeenth century to familiarity, which bred a somewhat premature contempt. Raleigh, disappointed in

Virginia, had developed an obsession—it was no less than that—about a rumoured kingdom, rich in gold, in the hinterland of Guiana. After his years at Court and in the Tower, Raleigh was not very well qualified as a *conquistador*. He was forestalled and out-manœuvred by Antonio de Berrio, who was twenty years his senior. His attempts to ascend the Guiana rivers in search of El Dorado were inevitably failures and led eventually to his death on the scaffold. Raleigh's enthusiasm, however, expressed in one of the most eloquent of all his writings,[8] communicated itself to others, and a series of attempts were made by his compatriots to establish colonies. The Guiana coast—swampy, hot and fever-ridden—was a singularly unsuitable place for inexperienced settlers. The early English attempts either failed or were destroyed by the Spaniards; only the Dutch succeeded in getting a foothold, on the Essequibo in 1616 and on the Berbice in 1624. The English failures, however, had important indirect results. Disappointed or dispossessed settlers, looking for alternative sites, lighted upon fertile islands in the Lesser Antilles. The Spaniards had left these islands alone, largely through dislike of the savage and intractable people who inhabited some of them. English landings on Dominica and St Lucia were beaten off by these Caribs, but St Kitts was successfully occupied by English and French settlers, acting separately but at first amicably. Most important of all, the settlement of Barbados, then uninhabited, was begun in 1624.

The financial backing for these undertakings came from informal merchant syndicates, of which the principal organizers were Thomas Warner, an old Guiana man, and Sir William Courteen, a London merchant with Dutch connections. As in New England, sharp promoters tried to exploit official ignorance of American geography, and over-lapping grants were the result. In order to oust Courteen the Warner group secured the support of a prominent but impecunious courtier, the Earl of Carlisle, who in 1627 obtained a patent from Charles I creating him Lord Proprietor of the Caribbees. This was the first appearance of a new type of English colonial organization, the pro-priety. It was the application to America of a form of grant long obsolete in England—a quasi-feudal grant of territory and jurisdiction to a prominent nobleman. Obviously a peer could obtain grants of this kind from the Stuart kings more easily than a group of merchants; and it was perhaps thought more appropriate that settlements in exposed positions should be made by feudal grant in the old tradition of knight-service rather than by trading companies. The Carlisle grant led to constant quarrelling among the heirs of the earl and the lessees of their rights; but in spite of political uncertainty, Barbados flourished. In the early years, apart from food the colony produced mainly tobacco, cotton and various dyes, fustic, indigo and others, important in view of the persistent attempts in the English cloth trade to change from the export of undyed cloth to that of the finished article. In 1640 sugar planting was introduced, mainly at the instigation of Dutch traders who had learned the methods of cultivation and manufacture from the Portuguese in Brazil. Sugar soon became the principal product. Its price was high and the European market apparently insatiable. By 1660 the exports from Barbados to England were considerably greater in value than those of Virginia and very much greater than those of New England; and Barbados was already known as 'the brightest jewel in His Majesty's crown'.

The French meanwhile, through their government-sponsored monopoly, the *Compagnie des Iles d'Amerique*, had settled Martinique and Guadeloupe, by similar methods and with similar results. These sugar islands, both English and French, were sheltered from effective Spanish interference partly by their windward position, which made them difficult of access from the Spanish centres; and partly by the fact that the Spaniards were desperately defending themselves against the pillaging fleets of the Dutch. Both English and French governments welcomed the settlement of islands which not only needed little defence, but also fitted neatly into the mercantilist theory of production and consumption, as the mainland colonies, in varying degrees, had failed to do. The islanders, however, not only depended indirectly on Dutch warships to protect them; they depended directly on Dutch traders to buy and transport their sugars and to supply their manufactured needs. Moreover, English and French West Indian products were similar, and competed in the European market. The directors of economic policy in an age of hardening mercantilism inevitably resented these limits on national profit. The story of the new American empires, more particularly the island empires of the West Indies, in the later seventeenth century and throughout the eighteenth, was to be filled with these struggles. Each metropolitan government strove to eject the Dutch from their position of commercial advantage; to bring its own colonies under planned mercantile control; and to annex, beggar or destroy the colonial possessions of its rivals.

Part III

THE FRUITS OF DISCOVERY

CHAPTER 14

THE LAND EMPIRE OF SPAIN

BY THE MIDDLE of the sixteenth century all the chief centres of native American civilization were in Spanish hands. That is not to say that all the territory subdued by Spanish arms had been effectively occupied. Many thousands of square miles in 'Spanish' America were never penetrated, much less occupied, by Europeans. The *conquistadores* left the forests and the prairies to their primitive occupants; but with unerring instinct and audacity they struck directly at the cities, and captured them all. No other military outcome, in the long run, was possible. More remarkable than the military fact of conquest, was the relative ease with which the Spaniards established a permanent, organized and—despite the efforts of the Crown—often brutal dominion. Resistance continued after the conquest, especially in Peru, where civil strife between Spanish factions encouraged it. Manco, the last reigning Inca, maintained an independent court in the mountain fastness of Vilcabamba for many years. The viceroyalty of Peru was not reduced to general order and obedience until the time of Francisco de Toledo in the fifteen-seventies, and then only by means of an extensive resettlement of disaffected Indians, and the execution of Túpac Amarú, the last recognized Inca prince. Resistance, however, was rarely effective over a wide area. It was usually paralysed by apathy, by treachery, by lack of leadership and co-ordination. Only remote and primitive peoples such as the Araucanians of Chile and the Chichimecas of the northern frontier, maintained themselves in real independence over a long period. Elsewhere, having seized the great ceremonial centres, the *conquistadores* successfully converted the tributary villages into *encomiendas*. They assumed the privileges of the chiefs and priests whom they had killed or displaced. The villagers, with sullen obedience, rendered to their new masters the service and the tribute which they had formerly paid to Indian overlords.

Encomiendas provided a firm social and economic basis for colonization. Indian tribute supplied food for the conquerors during the initial period of organization and settlement, and a steady income for the leaders. With Indian labour they built the towns in which they were to live, small and humble at first, but complete with dwellings, public buildings and churches. The *encomienda* system, however, was only a starting point. It provided only for a fortunate few, and obviously could not supply all the types of food, tools and clothing which a European society demanded. As fresh immigrants arrived, in a steady trickle with every trans-Atlantic fleet, there grew up, beside the Indian economy based on communal agriculture, a new and characteristically Spanish economy, whose principal and most lucrative occupations were stock raising and silver mining.

In the arid uplands of Castile from which most of the *conquistadores* came pastoral pursuits, the grazing of semi-nomadic flocks and herds, had long been preferred to arable farming. The New World offered limitless grazing. The demand for beasts of burden, especially mules, in a land where most transport hitherto had been on the backs of men, was insatiable. Mendoza, the first viceroy of New Spain, introduced the merino sheep, the basis of an incipient woollen industry, which earned a bad reputation for ill-treatment of Indian workmen in its *obrajes*. Horned cattle, besides being a source of food, produced valuable and exportable commodities: hides, for saddlery and protective clothing, and tallow for making candles and coating the hulls of ships. Cattle raising suited the temperament of the *conquistadores*; it called for daring horsemanship and periodical bursts of great energy, but not for sustained or careful effort. Grazing rights, to those who had the capital to stock them, were granted initially in terms of radius from a given spot, and little attempt was made to survey boundaries. The beasts were turned out on open range and multiplied prodigiously. Carcasses, when hides and tallow had been removed, were often left to rot where they lay. Beef became so plentiful that no Spaniard need starve or work for wages. Great men who owned cattle ranges could keep open house and feed great bands of retainers, ready to defend their interests against rivals or to follow them in new *entradas*.

First *encomiendas* and then stock ranches produced the accumulations of capital which made possible the large-scale mining of precious metals. Gold and silver mining in the early days of the conquest had been a simple affair of prospecting and washing in likely streams; but about the middle of the sixteenth century immensely productive silver veins were discovered at Zacatecas and Guanajuato in New Spain and at Potosí—richest of all—in what is now Bolivia. The discoveries produced lawless and exciting silver rushes, and special courts were hastily set up in the mining camps to register claims and settle disputes. Some Spaniards, and more Indians, worked small claims by hand; but the larger and more productive mines were operated by capitalists on a fairly large scale. Various forms of mass-production took the place of the primitive washing process, and extensive plant—extensive for those days—was set up for extracting the silver from the ore, usually by a mercury amalgamation process. The Crown claimed a share, usually one-fifth, of all metal produced. A considerable body of officials was employed to weigh, test and stamp the silver ingots as they issued from the works, and to take out the royal share which, after authorized disbursements, was shipped to Spain, along with the larger quantities of bullion sent home by individuals, either as an investment or in payment for European goods imported.

The new Spanish economy in the Indies depended on the old Indian economy for much of its food—particularly grain, vegetables and poultry, all mainly produced by Indians—and for almost all its labour. In the first half-century after the conquest, the Spaniards grew accustomed to an extremely lavish use of labour. They conceived ambitious building projects, and carried them out with the same ferocious determination which they had displayed in the conquest itself. Later in the century, the development of mines created a great demand for pick-and-shovel labour; some of this demand was met by the import of negro slaves, but most of the work was done by Indians. Other industries—woollen weaving, sugar making, shipbuilding, and so on—increasingly employed semi-skilled Indians. As the demand for labour in Spanish industry increased, however, the Indian population which supplied it rapidly declined. There were two main reasons for this. One was the damage caused to Indian cultivation by domestic animals. Cattle on open range, despite repeated legislation and the efforts of colonial courts to protect Indian property, strayed on to the unfenced village farms. The hedges of closely planted cactus which are so conspicuous a feature of rural Mexico today were the Indian answer to this attack; but a tardy and inefficient answer. The spread of stock ranching was a major cause of depopulation in central Mexico, and over-grazing one of the causes of spreading soil erosion.[1] In Peru, horned cattle were less numerous, but sheep, and pigs rooting in the potato patches, created similar conditions in many highland areas. Peasant cultivators, who saw their crops repeatedly destroyed by great herds of grazing, trampling beasts, could avoid starvation only by moving to remote and less attractive areas, or else by seeking employment in Spanish settlements. In the towns, however, they encountered an even more serious danger, that of infectious disease. Smallpox had come into Mexico with Cortés' army, and together with typhoid—contracted through drinking the lake water after the aqueducts had been cut—had sapped the resistance of the defenders of Tenochtitlán. Thereafter European diseases, from which the Indians had no immunity, reduced the native population at appalling speed. Major epidemics

229

occurred in the fifteen-twenties immediately after the conquest, in the fifteen-forties and again in the fifteen-seventies. Crowded concentrations of labour in the mining camps bred infection, which was then carried by the miners back to their home villages. A well-documented study gives the following approximate population figures for central Mexico: 1519—11,000,000; 1540—6,427,466; 1565—4,409,180; 1597 —2,500,000.[2] Other writers differ in their estimate of numbers, and no comparable detailed information is available for Peru; but there is general agreement on the downward trend. Communal agriculture broke down in many places. Ancient irrigation works were abandoned, and many areas, particularly in the coastal plain of Peru, reverted to desert. The decline of population went on for over a hundred years; not until well into the seventeenth century was there any clear sign of recovery.

A developing European society thus found itself faced, in the late sixteenth century, by periodical shortages of grain and a continual and growing shortage of labour. The official remedies for grain shortage were standard and obvious: attempts to control marketing and prices, and the establishment of government granaries in the main centres. European landowners also found it increasingly profitable to grow some grain themselves. Favoured localities such as Puebla in New Spain and Antioquia in New Granada from a fairly early date produced wheat for sale in nearby cities, or at the ports for victualling ships. Towards the end of the century more and more estates included some arable acreage. This inevitably increased the pressure on Indian village holdings. Strict legislation prohibited the seizure of Indian land and limited its transfer in other ways; but headmen could be bribed, and no legislation could prevent alienation by agreed, or apparently agreed sale. Peasants who lost control of their land had usually no alternative but to remain on it as labourers and semi-servile tenants. Goods and money were often advanced to such tenants by landowners on the understanding that the advances would be repaid in labour. This practice led to peonage, debt slavery, which local custom sealed as an inescapable hereditary burden. Arable farming on a large scale by Spaniards contributed, therefore, to the decay of Indian communal agriculture, and the spread of self-contained European-owned *latifundia*.[3]

For labour shortage there appeared no remedy but organized compulsion. The wages of regular labourers in mines and industrial undertakings, it is true, rose steadily in response to demand; but most Indians preferred their old communal ways and would not willingly work full time for wages. Forced labour had always been a feature of the American economy. The Indians were accustomed to it from pre-conquest times; most Spaniards in the New World thought it not only economically essential, but, under proper safeguards, positively salutary, part of the civilizing process. Repeated and detailed legislation on the subject, by both royal and viceregal governments, expressed a genuine and conscientious wish to protect Indians from hardship and unreasonable exploitation, and a natural suspicion of the feudal implications of the *encomienda* system; but it also reflected the fear of economic collapse and the necessity of making the most economical use of a dwindling population. The first attempts, in the New Laws of 1542, to abolish *encomiendas* provoked a fierce outcry, and were abandoned; but as *encomenderos* died, the Crown wherever possible took over their grants, so that the number of *encomiendas* steadily diminished. From the middle of the century, moreover, the rights of *encomenderos* were restricted to the receipt of tribute in accordance with a fixed assessment, and they were forbidden to exact forced labour from the Indians of their grants. Instead, all unemployed Indians were to be compelled to offer themselves publicly for wage-earning employment. This naïve decree naturally produced little result; and in the fourth quarter of the century the viceregal governments proceeded to organize, carefully and in detail, the system of forced labour rotation known in Peru as *mita* and in New Spain as *repartimiento*. The system was not new; it had long been used in a casual and *ad hoc* fashion to recruit labour for public works; but Enríquez in New Spain and Toledo in Peru made it permanent, regular and general. Every Indian village, through its headmen, was required to produce a fixed proportion of its male population, for a fixed number of weeks, in rotation throughout the year. The labourers were allocated by the local magistrates either to public works, or to private employers engaged in vital occupations such as silver mining or food production; and were paid by those employers according to a fixed scale of wages. Employers thus gained a regular but inefficient and constantly changing labour force; Indians were compelled, for several weeks in each year, to do uncongenial work in strange surroundings far from home; and the villagers lost a proportion of the men available for communal farming, so that at home also they had to work harder in order to live. For the individual Indian, the only way of escape from the alternating compulsion of Spanish employer and village community was to accept the implications of a money economy, move to a Spanish settlement, put on Spanish clothes, and become a wage-earner or, if his resources and skill allowed, a craftsman or small capitalist. This, of course, was what many responsible Spaniards considered to be the ultimate and sensible outcome.

Spanish opinion, however, was divided. The conquest had been a spiritual as well as a military campaign, and the first and most outspoken opposition to the rule of swordsmen had come from the soldiers of the Church, the friars of the missionary Orders. The Franciscans were the first in the field in New Spain, as the result of a request made to the Emperor by Cortés himself. The first Franciscans sent out, in 1524, the famous Twelve under Fray Martín de Valencia, and many of their successors, were strict Observants, carefully trained for their task. The same is true of the first Dominicans, who, under Fray Domingo de Betanzos, went out in 1525. They were picked products of Church reform in Spain. They represented the radical churchmanship of Cisneros, to which their immediate successors were to add something of the humanism and learning of Erasmus. Fray Juan de Zumárraga, nominated by Charles V as the first bishop of Mexico in 1527, was a conspicuous admirer of Erasmus. The doctrinal books printed in Mexico under his direction, the *Doctrina Breve*, and the *Doctrina Cristiana* prepared as a catechism for Indian use,[4] both show the profound influence of Erasmian thought. Both insist on the primacy of faith over works and advocate the unlimited diffusion of the Scriptures. The men who began the spiritual conquest of Mexico were thus daring religious radicals; but they were also members of a spiritual army whose leaders stood close to the throne. In the first decades of Mexican settlement they had almost a free hand, usurping, by royal direction, the pastoral and sacramental duties normally entrusted to secular clergy. Their leadership in the spiritual conquest ensured its efficiency and speed. Their impact upon colonial society in New Spain, despite the smallness of their numbers, was of explosive force.

The conversion which the missionaries sought to achieve was more than a mere outward conformity. Baptism was to be preceded by careful instruction in the faith, by preaching, by catechism, and by the establishment of schools in which the sons of leading Indians might be educated in Christian doctrine and European ways.[5] The teaching, catechizing and baptism of many hundreds of thousands could be achieved, by the small numbers of friars available, only by concentrating the Indians in urban communities close to the nucleus of church and convent from which the missionaries directed their enterprise. Naturally the friars settled in places where urban communities already existed; but outside the old capitals such concentrations of population were rare. The great majority of Indians lived in scattered hamlets among their cultivations. Much of the energy of the missionaries was therefore devoted to persuading or compelling the Indians to move into new towns built around church and convent and reserved for Indian habitation. By these means, they argued, new converts could have not only the moral advantages of urban life and missionary teaching, but also the economic and social advantage of segregation from lay

Spaniards. A policy of racial segregation was advocated, not for the convenience of Europeans, but in order to protect Indians from the exploitation and demoralization which might follow from too close contact with Europeans, and to keep them under continuous ecclesiastical supervision.

The success of the friars in establishing their ascendancy over the Indians was extraordinary, and can be explained only in terms of Indian psychology. The Indians were accustomed to living in accordance with an intricate and continuous ritual which governed all their communal activities, including the all-important processes of agriculture. Ceremonial and work were intertwined and inseparable. The Spanish conquest, with its destruction of temples, its prohibitions of pagan dances, its forceful proselytizing, weakened and in some places destroyed the old ritual organization. Work—whether forced labour for an *encomendero*, or wage labour, or even subsistence agriculture—ceased to be part of a socio-religious ceremonial system and became a mere profane necessity. A void was created in the spiritual and social life of the Indians, which could be filled, though partially and often superficially, by the ritual of the Church and the activities of church-building. The friars understood this necessity; and the very numerous and very large churches which were built, all over New Spain, though they owed their massive strength to considerations of defence, also owed their magnificence to a desire to replace the lost splendour of the pagan temples. Similarly, the splendour of ecclesiastical ritual—far more elaborate than was usual in Europe—was an attempt to meet the Indians' longing for the old ceremonial life which they had largely lost. As a result, in New Spain those Indians who were in close contact with missionaries acquired a new theocracy, a new priesthood and a hybrid religion. The cult of the Virgin was superimposed upon, and confused with, the cults of earth-mother and corn-goddess. The war-gods were forgotten, because they had proved so patently powerless against Spanish steel. Pagan fertility rites were Christianized, by the inclusion of a preliminary Mass and a procession through the village with the images of saints, or of local gods—for the distinction was often little understood. The outward sign of this intermingling of cults can be seen to this day in sixteenth-century churches decorated by Indian craftsmen. Angels are carved wearing feather bonnets, and the Madonna is depicted with the swarthy skin and lank black hair of an Indian.

The policy of the Orders necessarily interfered with the control of Indian labour upon which Spanish economic activity depended. It involved the preservation, and indeed the extension, of Indian communal agriculture, for the support of the mission towns. Moreover, the demands of the missions for Indian labour, and their success in securing it, for the purpose of building churches, cloisters and new dwellings, competed directly with the demands of lay Spaniards; and their exemption from episcopal jurisdiction was a constant source of friction within dioceses. Inevitably the friars on one hand, the secular clergy and Spanish employers on the other, became embroiled in a complex struggle for colonial power. Under Charles V the friars had very much their own way. Under Philip II, government policy changed and the decision went against them. It could hardly have been otherwise, in view of the imminent labour crisis. The Indians were to be Hispanicized as well as Christianized. Secular clergy—some of whom were now being trained in the new American universities—were to minister to their needs. The cloisters were to be brought under episcopal discipline. The friars' dream of a separate, specifically Indian Christian community was to be abandoned; only in remote provinces, Paraguay, New Mexico, California, could self-contained mission towns survive. The Indians were to be members—subordinate members, to be sure—of a centralized and integrated society of European type. Even within their own villages, the *corregidores de Indios*—district officers, as we should say—were instructed to supply them with European clothing, tools and seed, and to encourage them to produce and to market crops acceptable to European taste.

Spanish attempts, lay and ecclesiastical, to Europeanize the Indian population, achieved their greatest success in central Mexico. Cortés' decision to rebuild Tenochtitlán, to associate its prestige with Spanish government rather than leaving its ruins as a monument to Aztec grandeur, was highly significant. It became a mixed city, in which Spaniards and Indians lived side by side in their respective *barrios*. The rebuilding, though it strained the local labour resources to the limit, began a fruitful intermingling of Spanish and Indian ways which has remained characteristic of much of Spanish North America to this day. Similar mingling took place in smaller towns, even in villages. Both lay Spaniards and clerics played a part in the process of Hispanicization. Indian society had a great tradition of craftsmanship in its own right. Indians easily learned European crafts. They could enter craft guilds in the cities as apprentices and become masters along with Europeans.[6] Many became skilled stone-masons, carvers, silversmiths. In the mines, Indian foremen often understood technical processes better than the Spaniards who were employed as overseers. Some Indians set up on their own, as miners, as traders, or as muleteers operating strings of pack animals. Such Indians, working in and near European centres, were protected against ill-treatment—though not, of course, against disease—and could become modestly rich. So could the village headmen who organized the labour supply. Only those who stayed in the villages and tried to carry on in the old way had the worst of both worlds.

Racial mixture played a major part in the process. Many Spaniards took Indian wives or mistresses. Their offspring were treated in most ways as Europeans, and were exempt from tribute and *repartimiento* labour. Today Mexico is a predominantly *mestizo* country, where the majority of the people are of mixed blood and mixed traditions, and take pride in both strains of their ancestry.

In Peru the interaction of European and Indian ways was much slower and less complete. Pizarro, in removing his capital from Cuzco to the new city of Lima, emphasized the division between Spanish coast and Indian mountain. The Hispanicizing process was less intense, the Indians more resistant, the mitigating and mediating influence of the missionary Orders less effective. By the time that Peru was conquered, Erasmian radicalism within the Spanish Church had lost much of its vigour. Peru received no picked band of zealots comparable with the Twelve. Christianity, in so far as it was accepted at all, was accepted as a second and separate ritual, while the traditional worship was carried on as well, sometimes secretly and sometimes in the open. For two hundred years after the conquest the ecclesiastical authorities found it necessary to send out periodical *visitadores de idolatría*, in a vain attempt to suppress pagan rites. Apart from these occasional persecutions, the Indians, so long as they paid their tributes and performed the labour demanded of them, were left to themselves; though economically, of course, their village life suffered from disintegrating forces similar to those in Mexico. They lost much of what was best in their old culture, without acquiring much of the culture of Spain. Some of the survivors of the Inca aristocracy, it is true, adopted Spanish ways and lived in comparative wealth and comfort as landlords, even as *encomenderos*. They tended, however, either to abandon their Indian ties altogether, or else to revert violently and become leaders of Indian revolt. The Hispanicized Inca aristocrat, like the Spanish missionary, failed to bridge the gap between Spaniard and Indian in Peru. Peru became, and still remains, a country with a Spanish, devoutly Catholic, ruling class, and an Indian, largely pagan, peasantry.

These social upheavals were inherent in the clash and mingling of two such different cultures, and probably no effort of policy could have averted them; but governmental policy had a part to play, in directing, organizing, mitigating, sometimes restricting. It was the central government, for example, which in the fifteen-seventies deliberately slowed down the process of expansion in order to concentrate upon the consolidation and exploitation of what had already been won. The Spanish sovereigns were active participants from the beginning in the organization of empire; they were never content merely to confirm the actions and enact the policies of men in charge on the spot.

The general aims of royal policy in the Indies can be summarized under four main heads: to spread the Catholic faith; to draw the maximum possible revenue, compatible with good administration; to assert and extend the direct authority of the Crown; and to do justice. The first aim was standard policy, from which no Spaniard—indeed, *mutatis mutandis*, no European could dissent. Similarly, no one in the sixteenth century denied that an imperial government might tax conquered provinces, especially when—as the Spanish government constantly proclaimed—the revenue was needed for European wars in defence of the faith. The assertion of direct authority was a natural aim and duty of any government, particularly a government such as that of Castile, which had bitter experience of feudal and municipal indiscipline, and good reason to fear their reappearance overseas. To do justice was traditionally the prime duty of every monarch; and the Spanish monarchy carried over from the age of feudalism into the age of sovereignty a keen sense of its judicial obligations. The problem of defining and maintaining the respective legal rights of Indians and settlers was a matter of deep concern, amounting at times almost to obsession, for the kings and their immediate advisers. The Indies were regarded as kingdoms of the Crown of Castile, separate from the kingdoms of Spain and administered through a separate royal council. The Indians, from the moment of conquest, became the direct subjects of the Crown, not of the Spanish State or of any individual Spaniards. They were to be converted to Christianity as soon as possible, of course; but their conversion was to be free, not forced, and when converted they were to be admitted to the sacraments. They must, of course, render loyal obedience to the Crown, and contribute, by their labour and their taxes, to the well-being of government and society. Subject to these basic requirements, they were free men, and might not be enslaved. Their land and property were their own and might not be taken from them, save by fair and willing sale. Their headmen were to be confirmed in office and treated as minor officials. They were entitled to the full protection of the law, and might sue Spaniards and be sued by them. Among themselves, their own laws were to be respected except where they were clearly barbarous or repugnant to the Spanish laws of the Indies.

By the middle of the sixteenth century, not only had these main lines of Crown policy been clearly indicated; the main instruments for enforcement had been chosen. Success depended upon replacing the self-appointed captains and governors of the initial conquest by reliable officials appointed by the Crown. Such officials could be recruited in sufficient numbers only from the legal profession and from the law schools of the universities, where the authoritarian principles of Roman law were by this time fully entrenched. The standing committee of the Council of Castile, set up in 1511 to deal with the business of the Indies, and formally constituted in 1524 as the separate Council of the Indies, was a predominantly legal body. It combined, in the manner characteristic of Spanish institutions at that time, the functions of a supreme court of appeal in important cases with those of an advisory council and a directive ministry for the supervision of colonial affairs. It drafted all colonial legislation, subject to royal approval. Below the king, the empire had a legal bureaucracy at its head.

In the Indies, as in Spain, the school-trained lawyer was the natural and trusted agent of a centralizing policy. One of the most striking characteristics of Spanish colonial government was the great power and prestige of the professional judiciary. Ten *audiencias* were established in the Indies in the course of the sixteenth century.[7] Primarily courts of appeal, they acted also as cabinet councils to advise the civil or military governors of their respective provinces. They might hear appeals against governors' decisions and actions and might report independently to the Crown. They were expressly charged with the protection of Indian rights, and provided a powerful connecting link between a paternal royal authority and a subject people of alien culture. No better device could have been found, in sixteenth-century conditions, to check the centrifugal tendencies of an avaricious and disorderly colonial society. The *audiencia* judges were necessarily, in the absence of colonial law schools, peninsular Spaniards, differing widely in training, temperament and interests from the general run of conquerors and settlers. Some of them, as might be expected, came to accept the interests and ways of life of colonial Europeans, and competed greedily for the available pickings; but there were always some who stood by the spirit of their professional training and the letter of their instructions, in the face of the most bitter local opposition and unpopularity.

Not only the higher courts, but the provincial treasuries also, were staffed from an early date by officers appointed by the Crown, replacing the original appointments made by the conquerors. The treasury organization was carefully separated from the general administrative and judicial system of the colonies. Each provincial capital had its treasury office, its strongbox, its staff of officials—treasurer, comptroller, factor. The officials were responsible for the collection of direct taxes such as the fifth on precious metals; for the collection of tribute brought in by the Indian villages held by the Crown (and its sale, if paid in kind); for disbursements, such as official salaries, authorized in advance by the Crown; and for the regular remittance of the surplus to Spain.

Treasury officials were directly responsible to the *contaduría* section of the Council of the Indies. No payments might lawfully be made from the colonial treasuries without the prior authorization of the Crown, so that no viceroy or governor could hope to establish a private kingdom with public money.

Each province had its governor, and the governors of the two greatest provinces—Mexico and Peru—enjoyed the title and dignity of viceroys. They might be lawyers, ecclesiastics, or—more commonly—aristocratic soldiers. The powers of a viceroy were great, and his stipend generous enough to place him above petty venality. He was in no position, however, to make himself dangerously independent. He could not spend public money or dispense royal patronage on his own authority. Apart from a small personal guard, he had no armed force at his command. He could raise an army to repel invasion or put down insurrection, by calling out the *encomenderos* and their men; but in order to pay troops he was required, at least in theory, to write to Spain for prior approval. Moreover, he was watched and to some extent checked by the *audiencia* judges, and like all other officials had to submit to a *residencia*, a judicial investigation of his tenure of office, at the end of his term. If he quarrelled with his *audiencia*, he could not be sure that the Crown would support him. By this uncertainty, by setting everyone to watch everyone else, the Crown characteristically maintained its own ultimate control.

Not only did the Crown appoint the higher officials in courts and counting-houses; its surveillance extended more and more to the details of local government. In Indian districts the gradual resumption of *encomiendas* by the Crown made way for the appointment of salaried *corregidores*—local magistrates or district officers—to supervise the village headmen. In the Spanish community also, the Crown steadily broke down the power of the 'old conquerors' in their own strongholds, the corporate towns. Spanish society, in the Indies as in Spain, was strongly urban in character. Leading men, though they drew their income from land, flocks and herds, or mines, preferred to live in towns. The municipalities which the conquerors established were, in the early years, the only institutions of settled government. The revolt of the *comuneros* in Spain, however, had made a lasting impression on the young Charles V, leaving him more than ordinarily suspicious of the privileges and pretensions of municipal corporations, and of the local magnates who usually controlled them. The towns of the Indies, therefore, got titles and armorial bearings, but little else, by grant from the Crown. Their power of raising local taxes was severely limited, their *procuradores* were forbidden to meet together without express royal permission, and any tendency towards concerted action was sharply discouraged.

Nothing in the nature of a colonial assembly or *cortes* was allowed to develop. At an early date, also, the Crown secured control of the internal composition of the major town councils. Where at first the annual *regidores* had elected their successors, year by year, subject to the governors' approval, the Crown increasingly appointed *regidores* for life. By the end of the sixteenth century elections had ceased in all important towns. Many of the men who received these local offices from the Crown, it is true, were 'old conquerors' or settlers; but others came straight from Spain with their letters of appointment in their baggage. Conscious of favours received, and hopeful of favours to come, they were unlikely to become champions of local independence.

Bureaucratic centralization, in a vast and scattered empire with slow and hazardous communications, naturally created its own problems. In the Spanish Indies it was achieved at the expense of local initiative and speed of action. The Spanish monarchs—with some reason—never fully trusted their colonial officers. All important decisions, and many unimportant ones, were made in Spain. A request to Spain for instructions could not be answered in less than a year, at best. Two years was more usual; and the answer, when it came, might be merely a demand for more information. The volume of papers crossing the Atlantic in both directions mounted steadily. A system of checks and balances, of report, counter-report and comment, certainly ensured that all parties got a hearing and that government was fully informed; but equally certainly it impaired administrative efficiency, encouraged endless argument, and led to indecision and delay. In the Indies, there was no jurisdiction which could not be inhibited and no decision which could not be reversed. Appeals and counter-appeals might hold up essential action for years, until the occasion for it was forgotten. Even when the government had made up its mind and given a firm instruction, the conventional formula 'obey but not enforce' might still excuse procrastination if the decision were unpopular.

With all these qualifications, the achievement of Spanish conquest and government was an impressive one. Orderly and prosperous kingdoms were created. The Crown was loyally served by its lawyers, as well as by its soldiers and its priests. A great body of Statute Law was enacted, governing the relations between conquerors and conquered, and asserting the authority of Crown and royal courts over them all. Much of this legislation—the New Laws of 1542, for example, and the *Ordenanzas sobre descubrimientos* of 1573[8]—was a model of enlightenment for its time. That it was imperfectly enforced is true, and not surprising. Most sixteenth-century legislation was imperfectly enforced; but at least the generous provision of courts, staffed by salaried professional judges who might be expected to be reasonably impartial, ensured that the royal decrees were more than mere pious exhortations. Spanish imperial government was paternal, conscientious, legalistic; it was no more oppressive, nor more corrupt, than most contemporary European governments; in some respects, at least in intention, it was remarkably humane. Its achievements, as colonial empires go, were to prove remarkably enduring.

Imperialism, however, lays burdens, both economic and political, upon the homeland of the conquerors, and its rewards are often illusory. Many Spaniards—*conquistadores*, settlers and officials—made fortunes in the Indies which they could hardly have dreamed of in Spain; but the steady drift overseas of men of courage and ability was a serious loss to Spain. The silver of the Indies, the most valued prize of empire, which paid the armies of Italy and Flanders, in the end created more problems than it solved. The great increase in the amount of silver in circulation in Spain, and in due course throughout Europe, the consequent rise in commodity prices, and the upsetting of the established bimetallic ratio, together caused great confusion and great hardship. Since the rigidity of the Castilian economy made it impossible for industry and agriculture to respond adequately to the stimulus of rising prices, the result was to place Spain at a serious disadvantage in international trade.[9]

Of specie remittances to Spain, between a quarter and a third were Crown revenue under various heads of taxation. Until about the middle of Philip II's reign this Indies revenue was not a major item in the total receipts of the Crown, not more than about ten per cent in most years. In the last two decades of the sixteenth century it mounted rapidly, and in one year, 1585, reached twenty-five per cent. Moreover, the income which private individuals drew from the Indies helped to increase the yield of taxation in Spain. The Indies revenue, therefore, though much smaller than most contemporaries, Spanish and foreign, supposed, was important enough to affect royal policy considerably, and to produce effects more insidious than monetary inflation alone. A nation cannot live, or fancy itself to be living, by the efforts of subjects overseas, without some demoralization of its public life at home. As early as 1524 the *Cortes* of Castile had protested against the proposal to sell the Moluccas to Portugal, on the ground that the possession of the islands secured to the Emperor a steady income, independent of taxation. The deputies were prepared to relinquish their only political bargaining counter, the control of financial supply, in order to relieve the immediate burden of taxes. According to the economic theories of the time the argument was reasonable; but it augured ill for the future of constitutional liberties in Spain. The possession of the Indies encouraged Philip II and his successors more and more to ignore unwelcome advice from the *Cortes*, from the nobility and from public opinion generally, in

Castile; and public opinion grudgingly acquiesced in the growth of absolutist practices born of successful imperialism. Bureaucratic absolutism spread, as it were by contagion, from the Indies to Castile, where it was naturally more directly felt, more burdensome, less tempered by distance and procrastination. The possession of the Indies also helped to make permanent the preponderance of Castile, the most warlike, the least productive, in many ways the most backward of the Iberian kingdoms, over the rest of the peninsula. Finally, exaggerated estimates of the value of the Indies intensified the fear and hostility which Hapsburg policy produced in many parts of Europe, while encouraging the Spanish Crown to pursue an international policy which it could not afford to maintain, and which was to lead it to impoverishment and defeat.

CHAPTER 15

THE SEA EMPIRES OF PORTUGAL
AND HOLLAND

THE merchant principalities of Indonesia soon recovered from the shock of the Portuguese intrusion in the early sixteenth century; and as the fighting peoples of the islands grew accustomed to European methods of warfare, and themselves increasingly made use of fire-arms both ashore and afloat, the Portuguese lost their early reputation for invincibility. They were few in number and far from home; their strongholds were widely scattered, precariously held, and cut off for part of every year from the viceregal capital at Goa. They soon found their place, not as a conquering empire, but as one of many competing and warring maritime powers in the shallow seas of the archipelago.

The principal Portuguese bases in the East Indies were Malacca and Ternate.[1] Malacca had been captured outright in 1511 and was ruled by a Portuguese governor. It was a harbour of importance, potentially dominating the shipping of the strait; but Portuguese warships in the area were too few to make this domination continuously effective, and other centres quickly rose to prominence and prosperity, as native trade avoided Malacca and sought other markets. The Sultan of Malacca, defeated and exiled, moved down the coast to the marshy islands of the Singapore Strait, and there began to build up the principality which became Johore. Opposite Malacca, the Sultanate of Atjeh grew in power and strength by selling Sumatran pepper to Javanese and Arab traders, and steadily extended its territorial power in northern Sumatra Much of the pepper which found its way to the Persian Gulf and the Red Sea came from Atjeh. Enterprising in business, warlike and fanatically Muslim, the Atjenese had become by 1530 very dangerous neighbours both in war and in trade. In 1537, in 1547 and in 1551 they assaulted the fortress of Malacca itself. Malacca had no allies in the area, except for an intermittent contact with the pagan Bataks of inland Sumatra, who were stubbornly resisting the proselytizing power of Atjeh. The Portuguese had little to offer to an ally; they were fully occupied in defending themselves and their trade. Not until 1587 did they gain, by a peace treaty with Atjeh, a period of respite in western Indonesia.

At Malacca the Portuguese were well entrenched and defended. In the Moluccas, and in eastern Indonesia generally, their position was weaker. They never conquered or ruled the island of Ternate. Their presence there was regulated by a treaty with the Sultan, which granted them a monopoly of the export trade in cloves and the right to occupy and fortify a limited factory area. They were always dependent in some degree, therefore, on the Sultan's good will. A series of able and energetic sultans of Ternate profited by Portuguese spice-buying and by Portuguese armed support against the rival sultanate of Tidore; but except for the factory area they gave up no sovereignty and tolerated no Christian proselytizing. The religious policy of Ternate caused considerable embarrassment to the governors of the Portuguese settlement, and led to trouble with Christian missionaries, especially, in the middle of the sixteenth century, with the Jesuits. Some of the most active Jesuit missionaries in the East were not Portuguese, but Italians, Flemings, or Spaniards; owing an international loyalty, they had no particular care for the political or commercial interests of Portugal and were bitterly critical of an alliance with an aggressive and persecuting Muslim power. Their influence contributed to a steady deterioration in the relations between the Portuguese and their neighbours in Ternate.

One way out of the dilemma in which the Portuguese governors found themselves was the establishment of missions and factories in other islands. When the Portuguese first arrived in the area, Tidore and Ternate had been the only producers of cloves on a commercial scale, but Portuguese buying had raised the price, and clove plantations quickly spread to Halmahera and the Banda Islands, to Amboina and Buru. In the second quarter of the sixteenth century the new plantations were in full bearing, and their product was mostly purchased by Javanese merchants. In order to avoid contact with the Portuguese at Ternate, these native traders used as their principal entrepôt the Muslim city of Brunei on the north coast of Borneo, which, by handling cloves and nutmeg for export to China and to India, grew in wealth and prominence and became a rival to Ternate, just as Atjeh, by handling pepper, became a rival to Malacca. Both to escape from dependence on the Sultan of Ternate and to retain their control of the clove trade, therefore, the Portuguese sought to extend their commercial, political and religious influence in the other islands of the Molucca group. In all the islands except Tidore and Ternate there were large pagan populations, not yet Islamized, which presented an opportunity for Christian missions. The great St Francis Xavier visited Amboina in 1546, and some success was achieved there and in western Halmahera in the establishment of missions and in conversion; though

THE AGE OF RECONNAISSANCE

the conversions were mostly of a politic kind. The pagan villagers throughout the area were willing to accept, at least outwardly, the religion of the power, whether Muslim or Christian, which appeared predominant at the time, and for the most part apostatized one way or the other with equal ease. In the Banda Islands Muslim missionaries outnumbered and out-preached the Christians; and the Bandanese, though willing to do business with the Portuguese, would not permit the erection of forts or the monopolizing of their trade. Amboina was more friendly and more receptive, and in the early fifteen-sixties preparations were made for building a Portuguese fort there. These moves produced a sharp reaction in Ternate, and in 1565 the Sultan's forces invaded Amboina. A few Amboinese Christians clung to their new faith, and suffered martyrdom. The viceroy at Goa, in response to appeals from the missionaries, dispatched a fleet which temporarily restored Portuguese power in the island. Emboldened by this success, the governor at Ternate withheld from the Sultan Hairun his due share of the profits of the clove trade; and then, in 1570, under cover of a meeting for negotiation, had him assassinated. The succeeding Sultan, Baabullah, declared war and besieged the fortress at Ternate. No further help came from Goa or Malacca; and in 1574 the fortress fell. The Sultan of Ternate thus became the dominant power in the Moluccas; only in Amboina the Portuguese, with native support, held out against him. When a few years later, Drake arrived at Ternate, he found the power of the local Portuguese at its lowest ebb since Alboquerque's time. Their political position in eastern Indonesia, and the continuation of some of their missions, had been saved only by a hasty alliance with the Sultan of Tidore; by the union of the Iberian crowns in 1580, which gave them the support of Spanish forces based at Manila; and by the opportune death of their enemy, Baabullah, in 1585.

The crusading tradition of the Portuguese, and the uncompromising orthodoxy and vigour of their missionaries, severely hampered their commercial and diplomatic endeavours. In an area where Islam was the dominant religion and was spreading rapidly among both Hindu and pagan peoples, the Portuguese often found themselves committed beforehand to religious hostility, in places where their interests would have been best served by commercial treaties. This was particularly so in Java, the great island lying at the centre of the trade and politics of the whole archipelago. The old Hindu empire of Majapahit, which had once covered most of the archipelago, had long been breaking up, and by the early sixteenth century Hinduism was confined to Java and Bali. In the first thirty years of the century a series of Muslim merchant princes established themselves on the north coast of Java, at Bantam,

Jacatra, Japara, Surabaya, and other harbour towns. These maritime sultans were bitterly hostile to the Portuguese conquerors of Malacca; only at Bantam were the Portuguese allowed to trade, and that not until 1545. Sea passage along the coast of Java became so dangerous that at some periods in the sixteenth century the Portuguese even routed their trade between Ternate and Malacca to the north of Borneo, swallowing their pride and concluding agreements with the Sultan of Brunei for this purpose. The north Javanese sultans effectively prevented any junction between the Portuguese and the declining Shivaitic rulers of inland Java. Eventually, about the middle of the century, the inland kingdom went over to Islam, with unexpected political results; for a new, invigorated, Islamized empire in central Java grew up, under the name of Mataram, and began a series of aggressive wars against the coastal sultans. This offered an opportunity to the Portuguese; since Mataram was exclusively a land power, indifferent to maritime trade, the Portuguese might support its rulers against the coastal towns and, if successful, might secure, by agreement, a monopoly of the Java trade. They did, in fact, inflict a number of naval defeats upon the coastal sultans, already threatened by Mataram on the landward side. They were not strong enough, however, to intervene decisively, and they were too deeply committed against Islam in general to make a permanent and effective alliance with a proselytizing state such as Mataram. Eventually it was not the Portuguese but the Dutch who profited by this opportunity.

The situation of the Portuguese in the East Indies was always insecure. They were not an important territorial power; their political and religious influence was comparatively small. On the other hand, their shipping was formidable by local standards; most of the Indonesian powers at one time or another sought their support in war, and their maritime trade remained successful and profitable well into the seventeenth century. They owed their continued commercial success not only to their armed strength at sea but to the extent and variety of their enterprises. Their ships went everywhere in the East. In the intricate and constantly changing pattern of relations, disaster in one place would usually be balanced by unexpected good fortune in another. Commodities from many islands were concentrated, for transhipment, in the Portuguese harbours of the Malabar coast; the profits of many complicated trades supported the raffish splendour of Golden Goa.[2]

Goa was a big and well-defended city, a territorial power of some importance, and a strong naval base. It was in regular contact with Europe and was the principal—the only important—eastern terminus for the direct sea-borne spice trade to western Europe. Here, if anywhere, Portuguese imperial power seemed secure. It was, however, a limited power. Just as in Indonesia there were many sources of spices, so in India there were many ports of transhipment, over which the Portuguese had no control. They never succeeded in establishing the monopoly which Alboquerque had planned. In India, as in Indonesia, they were one territorial and commercial power competing among many. Moreover, in the course of the sixteenth century the balance of power in India changed to their disadvantage.

When Alboquerque took Goa, the power of the Muslim sultanates of central India had been counterbalanced by that of Vijayanagar, the formidable and fabulously rich Hindu kingdom in the south, whose territories stretched from the Kistna to Cape Comorin. After the death of Krishna Raya in 1529, this kingdom entered upon a steady decline. Finally it was defeated and dismembered by a league of the central Indian Muslim sultanates, Bijapur, Ahmadnagar, Golconda and Bidar. The battle of Talikot in 1565 marked the end of the kingdom of Vijayanagar as a potent political force and placed the Muslim princes in undisputed command of most of central and south India. One of the inevitable results of this Muslim victory was an agreement among the sultans to drive the Portuguese out of Goa and the other coastal fortresses. The attack on Goa began in 1569; its defence against heavy odds was one of the most brilliant military feats in Portuguese history, and entitled the viceroy Luis de Ataide to rank among the great soldiers of his time. Command of the sea—the only route by which reinforcements could come—saved the Portuguese garrisons from annihilation; but only after two years of fierce fighting did the sultans abandon their attempt.

Meanwhile in north India even more momentous events had been taking place. At the time when the Portuguese arrived in India, the sultanate of Delhi, under an Afghan dynasty, had been passing through a period of disorder and decline, and the Hindu Rajput princes had recovered something of their old power; but in 1524 the supremacy of Islam was restored by a fresh invasion. The invader was Babur, a descendant on his father's side from Timur the Lame and on his mother's from Chinghiz Khan. Babur entered India to recapture the old possessions of his family with a small army of central Asian horsemen and—significant and decisive innovation—a battery of Turkish artillery. He possessed himself of the Delhi kingdom in two major battles. At Panipat in 1526 he defeated and drove out the Afghan sultan; and at Kanua in 1527 he broke up the Rajput confederation. Babur was the founder or re-founder of the Delhi empire of the house of Timur, miscalled by Europeans the Mughal empire—the most powerful state in India, ruled by a series of able and vigorous princes. The Mughal emperors were not, therefore, native to India, any more than the

Portuguese. They were of central Asian origin; their mother-tongue was Turki; the official and literary language of their court was Persian. With one notable exception they were orthodox and often persecuting Muslims.

Since the Mughals were exclusively land warriors and the Portuguese were fighters by sea, the first contacts between them were indirect. They arose from the attempts of Babur's successor Humayun to extend his authority over the independent Muslin sultanates of north India, in particular the maritime state of Gujerat, which at the time was in a state of chronic disorder and civil war. The ruler of Gujerat, threatened with invasion by the Mughal, asked for Portuguese help, and in 1535 the Portuguese, in return for a promise of military assistance (which they never fulfilled) received a site for a warehouse and fortress at Diu and other territorial concessions. Shortly afterwards Humayun abandoned his campaign; but the Portuguese remained at Diu and beat off all attempts of the Sultan of Gujerat to dislodge them. Diu became, after Goa, one of the most important bases of Portuguese power in India.

Humayun's successor on the Mughal throne was Akbar, the greatest of his line and one of the most remarkable sovereigns of any time. So vigorous a ruler clearly would not tolerate a source of constant disorder in Gujerat. The Portuguese, appreciating by this time the power which the Mughals wielded, refused to be enticed into any alliance against Akbar. To the emperor it must have been a source of great vexation to find important harbours like Diu and Bassein in the hands of alien merchants; but he saw at once that the Portuguese could not be dislodged without the use of a fleet, which the Mughals never possessed. When, therefore, Akbar reduced Gujerat to obedience in 1572–3, he entered into courteous relations with the Portuguese and left their warehouses alone. In 1578 a Portuguese ambassador was accredited to Akbar's court, and in 1580 the first Jesuit mission visited the Mughal capital. Akbar was characteristically interested in all religions, and like Kublai Khan in the thirteenth century was disposed to give Christians a fair hearing. In this, however, he stood alone. The Portuguese could not hope for a like tolerance after his death. Their own crusading tradition, indeed, made it difficult for them to maintain for long normal civil relations with a Muslim state.

When Vasco da Gama first reached Calicut and was asked by its ruler what he had come to seek, he is said to have answered tersely, 'Christians and spices.' There were, of course, considerable numbers of Nestorian Christians in south India. Da Gama's followers even confused Hindus with Christians; at least they were prepared to regard all who were not Muslims as potential Christians. Since the crusading zeal of da Gama, Alboquerque and their like took the form of a commercial and religious war against Islam, and since when they arrived the struggle between Hindu and Muslim in south India was still undecided, it is surprising that the Portuguese did not make more serious efforts to come to an understanding with the Hindu communities. In dealing with these communities, however, they displayed an obtuseness which prevented them from making either trustworthy allies of the neighbouring rulers or loyal subjects of the inhabitants of their own harbour towns. The caste system, for example, was a mystery to them. Even Alboquerque, usually punctilious in such matters, on one occasion asked the Raja of Cochin to have some men of low caste, who had assisted the Portuguese, raised to a higher caste, and took offence at the Raja's refusal. That such matters were beyond a prince's power seems never to have occurred to him. Brahmin notions of ceremonial purification caused constant trouble. Portuguese admirals attributed the refusal of Brahmins to dine on board their ships to the fear of poison, and were quick to take offence at the ceremonial cleansing which had to be undergone by Brahmins who visited Portuguese ships. It is true that, within the Portuguese enclaves, Alboquerque and his immediate successors interfered very little with native religious custom, except for attempts to suppress the rite of *sati*; but missionaries followed upon the heels of the merchant crusaders. The relations of the Portuguese commanders to the Church inevitably changed as ecclesiastics became a larger and larger proportion of the white inhabitants; especially since the Jesuits, shortly after the foundation of their Order, selected Goa as their principal headquarters outside Rome. In 1540 came the royal order for the destruction of all Hindu temples in Goa. The early intermittent work of the friars, mainly Franciscan, who came out with the annual fleets blossomed into a native church under the apostolic teaching of St Francis Xavier, who reached India in 1542. Independently of the apostolate of St Francis, there emerged a system of civil regulation designed to exclude all non-Christians from public office. In 1560 the Inquisition arrived to deal with apostates and heretics. The accession of a Spanish zealot to the Portuguese throne in 1580 increased the official pressure upon the native religions. Even the Nestorians—the 'St Thomas' Christians'—received no encouragement, and indeed after the arrival of the Jesuits were treated more harshly, as heretics, than were Hindus. The Synod of Diamper in 1599 officially denounced Nestorius and his errors and for a time extinguished the Indian Nestorian Church as an organized community in Portuguese territory.

The fervent apostolic mission of St Francis and his followers was one of the outstanding achievements of the Counter-Reformation Church. To this day, throughout Ceylon and in many of the Malabar towns, there are considerable numbers of Catholic Christians who bear Portuguese baptismal names and who are conscious enough of their separate communal existence to wear a distinguishing dress. They have always been, however, a relatively small minority of the whole population. Muslims were hardly touched by Christian preaching. Hindus and Nestorians were too numerous, too civilized and too deeply attached to their own ways to be converted *en masse* by a handful of European friars, however devoted. Moreover, the Catholic attitude towards other religions was alien to the normal tolerance of Hindus. The majority of conversions were made among persons of low caste seeking to escape from the pressure of the caste system. The result of the zeal of Crown and missionaries was often to make the Portuguese hated, not only as pirates, but as religious persecutors. By one of the unexpected coincidences of history, in the same year—1599—in which the Synod of Diamper condemned the ancient church of Malabar, the London merchants met in Founders' Hall to establish an East India Company.

At the end of the sixteenth century, then, the Portuguese maintained small though strong bases on the west coast of India, and more precarious footholds in the East Indies. They conducted a widespread, varied and profitable trade in eastern products, and monopolized the trade between India and Europe by the Cape route. They had no monopoly of the purchase of spices, and no control over their production. Eastern products in large quantities still went to the Mediterranean by the old routes, and though the Portuguese preyed intermittently upon this trade, they could not prevent it. Their position depended upon their sea-borne strength; and the efficiency of their shipping was declining both absolutely and relatively to other European powers. The appearance in eastern waters of an enemy who could defeat them at sea would damage their power and their trade severely. The Turks had several times tried and failed. In the end it was a European enemy who succeeded.

The Dutch East India Company, like most trading corporations, at first acquired territorial possessions slowly and with reluctance. Theorists and politicians in Amsterdam attributed the decline of Portuguese wealth and power to the dissipation of energy in territorial conquest, and warned the company against a similar mistake. The official policy of the directors was to stick to trade and to avoid entanglement in Indonesian politics; and the admirals of most of the early expeditions behaved with a circumspection and courtesy which contrasted sharply with Portuguese arrogance. They soon discovered, however, that spices were cheap and plentiful throughout the islands. There were many alternative sources of supply and many routes of shipment to India, the Near East and Europe. If the Dutch company were to become one more among many competing carriers, the result would be to raise prices in Indonesia and probably to glut the European market. To ensure a cheap and regulated supply in the East and a steady high price in Europe, a monopoly was necessary. This could be achieved only by doing what the Portuguese had failed to do; by controlling all the main sources of supply. Some of the ablest of the company's officers in the East favoured an aggressive policy almost from the start. Coen, the founder of Batavia, declared the section of Java from the frontier of Cheribon to that of Bantam, and from the Java Sea to the Indian Ocean, to be company's territory. He could not enforce his claim, and neither the directors nor the Indonesian princes took it seriously; indeed, throughout much of the seventeenth century the Dutch could not wander far from the town without danger from Bantamese dacoits. Some of Coen's successors, however—van Diemen and Speelman particularly—made far wider claims, and eventually their policy prevailed. Circumstances compelled the company to secure commercial mastery by territorial dominion.

The general plan inherited from Coen by his successors was to make Batavia a central mart for inter-Asiatic trade and the general warehouse of eastern goods for export to Europe. Since Dutch commercial interests extended throughout the East from Nagasaki to the Persian Gulf, the plan of forcing trade through Batavia involved much unnecessary sea transport by long indirect routes; but as usual at that time, considerations of convenience were expected to give way to considerations of monopoly. A centralized monopoly was the easiest to protect. As a would-be monopolist, the company sought to close the eastern seas, as far as possible, to other European ships, Portuguese and English especially, and to reduce native shipping to the auxiliary rôle of supplying local products without competing in the carrying trade on the main routes. Such a system could be enforced only by armed fleets, and maintained only through a vast network of fortified posts. The establishment of posts and bases called for treaties with the local rulers. Constantly troubled by harem intrigues or succession wars, or needing support against the Portuguese or against local neighbours, the Indonesian princes called all too readily upon the Dutch to intervene in their quarrels. The company, with its stable organization and its inexorable demand for profit, took payment in the form of permanent commercial concessions. It thus established an economic stranglehold and gradually reduced the princes first to subordinate allies and then to vassals. Eventually the Dutch found themselves not only following in the footsteps of the Portuguese, but acquiring far more actual territory than the Portuguese ever possessed.

One of the major objects of the company's policy was to secure control of the western approaches to the archipelago. Batavia itself commanded the Sunda Strait. In the Malacca Strait, Portuguese and Atjenese, though mutually hostile, resisted the Dutch for many years; but in 1641 van Diemen took Malacca, and in 1663 Maetsuycker, by assuming the protection of a league of its discontented vassals, procured the downfall of Atjeh as a powerful and organized state. Further west, the Dutch had fastened their grip upon Ceylon in 1640, allying themselves with the inland kingdom of Kandy against the Portuguese factories on the coast. The Sinhalese monarch, like many of the Indonesian princes, incurred a heavy war debt to the company, which he paid in instalments of elephants and cinnamon. The Dutch seized the coastal settlements, Colombo, Galle, Batticaloa, Trincomalee, and by 1658 the last Portuguese were expelled. Ceylon had long been an important half-way house of Indian Ocean trade. Dutch control of its most important harbours placed the company in a strong position to monopolize trade across the Bay of Bengal and to discourage—though not to prevent—other European trade with the Coromandel coast.

These successes assured the Dutch monopoly of the most valuable part of the eastern trade, the trade in spices with the Moluccas; for though the Spaniards hung on at Tidore until 1663, they were clearly fighting a losing battle. The Banda Islands had been conquered by Coen in 1621. The inhabitants had been killed or enslaved and the land distributed among the company's servants or nominees, who undertook to sell all their produce to the company at the company's prices. Amboina was similarly absorbed in 1647, after a long series of *hongi* raids by armed fleets of native mercenaries, employed by the Dutch to destroy all clove production in excess of the company's requirements. In 1650 a rising against the Dutch factors at Ternate—where they had originally been welcomed as allies against Tidore—led to reprisals, and in 1657 the Sultan was compelled to an agreement whereby, in return for a Dutch pension, he undertook to prohibit the cultivation of spices in all islands subject to him, leaving spice growing entirely to islands in the possession of the company. The immediate effect of the subjection of Ternate was to increase the wealth and prestige of another rival, Macassar, whose Sultan was supplied with arms by Portuguese and English traders; but Macassar too was taken in 1669 by a Dutch fleet and a large force of Buginese mercenaries under Cornelius Speelman. The Sultan of Macassar agreed to sell all the exportable produce of his kingdom to the company, and granted the Dutch a monopoly of the import of manufactures and all Chinese goods.

There remained the central problem of the control of Java. The safety of Batavia depended in large measure upon the mutual jealousy of the sultanates of Mataram and Bantam, both of which had claims to the Batavia territory. As a maritime State, Bantam had backed the losing cause of the English in 1618, in the hope of recovering Batavia, and remained bitterly opposed to the Dutch. Mataram, much the larger and stronger of the two, was an inland state whose rulers had little appreciation of the importance and value of maritime trade. While despising the Dutch as mere merchants, they tolerated them as customers for rice and welcomed their wars on the coastal sultans. In 1646 the *Susuhunan*—'he-to-whom-everything-is-subject'—of Mataram agreed, in return for a formal recognition of his suzerainty over company's territory, to the exclusion of Javanese traders from the Spice Islands. Step by step the Dutch destroyed maritime intercourse between Mataram and the outside world. Traders and shipbuilders lost their occupations, and the Javanese became almost entirely a race of cultivators; the only customer for their export crops being the Dutch company. In 1675 the Dutch, further to secure the food supply of Batavia, intervened in a succession dispute in Mataram, and secured from the victor an agreement closing the vassal ports of Mataram to all other foreigners, granting a monopoly of the opium trade, and ceding a considerable tract of inland rice-producing territory to the company. In 1680 they picked a quarrel with Bantam, and after inflicting a crushing naval defeat upon the Sultan, insisted on his abandoning his territorial claims, granting a pepper monopoly to the Dutch, and closing his ports to other foreigners. By the end of the century the company not only controlled all the ports of Java, but possessed a large tract of inland territory from coast to coast. Many maritime princes and their subjects, forced from their livelihood, took to piracy; but none was strong enough to challenge the company directly. The way was prepared for widespread annexation and the development of a great territorial empire.

One incidental achievement of the Dutch company must be mentioned: the establishment of a colony at the Cape of Good Hope. This was the only true colony founded by the Dutch in the Old World in the seventeenth century. It was planted in 1652, not as a trading station, but as a strategical support to the Indies commerce and as a convenient halting-place where the company's ships could take in fuel, water and fresh provisions. The company, while retaining all freehold, offered stock and leases on easy terms, and soon attracted a considerable number of settlers. Most of these *boers* were peasants from Holland and elsewhere, who were eager only for land and did not resent the political and commercial restrictions placed upon them by the company. Within a few years the colony was producing wine and provisions in considerable quantity and had become a valuable asset. Politically it formed one of the nine governments into which the Dutch Indies were divided, under the general administrative supervision of Batavia; the others being Ternate, Coromandel, Amboina, Banda, Ceylon, Malacca, Macassar and the north-east coast of Java.

Dutch colonial policy in the seventeenth century displayed little of the careful stewardship which was to be its characteristic in later times, and still less of the missionary paternalism and care for native rights which, officially at least, distinguished that of Spain. The company was unwilling to bear the expense of any but a purely commercial administration. The government at Batavia stood at the head not of a territory, but of a number of widely-scattered establishments. Just as the company at Amsterdam was organized as a firm of shipowners of whom the governor-general was the paid agent, so the company's employees under the governor-general in the East held commercial, not administrative rank, as merchants, junior merchants or clerks, though their actual work might be as director of factories, commandants of forts or residents at the courts of native princes. At the elbow of the governor-general, and second only to him in importance, stood an executive officer known as the director-general of trade.[3]

Although the company, as its activities expanded, could not avoid acquiring territory in the interests of its profit and safety, it delegated the responsibilities of administration wherever possible. The immediate neighbourhood of Batavia was under direct Dutch rule; but in the other possessions of the company in Java the duties of government were entrusted to regents, in theory the company's servants, in practice petty feudal lords, vassals of the company as they had formerly been vassals of Mataram. The regents had to obey the orders of the company's European officers; but as a rule these orders only concerned the delivery of produce. In all other respects they ruled as little local tyrants, very loosely supervised, but sure of the company's support if their authority were resisted. The more distant princes of Java in the late seventeenth century still boasted a more or less fictitious independence, ruling under the suzerainty or protection of the company or in subordinate alliance with it. The senior Dutch officer at the court of each of these protected princes—the 'resident'—exercised both civil and criminal jurisdiction over the company's servants and other Europeans living in the principality. He administered Dutch law, with the local modifications contained in the statutes of Batavia. In respect of the native princes and their subjects, the functions of the 'residents' were primarily commercial. Interference with native justice was exceptional. Non-European foreigners, of whom the Chinese were by far the most numerous, lived under the jurisdiction of their own headmen in accordance with the normal custom throughout the East.

Outside Java, the same gradations of Dutch rule, direct and indirect, existed. Except for harbour towns and factories, only the small but important spice-producing areas of Amboina and the Banda Islands were administered directly by the company. In Ternate, in Macassar and elsewhere, Dutch interests were protected as in Java, by treaties of alliance or protectorate enforced by Dutch 'residents'.

The company derived its revenue in the first instance from the profits of trading; but since its trade was a jealously guarded monopoly, it began, as soon as its growing power permitted, to regulate production in order to maintain prices, and to confine the production of especially valuable crops to areas under its own control. From the regulation of production to the levy of tribute in kind under colour of trade was but a short step. The principal duty of the regents in occupied Java was to supply to the company, free of cost, fixed quantities of pepper, indigo and cotton yarn. The treaty with the *Susuhunan* of Mataram in 1677 required that prince to deliver annual consignments of rice at a fixed price. The Sultan of Bantam by a similar treaty was compelled to sell to the company, at its own price, the whole pepper crop of his kingdom. In theory a distinction was maintained between 'contingencies', which were undisguised tributes in kind, and 'forced deliveries', trading contracts exceptionally favourable to the purchaser; but in practice these two sources of revenue, which came to supply the bulk of the company's income, were confused both with one another and with the proceeds of ordinary trade. Compared with these tributes, open and disguised, taxation in the ordinary sense was unimportant. As a rule only Europeans paid direct taxes in money, and Europeans were the chief contributors under most heads of indirect taxation; but natives under Dutch rule were liable to forced labour, particularly for harbour works. In the Banda Islands the Dutch resorted to slave labour for the cultivation of spices, after the extirpation of the native population.

In social life, discrimination against Asiatics as such was unknown either in law or in practice, and mixed marriages were common; though the company discouraged non-Europeans and half-castes from going to Holland. There was sharp discrimination in law against non-Christians. In Batavia the public exercise of any worship except that of the Dutch Reformed Church was forbidden. In practice, despite the protests of the ministers, Hindus, Muslims and Chinese enjoyed complete freedom of worship immediately outside the walls and—as far as the company was concerned—elsewhere in the Indies. Like most Protestant Europeans at that time, the Dutch showed comparatively little interest in missionary work. The great variety of Indonesian dialects, moreover, made systematic preaching among the natives impossible. Throughout the seventeenth century Portuguese remained the chief *lingua franca* of the archipelago; and the few native converts to Calvinism came mostly from among Portuguese-speaking Catholics.

In sharp contrast, Islam under Dutch pressure displayed a great and growing vitality. Behind the moral force of Muslim preaching lay the political force of the empires of Turkey, of Persia and of north India. From time to time the Indonesian princes, in particular the *Susuhunan*, tried to arouse the interest and sympathy of these mighty states in the affairs of the Far Eastern Muslims. Had they succeeded, considerable damage might have been done to European interests in the Near and Middle East. The attempts failed; but even so, the hold of Islam upon the Indonesian peoples grew steadily stronger. Apart from the Hindus of Bali, the only Asiatics in the archipelago who remained unaffected were the Chinese, whose numbers and whose influence increased steadily under Dutch rule and have continued to increase ever since. In general, the influence of the Dutch invasion, irresistible in commerce and powerful in politics, was much weaker in ordinary social life, and in religious affairs almost negligible.

The trade of the Indian mainland was, for the Dutch, secondary to the more lucrative trade with the East Indies. They possessed a factory at Pulicat on the Coromandel coast, from which they ran a flourishing trade in cotton cloth with Java; but they were never particularly interested in Malabar or in north India. Their long blockade of Goa was intended to cut off Portuguese trade with Europe rather than to capture the town itself. For the most part they left western India to the English company, whose factory at Surat, established with the permission of the local Mughal viceroy, enjoyed a long and on the whole prosperous career as a depot for cotton, muslin, saltpetre and indigo from the interior of north India. The occasional misfortunes of Surat were the results either of local famines or of temporary losses of Mughal favour. The English were blamed and punished in 1623 for piracies committed by the Dutch against pilgrim ships plying to Mecca; and again in 1636 for the similar piracies of English captains, authorized by Charles I to visit India in contravention of the company's charter. Apart from these interludes the factors at Surat drove a profitable and peaceful trade as long as the Mughal power protected them; and the company's ships made some small return by policing the pilgrim route and by privateering against Dutch and Portuguese, under letters of marque from the Emperor.

The English also traded on the Coromandel coast, and there also they sought the protection of great overlords such as the King of Golconda, rather than relying upon agreements with the petty rajas of the coast. From 1634 the policy of the English company was to maintain a 'permanent residence' at the court of Golconda; but this 'residence', unlike those of the Dutch in Java, was diplomatic, not supervisory. It was with the permission and approval of the ruler that Francis Day, factor at Masulipatam, turned the flank of the Dutch in 1639 by founding a factory at Madras, and by building a fort there despite the opposition of his directors. In 1658 the company, strengthened and encouraged by Cromwell's charter of the year before, made Madras its headquarters for eastern India.[4]

1658 was the year of the accession of Aurangzeb, the last great Mughal emperor, a grim and earnest Muslim fanatic. Throughout the first half of the seventeenth century the policy and practice of the English company, as far as Indians were concerned, was peaceful unarmed trade. Its resources were at first too small to support a more aggressive policy. It relied upon the great Indian powers for protection, not only against banditry, but to some extent against the intrusion of other Europeans on land. On the high seas its ships could look after themselves. But an armed monopoly was the implied object of the English company, as of most European trading companies, and changes in the political situation in India eventually brought about an overt change in the company's policy. Aurangzeb's religious persecution alienated the Rajput princes, in Akbar's time the strongest supporters of the empire, and provoked widespread risings among Hindus from the Punjab to the Deccan. The military efficiency of the empire, no longer reinforced by immigrants from central Asia, was declining. In central India a predatory Hindu power, the Maratha confederacy, raided the Mughal provinces and through years of guerrilla warfare resisted or evaded the unwieldy imperial armies. In 1664 the Marathas raided Surat. They sacked the town, but were beaten off by the company's men from the walls of the English factory. For the first time the Mughal had failed to protect his clients, and the company began to look round for means to defend itself. The first requirement was a defensible base, if possible outside the imperial jurisdiction. Such a base lay ready to hand. Bombay had come into Charles II's hands as part of Catharine of Braganza's dowry. His ships had taken possession in 1665, after a protracted dispute with the resident Portuguese, and in 1668, finding the town an expensive liability, he leased it to the company. Aungier, the president at Surat, began the work of developing and fortifying the harbour. He established a gunboat squadron as a protection against local pirates and boldly entered into treaty relations with Sivaji, the Maratha chieftain upon whose flank he was entrenched. By 1677 the trade of Bombay already rivalled that of Surat. The old dependence upon Mughal favour was broken and the company had embarked upon a career of trading sword in hand.

The same growing forces of disorder afflicted eastern India also.

Madras was threatened by Sivaji in 1677. In Bengal, the small and struggling English factories protested vainly against the exactions of a semi-independent Mughal viceroy, until another local leader, Job Charnock, established a defensible base at Calcutta in the swamps of the Ganges delta in 1686. Charnock's quarrel with the viceroy in Bengal soon widened into a general war against the Mughal empire. The policy of unarmed trade was thus abandoned, and the company looked to its servants 'to establish such a polity of civil and military power, and create and secure such a large revenue as may be the foundation of a large, well-grounded, sure English dominion in India for all time to come'. This change of policy was made in conscious imitation of the Dutch. It was premature, however, to declare war and send a puny expedition of a few hundred men against an empire which maintained in the field an army of at least a hundred thousand. Aurangzeb's officers seized the company's factories at Surat and Masulipatam and cast its agents into prison. Probably only appreciation of English power at sea and the consequent threat to the pilgrim route saved the factors from expulsion. As it was, the company sued for peace, and in 1690 obtained a fresh licence to trade at the cost of humble submission and a heavy fine. In the same year Calcutta, abandoned during the war, was reoccupied, this time permanently, and the first buildings of a great city began to appear on the fever-haunted banks of the Ganges.

Although the Mughal empire was still too strong for the English on land, its power was fast declining. Aurangzeb's reign saw the greatest territorial extension of the Mughal power and the beginning of its disintegration. During his long absences on campaigns in south India he lost much of his control over Delhi and the north. His *subadars* became semi-independent feudatories, and his last twenty-five years were a weary and losing battle against growing anarchy. The Marathas paved the way for European political intervention in defence of commercial monopolies. The same train of events which had turned Aurangzeb into a wandering soldier, was to drive the English company in the eighteenth century to political intrigue and military adventure. From being a mere commercial undertaking it was to become a territorial overlord and a gatherer of tribute on a vast scale; and the East India 'interest' was to become one of the most powerful and corrupting influences in English public life.

CHAPTER 16

THE PLANTATIONS AND THEIR TRADES

THE achievement of Portugal in the sixteenth century included not only a maritime and commercial empire in West Africa, India and the East Indies, but a complementary land empire in Brazil. This string of scattered coastal settlements grew slowly, in contrast with the speed of eastern penetration. Neither gold nor diamonds were found until late in the seventeenth century, and pioneering in the Tropics held little attraction for men who could, if they chose, engage in the commerce of the East. For the first thirty or forty years after Cabral's landfall, Brazil was valued chiefly as a source of wild brazil-wood for use in the dyeing industry, and as a dumping-ground for transported criminals. Jealousy of French woodcutters and settlers, and suspicion of Spanish encroachments in the Río de la Plata area, first prompted John III in 1549 to establish a royal government at Bahía and actively to encourage settlement. Tomé de Souza, the first captain-general, had already considerable experience of war and administration in Africa and the East. The formidable expedition which accompanied him to his post included, besides soldiers, settlers and officials, six Jesuits under Manoel de Nobrega. Members of this newly-founded Order were to play a prominent part in the growth of Portuguese empire in the New World as in the Old, and their missions among the primitive Tupi-Guaraní peoples were to set a characteristic stamp upon the whole history of interior Brazil. Nobrega remained in Brazil until his death in 1570. His ministry overlapped and influenced the government of Mem de Sá, captain-general from 1557 to 1572. Mem de Sá was the most forceful and effective of the founders of colonial Brazil. His government succeeded in attracting considerable numbers of Portuguese settlers. He finally evicted the French, and founded in 1567 the settlement of Rio de Janeiro near the site of the principal French encampment. He was the first captain-general to devise and enforce a consistent native policy, intended to discipline the warlike, to convert the heathen, to protect those who submitted against enslavement and ill-treatment; in particular, to abolish cannibalism and to induce the Indians to settle in agricultural communities.

Portuguese society in Brazil was markedly rural in character. There were no Mexicos or Limas, and most of the 'towns' were mere hamlets. Apart from subsistence crops—native cassava and introduced maize—and the dye-wood which grew wild, the principal product was sugar, introduced from Madeira. Sugar was best grown, in Brazil as elsewhere, on relatively large estates, with slave labour. The Brazilian Indians proved unsuitable for estate labour, but the Portuguese were better placed than other Europeans for obtaining slaves from West Africa, and by the end of Mem de Sá's government the pattern of 'great house', slave quarters and cane-fields was generally established. By 1580 there were some sixty sugar mills in operation. The population of the settlements amounted to roughly 20,000 Portuguese, 18,000 settled Indians, and 14,000 negro slaves. As in Spanish America, inter-racial unions of one sort or another were frequent, and numerous half-castes came to swell the settled population, a thin scattering of people, confined to a narrow coastal fringe. The hinterland, the harsh and mountainous *sertão*, offered little attraction and was left untouched.

The union of the Iberian crowns in 1580 made little difference to this easy-going rural society. The influence of Spanish bureaucracy affected it only indirectly, incompletely and by slow degrees, while the demand for sugar in Europe increased year by year. The sugar areas of Brazil reached a peak of prosperity when the rest of the Portuguese empire was declining under Spanish rule and Dutch attack.[1] In 1623, on the eve of the first Dutch invasion, the Portuguese Crown controlled the coast from the Amazon delta to the Bay of Paranaguá. The northern area from the Amazon to Cape São Roque was still very sparsely inhabited, but an administration of sorts was carried on from a headquarters at São Luis do Maranhão. Most of the population was on the coast south of Cape São Roque. The most populous areas were Recife, Olinda, and their surrounding district, in the north-east captaincy of Pernambuco; the capital Salvador and its neighbourhood, in Bahía; Rio de Janeiro; and the highland plateau of São Paulo in the south. Pernambuco was the most flourishing sugar-producing area, followed by Bahía. Bahía was the seat of the governor-general, a bishop, and an *audiencia*. The other captaincies were administered by governors, mostly appointed by the Crown, though some were still appointed by semi-feudal proprietors—*donatarios*. The town councils or *senados da camara*, everywhere except in the capital, were the most influential and powerful organs of local government, and the colony as a whole was to a considerable extent self-governing, subject to the general religious and commercial regulations laid down in Lisbon or Madrid. There were some sixty or seventy thousand settlers of European or part-European origin, about half of them concentrated in Pernambuco, and about

350 sugar mills. Most of these were small cattle-driven machines; but even a small mill of this type, with the fields which supplied it with canes, would require four or five Europeans and twenty or thirty slaves to operate it. The largest mills employed four or five times this number. The aboriginal Amerindians had been killed, enslaved, or driven away from the immediate neighbourhood of the Portuguese settlements, except where they had been grouped together in villages under the administration of Jesuit missionaries. Labour for the sugar plantations was mostly supplied by negro slaves from West Africa and Angola, which furnished about 8,000 annually for Brazil and nearly as many for Spanish America.

Brazil was the chief source of the sugar consumed in Europe. Most of the trade in sugar and slaves between Brazil and Portugal or between West Africa and Brazil was still in the hands of Portuguese merchants and contractors, many of them of Jewish origin; but the export of sugar from Portugal to the rest of Europe was handled by Dutchmen, and Dutch skippers also plied a clandestine trade with the Brazilian ports. The local Portuguese connived at this trade, and resisted the attempts of the Spanish bureaucracy to prevent it. Merchants in Portugal, also, lent their names to Dutch commercial enterprises, on a commission basis, during the periods when Dutch trade to Iberian ports was officially forbidden. Dutch trade both to Portugal and to Brazil expanded rapidly during the years of the Truce. The mercantile Dutch had a clearer, a more sophisticated understanding than most Europeans —except perhaps the Portuguese themselves—of the nature of New World possessions as sources of profit. Usselincx, the pamphleteer and proponent of the Dutch West India Company, was among the first to point out in public discussion that the colonial wealth of the Iberian kingdoms was not simply a matter of gold and silver mines; that sugar, indigo, cochineal, tobacco, dyewoods, hides and pearls were together more valuable than precious metals; and that the population of the New World, European, Indian and *mestizo*, represented a vast and potentially very profitable market for European goods. He pointed to Brazil as an instance of a territory which produced no precious metals but a great deal of wealth in other forms. The policy which he urged upon his countrymen was a concentration upon peaceful settlement in productive but unoccupied parts of the Americas, in order to create other Brazils under Dutch management. How this was to be achieved without fighting Spain, he never explained. In fact, when the Dutch West India Company was incorporated after the expiry of the Truce, its activities included not only trade in any part of the Americas where goods could be sold and cargoes purchased, not only the peaceful settlement of New Netherland on the banks of the lower Hudson, but also, against Usselincx' advice, a large-scale naval war of plunder and attrition against Spanish-American harbours and trade, and a series of determined campaigns for the conquest of Portuguese Brazil.

The Dutch capture of Bahía in 1624 was short-lived, for a powerful fleet sent from Portugal re-took the place in the following year. It was in the next five years that Piet Heyn and other Dutch admirals achieved their greatest successes against Spanish shipping in the Caribbean, and amassed the plunder which was to finance the renewed offensive against Brazil in 1630. This second attack was directed not against Bahía, but against Recife in Pernambuco. The Iberian crown, weakened by losses in Europe and America, could no longer afford to counter-attack, and between 1630 and 1643 the whole captaincy of Pernambuco, and the north coast to the mouth of the Amazon, came under the rule of the West India Company. In these years also the company seized the Portuguese slaving-stations in West Africa—Gorée, Axim, Elmina, São Paulo de Luanda and Benguela—and so secured for Dutch Pernambuco, and denied to Portuguese Bahía, the supply of slaves without which the sugar plantations of Brazil were unworkable.

Despite all its strategic and commercial advantages, despite the energy, the ability and the humanity of the governor-general, Johan Maurits of Nassau-Siegen, Netherlands Brazil was a political and economic disappointment.[2] It was never at peace. Formal Dutch expeditions against Bahía, and Portuguese assaults on Recife, were alike unsuccessful; but a constant guerrilla warfare was kept up, in which the Bahía Portuguese had the advantages of local knowledge. The Dutch, for their part, made valuable allies among the Amerindians, some of whom thus found means of expressing a long-standing hostility to the Portuguese. The fighting on both sides was very destructive. The combatants sought to cripple one another by wrecking machinery, burning cane-fields, and kidnapping slaves. The damage to the Brazilian economy was widespread and lasting. This, among other circumstances, made it difficult to attract the Dutch and German peasant immigrants to whom Usselincx and other theorists had looked for the basic population of Dutch colonies. The United Netherlands were themselves constantly at war, but they were successful and prosperous. There was little inducement for artisans and farmers to leave home, to undertake physical labour in an equally war-torn tropical colony. Few Dutchmen, other than soldiers, traders and officials, went to Brazil, and those who did go there resided for the most part in the towns. Sugar production could be maintained only with the help of the resident Portuguese who ran the mills and the estates; and their co-operation could be secured only by means of wide concessions, in particular a measure of freedom of Catholic worship, and freedom to sell their sugars as they pleased. For a monopolistic company run by zealous Protestants, this was a high price to pay. The Dutch themselves were frequently at odds about it; nor did they succeed thereby in attracting the loyalty of their Portuguese subjects, who constantly looked to Bahía for support. The restoration of the Portuguese monarchy in 1640 was initially welcomed by the Dutch, as a division and a weakening of their enemies' forces. The company was encouraged to cut down its heavy burden of expense in Brazil by recalling Johan Maurits in 1643, and by reducing the strength of the Pernambuco garrison. The Dutch were, in effect, staking their future in Brazil on the maintenance of peaceful relations with Portugal. In this they miscalculated. The restoration had quickened Portuguese national pride. In 1645 an energetic revolt broke out in Pernambuco, supported from Bahía. In 1648 the governor of Rio de Janeiro, Salvador de Sá, an able and enterprising sea commander, recaptured Luanda and began the expulsion of the Dutch from the slaving-stations of Angola.[3] Both the prosperity and the safety of Recife were threatened. The company was in financial difficulties, and support in the Netherlands for its policy was neither unanimous nor enthusiastic. Many Dutchmen preferred privateering or unorganized private trade to organized monopolies, and resented the expense and trouble incurred in colonial administration. Moreover, relations with Commonwealth England, exacerbated by commercial rivalry, were deteriorating, and in 1652 broke out in open war. Despite the enormous disparity between Portugal and the Netherlands in wealth and seaborne strength, the company was unable to support its Brazilian government adequately. In 1654, after a struggle whose outcome remained uncertain almost until the end, the Dutch were finally expelled.

Dutch rule in Brazil was thus a relatively brief interlude in the history of that country, just as the ravages of the West India Company's fleets were a brief interlude in the history of the Caribbean. The company itself went bankrupt in 1674, after little more than fifty years of business life. Its activities during that period, however, had widespread and lasting consequences. It was the catalyst whose presence enabled both French and English to establish themselves in the West Indies and on the American mainland, in permanent and profitable settlements, without serious opposition. Dutch traders had served the early tobacco colonies, buying the crop and providing the settlers with goods on long credit. A little later, sugar planting spread through the West Indies, again mainly at the instigation of Dutch traders who had learned the methods of cultivation and manufacture from the Portuguese in Brazil. Sugar was far more valuable than tobacco, the price of which was falling in a glutted market. The Dutchmen sold to West Indian planters the equipment needed for crushing, boiling and pot-crystallization, and taught them a little later the washing processes which turned brown sugar into the much more valuable white or 'clayed' product. Dutchmen often advanced the capital, bought the crop, and carried it to Europe. They also supplied, from the former Portuguese barracoons in West Africa, the slave labour needed for the heavy, unskilled and repetitive field work of sugar plantations. With Dutch help many of the West Indian islands became little Brazils, all the more profitable because of the havoc which war had caused in the trade of Brazil itself.[4]

Both French and English had profited by Dutch precept and example; their planters depended for several decades upon the Dutch as suppliers of goods, as customers, and as carriers. Both, true to mercantilist principles, as soon as they felt strong enough, turned upon the Dutch and sought to exclude them. The English Navigation Act of 1651 was an act of economic war against the Dutch, and in 1652 it led to real war. Similarly, the Acts of Trade under the restored Stuarts were frankly aimed against Dutch trade; but they had at the same time a more general purpose; the systematic application of mercantile principles to an integrated colonial empire. By the specialization of its various parts, this empire was to be made a stronger competitor in peace and a more powerful adversary in time of war. The principles in themselves were clear and consistent. The colonies were to be given a monopoly of the home market for their characteristic products. Conversely, having been founded for the benefit of the mother country, they were to produce goods which England could not produce, in particular certain kinds of raw materials, and were to be discouraged from making manufactured goods which they could obtain from England. All exports of the most valuable colonial products were to be sent to England; it seemed reasonable that if colonial producers were to be given a guaranteed market in England, then England could insist on a corresponding monopoly. England was to control the carrying trade; since the successes of the Dutch apparently defied free competition, strangers must be excluded from the colonial market by law and by force. The colonies, nevertheless, were to be outside the fiscal boundaries of England, for the Crown could not afford to forgo its dues; colonial products always paid customs, though usually the duties were lower than those levied on comparable foreign goods, and in case of re-export to the continent of Europe part of the duty might be repaid as a 'drawback'. The navy and merchant marine were to be enlarged, for it was useless to proclaim a monopoly of colonial trade unless the empire had the ships to carry and defend that trade.

The Navigation Act of 1660 provided that no goods should be imported into or exported from any English colony except in English or colonial ships; and that 'enumerated' commodities—sugar, tobacco, cotton, indigo, ginger and dye-woods, all West Indian products— should be shipped only to England or to another English colony. An English or colonial captain in the colonial trade was required under the Act to deposit a bond at his port of departure, as security that he would not carry enumerated goods to an illegal destination. The Staple Act of 1663 laid down that goods, English or foreign, intended for the colonies must be shipped from an English port. The only important exceptions to this rule were Madeira wine, and salt for the Banks fisheries. The Plantations Duties Act of 1673 laid a substantial duty on all 'enumerated' commodities shipped from one colony to another; its purpose was to discourage illicit sales to foreigners under colour of inter-colonial trade. A special official—the Clerk to the Naval Office— was appointed in each colony to enforce the Acts; and offences against them were punishable by the Courts of Vice-Admiralty, set up in the colonies by the consolidating Navigation Act of 1696. The immense development of English merchant shipping in the later seventeenth century made the Acts of Trade appear to contemporaries realistic as well as reasonable; and the need of naval protection induced the colonists, at least in principle, to accept them. Naval protection was both necessary and real. The north Atlantic was infested with pirates, not only the freebooting outlaws of the Caribbean, and not only Dutch or French privateers in time of war, but powerful fleets maintained by the North African sultans for the purpose of preying upon European shipping. Many an English or colonial sailor ended his days pulling an oar in an Algerine galley. England maintained constant naval patrols along the main shipping routes, and even for a time a fleet base at Tangier. A frigate squadron was based on Jamaica—which had been taken from the Spaniards in 1655—for operations against the West Indian buccaneers. Convoy escorts were provided during the wars with the Netherlands and later with France. Sea power was the key to English imperial policy; and sea power enabled the English government, to a considerable extent, to enforce the Acts of Trade.

The West Indian sugar colonies were ideally adapted to the economic concept of empire embodied in these enactments. By 1660 growing industrial and commercial activity in England had absorbed much of the agrarian unemployment of half a century before. Men were in demand. The old desire to get rid of surplus people had given way to its opposite, to a fear of depopulation. For mercantile theorists the ideal colony was one where a small number of English planters supervised a large non-English labour force in producing tropical commodities. The labour force itself was an article of trade with a prominent place in the mercantile scheme. When the Portuguese recovered their place in the slaving-stations in Angola in 1654, the English, in close alliance, secured trading rights there. Ten years later they followed up this diplomatic advantage by naval aggression, and seized the Dutch barracoons at Gorée and Cape Coast. To exploit these sources of slaves, a chartered monopoly was granted in 1660 to the concern which later (in 1672) became known as the Royal African Company. The company was not a financial success—like most such organizations, it was cheated by its own servants[5]—but its failure to supply slaves in adequate numbers was more than made up by the activity of English interlopers. The profits of the trade in slaves and sugar justified the legislative care bestowed upon them. Despite their repeated protests against restrictions and monopolies, the West Indians grew rich and the merchants who dealt with them grew richer still. At the end of the seventeenth century the West Indies supplied nine per cent of English imports, as against eight per cent from the mainland colonies; they took more of English exports than the mainland (four per cent as against less than four per cent), and they accounted for seven per cent of the total English trade, as against six per cent by the mainland.[6] Their value proved so great and enduring that even Adam Smith—no friend of colonies in general—had to admit, three-quarters of a century later, that, 'The profits of a sugar plantation in any one of our West Indian colonies are generally much greater than those of any other cultivation that is known either in Europe or America.'

The mainland colonies, though they too attained modest prosperity in the later seventeenth century, fitted less readily into the mercantile scheme. Tobacco, it is true, occupied a place in imperial commerce similar to that of sugar, though humbler, and Virginia imported slaves to grow it; though in order to establish the Virginian industry it had been necessary originally to prohibit tobacco-growing in England. The colonies further north neither could nor would conform to the pattern. Their people could offer little that was wanted in England. Furs, which had been a valuable export from New England, became scarcer as settlement extended and drove the fur-bearing animals away. New England timber was a valuable stand-by in emergency, and became the chief source of very large masts; but the cost of transport across the Atlantic made it too expensive to replace normal supplies from the Baltic in ordinary times. New England fish was unwelcome in Old England. For the rest, the New Englanders produced barrel-staves and provisions, which they either consumed themselves, or sold in the West Indies—butter, beef and flour for planters, salt fish for the slaves. They imported enumerated goods from the West Indies—English, French or Spanish—and re-exported them to continental Europe. They established local industries, such as iron-founding and felt-making, in direct competition with imports from England. Under the protection of the Navigation Acts they built up and operated their own very efficient merchant marine; but in defiance of the same Acts they traded freely with foreign powers and foreign colonies, even when those powers were at war with England. Until 1654 New Amsterdam was a major centre for clandestine foreign trade with the English colonies. In that year it was taken, with its hinterland, by an English fleet, without the formality of a declaration of war, and renamed New York. By this act of aggression England secured a back door, by way of the Hudson, to the fur-bearing region of French Canada, as well as stopping a leak in the mercantile system. Many ports in the West Indies remained open, however, and New England smuggling continued to flourish. New England, moreover, though it imported no slaves, continued to attract honest but landless free men whom Old England could ill spare. Orthodox economists in England regarded the New England colonies at best as unprofitable, at worst as a positive disadvantage, to the empire as a whole. Their unprofitableness might have been borne, for New England was still a relatively minor factor in imperial prosperity. Far worse, in the opinion of Restoration statesmen, was the semi-autonomous character of the government of Massachusetts, the independent language which it used on occasion in reply to explicit royal orders, and the obstructions which it placed in the way of commissioners sent to enforce them.

The English empire was the only European colonial empire at that time in which representative institutions played any significant part, as indeed was natural, since England, unlike Spain and France, embarked on the settlement of colonies in a period when the idea of representative government was gaining strength in the mother country. Nearly every colony had an elected legislative assembly; the chief exception was New York, which had no assembly until 1689. The franchise was limited in all the colonies—as it was in the English shires—to freeholders. Except in town government, which was democratic in the classical sense of the word, indented servants, and landless people generally, had no vote. Nor, of course, had slaves; slavery, though its practical importance varied greatly, was recognized by law in all the colonies. Even the New Englanders sometimes enslaved recalcitrant Indians, and slavery caused liberty-loving Englishmen no serious searchings of conscience. The English parliament legislated for the empire as a whole, particularly in matters of trade; it did not concern itself with the internal affairs of individual colonies, and the local validity of its enactments was sometimes disputed, especially in New England. Colonial assemblies voted their own taxes and made their own local laws, with the governors' assent. They could—in theory at least—be required by the

Crown or by Parliament to pass specific Acts; and after the Restoration the Crown lawyers began to argue that all colonial Acts must be approved by the Privy Council. The constitutional position of the colonial assemblies in general was much less secure than that of the English parliament; but like Parliament they tended to encroach on the royal prerogative, and one of the characteristics of a good governor was his ability to manage an intractable assembly.

Within this general framework, degrees of local autonomy varied greatly. In formal law there were three broad groups of colonies: Crown colonies, proprieties and charter colonies. Up to the Civil War Virginia had been the only Crown colony. During the war and interregnum several other grants lapsed or were suppressed. Barbados and the Leeward Islands became Crown colonies. Jamaica had been captured by a formal naval operation, and after a few years of military rule naturally became a Crown colony too. In all these colonies the Crown appointed the governors, executive councils, judges and other high officials. The councillors almost always, and sometimes the governors, were resident planters; but more commonly the governors came from England. They were appointed by letters patent and held office during the king's pleasure. Proprieties differed from Crown colonies in that in them the person of the proprietor was interposed between the Crown and the colonists. He appointed the governor and higher officials, and they took an oath of loyalty to him. The proprietors were for the most part courtiers and there was never any question of proprieties setting up as semi-independent states. In practice, the internal government of the proprieties was very like that of the Crown colonies. By the middle of the century proprietary grants were widely felt to be anachronisms. Only one of them—Maryland—survived the Civil War as a going concern, and the Privy Council constantly petitioned Charles II not to grant any more. He did in fact grant several: Carolina in 1663 to a syndicate; New York and New Jersey in 1664 to James, Duke of York; and Pennsylvania in 1681 to the Quaker William Penn. Pennsylvania was the first inland colony in English North America. The last English propriety to be granted in America was Georgia, founded in 1732 as a home for insolvent debtors. The proprietary form of government never established itself in New England, except for a brief period in Maine under Gorges. Massachusetts, Connecticut and (after 1663) Rhode Island were charter colonies; that is, they each possessed a royal charter similar in form to the charter of a joint-stock trading company, permitting the freeholders of the colony to elect their officers as the shareholders of a company did. There were no officials appointed by the Crown, and no representatives in England upon whom the Crown could bring pressure. Charter colony government was the nearest approach to responsible self-government in any of the colonial empires of the time.

The jealousies and differences between colony and colony; the independent or evasive attitude adopted by some colonial assemblies; the insolent disregard of royal orders in Massachusetts and elsewhere; the difficulty of enforcing mercantile regulation; all these circumstances revealed, in the opinion of the Lords of Trade, 'the necessity of bringing those people under a more palpable declaration of their obedience to His Majesty'. The Restoration governments sought at first to strengthen colonial administration in two ways: by converting the proprieties into Crown colonies and by inserting royal officials into the charter colonies. The revocation of a proprietary patent was largely a matter of finding a legal loophole. The colonists had no great love for their proprietors— usually mere absentee receivers of rents—and were willing enough to come under Crown administration. New Hampshire and Bermuda became Crown colonies in Charles II's reign. New York, New Jersey and Delaware followed in 1685 by the fact of their proprietor becoming King. From 1689 the Crown insisted on approving the appointment of governors in the remaining proprieties, so that the power of the proprietors was correspondingly weakened. The few proprieties which survived into the eighteenth century became bywords for corruption and incompetence. In the charter colonies, however, the situation was very different. The charters had all been issued to groups of malcontents at a time when oversea settlement was a matter of relatively small interest to the home government, and were drawn in very wide terms. After the Restoration, officials such as Nicolls, the captor of New York, who was sent on to New England as a commissioner to investigate the manner of government there, and Randolph, sent out from England in 1678 as collector of customs for New England, met with studied and sometimes insolent obstruction, particularly in Massachusetts. The wording of the charters gave some legal colour to this independent attitude. The King's advisers were warned that the colonists, or at least the ruling oligarchies among them, were jealously attached to their charters, and might even take up arms to defend them.

This legal nettle was not firmly grasped until 1684. The Massachusetts charter was withdrawn in that year, as a result of *quo warranto* proceedings, broadly on the ground that the colony had aspired to become an independent body politic. Connecticut and Rhode Island followed shortly afterwards. There was no resistance. When it came to the point, the New Englanders preferred submission with protection to a precarious independence. James II proceeded to unite the northern colonies, for purposes of administration and defence, in a single dominion, and to appoint a governor-general with power to suspend the colonial assemblies and to govern through a nominated council. The governor-general's instruction in many ways resembled those issued to the Spanish colonial viceroys, especially where they concerned the courts and the arrangements for judicial appeals to England. They represented an experiment in administrative reform at the expense of constitutional tradition. In 1688, however, James II lost his throne, a corresponding revolution broke out in New England, the assemblies resumed their sittings, and the governor-general was shipped home. A series of constitutional compromises followed the accession of William III. Connecticut and Rhode Island, which had never given much trouble, recovered their charters in 1690. Massachusetts, the most recalcitrant colony, also recovered its charter, but in a modified form. The governor was to be appointed by the Crown and the Church membership test for the franchise was to be abolished.

The Crown, therefore, failed to achieve James II's administrative ideal, of great centralized viceroyalties governed from Whitehall. The efforts of the later Stuarts had, however, brought about a certain measure of centralized control. In 1696 William III set up a permanent Board of Trade and Plantations to replace the Privy Council committees which had hitherto looked after colonial affairs; though executive power remained, as before, with the Privy Council itself. A general customs organization was created, staffed by officers appointed in England, backed by vice-admiralty courts to enforce the Acts of Trade. The Crown appointed the governors and certain other officials in nearly all the colonies. On the other hand, the elected assemblies retained most of their old power. They frequently approached their responsibilities in a suspicious and narrowly local spirit, which perpetuated inter-colonial quarrels and impeded administration. In some of the old Crown colonies—Virginia, Barbados, Jamaica—the assemblies had been induced at an early date to grant to the Crown a permanent, though inadequate, revenue by indirect taxation. Most assemblies, however, obstinately refused to do this. They voted year by year, reluctantly and stingily, the taxes from which the entire cost of government, save only naval defence, had to be met. Most colonial governors were frustrated in their efforts towards sound administration by the lack of an assured revenue. Even their own salaries were at the mercy of capricious assemblies, to which they were not responsible and which they could control only with great difficulty. Haggling, friction and frustration, for another three-quarters of a century in most of the mainland colonies, for longer still in the West Indies, were to remain characteristic of English colonial government. It was not oppressive; but it was always weak, often incompetent, and usually more or less corrupt.

One chief factor held the empire together—apart, of course, from old associations. That was the fear of invasion or encirclement. The Dutch possessions in North America had been swallowed up, but the Spaniard still ruled the largest and richest of the New World empires; the French colonies were growing in power and population and appeared as dangerous enemies in the north and west; the Indians were a perpetual menace on the frontiers. At the end of the century it seemed possible that all three might combine against the English on the Atlantic seaboard.

French colonization in the seventeenth century was less spontaneous, more planned and regimented, than English or even Spanish expansion —for the Spaniards, too, were expanding in New Mexico and up the Pacific coast. The various companies under whose auspices settlement had been organized were all controlled and subsidized by the Crown, and in Colbert's time the Crown relieved them of their administrative powers and assumed direct responsibility for colonial government. By 1678, Colbert had already done in the French empire what James II failed to do in the English. Each colony was ruled by a military governor appointed by the Crown. These soldiers were assisted and at the same time watched by civil governors—*intendants*—who handled all financial and economic business. Governors and *intendants* together were advised by nominated councils which also served as courts of appeal, though they had none of the independent powers of the Spanish *audiencias*. The system was simpler and cheaper than the elaborate bureaucracy of Spanish America, quicker and more efficient than the creaking English representative system. The economic policy of colonial France was a mercantilism even more rigid and consistent than that of the English Restoration governments, and despite shortage of shipping and the persistence of Dutch and New England smugglers in the West Indies, the French government made strenuous efforts at enforcement. Unlike the English government, it had also a positive emigration policy. Colbert retained the system of feudal *seigneuries* established in Richelieu's day, but made them conditional upon effective occupation. The French, unlike the English, never thought of allowing their colonies to be peopled by paupers, felons and religious dissidents. On the contrary, everything possible was done to attract eligible settlers, especially to Canada. Demobilized soldiers were pensioned with land for farms in Canada and settled along the Richelieu River and at other strategic points. Tools, seed and stock were provided at government expense; and the government even provided free passages to Canada for women who were willing to marry settlers there. These provisions were not without effect; the population of French Canada trebled under the Colbert régime. Even so, at his death in 1683, the total number was only about 10,000. The subsequent steady increase was due more to the fecundity of the settlers than to a steady increase in emigration. The military efficiency of the population was very high, despite its political and economic primitiveness. The settlers were at once adventurous and disciplined, and their liability to military service was a reality, in sharp contrast with the English colonial militias, which were divided among a dozen separate governments, seldom mustered, and accustomed to cavil at the orders, or rather the entreaties, of the King's representatives.

As explorers by land, the French in America at this time far outshone their English contemporaries. By 1673 Jesuit missionaries had visited most parts of the Great Lakes region and were striking southwards to the headwaters of the Mississippi and its affluents. In 1682 La Salle made his great journey by water down the whole length of the Mississippi to the Gulf of Mexico and opened up a whole vista of strategic and economic possibilities. La Salle lost his life in 1687, while still a young man, in a premature attempt to plant the colony of Lousiana at the mouth of the Mississippi. His adventurous imagination presented to his countrymen the project of connecting Louisiana with Canada by a chain of French settlements. The whole distance could be covered by several alternative water routes, with comparatively short portages. Communications could be safeguarded by forts covering the principal portages and the narrowest stretches of water. Nothing came of La Salle's dream in the seventeenth century, for Colbert's death was followed by a period of stagnation and neglect in the colonial policy of France; but in the eighteenth century the project was pursued with great vigour, and might have set close limits to the slow westward expansion of English settlement had the French in America been more numerous.

The courage and initiative of explorers are not enough, in themselves, to found an enduring empire. Even Colbert failed to make the solid work of settlement attractive to adventurous Frenchmen, for the restrictive feudal structure of Canadian settled society constantly drove the more enterprising out to the wilder frontiers. Many of these hardy traders and trappers adopted Indian ways, took Indian women, and produced in a generation or two a characteristic type, the half-caste *coureur des bois*. At the same time, the ill-defended monopolies of the trading companies attracted interlopers, who were often the companies' dismissed or disgruntled servants. Two such malcontents were largely responsible for the most severe blow which befell the French monopoly in Canada in the seventeenth century—the foundation of the English Hudson's Bay Company. An overland route to the shores of Hudson's Bay was first discovered by two French fur traders, Radisson and Groseillers. These men tried, but failed, to persuade the authorities in France to develop a trade in furs from Hudson's Bay; but they found a backer in England, in that restless royal adventurer, Prince Rupert. The result was the incorporation in 1670 of the Hudson's Bay Company, trading directly to the Bay by sea. This enterprise was the first serious attack on French leadership in the fur trade; and is the only Stuart incorporation which survives as a working concern today.

Twelve years of financial good fortune followed the company's foundation, and in those years forts were established to exploit the trade of the whole southern and south-western shore of the Bay. Serious French counter-attacks began in 1682. In the general war following the English revolution of 1688 the French achieved widespread success. Frontenac, able and vigorous governor of Canada, recaptured Nova Scotia, overrun by the New Englanders in 1691, frightened the Iroquois tribes into temporary peace, and kept the frontiers of New England and New York in constant fear of combined French and Indian raids. Much of the bitterness of colonial warfare arose from this habit of employing Indian auxiliaries, with their traditionally barbarous methods of fighting and of torturing prisoners. At the same time a brilliant sea commander, d'Iberville, ravaged the English settlements in Newfoundland and all but destroyed the company's hold in Hudson's Bay. The favourable colonial terms secured by France in the Treaty of Ryswick were due largely to the successes of these men.

By the end of the seventeenth century the general lines of the final struggle for power and trade in America were already apparent. The Dutch were beginning to drop out, weakened by unequal war in Europe. The power of Portugal was localized in Brazil and unlikely to expand elsewhere. To some observers at least, the Spanish Empire seemed on the verge of collapse. In fact, despite commercial weakness and a top-heavy bureaucracy, it was to outlast the others as an imperial unity; but its part in the eighteenth-century struggle was to be largely passive. Of the major fighting competitors, each had its weaknesses. The English Empire obviously suffered from lack of unity and discipline; but the French Empire had the more serious defect of lack of people.

CHAPTER 17

MIGRATIONS AND DISPERSALS

THE Reconnaissance was a movement not only of discovery and trade, but of migration on a scale which Europe had not known since the Dark Ages; a migration of whole communities, men, women and children, animals and cultivated plants. The migration was sea-borne, at least initially, and its tide set for the most part from east to west across the Atlantic. The Europeans who went to West Africa or to the East were few in number, and were mostly temporary residents; a handful of factors, a few bands of soldiers, sent to man scattered trading posts and forts. Their influence on the great settled populations of the East in the sixteenth and seventeenth centuries was very small. Even the Cape of Good Hope, though a true colony of settlement, for long maintained only a very small population. In the Americas, on the other hand, the whole ethnographic pattern as well as the economic and social structure was radically altered by immigration from the Old World.

The trans-Atlantic emigrants can be classified in three broad groups. The first in time consisted of people from south-western Europe, mostly Spaniards, who settled in the West Indies, in Central America, in Mexico, and in highland regions with their coasts in South America. They chose for the most part areas already settled by agricultural populations, as was natural, since they intended to live by the fruits of native labour, and in the process to evangelize and in some degree to Europeanize the people who provided that labour. They became a privileged caste. Their numbers were considerable, crossing the Atlantic in a steady stream, perhaps a thousand or two in a year throughout most of the sixteenth century;[1] enough to raise fears of depopulation in Spain itself. For the Amerindian peoples their intrusion was a major demographic catastrophe. In most of the Antillean islands the natives quickly dwindled under the impact of an aggressive alien culture, with its diseases and its animals. They could not adapt themselves to living beside Europeans; they could not retreat, as the Plains Indians were to retreat centuries later, with the dwindling buffalo herds; there was nowhere for them to go. Within a century they were extinct, and a new society of immigrants from the Old World had taken their place. On

273

the Mexican mainland, also, conquest was followed by depopulation, a steady decline throughout the sixteenth century, punctuated by abrupt downward plunges due to epidemics. The settled peoples of central Mexico, however, were more civilized, more resistant, more adaptable; they had more elbow-room. Many minor migrations took place among them after the conquest. The lowland population declined more rapidly than that of the highlands,[2] a circumstance which may have been due to introduced malaria, but which may also indicate migration. In the fifteen-thirties considerable numbers of Nahuatl-speaking people migrated from the sheep-infested central plateau, in the wake of Nuño de Guzmán's army, to the sparsely inhabited hills of the Pacific provinces. Other groups retreated into semi-desert areas in the north. Detailed study of population movements in Andean South America has not yet been attempted, but the scanty evidence available suggests a similar pattern there, of rapid depopulation and local migration to more remote areas. Throughout the settled mainland provinces, depopulation was general and disastrous, but nowhere complete. In the seventeenth century population began to recover; but some areas, particularly on the coasts, remained permanently deserted, and the rising population in most places was not pure Indian, but mixed. Among the European immigrants there were more men than women. Many Spaniards took Indian wives or concubines. A *mestizo* population grew up, which in many parts of the Americas came to outnumber both Europeans and Indians. Except in the south of South America, where the original native population was sparse and primitive, most countries in Spanish America today are inhabited largely by people of mixed descent.

The second great stream of emigrants consisted of people from north-western Europe, mostly English, who settled in the outer islands of the Antilles and on the Atlantic seaboard of the North American continent. These areas were either uninhabited, as Barbados was, or else inhabited by a relatively sparse and primitive population which lived by rudimentary cultivation, by hunting and by fishing. The native peoples neither could nor would provide labour for farms and plantations or tribute for the support of an intrusive overlord group; nor were the intruders particularly interested in evangelizing the Indians. Among the settlers of New England, it is true, were many who had migrated for conscience' sake, and their number included religious leaders of profound conviction and spiritual power. They left England, however, as dissenters against the state church, not as missionaries. They sought space and freedom to fashion and to govern a church to their own liking, without interference from royal or episcopal authority. For this purpose a remote and sparsely inhabited wilderness was a positive advantage. Having set up their wilderness church, their next care was to guard its new and hard-won orthodoxy with stern discipline, rather than to spread its influence. Some dissident groups—the Quakers, for example—showed some interest in carrying the Gospel to the Indians; but Quakers themselves got short shrift in Massachusetts. In general the churchmanship of New England was defensive rather than expansive. In Virginia, where the Church of England became established on familiar English lines, the immigrants showed a similar indifference to missionary opportunity. Effective proselytizing among the Indians would, indeed, have been impossible there, because of the lack of trained clergy. The North American Indian, moreover, was an unpromising neophyte. Even in Canada, where the French Jesuits did make strenuous efforts at conversion, and in some instances suffered gruesome martyrdom, the permanent results of their evangelizing were very slight.

The founders of English America settled as fishermen, traders, farmers, planters, producing subsistence crops and, in some places, cash crops for export, usually on a relatively small scale. They created communities which, in pioneer conditions, were necessarily homogeneous and close-knit. This is not to say, of course, that their society was in any modern sense egalitarian. They carried with them the familiar distinctions between gentleman and mechanic, between landlord and peasant, between master and man. The leaders understood from the start, however, that they must recruit their labour force from among their own countrymen, or at least from among other Europeans; they must offer opportunities for homestead immigrants, for the land-hungry and the unemployed. This they succeeded in doing, chiefly through the device of indenture. The flow of north European migrants to America in the seventeenth century, though a mere trickle compared with the torrent of succeeding centuries, was considerable and continuous. Between 1643 and the end of the century the population of Massachusetts grew from about 16,000 to about 60,000, that of Connecticut from 5,500 to over 20,000, that of Virginia from 15,000 to 60,000. New York at the time of its capture had only 7,000 Europeans in its whole territory; at the end of the century there were nearly 20,000. The total population of the English mainland colonies at the end of the century was something over 200,000.[3] The French mainland population, as we have seen, was much smaller, though the *coureurs des bois* ranged over an immense area and exercised an influence out of proportion to their number.

The most remarkable migration of north Europeans, however, was to the outer islands of the West Indies in the sixteen-thirties and -forties. Homestead immigrants flocked into these islands, attracted by fertile land on very easy terms, and by the profits to be made by growing tobacco, indigo and cotton. Farming and planting, as in the mainland settlements, was on a small scale; planters relied for their labour on indented servants, who came in great numbers, hoping to secure land themselves at the expiry of their indentures. In 1640 the population of Barbados was equal to that of Virginia and Massachusetts combined: over 30,000 people, or 200 to the square mile, which by seventeenth-century standards was heavy overcrowding. St Kitts in the same year had 20,000. The society of Barbados and the Leeward Islands in the mid-seventeenth century, like that of Virginia and Massachusetts, was a European society transplanted to the New World. Unlike Massachusetts and Virginia, however, it failed to preserve its homogeneity. The change from tobacco to sugar about the middle of the century brought an abrupt change in migration. Sugar could not be produced on a small scale. Considerable capital was needed to set up a mill, and a plantation, to run economically, had to be big enough to keep the mill constantly supplied with canes throughout the crop season. Successful sugar planters, eager for all the land they could get, bought up the holdings of failing tobacco farmers, until most of the usable land in the settled islands was absorbed in fair-sized plantations. This removed the principal attraction of indenture; and the supply of voluntary indented labour dwindled and ceased. Work on sugar plantations was hard and uncongenial. Many indented servants actually in the islands ran away, to try their luck in Jamaica or on the mainland, or to join the buccaneers. Many died of hunger and hardship in this pitiful dispersal. The growing sugar industry, on the other hand, clamoured for more and more labour. Every conceivable method of propaganda was employed to recruit labour in Europe, especially in north Germany, where the Thirty Years War had left thousands homeless, ready with the credulity of utter misery to go anywhere that offered a ray of hope. Crimping became a regular trade in England and in the continental ports. More legally, but no less brutally, the English penal system was adapted to West Indian needs, and transportation became a regular punishment for vagrants, for political prisoners, and for many convicted felons. The effect was to create a class of semi-servile poor white labourers, miserable, desperate and despised. None of the methods of persuasion or compulsion sufficed. Eventually, as the Spaniards and Portuguese had done before them, the English and French planters found a solution of their labour problem in the purchase of slaves from West Africa.

Africans formed the third great wave of migration which resulted from the Reconnaissance. For many years poor white labourers in the West Indies worked with negro slaves, lived in similar circumstances, and interbred with them; but steadily, as sugar planting spread, the number of white labourers declined and the number of negroes increased. Barbados had a few hundred negroes in 1640; by 1645 there were over 6,000 negroes and about 40,000 whites; in 1685, 46,000 negroes and 20,000 whites, bond and free. By the end of the century the white population was down to 12,000. In the Leeward Islands the change began a decade or so later, but, once begun, was more rapid and more clearly complete than in Barbados. Jamaica, which never had a large white population, began to import slaves from the date of its capture by the English. On the mainland, Virginia and Maryland, unable because of cold winters to turn to sugar, imported slaves to work on the tobacco plantations; though there, since land was abundant, small farmers were not displaced to any serious extent in the seventeenth century. In the French islands also, the process of change, in the early years, was relatively slow. The white population of proprietors and *engagés*, though small, proved tenacious; but by 1700 the French islands had about 44,000 slaves and a white population of only some 18,000. Africans formed in most British and French islands the great majority of the population. The European planters in each colony became a small garrison; a garrison which believed, with reason, that its safety depended upon maintaining a rigorous, often savage discipline among its slaves.[4]

It is difficult to form, from contemporary accounts, any clear picture of this great body of people brought against their will from Africa. Of the African homeland of their slaves the West Indian planters knew and cared little. Even the slavers visited West Africa only as traders, enjoying limited and revocable privileges granted to them by the local rulers. Their knowledge did not extend beyond the coast; and the coast on which they operated was long and varied, with a deep and populous hinterland. The markets which chiefly supplied the West Indies lay on the great middle stretches of the coast: Sierra Leone, the Grain Coast (now Liberia), the Ivory, Gold and Slave Coasts, the Oil rivers of the Niger delta, Cameroon, Gaboon, Congo and Luanda. Naturally people from this great area spoke many languages and exhibited many variations of culture and custom; but they also shared many traits in common. Their languages belonged to one or the other of two great families, Sudanic or Bantu. The principal peoples in the heart of the slaving area were the Ashanti of the Gold Coast, the Dahomeans, the Yoruba, grouped under the Oyo Kingdom in what is now western Nigeria, and the Bini of the western Niger delta. All these peoples were composites of many smaller groups, welded through a long process of conquest into more or less homogeneous kingdoms, ruled by powerful, stable dynasties or groups of families. All were essentially agricultural, but they possessed also a considerable range of hand-craft industries, sophisticated art-forms—most notably carving, and the brass-founding of Ile-Ife and Benin—and wide trade connections overland. They had cities of considerable size, elaborate markets for the exchange of goods, a recognized means of exchange—cowrie shells—and crude but efficient systems of taxation. Slavery had long existed throughout the region. Prisoners taken in inter-tribal war were commonly enslaved, and wars were undertaken deliberately for the purpose. Slaves might also be recruited by kidnapping or by purchase. All the rulers of the area kept large numbers of slaves. In Dahomey a plantation system existed, resembling the régime which the slaves were to encounter in the New World. Apart from work in field or household, slaves were valuable for sacrifice and as export goods, with which the rulers and their sub-chiefs could purchase guns, gunpowder, hardware and European cloth from the deep-sea slavers who supplied the New World market.

Arrived in the New World, the Africans displayed the variety of their origins, and most West Indian accounts of plantation life give lists of types of slaves, with the characteristics ascribed to them: Senegalese, Coromantees, Whydahs, Nagoes, Paw-paws, Eboes, Mocoes, Congoes, Angolas, Mandingoes, and so on. The names are imprecise and often misleading; some of them refer merely to estuaries or ports of shipment. Beneath the variety of origin and language, and the real or supposed differences of character, the newcomers showed underlying similarities of behaviour. As might be expected of fighting peoples, they reacted against their enslavement and exile with a bitter and active resentment, very different from the sullen apathy of the Amerindian. The first serious servile mutiny in Barbados occurred in 1649; and throughout the history of New World slavery mutiny, or the fear of mutiny, was a constant feature of plantation life. There was no lack of leaders for such designs, for the recruitment of slaves by war or kidnapping did not discriminate on grounds of social status, and chiefs and shamans reached the New World with the rest. Overt risings, it is true, could usually be prevented or punished by stern repression, but individuals could and did express their resentment in other ways; by suicide, by infanticide, or by running away, especially in islands such as Jamaica where mountains and forests offered shelter to fugitive groups. Apart from these desperate acts, resentment found regular expression in calculated idleness, giving the owner the bare minimum of labour necessary to escape the whip; in wilful carelessness and destructiveness in handling the owner's property, whether tools, fences, buildings or stock; and in feigned stupidity. On the other hand, the natural resilience, physical strength and imitative capacity of the

278

African enabled him to adapt himself to adverse conditions and to acquire, given the opportunity, such European habits and skills as seemed to him desirable. Eventually negroes and mulattoes worked out, in the West Indies as in Brazil, a way of living which was not that of any single African group from which slaves were drawn, nor a composite of African folk-ways, but a characteristically West Indian—or Brazilian —amalgam. The process was slow; for plantation life discouraged inventiveness, and the purely African element was constantly re-inforced, for a hundred and fifty or two hundred years, by fresh importation.

The trans-Atlantic migrations of the Reconnaissance brought Euro-peans into close daily contact with utterly unfamiliar peoples, peoples with whom they had initially few points of contact, but for whose spiritual and material welfare they found themselves in some degree responsible. They had usually little to fear from these peoples, after the initial uncertainties of conquest and settlement, and much to gain as missionaries, as administrators or as exploiters of labour, from under-standing them. The rich, strange and varied cultures of the settled Amerindian peoples appealed strongly to Renaissance curiosity, and the desire to study them and write about them acquired urgency because of the possibility, recognized by some of the more perceptive and sympathetic Spaniards, that they might disappear. The modern science of ethnology may fairly be said to have begun in sixteenth-century Spanish America. Some Hispanicized Indians, with Spanish encouragement, wrote histories of their own people; notably Ixtlilxó-chitl[5] in Mexico and Garcilaso[6] in Peru, who wrote nostalgically of past glories. Spanish missionaries also wrote histories or descriptions of the Indians with whom they came into contact. Many of these works —as might be expected from the circumstances in which they were written—were undertaken not as academic studies but as polemics. Las Casas[7] and Motolinía[8] wrote in order to expose and denounce Spanish ill-treatment of the Indians, to support proposed legislation for their protection, above all to insist on their right to receive the Sacraments, after conversion, like other Christians. Las Casas especially dwells on the docility, the helplessness, and the intellectual capacity of the Indians; but despite their polemical purpose his works are mines of anthropological information. Diego de Landa, Bishop of Yucatán, indefatigable persecutor of idolatry and destroyer of Mayan manu-scripts, was fascinàted by the culture he helped to destroy, and his account of it is a classic of its kind.[9] On the other hand, Sarmiento's *History* of the Incas[10] is propaganda of another sort. It was commissioned by the viceroy Toledo to show that the Indians of Peru had lived under a bloodthirsty tyranny from which the Spaniards had rescued them;

but its author's lively curiosity and his use of Indian informants make the book, though naturally highly selective, a valuable source of information.

An exception to these generalizations, and by far the greatest sixteenth-century authority on Amerindian cultures, was the Franciscan missionary, Bernardino de Sahagún, whose *General History*[11] got him into trouble with his superiors and was not printed until more than two hundred years after its author's death. Sahagún spent most of his long life in New Spain, knew of the depopulation of the islands, and lived through the devastating smallpox epidemics of 1545 and 1575. His comments on these disasters were less apocalyptic than those of some of his brethren; he thought that the Indian population would survive in reduced numbers within an increasingly Spanish society. He found the prospect disquieting; for he feared that the secular aspects of Indian life—in which he saw much to admire and respect—might disappear, while their 'idolatrous' religion would persist, even if only in secret. He was profoundly sceptical of the mass conversions which took place during his time in New Spain. It was in order to make the work of evangelization more effective, by a thorough understanding of the Indians, that Sahagún set himself to describe their culture; but as the writing progressed, intellectual curiosity and human sympathy together took charge. The *History* covers, in systematic detail, every aspect of Aztec life: theology, philosophy, ritual, astrology and sooth-saying, government, economic activity, social customs, science and medicine, and the natural resources of the country. Only the last Book of twelve is history in the ordinary sense—a narrative of the conquest, unsparing in its condemnation of atrocities. Sahagún had outstanding qualifications for his task: long personal experience, profound know-ledge of Indian languages—much of his work was written in Nahuatl —and cool critical judgement. He made little use of 'authorities'. He quotes the Scriptures rarely and the Classics hardly at all—strangely, for a man trained in Renaissance Salamanca. On the other hand, he employed many Indian informants, and selected them carefully for their knowledge, intelligence and probity. In questioning them he used materials which they understood: their own pictogrammic records of the subjects to be discussed. He gives their names and their qualifica-tions, and where informants differ, compares their versions and gives his own objective comment. His method was both rigorous and imaginative. He was the first great European ethnologist.[12]

Most of the more developed Amerindian cultures were in areas colonized by Spaniards. As might be expected, the more primitive peoples encountered by other Europeans were less carefully studied. That genial humanist, Johan Maurits, showed an affectionate interest in the wild forest dwellers of northern Brazil, and was liked by them in return. His interest was shared by some among the *coterie* of artists and natural scientists who frequented his little court. Examples of Indian craftsmanship were collected in Brazil and later found their way into European museums. Some of the books about Brazil later printed in Amsterdam at Johan Maurits' expense, notably the lavish folios of Barlaeus,[13] contain, in addition to descriptions of flora and fauna, much ethnographical information. Neither the Dutch nor the Portuguese achievement in this field, however, compares with that of the Spaniards. In English America, the best account of an Indian culture in one period is one of the earliest: Thomas Hariot's *Briefe and true report*[14] which together with John White's drawings and the notes which Hariot wrote for the engravings in De Bry's *America*,[15] form an intimate record of the people whom the first Virginia settlers encountered. Hariot describes the villages of the Indians, their domestic habits, their crafts, their ceremonies and religious beliefs, most particularly their crops. He acquired some knowledge of the Algonkin language and taught English to some of his Indian informants. He was a careful observer, detached yet sympathetic, and he makes his Indians live as individuals. The coastal Algonkian people whom he described were primitive, and they formed only one among many woodland groups. For the woodland people of New England we have no such careful study. The New England settlers showed comparatively little interest in the Indians, except in so far as they were dangerous. Some considered that God's concern for their settlement had been lovingly manifested by striking the Indians with pestilence a few years before the migration, so making the waste places safe for His children.[16] Most Puritan divines considered the conversion of such primitive people to Christianity to be a hopeless task, and the Indians to be irretrievably the Devil's. To this generalization there were some exceptions, notably John Eliot of the Algonkin Bible;[17] but the inward-looking, heresy-hunting theocracy of New England could hardly be expected to foster the sympathetic detachment of the ethnologist. Some interesting information about Indians is to be found in Thomas Morton's *New English Canaan*.[18] Morton was an amusing rascal, a keen sportsman and a good naturalist who well described the game of the New England woods. He liked the Indians and got on well with them; but he loved a tall story, and certainly was no anthropologist. In general, the red man appealed to the imagination of the English—and, in a more sophisticated fashion, of the French—rather than to their scientific curiosity, in the Age of Reconnaissance. Pocahontas, *la Belle Sauvage*, provided a personal and appealing contact. The poetry and drama of the late sixteenth and early seventeenth centuries are full of echoes of this primitive New World. Essayists and philosophers—Montaigne the first, in his essay on the Cannibals—were quick to point the morals to be drawn from the newly-revealed world of primeval innocence. Montaigne's influence, through Florio's translation, is clear in *The Tempest*. The most moving of all pictures of the savage as he appeared to Europeans, with his mixture of characters, pathetic, endearing, repulsive, was drawn not by an anthropologist but by a poet of consummate genius.

The volume of description, scientific and literary, of the Amerindian stands in sharp contrast to the conspiracy of silence about that unwilling migrant, the African slave. A slave, even though legally a chattel, does not necessarily lack personality in the eyes of his owners; but in the Americas, the wholesale character of plantation slavery and of the trade in slaves robbed most Europeans of any sense of the humanity of the Africans whom they purchased and employed. Most writers on the subject concerned themselves only with the economic aspects of slavery, with the cost of slaves, their efficient management, their capacity for work. This is not to say that the European conscience was entirely easy in the matter, or that all Europeans accepted the legalistic sophistries used to justify negro slavery while condemning the enslavement of Indians. Some writers openly attacked all slavery and trade in slaves. Las Casas did so in his later years. An equally vehement critic, Fray Tomás de Mercado, in a treatise on commercial law and morality,[19] used arguments about the slave trade which anticipated those advanced by Wilberforce and Clarkson over two centuries later. The opponents of slavery, however, like its apologists, dealt in generalities, in this instance theological and legal. They did not, as a rule, write of negroes as persons; at most, they occasionally mentioned details of appearance or customs which struck them as quaint or interesting. There is one work on negro slavery and evangelization among slaves which contains serious ethnological information: the very rare treatise of Alonso de Sandoval,[20] printed at Seville in 1627. This book, like Mercado's, is a violent denunciation of the trade. Sandoval had been rector of the Jesuit college at Cartagena de Indias, and wrote of negro slaves from personal knowledge. Among much miscellaneous detail he gives a careful description of the tribal markings used by the Guinea and Angola peoples. Sandoval was exceptional. In general, neither poets, philosophers nor anthropologists paid much attention to the plantation slave in the Age of Reconnaissance.

The migrations of the Reconnaissance were movements of plants and animals as well as of people. European domestic animals—horses, cattle, sheep, goats and pigs—as we have seen, radically altered the economic life of the Americas; and since many of them ran wild, they also profoundly modified the native flora and fauna. Movement in the reverse direction, of animals as of people, was by comparison negligible. The llama and the vicuña were of little interest to Europeans. One domestic species which caught the attention of Spaniards—the Mexican edible dog—was an early casualty of the conquest, and became extinct. The only American beasts of economic importance carried to the Old World were the domestic turkey and the Muscovy duck (which has nothing to do with Moscow). The movement of cultivated plants, on the other hand, was a two-way exchange of great complexity. European emigrants took with them many of the plants with which they were familiar, both as cash crops and as daily sustenance. Of the food crops, wheat was by far the most important. It was widely introduced in the sixteenth century in favoured highland areas of the American tropics, such as the Puebla valley in Mexico; and in the seventeenth century was carried to temperate North America by English and French settlers. Rye, oats and barley, vital crops in Europe, were of much less importance in the Americas, where maize was already widely available as an alternative to wheat. Besides grain crops, European fruits were among the earliest introductions. Spaniards have long been lovers of orchards, skilled in the management of fruit trees—one of the gracious characteristics which they acquired from the Moors who ruled and civilized so much of medieval Spain. Few missions and few large houses in sixteenth-century colonial America lacked the dignity of a walled orchard, where European exotics could be tended and watered. The olive and the European vine proved difficult to establish—though many varieties of native grapes were found wild on the Atlantic seaboard—and oil and wine were major imports into the New World throughout our period. On the other hand, most of the familiar varieties of citrus were brought from Spain and widely and successfully grown from the early sixteenth century. To the Spaniards, also, the West Indies almost certainly owe the banana, and perhaps the edible plantain. A wild plantain grows in the Caribbean area, for which an economic use was found late in the seventeenth century; for its succulent stems, cut into junks and stowed in great bundles below the mizen chains, served as fodder for the animals upon which ships depended for fresh meat at sea. This wild plantain, however, is not the parent of the familiar cultivated varieties. According to Oviedo, the banana was brought to the West Indies about 1516 from the Canary Islands, where, presumably, it had earlier been introduced from tropical Africa by Portuguese or Spaniards. This is by no means certain. The plant seems to have originated in the East, and might have reached America by more than one route. Oviedo's description of a sweet fruit eaten raw clearly applies to the true banana, and not to the starchy plantain which requires cooking. The Spaniards may have introduced both; though Acosta,[21] writing of the mainland later in the century, considered the plantain to be a native Indian crop. Both banana and plantain have become essential articles of food in tropical America, and the banana in modern times a major export of the West Indies. They can easily be grown by peasants, in areas of adequate rainfall, and require comparatively little attention. They can be harvested throughout the year, and their food yield is prodigious.

Among introduced cash crops sugar was by far the most important. The economic and social revolutions following its introduction have already been described. It had an indirect effect upon the spread of food crops; for sugar planters imported slaves, and the ships which carried the slaves brought also some of the plants on which they were to be fed. Slavers victualled in West Africa chiefly with yams, which provided a cheap and abundant form of starchy food with excellent keeping qualities. There is one species of yam native to the New World: the yampee (*dioscorea trifida*); but though its tubers are of excellent flavour they are small and not very prolific. The much larger and coarser Guinea yams (*d. rotundata* and *d. cayenensis*) came from Africa, entered the West Indies in the early days of the slave trade, and quickly became established there. Oviedo describes them, under the name of *nname*, as recent arrivals in Hispaniola, and says that they were chiefly grown and eaten by negroes. They were largely superseded in the later seventeenth century by the superior greater yam, *dioscorea alata*, which came from India to West Africa and thence to America. The greater yam is well named. It produces immense tubers, sometimes over 100 lb. The cultivation of yams, though laborious, is not difficult in good soil; and their habit of burying their tubers deep in the ground gives them protection against rooting pigs. Without these high-yielding introduced root crops the feeding of great armies of slaves on the West Indian sugar plantations would have been impossible; and the peasant descendants of the slaves rely heavily on them today.[22]

The Europeans who emigrated to the New World, taking tools, seed and animals with them, did not establish their farms in a total wilderness. Almost everywhere they found some sort of cultivation, however sparse and rudimentary; and in favoured regions, as we have seen, they found highly complex and productive systems of cultivated crops. Some of these crops were native to the Americas, others probably introduced at some more remote time, probably across the Pacific. All were unfamiliar to Europeans; but European immigrants accepted many of them, at first buying them by barter or seizing them as tribute, and then cultivating them or causing them to be cultivated on their own farms or estates. African slave immigrants accepted them also, because often they had no alternative. Cassava (*manihot utilissima*) was among the earliest of these acceptances. Both sweet and bitter varieties grew, and still grow, in the West Indies and north-eastern South America. Sweet cassava is boiled or baked and eaten as a vegetable, and very insipid stuff it is. Bitter cassava is grated, washed, pressed and either made into bread or fried as *gharri*. The discovery of a method of leaching out the poisonous juice of this root must have been, for primitive folk, an event of the first importance. Vázquez de Espinosa[23] and Oviedo both describe the process, which is slow and laborious. The Spanish settlers in the islands ate cassava bread when they could get nothing better, and regularly victualled their ships with it, for it has good keeping qualities. As a food it is inferior to yams and still more inferior to potatoes; but it has a high yield, needs little attention, and will flourish in poor and arid soils where little else will grow. For these reasons it is a superficially attractive crop to a primitive peasantry, especially where good land is scarce and where long dry seasons occur. The precise manner of its introduction to the Old World is unknown; probably Portuguese slave dealers were responsible. It has become a major crop in many parts of West Africa, and the staple food of the poor there. While declining in the Americas it is steadily extending its range in the Old World and is probably a contributory factor in the spread of soil erosion.

The sweet potato (*ipomoea batatas*) was also first encountered by Europeans in the New World. Oviedo reported it from Hispaniola, Acosta from coastal Mexico, Hariot from Virginia. Like cassava, it grows quickly and has a fairly high yield, but it needs more water and better soil. Its keeping qualities are poorer and it cannot be used for bread. It is widely grown in eastern Asia, and is often said to have been carried there by Spanish ships sailing to the Philippines; though it might have made the crossing at some much earlier date; or equally possibly have originated in Asia and crossed the Pacific eastward in prehistoric times. There is no firm evidence. In the Spanish Indies, it quickly became a favourite among the negro slaves, and in the sixteenth century attracted considerable attention in Europe. In Spain it was candied in slices with sugar for sale as a sweetmeat and, tinctured by boiling with eryngium, as an aphrodisiac. The Spaniards in America propagated only the sweet varieties and neglected the larger, more starchy kinds. Oviedo says that by 1525 some of the varieties which he had known were already disappearing, as the Indians who had cultivated them died out. Yams, grown on negro provision patches, took their place.

All the agricultural societies of South America, not only the primitive groups of Brazil, Guiana and the islands, but the highly developed societies of the western coast and mountains also, were planting cultures, based economically on the use of tuberous-rooted cultigens. Of these root crops by far the most valuable were potatoes, native to the Andean highlands. Scores of species and varieties of *Solanum*, some wild and some cultivated, grew and still grow there, and many methods of preparation and use were known to the people of the region; indeed, the support of so elaborate a society and so dense a population at such high altitudes was made possible only by the development of improved polyploid potatoes, and by methods of preserving them, by alternate freezing, thawing and drying, in an easily transportable form. Europeans accepted the potato later and more slowly than they accepted the tropical crops of Central America, but the effects of the acceptance were even more widespread and significant. The story has been studied in detail;[24] it is an obscure story, complicated by early confusions with the sweet potato. John Gerard's celebrated *Herbal* of 1597, for example, which contains a whole chapter on potatoes, appears to muddle together these two quite unrelated plants. Nevertheless, it is certain that by the end of the sixteenth century the true potato, still little noticed, was becoming established in many places in northern Europe. The story which attributes its introduction into Ireland to Raleigh is at least plausible. In the seventeenth century it played a leading part in the process whereby European farmers, with the help of root crops, overcame winter starvation. It has since spread throughout the temperate regions of the world, and is a major article of diet almost everywhere among people of European descent. In some peasant societies it has become—like cassava in some tropical areas—the staple food of the poor, and the basis of immense increases in population; but, though a far better food, it is less reliable than cassava, and excessive dependence on it has in some places, notably Ireland, led to major disasters.

The Amerindian societies of North America were seed-sowing rather than planting cultures. In the more developed regions, maize and beans, supplemented by chilis and by various species of squash and other gourds, formed a crop complex admirably adapted to preserve soil fertility in conditions of hoe-cultivation. Maize was the staple; the squashes gave shade and conserved moisture round the roots of the growing maize; and the beans performed a double function, supplying protein in a diet impoverished by the killing out of game, and fixing nitrogen in the soil. From Middle America, their probable area of origin, maize and beans were diffused in all directions, and by the time of the European invasion they were grown in most parts of the Americas where agriculture was practised. In North America

east of the mountains they superseded less satisfactory plants such as the sunflower and the giant ragweed, formerly grown for their seed. In South America they supplemented the basic roots. Many varieties of maize were grown, both soft varieties eaten green and hard kinds used for grinding into meal and making bread. Maize is a nutritious and highly productive grain, adequate—like the potato —for the support of developed cultures and dense populations, but it is less tolerant than the potato. It needs good soil, good rain in the growing season, and hot sun for ripening. Europeans first encountered it, as a totally unfamiliar plant, in the New World. They took to it readily—though always preferring wheat—and carried the seed to Europe, where it has become an important food for men and for beasts. In some parts of south-eastern Europe it has spread at the expense of wheat and barley. In West and Central Africa it has become even more widespread, almost certainly by European agency, wherever soil and climate are suitable, and is a most valuable crop, rightly preferred to cassava and to many of the native millets.

Three cash crops of major importance remain to be noted: tobacco, cacao and cotton. The cotton-yielding genus *gossypium* has many species, but of cultivated species there are only four, two of Old and two of New World origin, and both in the Old and the New World cotton weaving preceded the crossing of the Atlantic by very many centuries. Cotton became an important plantation export crop in Brazil and the islands in the seventeenth century; in other parts of the Americas in the eighteenth and nineteenth. The story of cotton is not one of introduction from Old World to New or vice versa, but a far more complicated story of hybridization and borrowing in both directions.[25] The commercial cotton of modern Egypt, for example, came from crosses between Sea Island cotton and perennial *barbadense*, both of New World origin. Cacao, on the other hand, is certainly a native American plant, from which the highland Mayas and the Mexicans made the *chocolatl* which delighted the *conquistadores*. They prized it highly and used its beans as currency. Chocolate became a fashionable drink in Europe in the later seventeenth century, and under European management cacao became the staple export crop of great provinces on the Caribbean mainland. More recently trees were introduced into West Africa. Chocolate has become a common and important food, and a major crop upon whose cultivation and export large parts of West Africa rely as their principal source of cash income. Tobacco also is a plant of American origin. The Amerindians grew several species, though only one, *nicotiana tabacum*, is commercially important. They used it in pre-conquest times in all the forms known today—in pipes, in cigars, in cigarettes (rolled in corn husks) and as snuff. It was an important element in social and religious ceremony all over the Americas. Europeans took to it eagerly both as a social habit and as a drug. Like many other unfamiliar plants, it was advertised in the sixteenth and early seventeenth centuries as a panacea for distempers ranging from pox to rheumatism. The cured leaves became, as we have seen, a major export of European plantations in America, and the seed was sown in Europe itself before the middle of the sixteenth century. Even in England it became, for a short time about the turn of the century, a crop of some importance. Its cultivation spread round the world with remarkable speed, producing an immense range of characteristic local varieties.[26] It is probably the most universal vegetable product known to men. It has made more fortunes than all the silver of the Indies.

Civilization rests on discoveries made by peoples for the most part unknown to history. Historic man has added no plant or animal of major importance to the domesticated forms on which he depends. He has, however, greatly expedited the process by which domesticated animals and cultivated plants can be introduced from one part of the world to another; not always with happy results. The Age of Reconnaissance was a time of very rapid acceleration of the process. For centuries, for millennia before Columbus, crops, animals, and ideas had moved out from the hearth-lands, mostly in Asia, through the countries of the 'Fertile Crescent' or round the north shore of the Indian Ocean, westward into Europe, south through the Ethiopian highlands into tropical Africa, and (probably) east across the Pacific into America. Evidence in support of trans-Pacific crossings in pre-historic times, possibly in both directions, has lately grown steadily stronger. Only the Atlantic apparently presented, to prehistoric peoples, an impassable barrier. In historic times, the Norsemen for a relatively short period made crossings of the north Atlantic; but they do not appear to have carried plants or animals with them and their voyages had no permanent effect. In the Age of Reconnaisance, Europeans first leapt the barrier of the Atlantic, completed the circle, and initiated a much more rapid movement of men, plants, and animals which, in a few centuries, drastically altered the physical aspect of many regions, both of the Old World and the New. Like other features of the Reconnaissance, this movement provoked a ferment of scientific study. Mention has been made of the long series of Spanish descriptions of the New World, and of the sharpness of observation which they reveal. The same may be said of the Dutchmen—Barlaeus, Marcgraf, Piso—who wrote about Brazil; and French and English writers displayed the same heightened awareness of the complexities of natural detail. The seventeenth century was remarkable for the appearance in western Europe of a whole school of careful observers in the natural sciences, especially in botany, to a smaller extent in zoology. Natural science was still unsystematic, still in the stage of collecting and storing information rather than arranging, classifying and interpreting it; but the solid foundation was laid in the seventeenth century for the work of the great systematists of the eighteenth and nineteenth. In great part, the stimulus to undertake this study came from the discovery and settlement of the New World. The Age of Reconnaissance has no record more characteristic—and none worthier —than the splendid folio volumes of Sir Hans Sloane.[27] It was during his time as physician to the governor of Jamaica that Sloane amassed not only the information which was to fill a massive and authoritative book, but also the magnificent collection of specimens which was to be the nucleus of the British Museum.

CHAPTER 18

THE COLONIAL BUREAUCRATS

FEW European States in the Age of Reconnaissance had any tradition of a salaried professional civil service. The modest clerking establishments of medieval kings had been staffed by churchmen, who could be paid for their services with ecclesiastical preferment. The Church had usually accepted this arrangement, with the safeguards which Canon Law imposed for preventing or punishing the crime of simony. In the sixteenth century, however, the arrangement broke down. Both Reformation and Counter-Reformation worked against the secular use of ecclesiastical preferment. At the same time, the scope of governmental activity steadily widened. More and more officials were needed, and had to be recruited from among educated laymen. Universities and law schools were beginning to provide laymen with suitable grammatical and legal education; but such men expected to be paid, and few governments had the means to pay them. Taxation could not easily be increased, for grants of direct taxation were still regarded in most countries as extraordinary measures to meet particular emergencies, and indirect taxation tended to become fixed by custom. Custom, no less than government finance, made the payment to most officials of adequate salaries quite out of the question. Some offices— those of justices of the peace, for example, or *alcaldes de la Hermandad*— were unremunerated, the honour of service being deemed an adequate reward. Most officials, however, were remunerated by fees, some paid by the bodies—courts or councils—which they served, and some by private citizens who had business with those bodies. Their offices were not only posts of duty; they were licences to extract fees, with the accompanying tips and perquisites, from the public.

Patronage was the means by which kings and great noblemen encouraged the loyalty of their followers. A king was not only entitled, but was expected to reward those who had served him in court or camp; and if a man died poor in the royal service, his widow and orphaned children looked to the royal generosity for their support. The medieval form of royal liberality had usually been the grant of fiefs. The sixteenth-century form was commonly the grant of fee-earning office, coupled where necessary with permission to exercise the office by deputy. Grants were often made for life, sometimes for a term of lives. Officials appointed in this way could not easily be dismissed. Office in general (like landed tenure, with which in the past it had often been associated) was regarded as a form of property, in which the holder possessed at least a life interest. Subject to the terms of the tenure, the property could be let; with royal permission it might even be bequeathed, sold, or given away. Kings might, and often did, lay down rules about the age, experience and other qualifications required in holders of fee-earning offices; but equally easily they might permit an unqualified person to hold office, provided he found a qualified deputy.

Empires, however acquired, must be governed. One of the essential functions of effective colonial government is the provision by the metropolitan power of a body of loyal, competent and reasonably disinterested administrative officers. Obviously, in sixteenth-century conditions, the creation of such a service was extremely difficult. The problem was most acute and most urgent in Spanish America, where in the space of a few decades the Crown of Castile acquired kingdoms far larger in area and population than Spain itself. The Indies had been conquered by private investors and soldiers of fortune, who operated under Crown licence, but not in any close sense under Crown direction. They commanded their followers through personal loyalty or financial dependence rather than by virtue of public office. They dominated the native Indians by right of conquest supplemented and modified by missionary teaching. Left to themselves, they tended to establish communities based on the bastard feudalism which had become, in many parts of Europe in the fifteenth century, all too familiar. The Crown, on the other hand, was impelled by conviction, by the desire to draw revenue from the Indies, and by authoritarian habit, to break down this loose personal rule and to replace it by a centralized imperial administration, itself appointing all high officials and insisting on their being obeyed by virtue of their office; reserving to itself all major decisions; and demanding detailed, almost day-to-day information of all occurrences. Considering the circumstances of the time, the Spanish Crown achieved a remarkable success in all these aims, particularly the last. Nothing is more impressive in the archives of the Indies than the prodigious volume, the detail, and on the whole the accuracy of the reports which poured into the Council of the Indies with every east-bound fleet.

Naturally the maintenance of such a system called for a very large administrative and clerical staff, and officials of one sort or another formed, by the end of the sixteenth century, a considerable proportion of the European population in most of the towns in the Indies. Some of these officials were directly appointed by the Crown—indeed by the King himself, from lists of names supplied, with appropriate comment, by the Council of the Indies—and received annual salaries charged upon the provincial treasuries. These salaried officers can be divided, very roughly and with much overlapping, into three classes: political, comprising the viceroys and governors of provinces, whose qualifications for appointment were commonly, though not always, of a military kind; judicial, comprising the judges and procurators-fiscal of the high courts of appeal, who were always school-trained lawyers; and financial, comprising the officials—treasurers, comptrollers and factors—who had charge of the provincial treasuries. But these senior salaried officers formed only a small fraction of the whole body of colonial officials. A centralized bureaucracy required an immense body of secretarial officials—*escribanos*—to handle the paper work. Every *audiencia* employed one or more *escribanos de cámara*—clerks of the court. Viceregal and provincial governments employed *escribanos de gobernación*—colonial secretaries. Every town council had its *escribano de cabildo*, its town clerk, who kept the minutes, drafted letters and deeds, witnessed the signatures of the *regidores* and often unobtrusively guided their deliberations. The provincial treasury offices, the mints, the guilds and chambers of commerce—every institution which conducted any considerable volume of formal or legal business—employed *escribanos*, often with large subordinate staffs. In a turbulent society, in which governors came and went, the *escribanos* represented permanence, order, routine. Their signatures on documents guaranteed to the Crown that prescribed procedure, administrative and legal, was being followed. Standing between their official superiors and the public, they often wielded great, though unobtrusive, power. They received no salaries. The King, it is true, could raise what taxes he pleased in America, and spend the money as he wished; but all the silver of the Indies would not have sufficed to pay salaries to all these officers out of royal revenue. As in Europe, they were remunerated by fees according to an official tariff. In the larger settlements these fees, together with incidental perquisites, assured a comfortable living. The more senior notarial offices in the Indies were valuable and coveted appointments. Conversely, it was always extremely difficult to fill notarial offices in small and backward settlements. The system of payment by fees, therefore, was an additional factor tending to concentrate European population and activity in the big towns.

The Crown of Castile possessed, in the Indies, an immense new range of patronage. In the distribution of this patronage, royal liberality and royal gratitude had to be reconciled with the aims of efficient administration and maximum revenue. Among the *conquistadores* and their descendants in the Indies, no less than in Spain itself, the Crown was confronted with a great number of eager claimants for office, most of whom based their claims upon services, military or otherwise, performed by themselves or their fathers. Some *conquistadores*—a lucky few—received *encomiendas*. Others were given seats on town councils, with the prospect of municipal office in due rotation, which cost the Crown nothing; or else—a little later—were made *corregidores* of Indian settlements, which cost very little, since the salaries were small. *Conquistadores* and their sons, however, rarely had legal or notarial training; they made indifferent quill-drivers. *Escribanos* in the early years had to be recruited in Spain. In Charles V's reign the appointment of fee-earning officials was largely handed over to private patronage in Spain. Colonial offices were given to claimants about the court as rewards for long service, for political good behaviour, or merely for persistent importunity. The members of the Council of the Indies in particular, and the King's secretaries, often secured grants of whole series of offices. The recipients of such grants also received the right to appoint deputies. In practice this meant that they sold leases of the offices in their gift, for life or for a term of years, to men who proposed to go to the Indies, do the work and collect the fees. In this indirect and haphazard way the secretarial staff of colonial governments, provincial treasuries and appeal courts was recruited. No attempt was made to establish a uniform system of appointment until Philip II's time. Philip, less imbued with the tradition of royal generosity, more interested in administrative routine, and more conscious of the revenue possibilities of America, kept colonial appointments firmly in his own hands. He endeavoured, with some success, to end the practice of titular officials serving by deputy. Where his father had given away fee-earning offices for lease or private sale, he usually had them sold directly to the men who were to perform the duties.[1]

It is sometimes said that Philip II introduced the sale of offices into the Indies. It would be more accurate to say that he made the sale of some kinds of colonial office a Crown monopoly. In this sense his innovations may fairly be described not as an abuse, but as a reform. In the course of his reign most important fee-earning offices in the colonies—*escribanías*, police offices, offices in the colonial mints, and a great range of municipal offices—were withdrawn from private or local patronage and made saleable on behalf of the Crown. They were to be offered publicly for sale in the provinces where vacancies occurred. Provisional titles were to be issued, usually to the highest bidder, except that the viceroy might in exceptional cases recommend a highly suitable applicant, though not the highest bidder. All titles required confirmation by the Crown; applicants were required to forward to Spain not only receipts for purchase prices, but also sworn testimony of their honesty, competence and purity of lineage, and in the case of *escribanos* their knowledge of the complexities of notarial procedure. From the Crown's point of view the system had important advantages. It helped to prevent provincial governors and viceroys from using public offices as rewards and pensions for their own public adherents, and it brought in revenue. Provided that judicial offices were excluded from the practice (as in law they always were) the idea of sale did not offend a public accustomed to regard fee-earning office as a form of property. The proposition differed little in principle from the method normally employed in collecting taxes. In the absence of a salaried staff of collectors, this work was commonly done by 'farmers', speculators who paid the Crown a lump sum or an annual rent, usually considerably less than the estimated yield of the tax. Fee-earning office could be treated in the same way, as a kind of round-about taxation; and in theory, provided that proper safeguards were observed, the efficiency of government need not suffer unduly. Under Philip II the safeguards concerning the competence of applicants for office were, on the whole, strictly enforced, and on occasion the Crown refused confirmation of appointment to purchasers against whom complaints were made, returning to them the purchase price which they had paid.

The administrative system created by Philip II survived in its essentials for a century and a half after his death. His seventeenth-century successors, however, both by legislative modifications and by laxity in enforcement, greatly weakened the Crown's control over the system as a whole. In 1606, in an attempt to make colonial offices more attractive, Philip III enacted that all saleable offices should be automatically renunciable also. This meant that the holder of an office might resign in favour of a successor of his own choice. The Crown, upon every renunciation, exacted a fee, usually one-third of the assessed value of the office, and always reserved the right to confirm, or to refuse to confirm every transfer of office. This very important enactment had an immediate and profound effect upon the administrative service. Naturally it made offices more valuable and more expensive to buy; on the other hand, it made it easier to borrow money to buy offices. An aspirant to an official career could borrow the purchase price of an office, offering as security a mortgage upon the office itself, and engaging to renounce the office in favour of his creditor, should he default on the interest payments. This arrangement was perfectly legal. It called into being a whole class of speculators who might be described as office brokers, people who acted as middlemen for deals in public office and made loans to intending purchasers. Some offices were renounced from father to son and became hereditary. This was true especially of municipal dignities and other honorific posts; but in the administrative secretariat of the colonies such bequests were rare. In general, renunciation was a polite word for private sale. An aspirant to an administrative career in the Indies would buy a junior office with borrowed money. If he did well out of fees, in a few years he would sell his office, or turn it in in part payment for another more senior and more lucrative, and so on, until he was rich enough to invest in landed property, or lucky enough to secure a grant of *encomienda* or marry an heiress.

In the second half of the seventeenth century the system of sale and renunciation spread from fee-earning offices to the more senior salaried posts. For this there was no legislative sanction; it was an abuse by seventeenth-century standards and recognized as such. It was never very common. Records survive of the sale of seventeen provincial governorships and thirty-five reversions. Seats in the Council of the Indies were sold on two occasions, and once an *audiencia* judge was allowed to buy his appointment. These transactions were not only bad administration; they were bad finance, since they allowed officials to buy, for a very low cash price, fixed annuities charged against royal revenue. They nearly all took place in Charles II's reign, and are evidence of the financial desperation of the time, which the revenue of the Indies was quite inadequate to relieve.

The system of appointment by public sale and payment by perquisites outlasted the seventeenth century. It was modified, curtailed and reformed in the eighteenth, but it survived, at least in part, until 1812. It was generally accepted and little criticized. The great jurist Solórzano likened it to debasement of the coinage, legally permissible, politically deplorable, but unavoidable.[2] It was an essential characteristic of the old colonial system, and to the historian of that system it suggests certain general reflections.

The Crown, having seized control of appointment to colonial offices in the sixteenth century, largely lost that control in the seventeenth. Most offices passed from hand to hand—from head to head, in the Spanish phrase—subject to a royal confirmation which became more and more perfunctory.

The great majority of colonial officials began their careers under heavy burdens of debt. They were not merely tempted, they were almost compelled to extort illegal fees, to take bribes, or to embezzle money from the royal chest, in order to make a living as well as keeping up their interest payments. The distinction between perquisites and bribes, to be sure, was difficult to draw exactly; but bribery in one form or another was almost universal in the seventeenth century. The unashamed openness of the sale of offices, the publicly accepted scale of charges, was matched by the openness of corruption and the cynically recognized scale of bribes; the two phenomena must have been connected.

Corruption would have existed whether offices were sold or not. A more direct consequence of the system of sale was the multiplication of offices. From Philip II's time onwards the Crown constantly created offices with no other purpose than that of selling them. This practice mattered little when the offices were mere honorific dignities. It became a serious nuisance when the Crown created new fee-earning offices and then, by legislation and by elaboration of procedure, compelled the public to employ the officers so appointed. It became financially self-defeating when the Crown, to raise ready money, offered for sale supernumerary salaried posts. The growing burden of bureaucracy was in part directly attributable to the growing practice of selling offices; and the actual income in ready money to the Crown from this source was in the long run hardly worth the trouble.[3] It did not compare in importance with the main heads of taxation: silver tax, sales tax, native tributes, customs duties.

On the other hand, the system had its advantages. It discouraged nepotism among the high officials; this was one of Philip II's reasons for encouraging it. It offered the opportunity of an official career to men resident in the Indies; its restriction in the eighteenth century closed this avenue to many Creoles, and, as often happened in colonial circumstances, the reform was more unpopular than the abuse. It encouraged immigrants to settle down in the Indies and was an important source of capital for the economic development of the colonies. Many prosperous estates, especially in Mexico, originated in the profits of public office.

Despite all the abuses, the work of the administrative secretariat in the colonies throughout the seventeenth century showed a remarkable uniformity. The machine ground on, almost of its own momentum. These bureaucrats, passing their offices from one to another by private sale, were many of them the products of the universities and law schools of Spain or Spanish America. They might be rapacious and—within recognized limits—venal; but they had an *esprit-de-corps*, a training, a respect for precedent, a pride in their profession, which surmounted the shoddy, hand-to-mouth system which appointed them. The Spanish empire in the seventeenth century suffered from a crippling lack of resources and faltering direction at the centre; its administrative procedure was pettifogging, complex and slow; but, subject to these defects, by the standards of the time the government was well served by its officials. It had detailed and accurate information, regularly supplied; on the few occasions when it succeeded in making up its mind to give a definite order, it could usually in time get that order carried out, though only at the cost of immense persistence and effort. This degree of centralized control was dearly bought. Administrative costs absorbed an ever greater proportion of the Indies revenue. For the private citizen, the cost in time and money of even the simplest official business came near to prohibition. At the end of the century the whole life of the empire seemed in danger of strangulation, not only by external enemies preying upon its trade and cutting its communications, but by the host of internal parasites preying upon the livelihood of its people.

No other European colonial empire in the Age of Reconnaissance possessed a bureaucracy as elaborate as that of the Spanish Indies. Some features of the administrative machinery of the Spanish empire, however, were common also to the other empires. Payment of most officials by perquisites rather than by salaries was universal. The French and Portuguese Crowns sold colonial offices in much the same way as the Spanish Crown, though on a smaller scale and in a less highly organized way. The French were less particular than the Spaniards about excluding judicial offices from the system of sale. Many French offices, including some judgeships, were hereditary, the Crown collecting an annual rent or tax from the holders.[4] In England, the government did not, as a rule, sell offices on its own account; the practice had been forbidden by Statute as early as 1552, and in the seventeenth century both Parliament and the colonial assemblies became extremely suspicious of attempts to increase extra-parliamentary revenue. Nevertheless, in the later seventeenth century king and ministers regularly used their powers of patronage, at home and abroad, to gratify their friends, clients and supporters. Colonial offices were often granted by Letters Patent to men who had obligations and duties in England, who had no intention of leaving England, and who performed their colonial duties by deputy. The deputies either retained a share of the fees of office and remitted the remainder to their principals in England; or else took leases of the deputations of their posts and paid their principals a lump sum or an annual rent. The fees appropriate to one man's work thus had to provide income for two men. When James Mill called imperialism 'a vast system of outdoor relief for the upper classes', he was thinking primarily of India; but his description could fairly be applied, as far as public office was concerned, to the English colonies in the New World.

Offices were patented in all the English colonies of the Old Empire, but the practice began earliest, lasted longest and achieved its widest extension in the West Indian islands, where the pickings were greater and local political feeling less developed than in North America.[5] It began, like many other arbitrary practices, under the Commonwealth, as part of Cromwell's plan for bringing royalist Barbados to heel; formerly, governor and council had chosen their own officials. After the Restoration the practice became general, and Charles II for the first time allowed service by deputy. The principal civil officials affected in each colony were the secretary, the provost-marshal and, after 1676, the clerk of the naval office. The secretary had charge of all public records, including the Acts of the legislature, which he transmitted in due form to England. He was also responsible for the registration of titles to land and for many minor matters. The provost-marshal was a chief constable, entirely responsible in peacetime for the enforcement of law and the custody of criminals. The naval officer was originally a clerk appointed by the governor to assist him in the supervision of trade and the enforcement of the Acts of Trade. His place became a separate office with a name of its own about 1676. Besides taking bonds and giving certificates to clear ships and cargoes, he acted as an immigration officer and kept a register of incoming passengers and indented servants. The office of attorney-general also was sometimes patented, and in Jamaica the responsible and very lucrative office of receiver-general or treasurer. There were various other clerkships in the larger colonies which carried fees and were thought capable of supporting a patentee and one or more deputies. Colonial governors themselves were almost the only senior officials, except judges, who remained as a class outside the system. They were appointed (except under the proprietors) by commissions under the Great Seal; they received stipends and were not allowed to serve by deputy.

The patentees were a mixed lot, mostly friends of ministers, people (or protégés of people) who were politically useful, or simply people who were thought deserving of pensions. One of the latter class was Congreve the playwright, who for years held the office of secretary of Jamaica. He never went there, though he was punctilious enough to write to the governor requesting formal leave of absence. The deputies whom he appointed distinguished themselves in opposition to the government. Patentees deputed their offices as they chose; it was only as an act of rare courtesy that governors were consulted. There were no stated qualifications of training or competence, and no official confirmation was required. A deputation was a straightforward financial deal between patentee and deputy. Often sugar factors and other businessmen in England with West Indian contacts acted as brokers and go-betweens, charging a commission for their trouble. The deputies were usually resident in the colonies—planters, merchants, local politicians. Secure in their tenure so long as they paid for it, they often proved incompetent, venal and insolent. Governors could not hope to create a smoothly-running administrative team out of a group of officials all appointed by different patentees and virtually irremovable; if a governor tried to get rid of a patent officer's deputy on grounds of misconduct he could seldom count on the support of ministers at home. As might be expected, governors' letters to the Lords of Trade on the subject were full of exasperated complaint.

Governors were alone in their complaints. Until the late eighteenth century public opinion, both in England and in the colonies, accepted the system as normal. The Crown needed the patronage, the power to grant offices as pensions to its loyal servants. Colonial assemblies sometimes grumbled about patentees' fees, or protested against the appointment of notoriously disreputable or unpopular deputies; but there was no general objection to the appointment of officers by Letters Patent when coupled with automatic leave of absence. On the contrary, the system suited the colonists well. The only function of imperial administration vital to their interests was the defence of their coasts and their trade. Their loyalty to the English Crown was partly traditional and sentimental, partly the respect due to the power which protected them. So long as that power kept the seas—and bore the cost—they thought that they could manage the land themselves. They certainly had no wish to see their internal affairs administered by efficient and zealous officers sent from England. Still less did they want their governors to have the power of appointing officers on the spot, because such power would permit the creation of 'government' parties in the legislatures by the distribution of patronage. They preferred to see the executive power weak and frustrated, officials absentee and inactive, the day-to-day work of administration done by deputies chosen, for the most part, among local people, amenable to local pressure, often committed to opposition to the governor. It was not merely that the colonies preferred self-government to good government. At times they preferred no real government at all to the prospect of effective government by Englishmen. To many of them the fees sent home to the patentees were a moderate price to pay for the privilege of being left alone, to run their own particular rackets in their own local way.

The Age of Reconnaissance produced commercial as well as administrative bureaucracies. The practices of appointment by sale and payment by perquisite obtained not only in empires organized like those of Spain, France and England, territorially by provinces, but also in empires whose organization was primarily commercial: the Portuguese empire in the East, the Dutch empire, and the incipient private empire of the English East India Company. Captains of ships often purchased their commands. So sometimes did managers of factories, even governors of fortress towns. Directors of the great companies had in their gift clerkships and cadet-ships which they could either sell, or bestow upon the sons of men whom they wished to oblige. The perquisites, with which the servants of these great concerns were largely paid, mostly took the form not of fees but of shipping space. All big overseas trading concerns allowed their servants privileges of private trade; they had no effective alternative. All waged a constant struggle—with varying degrees of success—to keep these privileges within permitted or reasonable limits, to reserve enough space for the companies' own goods, and to insist on adequate attention being paid to the companies' interests as distinct from the interests of individuals. It was extremely difficult for these great organizations, operating with slow communications over great distances, to demand adequate standards of loyalty and honesty from clerks and managers whom they did not, and could not, adequately pay or supervise. This was one of the causes of the financial difficulties in which they repeatedly found themselves. The companies' servants made fortunes when the companies themselves were bankrupt.

In the Age of Reconnaissance, energy, exploring curiosity, acquisitive enterprise, missionary zeal, all outran administrative capacity. European rulers found it far more difficult to govern distant kingdoms effectively and economically, than to acquire them. The difficulty was partly financial, arising not only from lack of actual money, but from lack of financial machinery flexible enough to apply money quickly where it was needed. Carrying bar silver about the world in sailing ships was a cumbersome device for administrative purposes; the estimating and accounting procedures of the time were quite inadequate for the needs of vast and widespread organizations. Partly the difficulty arose from the comparatively rudimentary administrative experience and methods of the European kingdoms themselves. The organization of defence, the maintenance of order and property, the provision of courts for the settlement of disputes—these were the normal, traditional functions of rulers, to which ordinary revenue was supposed to be devoted. In order to enforce innovating legislation, to make its will effective in some particular field of national life outside the traditional fields, a government had to make a special and concentrated effort, often to appoint a special body of men for the particular purpose. There was no general machine, no permanent body of men available to keep up the pressure, to make the will of government effective continuously and simultaneously over a wide range of fields of activity. Much sixteenth- and seventeenth-century legislation, even in Europe, was ineffective; or rather, was effective only occasionally. Naturally the difficulties in the way of regular, continuous enforcement were still greater overseas.

Partly, again, the difficulty was one of loyalty. Loyalty and obedience to the king, to the king's magistrates and officers, or to feudal superiors, were duties which every good subject acknowledged; but they were duties of a relatively passive kind. A man must refrain from doing anything to the prejudice of his lord or the commonwealth. He must, to be sure, come to his lord's aid if summoned, and must render certain fixed dues and services; but there his obligations ceased. The loyalty of sixteenth-century officials—apart, of course, from the most senior and responsible—was similar to that of private men. An official occupied a place of trust and emolument. He had been given that place either because he had earned it by past services; or because he had bought it; or because he had been lucky in securing the patronage of some great man. He was expected to perform certain duties, to transact certain pieces of business according to rules, if and when he was called upon to do so, either by the government, or by a private person, such as a petitioner or a litigant. He received a separate fee for each job done. If he were a loyal and conscientious official he would do what he was asked to do, protect the royal interest to the best of his ability, and refrain from oppression or fraud. On the other hand, he did not think of himself as being in full-time employment, as being committed to the active and continuous service of the Crown and to the furtherance of its policies. If the Crown did not pay him, there was no reason why he should.

Throughout the sixteenth, seventeenth and eighteenth centuries, European governments slowly but persistently worked to overcome these difficulties; to make their civil services more active and effective instruments of their will; to recruit corps d'élite of professional, salaried officials imbued not only with personal loyalty to king or immediate superior, but also with that impersonal loyalty to the administrative machine which is characteristic of the good bureaucrat. The growing complexity of government in Europe would have made such a development necessary in any event; but the possession of kingdoms overseas gave it added point and urgency. In Europe, centuries-old custom ensured that social and governmental organization survived and worked in some fashion, even under weak rulers, even with the most sketchy and defective administrative machinery; but overseas everything was new and strange. Innovating legislation was not a special remedy in exceptional circumstances, but a constant need; and it had to be enforced, at a great distance, by men who could have no personal contact with their rulers. The empires, if they were to be effectively governed at all, could be governed only by bureaucratic methods. Kings, ministers, great officials, could not tour their overseas possessions in person, as they toured their European kingdoms. They could not question and supervise their colonial servants directly. They had to rely on written reports, to express their will in written orders. The empires of the Reconnaissance were held together by chains of paper; chains which made up in number what they lacked in individual strength. Men skilled in handling paper were the indispensable servants of imperial government. The members of the Council of the Indies, the Lords of Trade, the Directors of the great Dutch companies, were all bureaucrats on a grand scale. Philip II, that great king governing his vast and scattered dominions from a desk in the Escurial, was the very type of a bureaucratic ruler. The government of the Indies, and in varying degrees all the empires of the Reconnaissance, demonstrated what could be achieved by loyal and efficient bureaucrats when ably directed. It demonstrated also the frustration, the heavy cost, the loss of all sense of urgency, which a bureaucracy entailed when carelessly recruited and inadequately supervised. Bureaucracy, like absolutism, strengthened its grip upon the kingdoms of Europe, in part at least as a consequence of needs experienced and experiments conducted overseas.

CHAPTER 19

THE RIGHTS OF CONQUERORS
AND CONQUERED

THE establishment of European empires overseas created not only problems of administration, but also problems of political theory. Here again, Spaniards were the first in the field and the most vigorous in discussion. Sixteenth-century Spain led the rest of Europe not only in the practice of law and government, but also in the theoretical field of jurisprudence. Spanish jurists worked out a theory of sovereignty distinct equally from the narrow kingship of the Middle Ages and from the unbridled absolutism later described by Hobbes; a theory of a constitutional state, possessed of the right of legislation and unrestricted in its sphere of action, but restricted in its exercise of power by the man-made laws and customs of its subjects. They expressed a horror of absolutism, at a time when absolutism was everywhere gaining ground. Throughout the century, books insisting on the legal rights of free peoples, even in extreme cases advocating tyrannicide, continued to circulate freely, were read without scandal, and exercised considerable influence not only upon thought, but also on the actions of government. Inevitably in such an atmosphere, the discovery and conquest of a new world provoked juridical discussion.[1]

Officially the Spanish Crown based its right to rule the Indies on the bulls of 1493, in particular upon *Inter Caetera*, which granted to Spain 'islands and mainlands . . . towards the West and South . . . with all their rights, jurisdictions and appurtenances', excepting only lands already held by Christian princes. None of the lands subsequently colonized by Spaniards had Christian rulers, but all were inhabited. Of the inhabitants, though some were very primitive, all lived under some kind of political discipline, all appeared to obey recognized chiefs. Presumably those rulers all had some sort of title to the territory which they governed and to the obedience of the people who occupied it. The Crown lawyers argued that the titles of the native rulers were probably usurped; that their rule was tyrannical, and therefore indefensible; and that in any event the papal grant had overriding force. This was a highly contentious argument. The doctrine of universal papal dominion, in temporal as in spiritual matters, usually associated with the name of Henry of Susa (Ostiensis), was, it is true, well known to canonists in the fifteenth and early sixteenth centuries, but was certainly not universally accepted. It was a relic of the medieval conception of the world, as a homogeneous Christendom with an infidel fringe. According to Ostiensis, infidels might retain their lands and possessions only by the favour of the Church. If they refused to recognize papal authority, the Pope might direct the steps necessary for bringing them into obedience, even to the extent of appointing Christian rulers over them; with the proviso, however, that such appointed rule must be *politicum* only and not *despoticum*. Many sixteenth-century jurists, in Spain as elsewhere, rejected the Ostiensian doctrine not only because it was theologically unsound but because it was unrealistic. Ostiensis, writing in an age of Mediterranean crusades, had had in mind the Muslims of the Levant, militant enemies of Christendom despite ample opportunity of studying Christian doctrine. It might plausibly be argued that their infidelity was deliberate, malicious and punishable. The great discoveries, however, demonstrated more powerfully than any theory the error of regarding 'the World' and 'Christendom' as more or less coterminous. It was clearly absurd to call on the American Indians to acknowledge the authority of a Pontiff of whom they had never heard. The solemn pantomime of the *Requerimiento*[2] deceived nobody. Moral, intellectual and legal scruples about the justice of the enterprise of the Indies could be quieted only by arguments independent of the temporal sovereignty of the Pope.

Whatever views might be expressed about the Pope's authority in temporal matters, no one as yet openly doubted his spiritual jurisdiction. Whatever else they might purport to be, the bulls of 1493 were a clear instruction to the Crown of Castile to undertake the conversion of the American Indians to Christianity. No Catholic—and discussion of these matters was long confined to Catholics—could deny the right of the Pope to give such an instruction, or the duty of the Spanish monarchs to carry it out. To what extent, however, were they authorized to use secular means to this spiritual end? Could the duty of conversion be held to justify armed conquest, the deposition of native rulers—if indeed the Indians had legitimate rulers—the assertion of Spanish sovereignty over the Indians in general? This was the central question. If it could be answered affirmatively, it gave rise in turn to subsidiary questions. If the Indians should be reduced, by a just conquest, to the position of subjects of the Spanish Crown, what legal and political rights remained to them? Should they be 'converted' by compulsion? Were they to be subject to Spanish courts of law, civil or ecclesiastical? Might they be commended to individual Spanish feudatories, deprived of their land, put to forced labour, enslaved? The attempt to answer these questions involved a statement on the part of each writer of the nature of papal and imperial authority; of the force of Natural Law and the Law of Nations in determining the grounds for just war; of the efficacy of force in converting the heathen; and of the status, character and capacity of the Indians themselves.

The question of the validity of Spain's title to the Indies exercised some of the best minds of the sixteenth century. The most distinguished and in many ways most original discussion of the problem was contained in a series of lectures delivered at Salamanca in 1539 by the great Dominican jurist, Francisco de Vitoria.[3] Vitoria never visited America. His interest in the subject was academic in the best sense, and was concentrated on the rights and wrongs of war and conquest. He was probably the first serious writer to reject firmly and unequivocally all claim of Pope or Emperor to exercise temporal jurisdiction over other princes, Christian or infidel.[4] He considered that the Pope possessed a 'regulating' authority, recognized among Christian peoples, by virtue of which a single prince might be charged, to the exclusion of others, with the task of supporting missions among a heathen people. This regulating power might authorize certain secular acts, such as the provision of armed force for the protection of missionaries; but it could not authorize war or conquest. War, like all relations between independent states, was for Vitoria governed by rules of law. In this also he was highly original, one of the first thinkers to maintain that there was a Natural Law connection between all nations, and that this connection, while it did not issue in any authority exercised by the Whole over its parts, at any rate involved a system of mutual rights and duties. From this point of view the Law of Nations was conceived as a law binding *inter se* upon States which were still in a state of nature in virtue of their sovereignty, and binding upon them in exactly the same way as the pre-political Law of Nature had been binding upon individuals when they were living in a state of nature. Vitoria gave this newly-conceived Law of Nations the old Roman name, *Jus gentium*; but he re-defined the term, paraphrasing Justinian's well-known definition,[5] as the law *quod naturalis ratio inter omnes gentes constituit. Jus gentium* had originally meant that part of the private law of Rome which was supposed to be common to Rome and other peoples; for Vitoria (and for Grotius later) it came to mean a branch of public law governing the relations between one people and another. He was quite clear that the Indian peoples were 'gentes' in this sense; they formed organized and independent States; their princes ruled by accepted title, and were subject, equally with the princes of Europe, to *Jus gentium*. Just cause for waging war against them could be found, not in any papal edict, probably not in their idolatry or alleged barbarity or wickedness, but certainly if they transgressed the rules of International Law.

Vitoria's theory of international justice assumed, though without expressly stating, the now familiar doctrine of the equality of States. The principal rights possessed by every nation were those of peaceful commerce and intercourse with every other nation (provided that no harm were done to the natives of the land visited); and the peaceful preaching of the Gospel. The Spaniards originally shared with other nations the right to visit the Indies upon such errands. The Pope, however, in virtue of his regulating authority, had confided the task of evangelizing in the New World to the Spaniards alone, partly as the nation best fitted for the task, and partly to avoid strife, since the Spaniards possessed the subsidiary claim of prior discovery. The papal decree was binding upon all Christian princes, though not upon the Indians; but the Indians, equally with the Christians, were bound by the wider rules of the Law of Nations to receive the Spaniards peacefully and to hear the Gospel. The Spaniards, for their part, must behave as Christians, offer peaceful trade, refrain from provoking resistance, and present the Gospel fairly. The Indians would not incur the penalty of conquest merely by rejecting the Gospel after hearing it; but refusal to hear, refusal to admit strangers, unprovoked attacks on traders and missionaries—any of these offences would at once give the Spaniards a just ground for war and conquest.

The Law of Nations in Vitoria's thought, unlike modern International Law, did not require universal acceptance in order to claim universal validity. *Jus gentium* derived originally from Natural Law. The nearest approximation on earth to a formulation of Natural Law was 'a concensus of the greater part of the whole world, especially in behalf of the common good of all'. The supposed majority of peoples constituted by Christian Europe was considered, therefore, to be the guardian of Natural Law and to have a secondary right and duty (since the Indians were members of the 'natural society and fellowship') to exercise a paternal and benevolent guardianship over peoples living in ignorance or open defiance of Natural Law. Typical offences against Natural Law—quite distinct from offences against the Law of Nations— were tyranny, human sacrifice and bestiality; all of which crimes were attributed by the colonists to the Indians. Vitoria was somewhat sceptical of colonists' tales, however, and was unwilling to base a right of conquest on Natural Law offences alone.

The possibility that a majority of Indians might elect to live under Spanish rule; the duty of protecting converts from the dangers of persecution or relapse; the right of assisting a friendly nation in a just war against a neighbour (such as the war of the Tlaxcalans against the

Aztec confederacy, of which Cortés made such adroit use), all were recognized as possible minor justifications for Spanish armed intervention in the New World.

Vitoria's conclusions on Spain's right to rule were curiously tentative. He would have preferred an empire based on peaceful trade to one formed by conquest. He believed commerce to be at least as effective as conquest, in spreading the Gospel, in satisfying a legitimate desire for individual profit, and in increasing the royal revenue. He cited in support of this belief the successes of the Portuguese in the East. Nevertheless, he admitted that once the Spaniards were established in the Indies they could not withdraw and allow colonists and converts to perish. He thought that Spanish government, even in a purely secular sense, could be an advantage to the Indians: 'Those people are not unintelligent, but primitive; they seem incapable of maintaining a civilized State according to the requirements of humanity and law . . . their government, therefore, should be entrusted to people of intelligence and experience, as though they were children. . . . But this interference must be for their welfare and in their interests, not merely for the profit of the Spaniards; for otherwise the Spaniards would be placing their own souls in peril.'[6] Finally, 'The prime consideration is that no obstacle should be placed in the way of the Gospel. . . . I personally have no doubt that the Spaniards were compelled to use force and arms in order to continue their work there; though I fear that measures were adopted in excess of what is allowed by human and divine law.'[7]

Vitoria's justification of the Spanish title to the Indies could not be called enthusiastic. It revealed a penetration and liberality of mind remarkable in its time; but also an anxious searching of conscience, which was shared by many sensitive Spaniards throughout the life of the empire. It embarrassed the government; it called forth a reprimand from the Emperor and a strong hint to the Dominicans not to discuss such matters in public. Nevertheless, Vitoria's great academic prestige and his considered humanity could not fail to influence public opinion. Many of the legal principles for which he argued came to be embodied in imperial legislation, in the New Laws of 1542 and still more in the *Ordenanzas sobre Descubrimiento* of 1573. In a still wider field, Vitoria's attempt to formulate rules governing the conduct of civilized States, both towards one another and towards weaker peoples, was a permanent and valuable addition to European political theory. He was the principal founder of the study of International Law.

Most other writers on the Indies were less academic in their approach, less interested in justifying the conquest (which was a fact, and had to be accepted), more concerned with the nature of the lordship which the Castilian monarchs actually exercised. During the middle decades of the sixteenth century the Crown was bombarded with memorials on colonial policy, and the government of the Indies—more specifically, the treatment of the Indians—became the subject of a bitter pamphleteering war. The propagandists, very roughly, fell into two groups: those who wished to safeguard the freedom of the Indians and, by implication, the exclusive influence of the missionary friars; and those who wished to extend the liberty of action and the quasi-feudal authority of the Spanish settlers. Of the first group, the most famous and most influential was another Dominican, Bartolomé de las Casas. Las Casas spent most of his long working life in the Indies, as missionary, as bishop, and as writer. His writings and his whole life were governed by his affection for the Indians, his zeal for their spiritual well-being, his determination to defend their rights, his passionate indignation at the treatment which they received. His major works, the *Historia* and the *Apologética Historia*,[8] are full of valuable information; but because of their verbosity and their lack of orderly arrangement, have been little read. His numerous polemical writings[9] are vituperative, one-sided and at times extravagant. The best known of them, the *Brevísima relación de la destrucción de las Indias*, is a hair-raising catalogue of atrocities, which was gleefully translated into English and used as anti-Spanish propaganda under the Commonwealth. Nevertheless, taken as a whole, Las Casas' writings reveal a theory of man and of government which, through all the verbiage, is clear and consistent.

The key to Las Casas' thought was his insistence upon liberty. He laid down as the essentials of civilized existence that men should live in politically organized communities, but that subject to the minimum of restraint necessary to make such organization possible, they should be entirely free. He deduced this necessity from Aquinas' definition of Natural Law: *Lex naturalis est participatio legis aeternae in creatura rationis compote*. Men required absolute liberty in order that their reason, which naturally inclined them to live in peace together, to seek good and to avoid evil, might be unrestricted. If the free exercise of reason was a right according to Natural Law, it belonged as well to infidels as to Christians, and not even the Vicar of Christ, in his zeal for the extension of the Faith, might lawfully invade such a right. Las Casas insisted more strongly than any other writer of his century on free and willing conversion; to use any form of coercion in missionary activity was worthy only of Mahomet. He consistently denounced the Ostiensian doctrine as heretical, and maintained that the Pope in ordinary circumstances held no authority whatever over infidels, to punish their sins or to depose their princes.

Like Vitoria, Las Casas attributed to the Papacy a limited and indirect temporal authority in matters relating to the spiritual welfare of Christendom. The Pope might lay upon a prince the task of defending Christians against infidels who openly attacked the Faith, and might delegate the duty of carrying the Gospel to infidels who were ignorant of it. In this sense Las Casas attributed Spanish authority in the Indies to papal delegation; but that authority, he insisted, was delegated exclusively to the Spanish monarchs, not to Spaniards in general. Spanish conquerors and settlers in America had no authority, no special rights, save as agents and subjects of the Crown. Las Casas' views on colonial government were based, therefore, not on a theory of superior civilization, but on a theory of kingship—an older, and in some ways more primitive theory than that commonly held by the contemporary writers of the Spanish juridical school; for while writers such as Azpilcueta, Covarrubias and Molina attributed kingship to some form of secular election, Las Casas clung to the medieval idea of divine ordination.

The conventional medieval theory of kingship had assumed an authority autocratic but not despotic; an authority bounded by strict limits, but within those limits supreme. The law of God, the rights of subjects according to their station, the laws and customs of the realm, were held alike to be above the power of the king, whose duty it was to protect and enforce them; but in his own sphere of activity, the administration of justice and the protection of rights, the king had no peer. The kingly rank was ordained by God for the sake of justice and was never the property of the man who held it, but an office, with high and difficult duties. The more solemn the trust, the heavier the penalty for abusing it. So long as he performed his duties faithfully and confined himself to them, a legitimate king was entitled to the implicit obedience of all his subjects. If he seriously neglected or overstepped them he became, *ipso facto*, a tyrant, and might lawfully be disobeyed, deposed, and even killed.

The rules of government which a king observes and a tyrant disregards, which distinguish between a king, the true defender of the realm, and a tyrant, its would-be proprietor, are described at great length in Las Casas' writings. They fall into four principal groups. The king must provide justice and keep the peace; he must uphold and defend the Church and support its missionary work; he must maintain and respect the rights of his subjects according to custom, including both their property and their legal liberties; and he must preserve the realm and the royal authority, which is not his own, intact for his successors. Las Casas applied these rules not only to the Spanish royal authority in its 'natural realm', but to the imperial authority of the Crown in territory which it had acquired by conquest and in which, according to the theory and practice of its officials, the ordinary limitations upon kingship did not exist. In this, Las Casas' theory was revolutionary. He maintained that the Crown in the New World, through evil advice, had permitted its Spanish vassals not only to infringe the liberties of its Indian subjects, but also to 'blemish the realm'.

The pamphlet entitled *Erudita explicatio*[10] deals at length with this question of the alienation of royal property and jurisdiction, and denies emphatically the right of a king to grant away authority over any part of his realm, or any of his subjects or their property, or to alienate any of the property of the State, or, except in exceptional circumstances, any part of the royal patrimony. Las Casas interpreted alienation in the strictest possible sense. The sale of offices was an alienation of authority, and however general it might be, was unjust and illegal. *Encomiendas*, which gave to private persons a strictly royal jurisdiction and authority over the Indians, were contrary to reason, Natural Law and the laws of Castile.

The Indians, equally with the people of Spain, were for Las Casas the natural subjects of the Spanish Crown, and enjoyed, from the moment of their entering into the Spanish obedience, all the guarantees of liberty and justice provided by the laws of Castile. They owed also the allegiance and duties of Spanish subjects, and Las Casas maintained that intellectually they were fully capable of discharging those duties and of receiving the Catholic Faith. In his ideal missionary empire, therefore, the Indians would live in their own villages, ruled by their own *caciques*, under the supervision of royal officials who would administer justice, instruct them in European customs and discourage barbarous practices. The Church would proceed freely and peacefully with its work of evangelization and spiritual care. Europeans, as private persons, if they were to be allowed in the Indies at all, would live apart from the Indians, and live by their own labour. Las Casas allowed the colonist no privilege but that of hard work, and no special reward but that of spiritual achievement.

That Las Casas' ideal empire was far from American reality is obvious enough. The interests of *encomenderos*, proprietary officials and town councils were well entrenched. The early administrative experiments which the government authorized on the lines of Las Casas' theories, in Hispaniola and Cumaná, were—not surprisingly— failures.[11] His propaganda could not simply be shrugged off, however, as a fanatic extravagance. He had powerful friends. His vehement persistence could beat down both opposition and indifference. Some of his ideas were congenial to Charles V and his ecclesiastical advisers, and made a wide appeal to humanitarian feeling. The clauses in the

New Laws of 1542 which provided for the termination of *encomiendas* probably owed something to his urging; and his ideas also found support at Rome, notably in the bull *Sublimis Deus* of 1537, which condemned as heretical the opinion that the Indians were irrational and incapable of receiving the Faith. These indications of approval in high places help to explain the hatred with which Las Casas was pursued by Spaniards in the New World. The old conquerors and settlers considered his ideas a serious challenge not only to their livelihood, but to their respectability. These men were by no means all mere cut-throat adventurers. Many of them took serious pride in their achievements, and thought of themselves as champions of civilization and religion against a cruel and superstitious barbarism. These ideas also had their theoretical defenders, among whom the most distinguished was Juan Ginés de Sepúlveda.

Sepúlveda wrote his *Democrates Alter*[12] in 1542. He was then at the height of his reputation as a humanist, an Aristotelian scholar and a master of Latin style. Like many learned Spaniards, he had counted Erasmus among his friends. As with Vitoria, his concern with the Indies was academic, unaffected by personal interest. Like Vitoria, he founded his thought on the subject upon a highly individual view of Natural Law. The Ciceronian definition, which 'Democrates' quotes, was orthodox and familiar: *est igitur lex naturae, quam non opinio, sed innata vis inseruit*. But this *innata vis* could manifest itself in different ways. In the physical sense, *jus naturale est quod natura omnia animalia docuit*; such precepts, for example, as the duty of reproduction, or repelling force by force. On the other hand, *innata vis* had a rational aspect, as in Aquinas' definition: *participatio legis aeternae in creatura rationis compote*. This was the law, according to Sepúlveda, which impelled men to respect their parents, to seek good and avoid evil, to keep promises and to believe the teachings of true religion. If man was by nature rational, then the second form of law was as natural as the first. Sepúlveda's thesis required the complete conformance of these two aspects of Natural Law; and he arbitrarily assumed that no prompting of instinct which failed to conform to reason could be deemed truly natural.

Natural Law as reason was identified in Sepúlveda's thought with *Jus gentium*, the body of rules supposedly common to all organized peoples. Unlike Vitoria, Sepúlveda admitted no secondary Law of Nations, no rudimentary international law prescribing the natural and proper relations between States. He used the terms Law of Nations and Natural Law almost indifferently. Both were revealed by human reason, since reason impelled men to formulate a common opinion on all matters of universal importance. Sepúlveda did not rely, however, upon the reason of all men, nor even upon that of the 'greater part', as did Vitoria. His Law of Nations was to be found only among the *gentes humanitiores*, not among those on the margin of civilization; and even among civilized peoples, the duty of declaring what was or was not Natural Law was confined to the wisest and most prudent men of the higher races. The whole theory was a plea for natural aristocracy; the government of the lower races by the higher, of the lower elements by the higher in each race. Sepúlveda even denied that a people might strictly be considered to have legitimate rulers—in modern terms, to be a State—unless it was governed according to the opinions of its best citizens; though for purposes of maintaining the peace, Natural Law enjoined obedience even to bad rulers, and rebellion could have no legal justification against a prince whose title was legitimate according to the particular laws and customs of his people.

The corollary of natural aristocracy was natural servitude, since the more perfect should hold sway over the less. The Aristotelian theory, as interpreted by Sepúlveda, was made to constitute a general mandate for civilized peoples to subdue by force of arms, if no other means were possible, those peoples 'who require, by their own nature and in their own interests, to be placed under the authority of civilized and virtuous princes and nations, so that they may learn from the might, wisdom and law of their conquerors to practise better morals, worthier customs and a more civilized way of life'. Sepúlveda was too restrained a polemist to level at the Indians such a battery of abuse as, for example, the historian Oviedo had employed; but he did assert that the Indians lived in defiance of Natural Law, and pointed to their very inability to resist the Spanish invasion, as yet further proof of their inferior state and their need of strong and wise government, for their own good.

From these premisses Sepúlveda might have drawn conclusions embodying a purely secular title for Spanish rule in the New World. This he had no intention of doing. The spreading of the Faith appeared as a solemn duty to him as to all his contemporaries, and though his theological arguments were logically unnecessary in the general development of his thought, they presented no contradictions. *Compelle eos intrare* was the text underlying his missionary theory. Forcible baptism he considered unjust and useless; nor did paganism in itself provide a cause for just war; but the effective conversion of large bodies of pagans was impossible, except after long contact with Christians. The Indians would not accept Christianity immediately, upon the mere word of strangers, nor change their way of life in a few days. In order that they might learn from missionaries and prepare themselves for entry into the Church, it was necessary to place them under civilized government and tutelage, with or without their consent.

Civilization and Christianity went hand in hand. Conquest was a religious duty, an act of charity towards ignorant and unfortunate neighbours.

Natural Law in Sepúlveda's thought gave to the Spaniards a well-defined chain of rights of conquest and colonization in the New World. The principal rights entitling a nation to wage just war were four: the natural right of repelling force by force; the recovery of possessions which had been unjustly taken; the necessity of punishing criminals who had not been punished by their own rulers (since all men were neighbours and mutually responsible one for another); and the duty of subduing barbarous peoples by force if they refused to submit voluntarily to government by a superior race. This last right depended in its turn upon four causes: the naturally servile nature of barbarians and their consequent need of a civilized master; their habitual crimes against Natural Law; the plight of the subjects of barbarian rulers, who were the victims of oppression, unjust war, slavery and human sacrifice; and the duty of making possible the peaceful preaching of the Gospel. All Christian and civilized nations enjoyed these rights and owed these duties. The special rights and duties of Spain in the New World arose from three causes: the natural superiority of Spaniards over other Christian nations; the right of the first discoverer to occupy lands which had no legitimate ruler; and the decree of the Pope, at once a spiritual commission to convert the heathen and a temporal grant of legally unoccupied territory.

Almost all the arguments ever cited in favour of imperialism were used by Sepúlveda. Even the purely pragmatic argument of economic development found a place in his work; the Spaniards had introduced beasts of burden into the Indies, had developed the mines, and taught the Indians profitable methods of agriculture. Of course they had profited themselves also; though Sepúlveda had severe things to say about conquerors who were inspired 'auri inexplebili cupiditate'. The force of his arguments was undeniable. Their principal defect was that they tended to prove too much. His cold and harsh reasoning roused few answering echoes (save among the more percipient colonists, who rightly regarded him as the champion of their interest; the town council of Mexico sent him a letter of congratulation and thanks). Many of his contemporaries and most historians since his time thought him an apologist for naked slavery. His theory of natural servitude was repugnant to most Spanish theologians and academic jurists; the great Suárez disposed of it curtly: 'hactenus tamen, ut existimo, tam barbarae gentes inventae non sunt.'[13] Certainly Sepúlveda wrote in ignorance of colonial conditions, and used purely theoretical arguments to support a system which lent itself in practice to appalling abuses. Certainly also he admitted the justice of enslaving prisoners taken in rebellion or in the act of unjust war—a right of the conqueror generally admitted at the time. He added to this admission, however, the warning that enslavement was no longer a reputable practice among Christian peoples, and that many Indians must have resisted in good faith, thinking that they themselves had just cause for war. The enslavement of these people would certainly be unjust. Sepúlveda protested bitterly in his letters against those who accused him of brutality in this matter. His proposal was not to enslave, but 'to divide the Indians of the cities and the fields among honourable, just and prudent Spaniards, especially among those who helped to bring them under Spanish rule, so that these may train their Indians in virtuous and humane customs, and teach them the Christian religion; which may not be preached by force of arms, but by precept and example. In return for this, the Spaniards may employ the labour of the Indians in performing those tasks necessary for civilized life.' As the Indians grew better acquainted with Christianity and European habits they were to receive greater freedom —'liberius erunt liberaliusque tractandi ministri'; though Sepúlveda doubted that they would ever become capable of governing themselves in a European sense.

The circulation of *Democrates Alter* in manuscript produced a storm of protest, especially from the Dominions. Las Casas and Melchor Cano both wrote violent refutations. Permission to publish the book was withheld, and discussion of the questions which it raised ran on until 1550, when they were submitted by order of the Emperor to formal debate, in which Sepúlveda and Las Casas argued face to face before a panel of eminent jurists convened at Valladolid. The proceedings were protracted and inconclusive. The judges never produced a final report; but Sepúlveda, by implication, lost the argument, since he never received permission to publish. *Democrates Alter* was not printed until more than two hundred years later.

Sepúlveda and Las Casas, whatever the original springs of their thought, represented the two divergent yet complementary tendencies of the imperialist theory of their time. Both sought to modify royal policy and to limit the exercise of the royal will. The thought of both was firmly rooted in the Middle Ages. Sepúlveda wished to interpose permanently between the Crown and the Indians a benevolent aristocracy, who might exercise at first hand a paternal authority which the Crown could not conveniently exercise at a distance, and who would be entitled to use Indian labour in reward for their services. The feudal implications of this proposal in themselves made it unacceptable to a royal government always suspicious of aristocratic pretensions; but further, to proclaim Indians slaves by nature was to disown much carefully drafted legislation, royal and papal, and to eat fifty years of royal professions. Las Casas wished to impose upon the Crown, in dealing with conquered Indians, the same limitation which, in his opinion, the law of God and the laws of the land placed upon it in governing Spain; and further, to prohibit the used of armed force against Indian peoples in future. But a government which operated in the Indies as an irresponsible, though conscientious, absolutism could hardly be expected to accept a theory which limited its sovereignty and might even cast doubt upon its right to rule. To insist with Las Casas that Indians should be won over by persuasion only was to abandon all future conquests and admit the injustice of past ones. The full implications of either theory were more than any self-respecting government of the time could stomach.

In practice, the attitude of the Crown was governed chiefly by its determination to guard its possessions and assert its authority; by its need to raise revenue; and by its anxiety to avoid in future tumults such as those which had followed the promulgation of the New Laws in 1543. This is not to say that the debate at Valladolid was, for the Crown, a mere academic exercise. Charles V took it seriously, and forbade all further expeditions of conquest until the question of just war should be settled. It never was settled; but in the third quarter of the sixteenth century, the interest of the Crown coincided in many ways with the views which Las Casas had put forward. The empire needed a period of consolidation and peace, in which the newly-discovered mineral wealth of the Indies could be exploited and their administration improved. In order to put a brake on the restless mobility of the old conquerors and settlers, to prevent them from keeping the frontiers in a constant uproar, and in order to avoid further brutalities such as those of the early conquests which had recently received such unwelcome publicity, it was necessary to limit new *entradas* and to keep them under strict royal control. To this end, the *Ordenanzas sobre Descubrimientos* of 1573 were promulgated. Juan de Ovando, the President of the Council of the Indies at the time—an outstandingly able and conscientious official—was an admirer of Las Casas, and by his orders Las Casas' manuscripts were brought from their monastic repository at Valladolid and utilized by the Council in the drafting of the new code.[14] The *Ordenanzas* did not, it is true, entirely prohibit the use of force against the recalcitrant; nor did the suppression of the word 'conquest' and the substitution of the word 'pacification' necessarily ensure the use of peaceful methods. Nevertheless, the new regulations emphasized, in words which Las Casas himself might have used, the royal preference for persuasion and agreement in extending the bounds of its authority, and the importance of effective—because willing—conversion. They laid down stringent conditions for the grant of licences for new expeditions, and forbade with severe penalties the old type of freelance, unauthorized *entrada*. To this extent, at least, the Spanish Crown disowned the ruthless methods by which the greater part of its possessions in the Indies had been acquired.

In the more immediate problems of native administration in provinces already subject to Spain, also, the legislation of Philip II enacted many of the ideas to which Las Casas and his friends had given currency. Short of sacrificing authority or revenue, the King was genuinely anxious to discharge his conscience towards his Indian subjects, both by supporting the evangelizing and civilizing mission among them, and by protecting their material welfare. The Crown insisted, as strongly as any sixteenth-century government could insist, that in any acquisition or conquest, personal liberty and private property, whether of individuals or of corporations, existing at the time of the acquisition, were to be respected. This is today—or was until recently—an accepted principle of civilized conduct; but it was new and strange to an age in which personal lordship and plunder were still traditionally accepted aims of conquest. No doubt the enforcement of the royal wishes was often perfunctory or ineffective; but the Crown made generous provision of courts in which Indian grievances could be heard, employed and paid advocates to defend Indian causes, and instructed judges to enforce native customs and laws where these were not plainly barbarous or repugnant to the Laws of the Indies. The greatest viceroys, such as Francisco de Toledo and Luis de Velasco I, adhered faithfully, on the whole, to the principles laid down by the Crown, and some of them, Toledo especially, showed an interest, unusual in a colonial governor, in the political theories involved. Outside Spain and Spanish America, the colonizing peoples and governments were less articulate on the subject of native rights, but among them too, some of the best colonial administrators, from Governor Bradford in New England to Johan Maurits in Brazil, upheld similar principles. One of the more respectable characteristics of European imperialism has been a deep sense of responsibility—widely acknowledged though not, certainly, consistently discharged—towards subject peoples of alien race. This responsibility has been more than the mere politic clemency of cunning rulers; it has been felt as a moral duty, enjoined by religion and humanity, and often embodied in law. It has sometimes even been carried to a logical conclusion, in the promotion of civilized and prosperous independence. It grew, in large measure, from the thought of theologians and jurists in sixteenth-century Spain.

One of the most curious features of the discussion of native rights was the contrast between concern over the fate of the Amerindian and callous indifference to the trade in negro slaves. Las Casas is sometimes accused of having suggested the substitution of African slaves for the dwindling Tainos in Hispaniola. There is no evidence for the accusation; but it is true that few of the Spaniards who insisted on the personal freedom of the Indians had anything to say about negro slavery. There was, of course, a legal distinction. The Indians were the subjects of the King of Castile and were entitled to his protection. Africans were the subjects of independent kings. Europeans visited West Africa as traders, not as overlords. The enslavement of prisoners of war was a normal proceeding in many parts of the world; in fighting off the Barbary coast, for example, prisoners were regularly enslaved on both sides, and set to row in the galleys. If West African rulers made war among themselves and sold their prisoners to slave dealers, that was not the fault of the King of Spain. Some theorists suggested that slavers ought to satisfy themselves that the war in which their purchases had been captured was a just war; while gravely admitting that such an investigation would be difficult in practice. Others pointed out that negroes were stronger than Amerindians and better able to endure hard work; or that enslavement was a means of taking pagans away from pagan rulers, placing them under Christian masters, and giving them a chance of salvation; or again, that some negroes were Muslims, and so fair game. The incidental suffering made little impression upon people accustomed to sudden death by violence or disease. The trade was carried on under Crown licence, and there was little serious opposition either from missionaries or from government.

Nevertheless, there were always some consciences unsatisfied by legal or anthropological casuistry. Las Casas in his later years condemned *all* slavery. Mention has already been made[15] of the Dominican Tomás de Mercado and the Jesuit Alonso de Sandoval. Sandoval pointed out that slave-owners in practice made no provision for evangelizing among their slaves and often treated them with calculated brutality; and that tribal war in West Africa was often the result, not the cause, of the trade in slaves. Sandoval's book is one of the most uncompromising denunciations of slavery ever written. Official doubts of the lawfulness of slavery were expressed from time to time throughout the seventeenth century. The Heeren XIX—the directors—of the Dutch West India Company on several occasions consulted theological opinion on the subject, and were reassured that slavery had Biblical sanction. The Portuguese Overseas Council reported regretfully in 1673 that the Angola slave trade 'up to now has not been freed from scruples of a Christian conscience'.[16] Yet no protest against negro slavery in the Age of Reconnaissance produced any practical effect. The trade was immensely profitable; it was indispensable to the working of sugar plantations in Brazil and the West

Indies; it was carried on in remote places; its horrors were seen by relatively few Europeans, received little publicity, and so were little known; it removed some of the burden of labour from American Indians, for whom European Crowns were admittedly responsible, and shifted it to alien Africans for whom they felt no responsibility; and being a matter of commerce rather than of political and territorial government, it raised less pressing problems of international law.

International law, the problems of just war and just title to territory, lay at the heart of all these controversies. By the early seventeenth century, the need for a fresh approach to these problems was apparent to jurists everywhere in Europe. In the sixteenth century, discussion of title to territory in the Indies had been centred first upon the question of just war against primitive or heathen peoples, and then upon the rules which ought to govern the relations between conquerors and conquered. Much thought had been given to defining the authority of the Spanish Crown in the Indies, weighed against the rights of the aboriginal inhabitants. The associated problem of the rights of the Spanish Crown, weighed against the claims of rival conquerors, had received no comparable attention. It had not been an urgent problem. There were, in effect, no rival conquerors except Portugal; and the colonial questions at issue between Spain and Portugal were settled, without great difficulty, by treaties in 1494 and 1529 and by the union of the Crowns in 1580. Apart from areas voluntarily surrendered by treaties, the Spanish Crown claimed the whole of the New World, occupied or unoccupied, as its own. To this position it clung with great tenacity. In all official dealings it based its exclusive claim upon the bulls of 1493. As we have seen, however, many Spaniards and most foreigners considered the bulls, in so far as they purported to confer temporal sovereignty, to be invalid. Vitoria and other Spaniards, accordingly, had worked out more sophisticated theories, which in one way or another derived an indirect grant of temporal power from the papal commission to evangelize the heathen. By qualifying the papal grant in this way, however, the theorists denied the Crown any exclusive claim to empty, or nearly empty, places in the Americas; to lands, that is, which had no considerable heathen population to be converted and were not actually occupied by Spaniards. Catholic rulers, without necessarily implying disrespect to the Pope or hostility to Spain, certainly considered themselves at liberty to annex such areas, and in Vitoria's reasoning there was nothing to prevent them from doing so. Some Catholics outside Spain went further, and questioned the Pope's right to prohibit Catholic missions anywhere. Protestants, of course, rejected all papal authority, spiritual as well as temporal.

The juridical claim of Spain to a monopoly of settlement and trade in the Americas, therefore, was doubted by some Spaniards, and outside Spain was widely challenged. In the late sixteenth and early seventeenth centuries the growing strength of other maritime powers began to make this challenge effective. The Spanish retort was a bald 'what I have I hold', supported by force. Hence the search, among the jurists of the maritime nations, for principles of international conduct in overseas trade and settlement which, without proclaiming mere anarchy, would repudiate the claim of Pope or Emperor to a supra-national sovereignty, and would allow scope for the aspirations of their countrymen. For the English, the classic exposition (out of many which were put forth) came in a protest that the English were excluded from the West Indies *contra jus gentium*. The use of the air and of the sea was claimed as common to all mankind, and the Spaniards were told that 'Prescription without possession availeth nothing', that their claims would only be accepted where they were re-enforced by effective occupation. The French, in similar terms, protested that 'In lands which the King of Spain did not possess they ought not to be disturbed, nor in their navigation of the seas, nor would they consent to be deprived of sea or the sky.' The juridical position of these maritime powers was summed up, in terms as measured and as humane as those of Vitoria, by Vitoria's great successor, the Dutch jurist Grotius, who wrote not only in general terms on the just grounds for making war and the accepted rules of civilized people in conducting it, but also specifically on the right of unrestricted passage anywhere upon the high seas.[17] Step by step throughout the seventeenth century Spain was obliged by military reverses to recede from its claims of general dominion. A series of treaties, at Antwerp in 1609, at Münster in 1648, at Madrid in 1670, at Ryswyck in 1697, admitted the right of other nations to trade and settle in unoccupied parts of the Americas, or recognized specific acquisitions there. The division of unoccupied parts of the world, and of many parts occupied by weak or primitive peoples, between a group of competing and often warring European States, was recognized in Europe not only as a political and economic fact, but as an accepted juridical system.

CONCLUSION

By the middle of the seventeenth century the main geographical impetus of the Reconnaissance was spent; the first tentative charting of the size, shape and disposition of the continents had been in large measure completed. There were still, it is true, large gaps in European knowledge, even of coastlines. The Pacific coast of North America, north of Lower California, was almost unknown, and the longitudinal extent of the continent was the subject of wild and widely differing guesses. The Pacific coast of Asia was little better known, though a few Chinese and Japanese ports had been visited by European ships and there were flourishing European settlements in the Philippines. Of the thousands of islands scattered in the vast expanse of the Pacific, few had been sighted; and for all men knew, there might be whole continents there, still undiscovered. One such continent, indeed, was known to exist; the west coast of Australia had been sketched in rough outline by Dutch navigators who had learned to fear its dangers. It clearly belonged to a great land mass, whose dimensions were unknown, but which was generally supposed to include New Guinea. *Terra Australis Incognita*, the old southern continent of Ptolemy, also lingered in men's minds. The west coast of New Zealand, which Tasman had sighted, might be part of it; and Tasman himself—not a very careful explorer—had assumed Cook Strait to be a mere inlet. No man had seen the coast of the real Antarctic continent.

The main coastlines of the rest of the world—the Atlantic coasts of the Americas and the Pacific coast of South America; the whole outline of Africa; the southern coasts of Asia, and the Asian archipelagos; all these were known in varying degrees of detail to European navigators, and through maps to the reading public. Here and there European knowledge went behind the coastlines. Spaniards had explored by land most of Mexico and Central America, considerable areas of South America, and, very sketchily, parts of what are now the United States. In eastern North America, French explorers had travelled great distances in canoes, and acquired some knowledge of the great labyrinth of lakes and rivers used by Indian traders. In the Old World, on the other hand, there had been little inland penetration, and the interior of Asia was hardly better known to Europe in the seventeenth century than it had been in the thirteenth. A few Europeans had travelled inland in mainland Asia as ambassadors or adventurers, but they had stuck for the most part to the ancient roads regularly used by pilgrims, merchants and officials. Interior Africa, still more, was unknown save for a few visits to Egypt and Abyssinia. In general, the world outside Europe, as known to Europeans, was a world of coastlines, roughly charted, of scattered harbours connected by a network of seaborne communication.

Seaborne skill and strength had enabled Europeans to exploit their geographical knowledge and to settle here and there in all the known continents except Australia. The nature of their settlements varied greatly, but all alike depended upon metropolitan countries in Europe. None was fully self-supporting; none yet aspired to independence of the founding State, though some colonies had changed hands as the result of European wars and many more were to change hands later in the century. The hold of the European nations upon many of their outposts was still weak. Only a few relatively small areas could be said to be Europeanized, and the most potent factor in determining the nature of a European colony was the character of the native race among whom it was planted.

In some places Europeans had settled as a permanent resident aristocracy among more primitive, but settled peoples, living by their labour and to a limited extent intermarrying with them. This was the situation in Spanish and Portuguese America; though the areas under effective European government still covered only a small part of the immense areas claimed by Portugal and Spain, and no province was without its Indian frontier. In the West Indies also, Europeans formed a resident aristocracy, though the primitive labour force there was not native but imported.

In other regions, where the native population was too sparse or too intractable to furnish an adequate labour force, and where settlers did not want, or could not afford to buy, imported slaves, Europeans had cleared land and formed purely European communities, living largely by their own labour as farmers, fishermen or traders. A thin fringe of settlements of this type stretched along the Atlantic seaboard of North America; settlements with small harbour towns looking towards Europe, with a dangerous forest frontier not far inland. English and French America lagged far behind Spanish America in population, wealth and cultural attainments, but was growing rapidly in assertiveness and strength.

In the Old World, Europeans had concentrated their efforts upon regions known to produce articles of value, and seaborne commerce rather than empire had been their principal object. In West Africa, source of gold, ivory and slaves, the climate and the forest, no less than the hostility of the inhabitants, had deterred them from settling. In the East they had encountered numerous and civilized peoples, organized and well-armed States. Here there could be no question of invading, of settling as a resident aristocracy. They came as armed traders, sometimes as pirates, constantly quarrelling among themselves as pirates commonly do. Their impact upon the great empires of Asia had been very slight. The government of China, with its highly organized, deeply cultivated official hierarchy, barely condescended to notice the uncouth foreign hucksters in the Canton river. In the territories subject to the Mughal Empire, various European groups had secured footholds, as merchants residing on sufferance, as vassals, as allies and somewhat unreliable mercenaries, in a few places as minor territorial rulers, nowhere as overlords. With Persia they had little direct contact, save through the Dutch factory at Bandar Abbas. The Ottoman Empire, with conquests thrust far into eastern Europe, was obliged to pay serious attention to Europeans, for it faced them continuously on two fronts. In the Mediterranean and the Balkans they were traders and profitable customers in peace, military enemies in war. In the Indian Ocean, the Red Sea and the Persian Gulf, they were well-established armed interlopers, intercepting and diverting a great part of the commerce which had formerly been in Arab hands. As yet, however, the Turk was little influenced and not seriously threatened by European power. Among the smaller principalities on the southern fringe of Asia, European invaders had asserted themselves more effectively; but even here, except for a few small areas in south India and in the East Indian islands, actual European possessions were still confined to forts and trading factories.

Nevertheless, considering the relatively small size and loose organization of most European States, the achievements of two centuries of reconnaissance were remarkable. The objects with which the early discoverers set out had been in great measure achieved. The Turk had been taken in the rear, and his power, though great, no longer seemed overwhelming. Europe was connected by regular sea passages with the sources of most of the goods which Europeans most desired, and many of these goods were being shipped from European factories abroad, in European ships. The colonies which Europeans had established in places suited for European habitation seemed likely to endure and to develop. Moreover, wherever conquerors, planters or merchants had settled, churches had been founded, and there were Christian communities in every inhabited continent.

The success of the Reconnaissance, by its very magnitude, produced

323

in the later seventeenth century a dulling of geographical curiosity. Men no longer expected to find Atlantis. Few still seriously hoped to penetrate by a northern route to Cathay. Though many thousands of miles of coast remained uncharted, and whole continents still awaited the explorer, these little-known places appeared to offer little prospect of immediate gain. The business corporations which, in the seventeenth century, controlled most long-distance voyaging, would not dissipate their shareholders' capital in the profitless pursuit of knowledge. There is a striking contrast between the intense, expectant curiosity of a Magellan, a Sebastian Cabot, a Henry Hudson, and the perfunctory attention which Dutch navigators, a little later, gave to the coasts of Australia and New Zealand. The exploring freelance buccaneer—such as Dampier, for example—was an increasingly rare exception. On the whole, the seventeenth century, by contrast with the sixteenth, was an age of consolidation overseas, of trading and planting exploitation, rather than of original exploration.

Seventeenth-century concentration on distant trade and planting was accompanied by a fierce competitive pugnacity, to be expected in a mercantilist age which regarded foreign trade as another form of war. In their incessant fighting over trade and territory, most European governments, lacking adequate naval force, made free use of buccaneers and pirates. In both East and West Indies, any gang of cut-throats whose predatory activities could be made to serve an immediate national advantage, could secure letters of marque and could be sure of the support and countenance of one or another colonial governor. The result was the creation of great areas of savage, unorganized conflict, through which only the very well-armed or the very inconspicuous could move with any confidence. The indiscriminate employment of buccaneers, it is true, was a temporary phase. These ruffians soon became so serious a nuisance to peaceful traders among their own countrymen that even French and English colonial governors were in time induced to co-operate with naval forces in their suppression; though naval officers themselves were not above occasional piracy. In the later seventeenth century a series of treaties between colonial powers formally repudiated the old convention of 'no peace beyond the Line', and the practice of egging on pirates to attack other nations' harbours and shipping ceased to be regarded as a respectable expedient of international conduct, even in the West Indies. The gradual suppression of buccaneering, however, did not mean an end of fighting in the Tropics. It merely confined major hostilities to periods of formal war; and wars were frequent. Throughout the last decades of the seventeenth century and the whole of the eighteenth, tropical possessions were among the principal bones of contention in every major war, and among the principal prizes in every major treaty. It was a sign of the growing importance of tropical colonies and trade in the estimation of the western world, that the age of the buccaneers should be followed by the age of the admirals.

Seventeenth-century expansion overseas, increasingly concentrated upon commercial ends, savagely competitive, became also increasingly independent of religious motives. In the colonies of the Catholic powers in the sixteenth century the period of crusading war and plunder had been succeeded by a period of deep and thoughtful missionary fervour. In Spanish America especially, the Church had striven not only to convert but to teach the Indians, and to recruit and train an educated native priesthood. By the end of the sixteenth century the attitude of Spanish missionaries, and still more the attitude of the secular clergy, towards the Christian Indian had become less optimistic. The ideal of a native priesthood was in large measure abandoned, partly through conviction of its hopelessness, partly through social opposition from secular sources. The principle upon which Las Casas had insisted, that the Indian was potentially the spiritual and intellectual equal of the European, was less emphatically urged in the seventeenth century, both by theologians and by those who professed to know the Indian. The work of spreading the Faith went on, it is true, in hundreds of Franciscan and Jesuit missions, penetrating into remote regions of the Americas far beyond the limits of ordinary white settlement. In French America, Jesuit explorer-missionaries performed miracles of endurance and devotion, though often to little apparent effect. In the Portuguese East, also, the work of Jesuit missionaries went on steadily, though often discredited by the piracies which their countrymen committed. In Europe, the establishment in 1622 of the Propaganda—the Congregation for the propagation of the Faith—evinced the direct concern of the Papacy in colonial missions, in the training of missionaries, and once again in the creation of native priesthoods.

In the later seventeenth century, despite the efforts of the Propaganda, missionary enterprise began perceptibly to slacken. The growing weakness of Spanish and Portuguese colonial government and French preoccupation with European affairs together caused a loss of effective support. The general intellectual temper of Europe, also, grew less favourable to missions. The seventeenth century was a time of profound religious conflict, often expressed in war and persecution. It was also a time of deep and original religious thought; for the Church had to face not only the challenge of schism and dissent, not only the challenge of growing national absolutism, but also the intellectual challenge presented by mathematics and physical science. This last challenge was, as yet, only latent; but the intellectual and spiritual energies of

European Christendom were more and more directed to its own internal problems, less and less to the problem of how best to spread a simple, agreed version of the Faith among supposedly simple pagan peoples. Moreover, the main initiative in expansion was passing from the Catholic to the Protestant nations of Europe; and though many Dutchmen and Englishmen carried abroad religious convictions of an uncompromising kind, they showed considerably less skill and enthusiasm than their Catholic rivals in missionary enterprise. They showed, also, on the whole, correspondingly less care for the material well-being of peoples who came under their influence. It was not to be expected, in particular, that commercial concerns should spend much money or thought upon missionary work or upon the work of general welfare which commonly accompanies evangelization.

'Impiger extremos curris mercator ad Indos,
   per mare pauperiem fugiens, per saxa, per ignes.'

Horace's famous lines roused ready echoes among the men of the Reconnaissance; but, apart from economic enterprise, there were two characteristics of the Reconnaissance which commanded respect and which, together with high courage, gave a certain nobility to the whole movement, despite the plunder and the savagery. One was intellectual curiosity, disinterested zeal for the increase of knowledge; the other a sense of responsibility, of obligation, towards men of other races. Both were in eclipse, in the field of oversea exploration, in the later seventeenth century. Both were to revive in different and more effective forms later.

The prodigious advances made by Galileo and Newton in astronomy, in optics and in mechanics, and the increasing skill of craftsmen in applying scientific knowledge, were to place in the hands of navigators and explorers instruments of a range and accuracy formerly undreamed of, and so to lay the foundations of a new age of discovery. When geographical curiosity reasserted itself, as it did in the mid-eighteenth century, in the hands of Cook and his successors and the scientists associated with them, it took the form, not of a search for particular places of interest or value, but of a systematic and precise charting of the earth's surface in the interests of science. Eighteenth-century exploration, moreover, was backed not merely by individuals or trading companies, but by the power and resources of governments.

Science and technology not only sharpened the perceptions and improved the techniques of explorers; they also conferred upon European peoples ever-increasing military and naval advantages over the rest of the world. These reinforced the truculent and cynical greed with which European States in the eighteenth century often embarked on wars of colonial aggression. But just as the brutalities of the Spanish conquest in America had produced anxious searchings of conscience and movements for reform among Spanish theologians and officials, so in the late eighteenth and early nineteenth centuries the destructiveness of European imperialism was met by the revival of a feeling of responsibility. Chief among the symptoms of this revival were the growth of the great Protestant missionary societies, with their emphasis upon educational and medical work as well as upon evangelization; the profound revulsion against slavery and the trade in slaves; the repeated emphasis laid upon the creation—in India, for example—of an accessible and uncorrupt judiciary. Later still, this feeling of responsibility has shown itself in the development of the idea of trusteeship, and in deliberate attempts to build up, among subject peoples, workable modern systems of government and welfare. Inevitably the development of western education among dependent peoples has proved, from the imperial point of view, to be a Trojan horse; but it has rarely been discouraged for that reason. In recent years an enlightened realism about the political aspirations of such peoples has led to many more or less voluntary withdrawals of imperial control and the establishment, on friendly terms, of independent states. None of the ideas which prompted these acts were entirely new. All were suggested, in one form or another, in the days of Las Casas and Vitoria. The sense of responsibility which lay behind them, though intermittent and imperfect, was an essential characteristic of the Reconnaissance, and must have its place in the story along with the curiosity, the ingenuity, the vanity, the courage and the greed.

THE EAST INDIES

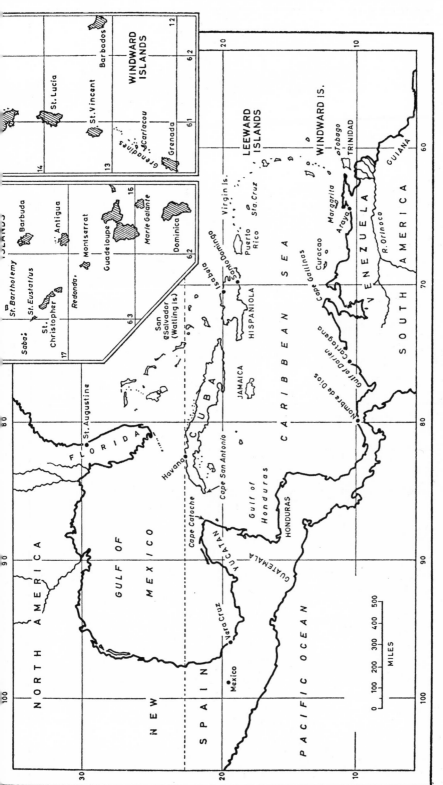

THE CARIBBEAN SEA

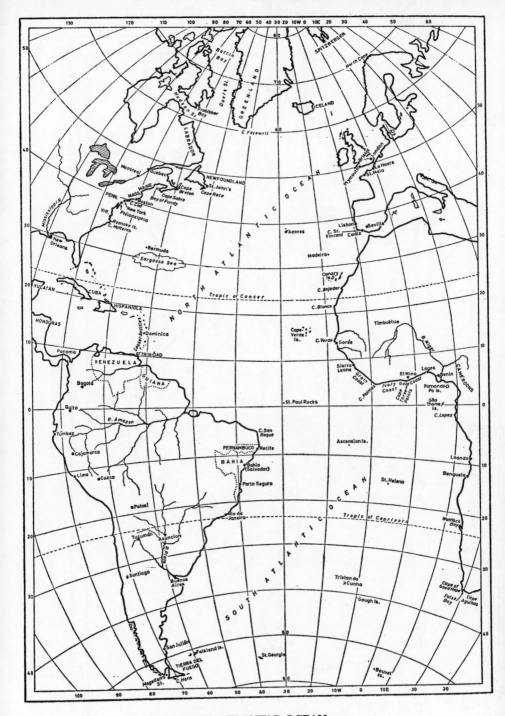

THE ATLANTIC OCEAN

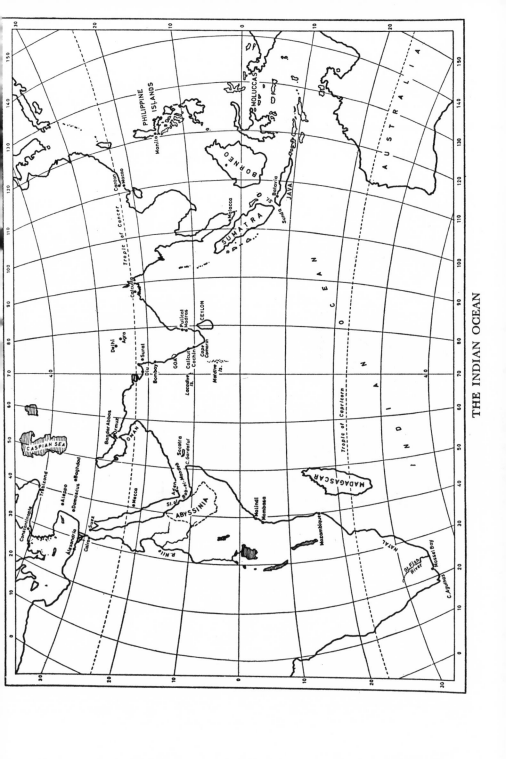

THE INDIAN OCEAN

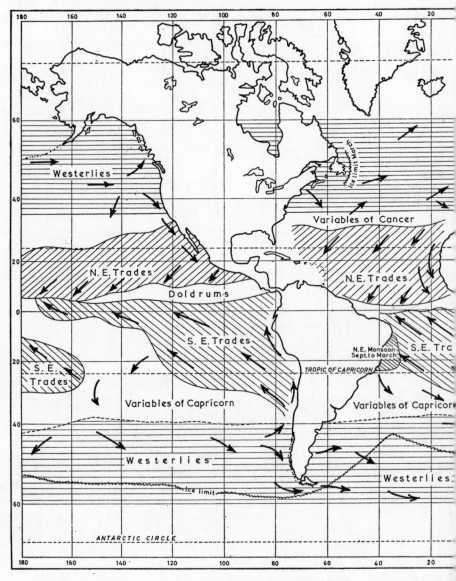

WIND CHA[RT]

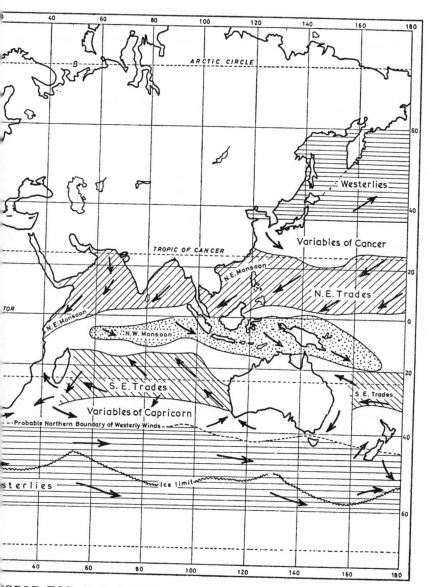

ORLD FOR THE FIRST QUARTER OF THE YEAR

NOTES

1. Gwyn Jones, *The Norse Atlantic Saga*, Oxford, 1964.
   T. J. Oleson, *Early voyages and northern approaches, 1000–1632*, Toronto, 1964.
2. R. A. Skelton, T. E. Marston and G. D. Painter, *The Vinland Map and the Tartar Relation*, New Haven, 1965.
   The original map is in the Yale University Library.
3. A. E. Nordenskiöld, *Periplus* (Stockholm, 1897), pp. 58–9 and plates XI–XIV.
   The original map is in the Bibliothèque Nationale in Paris.
4. E. W. Bovill, *The golden trade of the Moors* (Oxford, 1958), p. 91.
5. A. van den Wyngaert, ed., *Sinica Franciscana*, vol. I, *Itinera et relationes Fratrum Minori Saeculi* 13 et 14, Quaracchi, 1929.
   C. Dawson, *The Mongol Missions*, London, 1955. (Contains an English translation of Carpini).
6. Skelton, Marston and Painter, *op. cit.*
7. William of Rubruck, W. W. Rockhill, ed. and trans., *The journey of William of Rubruck*, London, 1900.
8. C. R. Beazley, *The dawn of modern geography* (3 vols., Oxford, 1906), vol. III, pp. 187–309, and bibliographical appendix, p. 542.
9. Francesco Balducci Pegolotti, *Libro di divisamenti di paesi e misure di mercatantie*, published under the title *La practica della mercatura*, A. Evans, ed., Cambridge, Mass., 1936. The (unique) MS. is in the Riccardian Library in Florence. An English translation of the section relating to Asia is in H. Yule, rev. H. Cordier, *Cathay and the way thither* (3 vols., London, Hakluyt Society), vol. II.
10. Marco Polo, H. Yule, ed., rev. H. Cordier, *The book of Ser Marco Polo*, 2 vols., London, Hakluyt Society, 1903.
11. Odoric of Pordenone, H. Cordier, ed., *Les voyages en Asie du frère Odoric de Pordenone*, Paris, 1891.
12. Sir John Mandeville, M. Letts, ed., *Mandeville's Travels*, texts and translations, London, Hakluyt Society, 1953.
13. Beazley, *op. cit.*, III, p. 528.
14. Ailly, Pierre d', E. Buron, ed., *Imago Mundi*, 3 vols., Paris, 1930.
    E. G. R. Taylor, 'Imago Mundi', *Scottish Geographical Magazine*, p. 47 (March, 1931).
15. *The Book of Roger* was completed in 1154. Few MSS. survive; one, written in Cairo, is in the Bodleian. It was first printed in 1592, in Rome, in a much abridged form. The first complete edition was printed in Paris, in French translation, in 1836.
16. N. H. Stevens, *Ptolemy's Geography*, London, 1908. A descriptive list of editions now in the Newberry Library. This is the best bibliography of Ptolemy in English. The first English translation is E. L. Stevenson, ed., *The Geography of Claudius Ptolemy*, New York, 1932.

CHAPTER I: ATTITUDES AND MOTIVES

1. Bernal Díaz del Castillo (A. P. Maudsley, ed. and trans.), *The true history of the conquest of New Spain* (5 vols., London, Hakluyt Society, 1908).
2. For the efforts of the popes to rally the European monarchies against the Ottoman empire, see L. Pastor (F. I. Antrobus, ed.), *The history of the Popes from the close of the Middle Ages* (20 vols., St. Louis, 1902–1930), II 277, III 19, X 170, 179.
3. For a penetrating discussion of these attitudes, see R. Menéndez Pidal (W. Starkie, ed.), *The Spaniards in their history* (London, 1950), p. 210 ff.
4. For this aspect of Prince Henry's character, see P. E. Russell, 'Prince Henry the Navigator', *Diamante*, XI, London, 1960.
5. A stimulating, if somewhat exaggerated, account of the mixed character of Iberian culture is A. Castro, *España en su historia, Cristianos, moros y judíos*, Buenos Aires, 1948.
6. M. Bataillon, *Erasme et l'Espagne, recherches sur l'histoire spirituelle du XVIe siècle* (Paris, 1937), Chap. 1.
7. Bernal Díaz, op. cit., cap. XXXIV: 'It may be, as Gómara says, that the glorious apostles Saint James and Saint Peter came to our aid and that I, being a poor sinner, was not worthy to behold them . . . but there were in our company more than four hundred soldiers and Cortés and many other gentlemen, and it would have been talked about . . .'
8. Bernal Díaz, op. cit., cap. LIX.
9. Ibid., cap. CCXII.
10. J. Burckhardt, *The civilisation of the Renascence in Italy*, Part IV.
11. Ibid., p. 154.
12. Gonzalo Fernández de Oviedo y Valdés (J. A. de los Rios, ed.), *Historia general y natural de las Indias*, 4 vols., Madrid, 1851–1855.
13. Peter Martyr Anglieri (F. A. MacNutt, ed. and trans.), *De Orbe Novo*, 2 vols., New York, 1912.
14. Fracanzano da Montalboddo, *Paesi novamente retrovati* . . . Vicenza, 1507, and many other subsequent editions.
15. S. Münster, *Cosmographia universalis*, Basel, 1544.
16. T. de Bry, *Grands Voyages*, 13 parts, Frankfurt, 1590–1634.
17. Gómez Eannes de Azurara (R. Beazley and E. Prestage, ed. and trans.), *The discovery and conquest of Guinea*, 2 vols., London, Hakluyt Society, 1896–99.
18. Schmeller, 'Über Valentim Fernández Alemão und seine Sammlung von Nachrichten über die Entdeckungen und Besitzungen der Portugiesen in Afrika und Asien bis zum Jahre 1508', *Abhandl. der Phil.-Philolog. Classe der K. bayerischen Akademie der Wissenschaften*, IV (München, 1847), p. 19.
    (Diogo Gomes' account as written down in Latin by Martin Behaim about 1483.)
19. Alvise de C'A da Mosto (G. R. Crone, ed. and trans.), *The voyages of Cadamosto and other documents on Western Africa in the second half of the fifteenth century*, London, Hakluyt Society, 1937.
20. J. M. da Silva Marques, *Descobrimentos portugueses: documentos para a sua história* (Lisboa, 1944), I, pp. 360–3.

21. J. Huizinga (J. S. Holmes and H. van Marle, trans.), *Men and Ideas* (London, 1960), p. 243 ff.

CHAPTER 2: COMMERCIAL EXPERIENCE AND FINANCIAL BACKING

1. F. Braudel, *La Méditerranée et le monde méditerranéen à l'époque de Philippe II* (Paris, 1949), p. 347.
2. Francesco Balducci Pegolotti, ed. A. Evans, *La practica della mercatura*, Cambridge, Mass., 1936.
3. E. W. Bovill, *The golden trade of the Moors* (Oxford, 1958), p. 116.
4. A. Schaube, 'Die Anfänge der venezianischen Galeerenfahrten nach der Nordsee', *Hist. Zeitschr*, C1 (1908), 37, 48 ff., 80 f.
5. J. Heers, 'Types de navires et specialisation des trafics en Méditerranée à la fin du moyen-âge', *Le Navire et l'économie maritime du moyen-âge au XVIII siècle principalement en Méditerranée*, M. Mollat, ed., Paris, 1958.
6. F. Braudel, op. cit., p. 429.
7. W. Heyd, *Histoire du commerce du Levant au moyen-âge* (Leipzig, 1885-6), I, 493 ff. The *Casa* has been thoroughly studied by H. Sieveking, 'Studio sulle finanze genovesi nel medioevo e in particolare sulla Casa di San Giorgio', *Atti della Società Ligure di Storia Patria*, XXV (Genoa, 1905), 149.
8. H. M. A. Fitzler, 'Portugiesische Handelsgesellschaften des 15 und beginnenden 16 Jahrhunderts', *Vierteljahrschr. f. Soz.-u. Wirtsch–Gesch.* XXV (1932), 209–50.
9. Heyd, op. cit., II, 530 ff.
10. A. E. Sayous, 'Partnerships in the trade between Spain and America and also in the Spanish colonies in the 16th century', *Journal of Economic and Business History*, I (1929), 282–301.
11. G. Arciniegas, *Los alemanes en la conquista de América*, Buenos Aires, 1941.
12. R. Carande, *Carlos v y sus banqueros*, Madrid, 1943.

CHAPTER 3: SHIPS AND SHIPBUILDERS

1. There are conflicting views about this. See J. F. Guillén Tato, *La caravela Santa María*, Madrid, 1927; and S. E. Morison, *Admiral of the Ocean Sea*, 2 vols., Boston, 1942.
2. F. C. Lane, *Venetian ships and ship-builders of the Renaissance* (Baltimore, 1934), p. 9.
3. Op. cit., p. 15.
4. Marino Sanuto (eds., R. Fulin and others), *I Diarii* (Venice, 1879–1903), vol. VIII, p. 474.
5. R. Morton Nance, 'The Ship of the Renaissance', Part I, *The Mariner's Mirror*, vol. XLI, p. 180; Part II, p. 281.
6. B. Gomes de Brito, ed., *Historia Trágico—maritima. Em que se escreven chronologicamente os Naufragios que tiverão as Nãos de Portugal, depois que se poz em exercicio a Navegacão da India.* (2 vols., Lisbon, 1735-36), especially II, 226; II, 532–3.
   J. Duffy, *Shipwreck and Empire* (Cambridge, Mass., 1955), p. 60.

7. W. H. Moreland, 'The ships of the Arabian Sea about 1500', *Journal of the Royal Asiatic Society*, Jan. and April, 1939.
8. J. Hornell, *Water transport: origins and early evolution* (Cambridge, 1946), p. 235.
9. J. Poujade, *La route des Indes et ses navires* (Paris, 1946), Chap. 5.
   G. F. Hourani, *Arab seafaring in the Indian Ocean in ancient and early mediaeval times* (Princeton, 1951), p. 103.
10. Sir W. Abell, *The Shipwrights' Trade* (Cambridge, 1948), p. 20.
11. The best evidence on the design of late medieval cogs is to be found in the municipal seals of northern European ports, especially those of Southampton (1400) and Amsterdam (1418). Cf. Nance, op. cit., p. 186.
12. A. van Driel, *Tonnage measurement, a historical and critical essay*, The Hague, 1925.
13. Lane, op. cit., p. 246.
14. E. K. Thompson, 'English and Spanish Tonnage in 1588', *The Mariner's Mirror*, XLV (1959), 154.
15. See the tables of trans-Atlantic tonnage in H. and P. Chaunu, *Séville et l'Atlantique*, vols. 2 and 3 (Paris, 1955).
16. B. Hagedorn, *Die Entwicklung der wichtigsten Schiffstypen bis ins 19 Jahrhundert* (Berlin, 1914), p. 102.

CHAPTER 4: SEAMEN AND SEAMANSHIP

1. Alice B. Gould, 'Nueva lista documentada de los tripulantes de Colón en 1492', *Boletín de la Real Academia de la Historia* (Madrid), vols. 85–88, 90, 92, 110, 111.
2. *The Journal of Christopher Columbus*, translated by Cecil Jane, revised . . . by L. A. Vigneras, London, Hakluyt Society, 1960.
3. García Palacio, *Instrucción Náutica*, Mexico, 1587.
4. Hawkins was one. Another was Francisco de Mello de Castro, captain of the *Nossa Senhora do Bom Despacho* in 1629–30. *Historia Trágico-maritima*, I, 4.
5. F. T. Tinniswood, 'Anchors and Accessories, 1340–1640', *The Mariner's Mirror*, vol. XXXI.
6. W. E. May, 'History of the magnetic compass', *The Mariner's Mirror*, XXXVIII.
7. D. W. Waters, 'Bittacles and binnacles', *The Mariner's Mirror*, XLI.
8. D. W. Waters, *The Art of Navigation in England in Elizabethan and Early Stuart Times* (London, 1958), p. 19.

CHAPTER 5: PILOTAGE AND NAVIGATION

1. Martin Cortés, *Breve compendio de la sphera y de la arte de navegar*, Sevilla, 1551.
   R. Eden, trans., *The arte of navigation. Conteyning a compendious description of the sphere* . . . translated out of Spanyshe, London, 1561.

NOTES

2. Michiel Coignet, *Instruction nouvelle des poincts plus excellents nécessaires, touchant l'art de naviguer* ... Antwerp, 1581.
3. *Prologue* to the *Canterbury Tales*, 390 ff.
4. B. R. Motzo, ed., *Il Compasso da Navigare*, Cagliari, 1947.
5. J. Gairdner, ed., *Sailing directions for the circumnavigation of England*, London, Hakluyt Society, 1888.
6. The earliest printed *portolano* known was printed at Venice in 1490. The earliest known printed rutter from north-western Europe was *Le routier de la mer*, ascribed to Pierre Garcie and printed at Rouen between 1502 and 1510.
7. Waters, op. cit., p. 32 ff.
8. R. Hues, C. R. Markham, ed. and trans., *Tractatus de Globis et eorum usu* (London, 1594). London, Hakluyt Society, 1888.
9. G. R. Crone, ed. and trans., *The voyages of Cadamosto*, London, Hakluyt Society, 1937.
10. E. G. R. Taylor, ed., *Brief summe of geographie*, by Roger Barlow (London, Hakluyt Society, 1931), pp. xv and xvi, and Appendix II.
11. J. Bensaude, ed., *Histoire de la science nautique portugaise à l'époque des grands découvertes. Collection de documents publiés par ordre du Ministère de l'Instruction publique de la République portuguaise*, 1914–1919.
    Vol. I: *Regimento do Estrolabio e do quadrante: tractado da spera do mundo. Réproduction fac-similé du seul exemplaire comun appartenant à la Bibliothèque royale de Munich*. Munich, 1914.
12. Pedro Nunes, *Tratado em defensar da carta de marear* (1537).

CHAPTER 6: CHARTS AND MAPS

1. E. G. R. Taylor, ed., *A Regiment for the Sea* and other writings on navigation by William Bourne, London, Hakluyt Society, 1962.
2. Above, p. 83.
3. E. L. Stevenson, *Portolan Charts, their origins and characteristics*, New York, 1911.
4. G. R. Crone, *Maps and their makers* (London, 1953), p. 53. Bianco's chart is in the Biblioteca Ambrosiana in Milan; Pareto's in the Biblioteca Nazionale in Rome; Benincasa's in the British Museum. Parts of all three are reproduced, with notes, in R. A. Skelton's *Explorers' Maps*, London, 1958.
5. In the Staatsbibliothek in Munich. See Skelton, op. cit., pp. 35, 47. On the oblique meridian. See H. Winter in *Imago Mundi*, vol. 2, 1938, and E. G. R. Taylor, ibid., vol. 3, 1939.
6. A. Cortesão, ed., *The Book of Francisco Rodrigues*, 2 vols., London, Hakluyt Society, 1944.
7. The chart is in the British Museum. See A. Cortesão, *Cartografia e cartógrafos portugueses dos séculos, xv e xvi*. 2 vols., Lisbon, 1535.
8. Not the Juan de la Cosa of the first voyage, the owner of the *Santa María*. Morison, op. cit., p. 144.
9. The de la Cosa chart is in the Museo Naval in Madrid; the Cantino in the Biblioteca Estense in Modena.
10. The Ribeiro chart, and most of the other charts mentioned, are reproduced in A. E. Nordenskiöld, *Periplus. An essay on the early history of*

charts and sailing directions, Stockholm, 1897. The development of Spanish and Portuguese cartography, respectively, is further illustrated by two splendid *fac-similé* collections:
Mapas españoles de América, siglos XV–XVII, publication sponsored by the Duke of Alba, Madrid, 1951.
Portugaliae monumenta cartographica, eds. A Cortesão and A. Teixeira De Mota, 5 vols., Lisbon, 1960.

11. For example, Pedro de Medina, *Arte de Navegar*, Valladolid, 1545, a book which enjoyed a considerable vogue; but Martin Cortés, six years later, showed an acute understanding of variation, and even suggested that it was caused by 'terrestrial attraction'.

12. The unique copy is in the British Museum.

13. E. G. Ravenstein, *Martin Behaim; his life and his globe*, London, 1908.

14. Edward Wright, *Certaine errors in navigation*, London, 1599.

15. Robert Dudley, *Dell' Arcano del Mare*, Florence, 1646.

CHAPTER 7: THE FIGHTING CAPACITY OF MEN AND SHIPS

1. '100 parts pure copper, 10 parts good latten, and 8 parts clean tin', according to Lucar.
The principal source of information on sixteenth-century guns is the *Colloquies* of Nicholos Tartaglia, published in Italian in 1546 and translated, with additions, by Cyprian Lucar, London, 1588.

2. M. Lewis, *Armada Guns*, London, 1961.

3. *The Arte of shooting in Great Ordnance*, by William Bourne, London, 1587.

4. B. Gomes de Brito, ed., *Historia Trágico-marítima*, 2 vols., Lisbon, 1735–36. Four of the most interesting accounts are published in English translation: C. R. Boxer, ed., *The tragic history of the sea*, 1589–1622. London, Hakluyt Society, 1959.

5. R. S. Whiteway, ed., *The Portuguese expedition to Abyssinia in 1541–1543 as narrated by Castanhoso*, London, Hakluyt Society, 1902.

CHAPTER 8: AFRICA AND THE INDIAN OCEAN

1. Pulgar, *Chrónica de los Reyes católicos*, II, lxii.

2. J. L. de Azevedo, *Epocas de Portugal económico* (Lisbon, 1929), p. 73.

3. João de Barros, *Da Asia* (Lisbon, 1945), I, vi, 2.
For the Guinea trade in general, see J. W. Blake, *European beginnings in West Africa, 1554–1578*, London, 1937.

4. Conde de Ficalho, *Viagens de Pedro da Covilhã*, Lisbon, 1898.

5. E. G. Ravenstein, ed., *A Journal of the first voyage of Vasco da Gama*, London, Hakluyt Society, 1898.

6. W. B. Greenlee, ed., *The voyage of Pedro Alvares Cabral to Brazil and India*, London, Hakluyt Society, 1937.

7. For a good contemporary account of navigation in Indian waters, see the sailing directions in Duarte Pacheco Pereira (G. H. T. Kimble, ed.), *Esmeraldo de situ orbis*, London, Hakluyt Society, 1937.

8. A. Cortesão, ed., *The Suma Oriental of Tomé Pires*, 2 vols., London, Hakluyt Society, 1944.

9. W. de G. Birch, ed., *The commentaries of the great Afonso Dalboquerque* (by his son, Afonso Braz de Alboquerque), 4 vols., London, Hakluyt Society, 1875–83.

1. C. Markham, ed., *The Guanches of Tenerife* . . . by Friar Alonso de Espinosa, 1594, London, Hakluyt Society, 1907.
2. *The Journal of Christopher Columbus*, translated by Cecil Jane, revised and annotated by L. A. Vigneras, London, Hakluyt Society, 1960.
3. Texts of the bulls and the treaty are in F. G. Davenport, ed., *European Treaties bearing on the history of the United States* (4 vols., Washington, 1917–37), vol. I.
4. Peter Martyr, *De Orbe Novo* (F. A. McNutt, ed. and trans., New York, 1912), I, p. 83.
5. By the Spanish envoy Pedro de Ayala. See J. A. Williamson, *The Cabot voyages and Bristol discovery under Henry VII* (Cambridge, Hakluyt Society, 1962), pp. 23, 228.
6. D. B. Quinn, 'The argument for the English discovery of America between 1480 and 1492', *Geographical Journal*, cxxvii, pt. 3 (1961), p. 277.
7. Williamson, *op. cit.*, p. 95.
8. H. P. Biggar, *Voyages of the Cabots and of the Corte-Reals*, Paris, 1903.
9. For a concise summary of this literature, see B. Penrose, *Travel and discovery in the Renaissance* (Cambridge, Mass., 1955), Chap. 7.
10. F. J. Pohl, *Pilot Major*, New York, 1944. Mr. Pohl gives English translations of the letters from Seville, Lisbon and the Cape Verde Islands. These letters are printed in the original Italian, together with the *New World* and the *Four Navigations* in *facsimile*, all with Spanish and English translations, in R. Levillier, ed., *Americo Vespucci y el Nuevo Mundo*, Buenos Aires, 1951. Levillier considers the *New World* and the *Four Navigations* to be genuine and the other letters to be forgeries; an opinion not now widely held among scholars.
11. C. E. Nowell, ed., *Magellan's voyage around the world; three contemporary accounts by Antonio Pigafetta, Maximilian of Transylvania and Gaspar Correa*, Evanston (Ill.), 1962.

1. J. Bayard Morris, ed., *The letters of Hernando Cortés*, London, 1928.
2. See Part I, Chapter 1, above.
3. The conquest of Peru did not produce eye-witness accounts of a quality comparable with those of Cortés and Bernal Díaz. Of those which survive, the best are: Pedro Pizarro, *Relation of the discovery and conquest of the kingdoms of Peru*, ed. P. A. Means, 2 vols., New York, 1921; and a series of shorter accounts collected in C. R. Markham, *Reports on the discovery of Peru*, London, Hakluyt Society, 1872.
4. C. R. Markham, ed., *The war of Las Salinas* by Pedro de Cieza de León, London, Hakluyt Society, 1923.
5. C. R. Markham, ed., *The war of Quito*, by Pedro de Cieza de León,

London, Hakluyt Society, 1913; *The war of Chupas,* by Pedro de Cieza de León, London, Hakluyt Society, 1908.

CHAPTER 11: ATLANTIC TRADE AND PIRACY

1. H. and P. Chaunu, *Séville et l'Atlantique,* 8 vols., Paris, 1955–6, contains detailed statistics of the trade.
2. W. W. Borah, *Early colonial trade and navigation between Mexico and Peru,* Berkeley, 1954.
3. J. A. Williamson, *Hawkins of Plymouth,* London, 1949.
4. Contemporary accounts of English exploits in the Caribbean are in I. A. Wright, ed., *Spanish documents concerning English voyages to the Caribbean, 1527–68.* London, Hakluyt Society, 1929.
    Documents concerning English voyages to the Spanish Main, 1569–80. London, Hakluyt Society, 1932.
    Further documents concerning English voyages to the Spanish Main, 1580–1603. London, Hakluyt Society, 1951.
    K. R. Andrews, ed., *English privateering voyages to the West Indies, 1588–1595.* London, Hakluyt Society, 1959.
5. E. Sluiter, 'Dutch-Spanish rivalry in the Caribbean area, 1594–1609', *Hispanic American Historical Review,* vol. 28 (1948), 179.
6. C. R. Boxer, *The Dutch in Brazil 1624–1654.* Oxford, 1957.

CHAPTER 12: NEW ROUTES TO THE EAST

1. The best summaries of the evidence are in H. Quirino da Fonseca, *Os Portugueses no mar* (Lisbon, 1926), pp. 724–32, and M. de Faria e Sousa, *Asia portuguesa* (Oporto, 1945), III, pp. 525–60.
2. Sir Richard Temple, ed., *The Travels of Ludovico di Varthema,* London, 1929.
3. M. L. Dames, ed., *The Book of Duarte Barbosa,* 2 vols., London, Hakluyt Society, 1918–21.
4. Gian Battista Ramusio was the most celebrated figure in Italian geographical literature of the sixteenth century. He spent more than thirty years collecting narratives of voyages. The first volume of his *Delle navigazioni e viaggi* was published in Venice in 1550. It includes Leo's *Africa*; the accounts of Cadamosto, da Gama, Cabral and Vespucci, all taken from the *Paesi*; Varthema's travels; Alvares' account of Abyssinia; descriptions of India and adjacent lands by Tomé Lopes, Duarte Barbosa and Andrea Corsali; the journeys of Conti and Santo Stephano; and Pigafetta's journal of the Magellan voyage. The second volume, which appeared posthumously in 1559, contains a composite version of several texts of Marco Polo; Hayton of Armenia; the Venetian missions to Persia; Paolo Giovo's book on the Turks; and, in a second edition (1574), the journeys of Rubruquis and Odoric, Heberstein's travels in Russia, and the apocryphal voyages of the Zeni to Greenland. The third volume (Venice, 1556) is devoted to America, and includes Peter Martyr's first three Decades; the entire 1535 edition of Oviedo; Cortés' second, third and fourth Letters; Cabeza de Vaca's account of his wanderings; the expedition of Coronado; the voyages of Ulloa and

Alarcón along the Pacific coast; Xeres' account of the conquest of Peru; Orellana's voyage down the Amazon; and accounts of the exploits of Verrazano and Cartier. Ramusio, like Hakluyt, was a careful and discriminating editor and translator. His collection is the most important single source of our knowledge of the Reconnaissance.

5. A. C. Burnell and P. A. Tiele, eds., *The voyage of Jan Huyghen van Linschoten to the East Indies*, London, Hakluyt Society, 1885.
6. Sir William Foster, ed., *The voyages of Sir James Lancaster to Brazil and the East Indies, 1591–1603*. London, Hakluyt Society, 1940.
7. Records of many of the sixteenth- and seventeenth-century Dutch voyages to the East are published by the Linschoten Vereeniging, the Dutch equivalent of the Hakluyt Society. Almost all writing of any value on these voyages and on the foundation and history of the Dutch East India Company is in Dutch. For references and for a concise account, see B. H. M. Vlekke, *Nusantara* (Cambridge, Mass., 1945), p. 91 ff.
8. W. Vogel, 'Zur Grosse der Europaischen Handelsflotten im 15, 16, und 17 Jahrhundert', *Forschungen und Versuche zur Geschichte des Mittelalters und der Neuzeit* (Jena, 1915), p. 319.
9. J. E. Heeres, *The part borne by the Dutch in the Discovery of Australia, 1606–1765*. Leyden, 1899.
10. H. P. Biggar, ed., *The voyages of Jacques Cartier*, London, 1924.
11. Hakluyt, *Principal Navigations* (12 vols., Glasgow, 1903–5), vii, 158 ff.
12. G. V. Stefansson, ed., *The three voyages of Martin Frobisher in search of a passage to Cathay and India by the north-west, A.D. 1566–8*, 2 vols.
13. Sir Albert Markham, ed., *The voyages and works of John Davis the navigator*, London, Hakluyt Society, 1880.
14. G. M. Asher, ed., *Henry Hudson the Navigator*, London, Hakluyt Society, 1860.
    Sir Clements Markham, ed., *The voyages of William Baffin*, London, Hakluyt Society, 1881.
    Miller Christy, ed., *The voyages of Captain Luke Foxe, of Hull, and Captain Thomas James, of Bristol*, London, Hakluyt Society, 1893.
15. Hakluyt, *Principal Navigations*, vol. II.
16. Koolemans Beynen, ed., *The three voyages of William Barents to the Arctic Regions*, London, Hakluyt Society, 1876.

CHAPTER 13: FISHING, FUR-TRADING AND PLANTING

1. D. B. Quinn, ed., *The voyages and colonising enterprises of Sir Humphrey Gilbert*, 2 vols. London, Hakluyt Society, 1940.
2. D. B. Quinn, ed., *The Roanoke Voyages*, 2 vols., London, Hakluyt Society, 1955.
3. Bacon, 'Of plantations', *Essays* (1625).
4. Hakluyt, 'Discourse of western planting', in E. G. R. Taylor, *Original Writings and correspondence of the two Richard Hakluyts* (London, Hakluyt Society, 1935), II, 211.
5. 'The general history of Virginia, New England and the Summer Isles', E. Arber, ed., *Travels and Works of Captain John Smith* (2 vols., Edinburgh, 1910), I, 278.

6. William Vaughan, *The Golden Fleece*, London, 1626.
7. Peter Force, *Tracts* (New York, 1947), II, 128.
8. Sir R. H. Schomburgk, ed., Sir Walter Raleigh, *The discovery of the large, rich and beautiful empire of Guiana with a relation of the . . . city of Manoa . . . performed in the year 1595 . . .* London, Hakluyt Society, 1848.

CHAPTER 14: THE LAND EMPIRE OF SPAIN

1. L. B. Simpson, *Exploitation of land in central Mexico in the sixteenth century, Ibero-Americana* 36, Berkeley, Calif., 1952.
2. S. F. Cook and L. B. Simpson, *The population of central Mexico in the sixteenth century, Ibero-Americana* 31, Berkeley, Calif., 1948. For detailed revisions of these figures, see W. Borah and S. F. Cook, *The population of central Mexico in 1548, Ibero-Americana* 43, Berkeley, 1960, and S. F. Cook and W. Borah, *The population of central Mexico 1531–1610, Ibero-Americana* 44, Berkeley, 1960.
3. F. Chevalier, *La formation des grands domaines au Mexique*, Paris, 1952.
4. García Icazbalceta, *Bibliografía mexicana del siglo* XVI (Mexico, 1886), pp. 6, 10; *Don fray Juan de Zumárraga*, Mexico, 1881.
5. For a detailed study of evangelizing methods, see R. Ricard, *La conquête spirituelle du Mexique*, Paris, 1933.
6. M. Carrera Stampa, *Los gremios mejicanos*, Mexico, 1954.
7. Santo Domingo, 1526; Mexico, 1527; Panama, 1535; Lima, 1542; Guatemala, 1543; New Galicia, 1548; New Granada, 1549; Charcas, 1559; Quito, 1563; Manila, 1583; for a general discussion of these institutions see C. H. Haring, *The Spanish Empire in America* (New York, 1947), chap. VII.
8. *Colección de documentos inéditos . . . de América y Oceanía . . .* (Madrid, 1864–81), viii, 484.
9. E. J. Hamilton, *American treasure and the price rise in Spain, 1501–1650*, Cambridge, Mass., 1934.

CHAPTER 15: THE SEA EMPIRES OF PORTUGAL AND HOLLAND

1. B. H. M. Vlekke, *Nusantara, a history of the East Indian archipelago* (Cambridge, Mass., 1945), 78 ff.
2. R. S. Whiteway, *The rise of Portuguese power in India 1497–1550*, London, 1899.
3. G. C. Klerk de Reus, *Geschichtlicher Ueberblick der administrativen, rechtlichen und finanziellen Entwicklung der Niederlandischen Ost-Indischen Compagnie*, Batavia, 1894.
   For references to works in Dutch on the organization and history of the Company, see Vlekke, op. cit., p. 103.
4. For the early history of the Company in India, see Sir W. W. Hunter, *History of British India 1500–1700*, 2 vols., London, 1899–1900.

CHAPTER 16: THE PLANTATIONS AND THEIR TRADES

1. F. Mauro, *Le Portugal et l'Atlantique au XVIIᵉ siècle, 1570–1670*, Paris, 1960.
2. C. R. Boxer, *The Dutch in Brazil 1624–1654*, Oxford, 1957.
3. C. R. Boxer, *Salvador de Sá and the struggle for Brazil and Angola, 1602–1686* (London, 1652), p. 252 ff.
4. The best contemporary account of this process is R. Ligon, *A true and exact history of the island of Barbados*, London, 1657.
5. K. G. Davies, *The Royal African Company*, London, 1957.
6. G. L. Beer, *The old colonial system* (New York, 1933), I, 13 ff.

CHAPTER 17: MIGRATIONS AND DISPERSALS

1. It is difficult even to guess the rate of growth of the European population of Spanish America. Emigrants to America were required to be licensed by the *Casa de la Contratación*. The surviving records suggest an annual migration in the sixteenth century ranging between 500 and 1,500; but for many years no records survive, and illicit emigrants were, of course, not recorded. C. Bermúdez Plata, ed., *Catálogo de pasajeros a Indias*, 3 vols. Sevilla, 1940.
2. S. F. Cook and W. Borah, *The Indian population of central Mexico, 1531–1610*, Berkeley, 1960.
3. W. R. Rossiter, ed., *A century of population growth*, Washington, 1909.
4. For a general account of these developments, and a select bibliography, see J. H. Parry and P. M. Sherlock, *A short history of the West Indies*, London, 1960.
5. Fernando de Alva Ixtlilxóchitl, A. Chavero, ed., *Obras históricas*, 2 vols., Mexico, 1912–13.
6. Garcilaso Inca de la Vega, C. R. Markham, ed., *The royal commentaries of the Incas*, 2 vols., London, 1869.
7. Almost all of Las Casas' voluminous writings contain anthropological material, but most of it is in the *History* and the *Apologetic History*.
   Bartolomé de las Casas, M. Serrano y Sanz, ed., *Apologética historia de las Indias*, Madrid, 1909.
   Bartolomé de las Casas, G. de Reparaz, ed., *Historia de las Indias*, 3 vols., Madrid, 1929.
8. Toribio de Benavente o Motolinía, D. Sánchez García, ed., *Historia de los indios de la Nueva España*, Barcelona, 1914.
9. A. M. Tozzer, ed., *Landa's Relación de las cosas de Yucatán*, Papers of the Peabody Museum of American Archaeology and Ethnology, vol. 18, Cambridge, Mass., 1941.
10. P. Sarmiento de Gamboa, *Historia de las Incas*, Buenos Aires, 1942.
11. Fray Bernardino de Sahagún, W. Jiménez Moreno, ed., *Historia general de las cosas de Nueva España*, 5 vols., Mexico, 1938.
12. For a modern appreciation of Sahagún's work, see Luis Nicolau d'Olwer, *Fray Bernardino de Sahagún*, Mexico, 1952.
13. Caspar Barlaeus, *Rerum per octennium in Brasilia*, Amsterdam, 1647.
14. The text is in D. B. Quinn, *The Roanoake Voyages* (2 vols., London, Hakluyt Society, 1955), 314.

15. Theodor de Bry, *America*, pt. I, Frankfurt, 1590. Details of this and subsequent editions are listed in Quinn, op. cit., 922.
16. Edward Johnson, *Wonder-working Providence of Sion's Saviour in New England*, London, 1654, in J. F. Jameson, ed., *Original narratives of early American history* (New York, 1906), 41.
17. K. S. Latourette, *A History of the Expansion of Christianity* (5 vols., New York, 1939), III, 218.
18. See p. 218 above.
19. Tomás de Mercado, *Tratos y contratos de mercaderes y tratantes*, Salamanca, 1569.
20. Alonso de Sandoval, *Naturaleza, policia sagrada i profana, costumbres i ritos, disciplina i catechismo evangélico de todos Etiopes*, Seville, 1627.
21. José de Acosta, *Historia natural y moral de las Indias* (1590), Mexico, 1940.
22. J. H. Burkill, 'The rise and decline of the greater yam in the service of mankind', *The Advancement of Science*, vol. 7 (1951), 443.
23. Antonio Vázquez de Espinosa, *Compendio y descripción de las Indias* (1621), Washington, 1948.
24. R. N. Salaman, *The history and social influence of the potato*, Cambridge, 1949.
25. J. B. Hutchinson, R. A. Silow and S. G. Stephens, *The evolution of gossypium*, Oxford, 1947.
26. E. Schiemann, *Entstehung der Kulturpflanzen*, Berlin, 1932.
27. Sir Hans Sloane, *A voyage to the islands Madera, Barbados, Nieves, St. Christopher's and Jamaica, with the natural history of the herbs and trees, four-footed beasts, fishes, birds, insects, reptiles, etc., of the last of those islands*, 2 vols., London, 1707–25.

CHAPTER 18: THE COLONIAL BUREAUCRATS

1. J. H. Parry, *The sale of public office in the Spanish Indies under the Hapsburgs. Ibero-Americana* 37, Berkeley, 1953.
2. J. de Solórzano Pereira, *Política Indiana*, VI, xiii, 2, 3, 4.
3. A. de León-Pinelo, *Tratado de Confirmaciones* (Madrid, 1630), II, 118.
4. R. Mousnier, *La vénalité des offices sous Henri VI et Louis XIII*, Rouen, 1946.
5. J. H. Parry, 'The patent offices in the British West Indies', *English Historical Review*, April, 1954.

CHAPTER 19: THE RIGHTS OF CONQUERORS AND CONQUERED

1. J. H. Parry, *The Spanish theory of empire in the sixteenth century*, Cambridge, 1940.
2. L. Hanke, 'The Requerimiento and its interpreters', *Revista de Historia de América* (1938), I, 25.
3. Vitoria's three *Relectiones de Indis* are printed in English translation as an appendix to J. B. Scott, *The Spanish origin of international law*, Oxford, 1924.
4. In *De potestate ecclesiae*, relectio I.
5. *Institutes*, I, 2, i.
6. *De Indis*, III, 18.
7. Ibid, III, 12.

8. See Chapter 17, note 7.
9. *Colección de Tratados de Bartolomé de las Casas, 1552–1553.*
   Biblioteca argentina de libros raros americanos, Vol. III (facsimile), Buenos Aires, 1924.
10. B. de las Casas, *Erudita et elegans explicatio questionis utrum Reges vel Principes jure aliquo vel titulo, et salva conscientia, Cives ac subditos a Regia Corona alienare et alterius Domini particularis ditioni subjicere possint,* Frankfurt, 1571.
11. L. Hanke, *The first social experiments in America,* Cambridge, Mass., 1935.
12. *Democrates Alter, sive de justis belli causis apud Indos,* in *Joannis Genesii Sepulveda Cordubensis Opera,* Madrid, 1750. Printed with Spanish translation by M. Menéndez y Pelayo in *Boletín de la Real Academia de la Historia,* vol. XXI, Madrid, 1892.
13. *De fide,* XVIII, iv, 5.
14. J. Manzano y Manzano, *La incorporación de las Indias a la Corona de Castilla* (Madrid, 1948), 203–206.
15. p. 282 above.
16. Boxer, *Salvador de Sá,* p. 239.
17. Hugo Grotius, *De juri belli ac pacis,* 1625.
    Mare Liberum, 1609.
    See W. E. Hall, *Treatise on International Law,* ed. by A. Pearce Higgins, Clarendon Press, 1924.

NOTES FOR FURTHER READING

THE great discoveries aroused eager public interest at the time, and books on the subject were among the 'best-sellers' of the sixteenth and seventeenth centuries. Accounts of voyages, descriptions of newly found territories, atlases, pamphlets and treatises urging exploration and settlement, and general annals of discovery, appeared in great numbers. The work of interpreting this great mass of evidence is still going on, and some of the questions which it raises are still matters of acute controversy. The story, moreover, is worth re-telling, and is constantly re-told, for its adventurous excitement as well as for its social, economic and scientific significance. The resulting literature is enormous, and of very uneven merit. Mention is made here of a small selection of books in English of a general character which may be found suggestive or useful for reference.

The best short general surveys are J. N. L. Baker, *A history of geographical discovery and exploration* (London, 1937), and for the later part of our period, E. Heawood, *A history of geographical discovery in the seventeenth and eighteenth centuries* (London, 1912). Interesting and important essays on the discoveries are contained in V. T. Harlow, ed., *Voyages of the great pioneers* (London, 1929), and A. P. Newton, ed., *The great age of discovery* (London, 1932). B. Penrose, *Travel and discovery in the Renaissance* (Cambridge, Mass., 1955), is a good narrative of voyages with an excellent survey of the literature.

The best accounts of medieval geographical knowledge are R. Beazley, *The dawn of modern geography*, 3 vols. (Oxford, 1896–1906); A. P. Newton, ed., *Travel and travellers of the Middle Ages* (London, 1930); and G. H. T. Kimble, *Geography in the Middle Ages* (London, 1938). On the legacy of classical geographers, the definitive work is J. O. Thomson, *History of ancient geography* (Cambridge, 1948).

Part I. There is no satisfactory single account of the development of shipping in our period. Most histories of sail concentrate attention on later centuries. For our purposes the best are R. C. Anderson, *The sailing ship* (London, 1926), and G. S. Laird Clowes, *Sailing ships; their history and development*, 2 pts. (London, 1931–36). A recent very readable sketch of the history of sail is J. de la Varende (trans. M. Savill),

348

Cherish the sea (London, 1955). There is a good chapter on ship-building by G. P. B. Naish in C. Singer, E. J. Holmyard, A. R. Hall and T. I. Williams, eds., *A history of technology*, vol. III. (Oxford, 1957). The same volume has chapters on gunnery and navigation. Among English books on navigation, with good chapters on our period, the most useful are J. B. Hewson, *A history of the practice of navigation* (London, 1951); E. G. R. Taylor, *The haven-finding art* (London, 1956); and L. C. Wroth, *The way of a ship: an essay on the literature of navigational science* (Portland, Maine, 1937).

On the cartography of the Reconnaissance, the literature is extensive and much of it highly technical. Two indispensable basic works are A. E. Nordenskiöld, *Facsimile-atlas to the early history of cartography* (Stockholm, 1889); and by the same author, *Periplus: an essay on the early history of charts and sailing directions* (Stockholm, 1897). Two notably good brief summaries are G. R. Crone, *Maps and their makers* (London, 1953), and R. A. Skelton, *Explorers' maps* (London, 1958)—the last profusely illustrated. For their beauty and technical perfection, as well as for their scholarly excellence, two collections of *facsimilé* maps and charts should be mentioned: *Mapas españoles de América, siglos XV–XVII*, sponsored by the Duke of Alba (Madrid, 1951); and A. Cortesão and A. Teixeira de Mota, eds., *Portugaliae monumenta cartogrcphica*, 5 vols. (with English text) (Lisbon, 1960).

Part II. A fascinating account of the African trade which helped to stimulate early Portuguese exploration is given in E. W. Bovill, *The golden trade of the Moors* (Oxford, 1958). The best survey in English of the Portuguese African voyages is E. Prestage, *The Portuguese pioneers* (London, 1933); of the African coastal trade, J. W. Blake, *European beginnings in West Africa, 1454–1578* (London, 1937). The story of the discovery of the sea route to India is well told in K. G. Jayne, *Vasco da Gama and his successors, 1460–1580* (London, 1910), and more recently and breezily in H. H. Hart, *Sea Road to the Indies* (New York, 1950); the effect of the discovery upon the maritime situation in the Indian Ocean is described in G. A. Ballard, *Rulers of the Indian Ocean* (London, 1928). R. S. Whiteway, *The rise of Portuguese power in India* (London, 1899), is still valuable. On Alboquerque, E. Sanceau, *Indies adventure* (London, 1936), is vivid and reliable.

Of the enormous and often controversial literature on Columbus the best and most convincing account is S. E. Morison, *Admiral of the Ocean Sea*, 2 vols. (Boston, 1942). It has the special merit of concentration on Columbus' achievements as a seaman. G. E. Nunn, *The geographical conceptions of Columbus* (New York, 1924), is a useful though somewhat technical study. A good, though perhaps unduly laudatory book on Vespucci is F. J. Pohl, *Amérigo Vespucci; pilot major*, New York,

1944. On Magellan and his successors the best short works in English are J. C. Beaglehole, *The exploration of the Pacific* (London, 1934), and F. H. H. Guillemard, *The life of Ferdinand Magellan and the first circumnavigation of the globe, 1480–1521* (London, 1890). Many books have been written about the Spanish conquests in America. Perhaps the best single volume is F. A. Kirkpatrick, *The Spanish conquistadores* (London, 1934). W. H. Prescott's two great literary classics, *The history of the conquest of Mexico* and *The history of the conquest of Peru* have their place in all bibliographies; there are many editions. More modern accounts of the principal episodes of the conquest are F. A. MacNutt, *Fernando Cortés and the conquest of Mexico* (New York, 1909), and P. A. Means, *Fall of the Inca empire and Spanish rule in Peru, 1530–1780* (New York, 1932).

C. H. Haring, *Trade and navigation between Spain and the Indies in the time of the Hapsburgs* (Cambridge, Mass, 1918); is still the best work in English on its subject. On European rivalries in the Caribbean, A. P. Newton, *The European nations in the West Indies, 1493–1688* (London, 1933), is excellent. J. A. Williamson, *The Age of Drake* (London, 1938), covers the English challenge to Spain in the late sixteenth century. More detailed information and bibliography is in *The Cambridge history of the British Empire*, vol. I (Cambridge, 1929). On the Dutch-Portuguese rivalry in Brazil the best and almost the only book in English is C. R. Boxer, *The Dutch in Brazil, 1624–1654* (Oxford, 1957).

Of the early exploration of North America, the best brief general account is J. B. Brebner, *The explorers of North America* (London, 1933). Of English voyages, Hakluyt's *Principal Navigations* is the principal monument. There are various editions, of which the standard one is in 12 vols. (Glasgow, 1903–5). On the French voyages, Francis Parkman, *Pioneers of France in the New World* and *The Jesuits in North America* (various editions) are classic works. E. G. Bourne, *The voyages of Champlain*), 2 vols. (New York, 1922), is a standard account; and Champlain's own *Works*, edited by H. P. Biggar, are published in seven volumes by the Champlain Society (Toronto, 1922–36).

Part III. Of many accounts and descriptions of European empires overseas, the following—in addition to some already mentioned—are useful general works: C. H. Haring, *The Spanish Empire in America* (New York, 1947); C. M. Andrews, *The colonial period of American history*, 4 vols. (New Haven, 1934–38); G. L. Beer, *The origins of the British colonial system, 1578–1660* (New York, 1908), and *The old colonial system*, 2 vols. (New York, 1922); G. M. Wrong, *The rise and fall of New France* (London, 1928); B. Vlekke, *Nusantara, a history of the East Indian archipelago* (Cambridge, Mass., 1945); W. W. Hunter, *History of British India, 1500–1700*, 2 vols. (London, 1899–1900); *The Cambridge History of the British Empire*; and *The Cambridge History of India*. Much illuminating discussion of the economic aspects of oversea expansion is to be found in three fundamental works in economic history; E. F. Hecksher (M. Shapiro, trans.) *Mercantilism*, 2 vols. (London, 1934); W. R. Scott, *The history of joint-stock companies to 1720*, 2 vols. (London, 1910–12); and E. J. Hamilton, *American treasure and the price rise in Spain, 1501–1650* (Cambridge, Mass., 1934). On the history of Christian missions, a vast store of information and an exhaustive bibliography are in K. S. Latourette, *A history of the expansion of Christianity*, 7 vols. (New York, 1943–47). II and III are the relevant volumes for our period.

No attempt has been made in this brief list to survey the great volume of published source materials for the history of the Reconnaissance. Some references are included in the footnotes. Most of the western countries which played a part in the story have societies devoted to the publication of relevant records; and particular mention must be made of the oldest and best known of these societies, the Hakluyt Society, which for over a hundred years has published annually two or three volumes of records of voyages and expeditions, in meticulously edited English translation. Without the work of this and similar organizations, a general survey such as the present one would be impossible.

INDEX

Baabullah, Sultan of Ternate, 244
Babur, 246
back-staff, 94
Bacon, Roger, 8, 9, 11
— *Opus Majus*, 8, 9
Baffin, William, 204
Baghdad, 42
baghlas, 42, 57, 139, 201
Bahamas, 150, 181
Bahía, 189, 259, 261, 262
Balboa, Vasco Núñez de, 157, 162, 163
Bali, 244, 255
ballast, 74
bananas, 283, 284
Banda Islands, 190, 200, 243, 244, 251, 253, 254
Bandar Abbas, 200, 323
Bantam, 197, 244, 245, 250, 252
Barbados, 222, 223, 267, 269, 274, 276, 277, 278
Barbosa, Duarte, 193
Barcelona, 40, 44
Barents, William, 206
Barlaeus, Caspar, 281
barley, 283
Baskerville, Sir Thomas, 185
Bassein, 247
Bastidas, Rodrigo de, 157, 162
Bataks, 242
Batavia, 199, 200, 250, 251, 252, 253
Batticaloa, 251
Bay of Bengal, 104, 144, 251
beans, 286
Behaim, Martin, 110, 150
Beirut, 43
Belalcázar, Sebastián de, 172, 174
Belem, 142, 143
Bengal, 257
Benguela, 261
Benin, 133, 136, 138, 278
— Bight of, 106
Benincasa, Grazioso, 102
Berbice, 222
Bermuda, 151, 217, 268
Berrio, 140

Berrio, Antonio de, 222
Betanzos, Fray Domingo de, 232
Biafra, Bight of, 133
Bianco, Andrea, 102
Bidar, 246
Bijapur, 144, 246
Bini, 277
binnacle, 88
Black Death, 6, 45
Black Sea, 38, 42, 43
blocks, 75
Boers, 252
Bombay, 256
bonnets, 78
Borneo, 160, 190, 243, 245
Boston, 219
botta, 64
boums, 42, 57
Bourne, William, 100, 123
Braganza, Duke of, 135
Brahe, Tycho, 2
Brahmins, 248
Brazil, 142, 155, 156, 158, 182, 186, 188, 189, 258, 260 ff., 281
Brazil Rock, 148
brazil wood, 182, 258
Bressan, Matteo, 68
Bristol, 69, 154
British Museum, 289
Brittany, 87
bronze, 45
Bruges, 55
Brunei, 243, 245
buccaneers, 324
Buenos Aires, 179
bureaucracy, 296, 297
Byzantine Empire, 22, 23, 24

cables, 75
Cabot, John, 154, 156, 157
Cabot, Sebastian, 96, 202, 204, 324
Cabral, Pero Alvares, 66, 98, 115, 122, 142, 155
cacao, 178, 188, 287
Cadamosto, Alvise da, 36, 47, 65, 91, 131, 132, 146, 147
Cadiz, 53, 55, 69, 180

Paraguay, 234
Paraguay River, 175
Paraná River, 179, 202
Pareto, Bartolomeo, 102
Patent Offices, 297 ff.
pearls, 187
Pecos, 175
Pegolotti, Francesco Balducci, 41,
  42
Pegu, 194
Peking, 42
Pelican, 196
Pennsylvania, 267
peonage, 230
pepper, 20 41, 42, 47, 48, 136, 188,
  190, 197, 242, 243, 252, 254
periploi, 12
Pernambuco, 259, 261, 262
perriers, 119
Persia, 24, 42, 46, 323
Persian Gulf, 138, 144, 200, 242,
  323
Peru, 31, 170 ff., 178 ff., 195, 227,
  229, 230, 231, 235, 238, 279
peruleiros, 179, 182, 202
Petrarch, 33
Philip II, King of Spain, 185, 234,
  240, 293, 316
Philip III, King of Spain, 294
Philippines, 160, 161, 194, 195
Phrysius, Gemma, 110, 111
Pigafetta, Filippo, 159
pigs, 174, 283
Pilgrim Fathers, 218
Pinzón, Vicente Yáñez, 155
pirates, 180
pita, 180
Pius II, Pope, 13
Pizarro, Francisco, 126, 171 ff.
Pizarro, Gonzalo, 173, 174
Pizarro, Hernando, 172, 173, 174
Plantations Duties Act, 264
plantains, 283, 284
Pliny, 9
Po, Fernando, 133
Pocahontas, 281
Pole Star, 77, 91, 93, 94, 133

Polo, Marco, 6 ff., 13, 107, 108,
  114, 150
Popayán, 174
Popocatépetl, 165
population
— of New Spain, 274
— „ West Indies, 276
— „ New England, 275
— „ Virginia, 175
port pilots, 84
Port Royal, 221
Porto Santo, 146
Porto Seguro, 155
portolani, 13, 85, 90, 101 ff.
Portugal, 20, 23, 25–6, 29, 33, 47,
  48, 50, 52, 64–6, 69, 81, 90, 96,
  104, 133–4, 136, 158
Posidonius, 12
potatoes, 171, 286
Potosí, 174, 179, 182, 228
Praecelsae devotionis (1514), 159
Prester John, 6, 35, 115, 138
printing, 34
Privy Council, 267, 269
procuradores, 238
proprieties, 267, 268
Ptolemy, 9, 10 ff., 92, 104, 107,
  108–9, 110, 112, 150, 321
— *Almagest*, 9, 10
— *Geography*, 9, 10, 11, 13, 108, 110
Puerto Bello, 178, 180, 181
Puerto Rico, 153, 185
Pulicat, 255
pumps, 71
Puritans, 218 ff.

quadrant, 91–2
Quakers, 275
Quebec, 221
Quechua, 170
querena italiana, 57
Quesada, Gonzalo Jiménez de, 174
Quetzalcoatl, 166
Quito, 172, 174

Radisson, Pierre Esprit, 271

Sierra Leone, 102, 131, 132, 133, 183, 277
silk, 20, 21, 40–2, 48, 50, 188, 195
silver, 45, 50, 178–9, 185, 188, 191, 195–6, 228–40
Singapore, 242
Sintra, Pedro da, 131, 133
Sivaji, 256–7
Slave Coast, 277
slave-trade, 182, 278, 282
slaves, 47, 136, 178, 182–3, 186, 189, 200, 229, 259–61, 265–6, 276–8, 282, 284–5, 317
Sloane, Sir Hans, 289
smallpox, 229
Smeerenberg Bay, 206
Smith, Adam, 265
Smith, John, 214, 217
smugglers, 182, 186, 187
Smyrna, 23
Smythe, Sir Thomas, 216
Socotra, 144
soil erosion, 229
Solís, Juan de, 156, 159, 202
Solórzano Pereira, Juan de, 295
Soto, Hernando de, 175
Southampton, 55
Southern Cross, 93
Souza, Tomé de, 258
Spain, 19, 26, 28–9, 31, 33, 39–40, 44–5, 51–2, 64, 66, 81, 90, 96, 104, 121
Speelman, Cornelius, 250, 251
spices, 20, 21, 41, 47–8, 50, 56, 143, 145, 190–2, 196–7, 199, 249, 251, 254
Spitzbergen, 206
square rig, 58, 61–3, 65–6, 78
squashes, 286
St Ann's Bay, 154
St Brendan's Isle, 148
St Eustatius, 188
St Germain-en-Laye, Treaty of (1632), 221
St Kitts, 222, 276
St Lawrence River, 154, 202, 203, 210, 221

St Lucia, 222
Staple Act (1663), 264
Strabo, 9, 12
Strait of Belle Isle, 202
Suakin, 138
Suárez, Francisco, 313
Sublimis Deus (1537), 311
Succession War (1474–9), 27, 134, 147
Suez, 38, 42, 144
sugar, 20, 41, 46, 51, 136, 147, 179, 182–3, 186–8, 223, 229, 259–60, 262 ff., 277, 284
Sulaiman the Magnificent (Ottoman Sultan), 24
Sunda Strait, 99, 198, 251
Surabaya, 245
Surat, 255 ff.
sweet potatoes, 285
Synod of Diamper, 248, 249
Syria, 23, 39

Tabriz, 42
Tainos, 115, 125
Talikot, Battle of, 246
tallow, 228
Tangier, 264
Tasman, Abel, 201, 321
Tasmania, 201
taxation
— in Spanish Indies, 240
— „ Dutch East Indies, 254
— „ English Plantations, 266, 269
Tehuántepec, 168
The Tempest, 282
Tenerife, 148, 183
Tenochtitlán, 164 ff., 234
Terceira, 180
Ternate, 145, 190, 196, 200, 242 ff., 251, 253–4
Terra Australis Incognita, 12, 109, 110, 201, 321
tides, 85 ff.
Tidore, 160–1, 190, 243–4, 251
Tierra del Fuego, 178, 196
timber, 45, 56, 57, 71, 147, 154, 265
Timbuktu, 5, 44

INDEX